Solus Jesus

A Theology of Resistance

Emily Swan & Ken Wilson

Read the Spirit
Canton, Michigan

For more information and further discussion, visit
SolusJesus.com

Cover art and design by Rick Nease
www.RickNeaseArt.com

Published by
Read the Spirit
42015 Ford Road, Suite 234
Canton, Michigan

Read the Spirit and Front Edge Publishing specialize in speed
and flexibility in adapting and updating our books. We offer
discounts on bulk purchases for special events, corporate
training, and small groups. We are able to customize bulk
orders by adding corporate or event logos on the cover and we
can include additional pages inside describing your event or
corporation. For more information about our fast and flexible
publishing or permission to use our materials, please contact
Front Edge Publishing at info@FrontEdgePublishing.com.

Contents

Dedicated to:

(Emily)

Rachel, the love of my life

Andrea, a true friend who suffered alongside me

Audrey, Gwendolyn, Kinley, Maggie, Vivian—my five nieces,
in hopes that our Christian faith will find new life
in your generation

(Ken)

Julia, my love

Jesse, Maja, Amy, Judy, Grace and Oceana—you taught me
more than I taught you (granted, there are more of you)

The memory of Nancy and Phyllis

All the people I've upset along the way, in hopes of
a future reconciliation

(Both)

The people of Blue Ocean Faith Ann Arbor, whose beauty and
spiritual maturity is awe-inspiring, and who gave us space to
write this book, especially our co-workers,
Caroline, Diane, Cassie and Penny

All who bear the marks of the scapegoat

Foreword

by Deborah Jian Lee, author of Rescuing Jesus: How People of Color, Women and Queer Christians are Reclaiming Evangelicalism

When I was a child, my grandmother would visit my family for weeks at a time. She had raised me as a baby, so even though I later lost my native Cantonese and she spoke very little English, we shared a deep connection. I loved her so deeply that when she would leave, I'd return to the room in which she slept and look for traces of her essence left behind— her smell, a forgotten bobby pin, the soft indentation in her pillow. Sometimes I would cry from missing her.

My grandmother used to live on a farm in Southern China and never received a formal education. She practiced Buddhism and cared deeply for her children and grandchildren.

She was also one of my greatest spiritual teachers. She surrounded me with a bounty of her love, the most powerful spiritual gift you can offer a child.

After I became a Christian in my teens, it baffled me to hear Christians invalidate my grandmother's love as a form of spiritual teaching. They asked if I worried that she, along with my non-Christian family members, would go to hell.

The deeper I got into evangelicalism, the more I saw the theological framework driving this belief, how it hurt the most vulnerable and dismissed their perspectives and theologies. I saw how it cut us off from experiencing the divinity, or the image of God, standing before us in different human beings.

I remember sitting in countless seminars about converting "non-believers" to our "absolute truth" and sensing the smallness of our collective imagination.

In *Solus Jesus*, Emily Swan and Ken Wilson subvert that theological paradigm. Their words validate the theology and spirituality that rises from experience, from the marginalized, from the least of these. Their proposed paradigm, *Solus Jesus*, argues for the authority of the living Jesus in us all. Drawing from personal experience and those who have long carved out theologies far from power, Swan and Wilson show how *Solus Jesus* can open a portal to the divine communion that is possible between all people.

Solus Jesus also maps out the damage done by theologies formed in enclaves of power and invites us to examine our own complicity and vulnerability to those harmful teachings. It speaks to those raised with a weaponized theology and works to disarm them by offering up Scripture through a different lens, demanding love, dismantling of harmful systems and collective action. For some, *Solus Jesus* will affirm and amplify the message they've known within themselves for so long. For others, this will challenge and disrupt their faith, but hopefully lead to a desire to claim theology as a tool for our collective liberation.

This is an important text for our time. We live in a culture that prizes ideas from people with access, power and the "right" education. From the stages of multi-million dollar church stadiums, we uplift spiritual leaders with fancy degrees, book deals and sizeable social media followings. Once again, we suffocate our souls by limiting whom we learn from. *Solus Jesus* points us to the edges of society, where vulnerability and experience breed spiritual vitality. It invites us to receive spiritual teaching in all its manifestations, even in the form of a grandmother's love.

Read *Solus Jesus* with an open heart, and prepare to be challenged and transformed.

Foreword

by David P. Gushee, author of Changing Our Mind

Beginning around 2010, a small number of U.S. evangelicals started publishing books that, in one way or another, dissented from the predominant anti-LGBTQ+ opinion in our religious community. Some of these books were by LGBTQ+ evangelicals themselves, like Matthew Vines and Justin Lee. Others were by people like Ken Wilson and myself—straight, white Christian men taking a stand for substantial reconsideration of the traditionalist position and its associated practices in church life.

In response to such books, as well as to a growing pressure for reconsideration (or for campus support groups, space to ask questions in denominations, or for a temporary freeze on exclusion in churches), the diffuse but very real evangelical power structure clamped down. Holding on to some version of the traditionalist position became even more non-negotiable in evangelical publishing, higher education, denominational service, and church life. Dissenters were pushed out—often brutally—and left communally, and even theologically, homeless. Painful exclusion was especially doled out to LGBTQ+ evangelicals.

A new trend has become apparent among some of these now-post-evangelical dissenters. They (we) have begun to theologize—have begun developing versions of post-evangelical theology. These post-evangelical theologies are deeply, self-consciously, and explicitly affected by the scalding experiences of their authors. As with much of the most

creative theology in Christian history, this new post-evangelical theology is emerging from a context of personal and
communal crisis, conflict, and loss.

When evangelical dissenters started challenging the traditionalist, anti-LGBTQ+ majority, most of us began our work
from somewhere within the overall theological framework
that gave rise to the majority anti-gay theology. We assumed
something like a *sola Scriptura* approach to biblical authority
and ethical epistemology; tried tackling the 6-8 "clobber
verses" that so dominated the traditionalist approach; and
attempted to argue that a modification of the Church's stance
on LGBTQ+ "issues" was possible without abandoning how
most evangelicals think and act. We did not leap to mainline
justice ethics or radical liberation ethics, and we were barely
touched by the first generation of the '70s and '80s gay/queer
theology.

Neither our elite scholarly adversaries nor most of the
evangelical rank and file were at all persuaded by our effort to
(mainly) play their game their way and somehow end up with
a different result.

Once the dust settled—once dissenters left or were exiled
from evangelicalism—some of us began to realize that the
problem goes deeper than an interpretive dispute within the
settled methodology of evangelicalism. Some of us began
to see that the settled methodology of evangelicalism is, in
itself, deeply problematic. To put it provocatively: Some of us
began to see that it is impossible to be fully and unequivocally LGBTQ+-inclusive within evangelicalism, because the
problem is evangelicalism—not LGBTQ+ inclusion.

This discovery has led in a variety of directions. Some
ex-evangelicals are now leaning in a liberationist, womanist,
feminist, social-justice, or queer-theology direction. In
relation to all of the aforementioned approaches, it seems that
almost everybody in this post-evangelical space is discovering,
often for the first time, *the role of power in biblical interpretation*—even the power involved in privileging the authoritative

interpretation of the written text of a translated Bible as *the way* of discerning truth.

Liberationist theologies had, for decades, zeroed in on power in biblical interpretation and theological construction: the power of colonizers, slaveholders, and conquerors; of (gulp) simply the unacknowledged power of those defined as white; of men, straight people, clergy and scholars; of the literate, educated, and wealthy. Groups that, for centuries, have had the Bible quoted at them by powerful people in order to harm them tend not to be naïve about the role of power in theology and biblical interpretation. Even when they embrace and love the Bible, they do so with a determination that they will read the Bible in a way that enables their group's flourishing—not its subjugation.

This power-aware, reading-from-the-margins biblical move is apparent in *Solus Jesus: A Theology of Resistance*, but so is much else. The critique goes much deeper, really—beyond evangelicalism and into significant aspects of historic Christianity. Here, for example, one finds a frontal attack on the *sola Scriptura* framework provided by Martin Luther and the majority strand of Protestantism for 500 years. One also finds considerable reconsideration of a theology of the Cross, with a very substantial engagement with René Girard and his "scapegoat theory" doing much of the heavy lifting.

The authors' deep Pentecostal background contributes a profound spiritual-experiential dimension, which also does a lot of work in the book. The authors suggest that it is the experience of Jesus directing us, as Christians—not mere exegetical parsing—that is the most reliable way for everyday Christians to listen for God's voice. The book offers numerous examples of supernatural experiences that contributed to directing, encouraging, and strengthening the authors amid the experience of embracing full LGBTQ+ inclusion (including self-inclusion, on the part of author Emily Swan) in the teeth of brutal Christian rejection.

Other theological resources make an appearance, and most notably Dietrich Bonhoeffer, who in a variety of ways continues to speak powerfully to our contemporary situation. Here, his interpretation of the Fall story—as an account of turning away from trust in God toward rivalry with God, in the determination of good and evil—plays an important role, as does his move toward "religionless Christianity," which resonates deeply for many of us wounded most acutely by religious people.

Solus Jesus is a post-evangelical theology of resistance—resistance to anti-LGBTQ+ Christianity; resistance to the theology, methodology and spirit that creates it; and resistance to any version of Christianity that teaches people to harm others in the name of Jesus—and then, when challenged, to claim victimization.

Born in a cauldron of faith and pain, *Solus Jesus: A Theology of Resistance* is a highly original, deeply provocative first stab at a post-evangelical, post-"gay debate" pastoral theology. It covers considerable ground, and some moves are more compelling than others. But the entire book is worthy of serious and prayerful consideration.

Foreword

by Brian D. McLaren, author of The Great Spiritual Migration

The ultimate authority for the Christian resides not in words on a page, but in the Word of God made flesh in Jesus Christ. This is the bold claim made by the book you now hold in your hands (or see on your screen): *Solus Jesus: A Theology of Resistance.* The claim shouldn't be controversial, but it is— and that is why this book is so important.

It is written, as all theology should be written, out of the crucible of experience, which includes painful experience. The particular crucible in which Emily Swan and Ken Wilson found themselves was the fierce debate over full inclusion of sexual minorities in Christian churches today.

As Christians formed in the evangelical tradition, Swan and Wilson were obliged to enter the LGBTQ+ debate as loyal adherents to evangelicalism's doctrine of *sola Scriptura* (Scripture alone). In other words, they could only use Scripture as a guide for faith and practice; contrary experience, scientific research, and moral qualms would have to be sidelined or minimized.

They found, as our mutual friend Phyllis Tickle predicted, that *sola Scriptura* could not bear the weight of this debate—unless they were willing to shut themselves off from the human suffering caused by upholding the traditional viewpoint.

But their consciences would not allow them to do so.

In other words, the authors' deep love for Scripture taught them an ethical mandate—to see others' suffering as their own, and to treat others as they would be treated. Guided by that Scripture-inspired mandate, they could no longer uphold the doctrine of *sola Scriptura*.

So they dared to trust that there was a better way to frame their approach to this issue—and to all of life. They came to see, as Martin Luther put it, that Scripture is like the manger on which Christ is presented to the world. Yes, the words of Scripture have inestimable value, but their value lies in their witness to the ultimate Word: the Word of God made flesh in Jesus.

This discovery is the treasure the authors articulate in *Solus Jesus: A Theology of Resistance*. Our task—whether facing the issues of LGBTQ+ inclusion, or care for this beautiful, fragile earth, or systemic racism or militarism—is not simply to marshal biblical texts to "prove" this or that position. Rather, our task is to position ourselves as humble and curious followers of Jesus and to discern the way, the truth, and the life in him.

In this way, *Solus Jesus: A Theology of Resistance* challenges us to see the authoritative Jesus in a fresh light, so that his life, message, death, and rising summon us to live in a new way as individuals and congregations. Here they blend the insights of two 20th-century giants. First, they draw from Dietrich Bonhoeffer, whose blend of no-frills discipleship to Jesus and intuitions toward a "religionless Christianity" have intrigued so many of us for years. Second, they draw from René Girard, a literary critic whose writings on the "scapegoat mechanism" provide a key for unlocking the mystery of a God weaning humanity off of the addictive drug of violence. Along with Bonhoeffer and Girard, they have been informed by a robust theology-from-the-margins (Kelly Brown Douglas, James H. Cone, and Ada María Isasi-Díaz, among others) with a partic-ular concern to counter readings of Scripture that betray an anti-Jewish bias.

The result is an invigorating and theologically informed vision of Jesus at the heart of their proposal. This Jesus manifests a God who is both completely good and thoroughly nonviolent—a God who became a victim of human violence to reveal the innocence of victims everywhere and for all time. The lens through which they see the story of Jesus beckons us to reimagine how we both share and live out the Gospel mandate, and in how we think about Christian conversion and the faith's relation to other religions.

But one particular theme running throughout this manuscript may prove the most challenging: that God can be reliably experienced by ordinary people, and that the faith of Jesus is deeply distorted without this experiential principle at its heart. The life experience that occasioned *Solus Jesus: A Theology of Resistance* is selectively revealed and reflected upon throughout this book, along with a vigorous defense of the legitimacy of lived experience as a priceless facet of Christian thought and decision-making. If they have an axe to grind, it is not the inadequacies of *sola Scriptura* (a task they have largely left to others); rather, it is the de-emphasis on experience that came in the wake of *sola Scriptura*, leaving the Church untethered from its mystical past, fracturing into tens of thousands of argumentative factions, and too often oblivious to the movement of the Holy Spirit in our day. You may be convinced—or not—but you will be challenged to think and rethink.

Authors' Introduction: A Slogan Whose Time Has Come

SOMETHING IS BUGGING us, and we think it's *sola Scriptura*—for 500 years, the sea in which most Protestant fishes have swum. *Sola Scriptura* (Scripture alone as the source of final authority in matters of faith and morals) began as an affront to the authority claims of the Roman Catholic Church hierarchy.[1] But *sola Scriptura* replaced one illusory certainty with another, and now is the time to consider an alternative: *solus Jesus*.[2] Which sounds naïve, we know. How could Jesus be the final authority in matters of faith and morals? Exactly. Why not?

But let's back up for a moment. *Solus Jesus: A Theology of Resistance* is a theological reckoning with what happened to us—Emily, Ken and our friends—at the hands of those committed to *sola Scriptura*. Or, to put it another way, it is a form of theological memoir. We hope *Solus Jesus* is more than that, but it is not less than that.

All theologies sprout from the soil of personal biography, and *Solus Jesus* is no different. Our stories converged at a

---

1 For a good summary of *sola Scriptura* in historical context, see *The Unintended Reformation: How a Religious Revolution Secularized Society* by Brad S. Gregory, 86-88.
2 *Sola Scriptura* is a Latin phrase, meaning "Scripture alone." Since Latin has gendered nouns, *sola* is feminine, to match *Scriptura. Solus* is the masculine form of the noun "alone," in Latin corresponding to the gender of the noun "Jesus." Hardly worth noting, though, especially since the gender of Jesus is not the point.

church that started in Ken's living room, several decades earlier. The church eventually affiliated with an evangelical denomination (Vineyard) that held the standard Reformed view on scriptural authority while also emphasizing the legitimacy—indeed, the centrality—of the wild and wooly realm of Holy Spirit leadings (dreams, visions, prophecies and the like).

Though Vineyard spawned one of the early "heal-the-gay" ministries in 1980, by 2001, Ken began listening to the experiences of LGBTQ+ people who were not seeking "healing" from their sexual orientation or gender identity. Their stories were changing him—and the church itself. By the time Emily returned—after four years on the mission field in Asia, to serve as a pastor with Ken—it was 2011, and the church was making slow but steady progress toward the full inclusion of LGBTQ+ people.

But it was also tortured progress.

Emily was still trying to convince herself that she was bisexual, not gay, and could manage to find a suitable husband or live happily single. Ken was trying to manage a conscience that could no longer enforce policies he knew to be harmful to LGBTQ+ people, even as he simultaneously recoiled at the thought of blowing up his beloved church by saying so. And he was looking for the scriptural basis for the inclusive pastoral practices that were emerging from his spiritual experiences and convictions.

That's when our dear friend Phyllis Tickle called into question the ability of *sola Scriptura* to bear the weight of such a change. Phyllis was known as an astute observer of the turbulent religious landscape. Privately, she was a Christian mystic. Like all mystics, she had a feel for the shifting winds of the Holy Spirit. At a prayer conference that we hosted, Phyllis said: "*Sola Scriptura,* as a plausible answer to the authority question, is over—and the stake in its heart is the gay issue."

That comment by Phyllis, offered in one of her *tour de force* expositions of the shifting grounds of authority in the Christian tradition, lay heavy on us.

As inheritors of *sola Scriptura*, we had already been reluctantly facing its myriad inconsistencies and oversold promises. But *sola Scriptura* was the *foundation* of our beloved religious tribe.

Hesitantly, Ken asked Phyllis to explain herself. The gist of her response follows:

Historically, the Christian Church abandons consensus readings of Scripture when the Holy Spirit indicates that they are past their due date. For example, different biblical texts can be marshaled to support both slavery and its abolition. Once we recognize the full humanity of slaves and the harm done to them by slaveholding, we shift the burden of proof, emphasizing the texts that support our Spirit-led abhorrence of slavery. When it comes to the full equality of humans who are women, the same: We de-emphasize the texts in support of gender hierarchy and emphasize the full-equality texts. But when the matter before us is the full equality of humans who are gay, lesbian, bisexual, transgender or queer, we're stuck. The texts that seem to address these questions are few, but univocal. We can't find a way to honor what we know the Spirit is saying in our hearts while maintaining that, yes, Scripture alone is our final authority in matters of faith and morals—*and* (a necessary corollary, if it's to make any difference) Scripture speaks plainly on such important matters as who it's OK to have sex with. Even if it *can* be done (many valiant efforts have been undertaken of late), the process is too tortured and the textual evidence too uncertain to support the survival of *sola Scriptura*.

The implications—both personal and theological—were unsettling. But we knew enough by then not to dismiss either our growing discomfort over the traditional discrimination against LGBTQ+ people in church or our experience of Jesus. If such was ill-advised, we were prepared—or thought we were—to live with the consequences.

We didn't know it then, but that was the beginning of our collaboration.

As a single, female pastor in married-male-dominated evangelicalism, Emily was already familiar with the effects of marginalization. But events unfolded, and the evangelical machine did what it does when threatened. Ken spoke openly in support of full LGBTQ+ inclusion. Emily met the woman who would become her wife: Rachel. The usual ugliness ensued and we now happily co-pastor a new, fully inclusive church in Ann Arbor, having worn out our Vineyard (and broader evangelical) welcome. That's the sanitized version. In subsequent chapters, as a more candid telling of our story illuminates our theological recalibration, we will offer it in less dispassionate detail.

Except for this introductory chapter and the Afterword, all other chapters were written in the voice of either Emily or Ken. While the voice of these chapters is singular, the content informed by our respective perspectives, each is also a collaboration. The book is the fruit of working together for several years, and especially going through an intense ordeal together on the way to planting a new church—one that inhabits what is perhaps a new allotment on the diverse Christian landscape.

We consider this a work of non-professional pastoral theology—non-professional because neither of us is academically credentialed in the discipline of theology. By this, we intend no apology. All of us are theologians to the extent that we seek to be students of God. The theological resources of the academy are now widely available, at least to those who read. In our sacred text, we see theology emerging on the fly, in much the way that we, as pastors, have had to do theology. Nothing here, so far as we can tell, is abstracted from our own pressing concerns or the pressing concerns of those we know and love. Wherever possible, we try to be transparent about the experience that informs our theology. We think that experience necessarily informs *all* theology, but too often the experience is hidden or unacknowledged.

A framework in three parts

You'll notice the book is presented in three major sections. Part 1 (Chapters 1-5) corresponds to the book's title, *Solus Jesus*. Part 2 (Chapters 6-11) corresponds to its subtitle, *A Theology of Resistance*. And Part 3 (Chapters 12-15) proposes a new way forward on four fronts: the meaning of the Gospel, the problem of religion, spirituality and inter-faith relations.

Part 1: *Solus Jesus*

Sola Scriptura can be regarded as a principle or a doctrine, but it has also functioned as a slogan. The dictionaries indicate that "slogan" is from a Scottish root meaning something like the rallying cry of an army or entourage. The Reformers did a lot of work to flesh out the theological implications of *sola Scriptura*—a highly nuanced effort that continues within these traditions to this day.[3] But beyond the academy, where most Christians live, *sola Scriptura* has always functioned as a rallying cry or an identity marker ("we are the people who regard Scripture alone as the final authority").

Solus Jesus is an alternative slogan, and this book is an early effort to flesh it out theologically. Part 1 can be understood as the basic proposal: that *solus Jesus* is an adequate and preferred response to the question, "Wherein lies authority in the Jesus tradition?" Except for Emily's Chapter 2, "*Sola Scriptura* and Power,*" we don't devote much energy to convincing the reader of the inadequacies of *sola Scriptura*. Those books have already been written and they make their case better than we could.[4] This is not a proposal for anyone satisfied with *sola Scriptura*—except perhaps to offer reinforcing fodder by negative example. It is a book for those who seek an alternative not already articulated by the major Christian

---

3 For a helpful, modern summary of the doctrine of *sola Scriptura*, see *The Shape of Sola Scriptura* by Keith A. Mathison, 255-281.
4 In particular, see *The Bible Made Impossible: Why Biblicism Is Not a Truly Evangelical Reading of Scripture*, by Christian Smith.

traditions (Eastern Orthodox, Roman Catholic, Reformed, Anabaptist, Anglican).

The adequacy of *solus Jesus* is grounded in the conviction that human beings can experience God. Somewhat reluctantly, we've included our own experience of God by way of example throughout the book. Experience is always concrete and particular, and simply talking about experience as an abstraction seems to do violence to that reality. So we took the plunge and recounted some of our own particular experiences where they seemed to pertain to the discussion at hand. This aspect of the book might be of intense interest or off-putting. Take it or leave it. Either way, we have sought to do so with discretion and a measure of humility.

Chapter 4, "In Defense of Experience," tackles the legitimacy of our embrace of experience directly. As does, in a different way, Chapter 5, "The Age of the Spirit." In Chapter 3, "Questions of Authority," we situate the experience of Jesus within a broader framework including Scripture, tradition, community and the like. Informed by the work of William Abraham, a United Methodist scholar, we call for regarding Scripture as a "means of grace" or "medicine for the soul." This, Abraham argues, is an older understanding that can be distinguished from a later view of Scripture as a "criterion of truth"—part of a broader philosophical quest for certainty that underlies *sola Scriptura*. Our use of Abraham's work is not intended to imply that he would support our proposal, as his work is part of a larger project called *Canonical Theism: A Proposal for Theology and the Church.*[5]

You will notice that Emily, in particular, draws from the work of theological voices speaking from the margins— including feminist, African-American, Latin American, postcolonial and First Nations writers. These voices inform her writing throughout. In a similar way, Ken has been informed by Jewish sources. Both of us also enjoy interacting

---

5 See *Canonical Theism: A Proposal for Theology and the Church*, edited by William J. Abraham, Jason E. Vickers, Natalie B. Van Kirk.

with scientific writers. The writing of this book has been an exercise in learning from each other's varied interests. And we both think that much more of our reflection needs to be shaped by these and other voices currently regarded as "from the margins" by much contemporary Christian thought. We regard our efforts here as no more than humble beginnings.

Part 2: A Theology of Resistance

If Part 1 represents our basic proposal, Part 2 represents our fleshing out an understanding of Jesus and its particular theological implications. We can imagine many different ways to do this work of elaboration depending on how one understands Jesus. This is one such effort, for starters.

As we read and experience Jesus, we see him leading a movement of resistance against powers that have the whole world in their grip. He offers an alternative "yoke" to these powers.[6] We understand Jesus, in line with the Hebrew prophets, as leading a freedom movement—out of oppression and into the goodness of God's realm. We believe discipleship to Jesus required resistance to religious powers of oppression within evangelicalism (driven by the love of money). We see these powers at work across the Christian landscape in our context. For those reading *Solus Jesus*, we imagine that the call to discipleship will require running afoul of these powers as well, hence our subtitle: *A Theology of Resistance*. This is our point of departure for Part 2.

Emily takes the lead here. In Chapter 6, "God of the Victim," she introduces the work of Dietrich Bonhoeffer, a German of privilege during World War II, who gave his life in solidarity with the Jewish people. We return to Bonhoeffer again and again throughout the book.

In Chapter 7, "Scapegoat Theory: Unlocking a Better Story," Emily introduces the work of René Girard, proponent of what

---

6 When Jesus offered his "yoke" as a lighter alternative, it is likely that he had the oppressive yoke of Roman occupation in view rather than the Mosaic Law, as has often been asserted by exegetes (Carte, 259-261).

has been called "mimetic theory" or "scapegoat theory." René Girard was a literary critic who made cross-disciplinary contributions to anthropology, psychology and theology. Girard's theory purports to explain the origin of religion, sacrifice and culture, elucidating categories of Christian thought as diverse as atonement theory, end times, the nature of the Satanic, the function of the Holy Spirit and ethics. His work is so expansive, so breathtaking in scope as to engender a reflexive skepticism.

Girard's core insight is as follows: Human society is grounded in the propensity of humans to control their otherwise escalating rivalries by turning on a vulnerable individual or group whose expulsion (by death, exile, marginalization and the like) restores a temporary state of equilibrium—until the next round of escalating conflicts resolves itself in yet another scapegoating event. What Girard calls the "scapegoat mechanism" is driven by the distinctively human capacity to imitate not simply external gestures, but internal states and, in particular, desire. We tend to borrow or mirror desire from each other—wanting what others want because they want it. This fuels the rivalries that could only be originally constrained by unconscious resort to the scapegoat mechanism. You will encounter this insight, elaborated in many different ways, throughout these pages. In our own encounter with Girard's thought, we found repetition—considering it from many different angles—essential to grasping its significance.

Our interest in Girard is also deeply personal. His theory is the one thing that offered explanatory power for an experience that was otherwise utterly baffling to us—our foray into the minefield of intense religious controversy. In Part 2, we add candid accounts of painful experience—Emily, as a queer woman facing the policies of exclusion that the traditional teaching requires; and Ken, as a pastor who couldn't bring himself to implement those policies. But this very personal interest in Girard was subsequently reinforced by national events—the appeal to white supremacy, sexism and the stirring of animosity toward the press, immigrants, Muslims, sexual minorities and other vulnerable groups in a successful presidential run. Scapegoat theory provides an important theological underpinning for reading the signs of our times.

Whether René Girard actually explains all that he purports to explain—the origin of culture, religion and sacrifice—is far beyond our ability to evaluate. It's also too abstract a concern to interest us. We tend to view Girard in the terms of one of his students: Sandor Goodhart, a Jewish scholar. Goodhart regards Girard as a prophet, a role he understands in the following way:

> *The prophetic, I often say, with a nod to Greek tragic writing, is the recognition of the dramas in which human beings are engaged and the naming in advance of the end of those dramas in order that we can choose to go there or not. (Goodhart, xx)*

Girard's core insight—the crucial, but largely hidden role played by the scapegoat mechanism in the human drama—is a prophetic one. Girard has discerned a thread running through much of the human experience that powerfully illuminates what otherwise remains hidden. That much we can embrace in Girard, and we suggest it's enough to blow your mind, too.

Part 3: A New Path Forward

Our final four chapters deal with four important implications of *Solus Jesus: A Theology of Resistance*. In Chapter 12, "The Gospel for Modern Ears," we step back to re-state the Gospel as we understand it through the lens of scapegoat theory—which we think offers an accessible and compelling message for modern people. In Chapter 13, "The Problem of Religion," we explore Dietrich Bonhoeffer's radical insight into how we think about and do morality—and how our ways are fundamentally flawed. Like many today, Bonhoeffer was deeply disillusioned by the moral impotence of the Christian religion in the face of the Shoah. In fact, shortly before his execution by the Gestapo, Bonhoeffer expressed his longing for a "religionless Christianity"—something that resonates with those similarly disillusioned today. René Girard also lived under the shadow of the Holocaust—born in neighboring France in 1923. We think Girard's thought illuminates Bonhoeffer's cryptic and elliptical comments on religionless Christianity. Together, Bonhoeffer and Girard help us understand the radical nature of the Jesus ethic, echoed by his irascible disciple, Paul.

In Chapter 14, "A Spirituality of Resistance: Pray and Act," we return to a theme running throughout the book: the importance of knowing Jesus experientially in order to be led and empowered by the Spirit who animates him. Resistance isn't just an act of opposition; it is primarily a matter of raising our sails to catch the wind of the Spirit. In most 20th-century attempts to understand Jesus as imaging the God of the marginalized, spirituality (the means by which we connect to God) took a back seat. But it is front-and-center in *Solus Jesus: A Theology of Resistance*. Indeed, a proposal of this sort only makes sense if God can be reliably experienced and is able to function as an active agent, advancing God's own cause. Here we consider a range of practices—from Pentecostal to monastic, from privilege-releasing to rivalry-reducing—which foster experience of God's good realm and empower us to cooperate with its unfolding.

The final chapter, "Jesus Among the World Religions," may be worth reading (or scanning) first, because it addresses an initial source of difficulty with the slogan *solus Jesus*. For many, *solus Jesus* conjures the sense of certainty and triumphalism associated with *sola Scriptura*. It conveys the "my God is better than your God" rivalry that seems to fit better in the world dominated by the scapegoat mechanism than the realm of non-rivalry that characterizes the goodness of God. We believe Jesus embodies the non-rivalrous nature of God and this is meant to characterize our engagement with other religious traditions.

A confident uncertainty

The quest for certainty, and religion's claim to offer it, then, is our bugaboo. Reading Martin Luther, one is struck not so much by his confidence (how could one oppose the power of the papacy without it?) but by his certainty.[7] Likewise, Luther's opponents display a shocking certainty. *Sola Scriptura* was a frontal assault on the claimed authority of the Roman Catholic hierarchy, which offered itself as a means of certainty. As such, it mirrored the certainty that characterized the Roman Catholic truth claims. The Church, represented by the pope and bishops, functioned as the final arbiters of truth. *Sola Scriptura* was an attempt to replace one certainty scheme with another. For the ensuing five centuries, we've witnessed a battle of competing certainties, and it's beaten our confidence in our own certainties down to a useless pulp. We view *solus Jesus* as a break with the quest for certainty. We aim, rather, for a more attainable goal—sufficient confidence to proceed.

Confidence to proceed rather than remain paralyzed? How can we leave home without it? But certainty? *Sola Scriptura* promised that if reasonable people read Scripture with open hearts, and observed a few interpretive guidelines, all would come to the same obvious conclusions. It didn't work out that way, did it? How can *we* now know that we know with certainty, knowing that so many of our betters asserted, with equal certainty, the superiority of contradictory truths—and by simple logic, they can't all be right? In its own way, that may be one of the greatest gifts to humanity of the long experiment called *sola Scriptura*.

---

7 The discussion of Luther's response to critics and other reformers in *Reformations: The Early Modern World, 1450-1650,* by Carlos M. N. Eire reveal the certainty of Luther's age in which he deeply participated. See Eire's chapter on Calvin, for example, 286-317.

A philosopher would say our epistemological posture (how we know what we know) has changed. It's not that we've achieved a new humility. We're more like the recovering alcoholic who can only gain sobriety by admitting that alcohol has them beat. Certainty claims have us beat.

How the truth claims of the Jesus tradition stack up against the grand claims of the other great world religions, well, that requires a posture—ultimate, provable, objectivity—that we simply have given up claiming as a kind of fool's errand. Clearly, the Jesus to whom the apostolic writings bear witness saw himself within the tradition of the Hebrew prophets and as one who stands in solidarity with the Jewish people. That the religion that claims him as a founder has been wracked with anti-Semitism in its Gentile-dominated expression is a source of deep—no, existential—shame. We have done our best to repent of this in our writing, and we eagerly open our hearts and our minds to our Jewish siblings who may help us further along that road.

As to the world religions of Islam, Buddhism and Hinduism (traditions that Jesus did not address directly, so far as we know), we seek a similar posture of humility. Surely the Golden Rule—love others as we would, ourselves, want to be loved—must apply to our neighbors in the world's great religions. We are guided by a confident uncertainty born of the conviction that a faith tradition can only be understood from within, by practitioners ("taste and see that the Lord is good"), which makes assertions of superiority in this realm— one tradition over another—suspect.

Jesus claimed a lordship of love over the authority claims of the Roman Empire, with its co-opted and subservient deities. What are their equivalents today? That is our primary task in applying the truth claims of Jesus, rather than seeking to assert or demonstrate the religious superiority of Christianity over other faith traditions. Rival empires abound in our world, and we have our own close at hand—American consumerist capitalism backed by a global economic and military juggernaut, with its co-opted and subservient deities—some of them dressed in Christian garb. Fortunately, to learn from Jesus and the light he offers only requires humility, sufficient confidence and a risk-taking willingness to proceed. Certainty, well—that's beyond our grasp, and any claims to it are riddled with illusion and presumption. Certainty fits the overreaching claims of empire, while the meek, eventually, inherit the earth.

Have you noticed that where *sola Scriptura* prevails, there is a great deal of pressured fussing about getting things right? That's because *sola Scriptura* yields to the demands of certainty—that we must find and adhere to a foolproof safeguard system that we mortals can maintain. It seems a fool's errand on its face, doesn't it?

But what if that pressure is wondrously off? And the wonder that removes it is simply a living Jesus exercising his considerable agency to make himself known? He does this through the means at his disposal and within the limitations imposed by our creatureliness. None of this removes the messiness that inevitably attends communication with human beings. But, perhaps the mess is just something to accept—a given, rather than a sign that something must be horribly wrong.

To that wondrously unpressured project, then, we now apply ourselves: *solus Jesus*.

Part 1: *Solus Jesus*

Here we present the proposal: it's enough to say a living Jesus is the final authority in Christianity. In support, we offer a critique of *sola Scriptura* as privileging the literate, tackle the vexing questions of authority that produced *sola Scriptura*, defend a robust role for experience, and situate *solus Jesus* within the age of the Spirit.

1

Our Rabbi Still

Ken

THE EARLIEST JESUS followers didn't presume to interpret the Bible "on their own," but rather always in the company of a rabbi, sage or teacher.[8] To this day, the Jewish Bible is frequently read in a version called *mikraot gedolot* ("Great Scriptures"), also known as the Rabbinic Bible. The biblical text is surrounded by commentary from many rabbis offering views that differ, views that may even conflict.[9]

The tradition of reading with the rabbis is rooted in the practice, evident in the Gospels, of young men (mostly) attaching themselves to a rabbi. They followed the rabbi's way, which included his interpretation of Israel's sacred texts. To assume that one could simply read and follow the Scriptures without a teacher would have seemed impractical and presumptuous—like a surgeon attempting a difficult procedure without training under a mentor. No, find a rabbi first.

The rabbi serves as an interpretive guide. The rabbi mediates the text to his disciples. The rabbi, under God, is the authority. And all of this takes place within the context of a relationship between teacher and students.

---

8 There is scholarly debate about the use of the term "rabbi" before the destruction of the Temple and the eventual emergence of Rabbinic Judaism. In general, it is thought that the term was applied more loosely during this earlier period.

9 This deference to rabbinic interpretation is expressed in the Jewish practice of reading Scripture in forms that provide commentary from many different rabbinic voices surrounding the text (Kushner, *xxi*).

What if this fundamental structure hasn't changed? In this case, *solus Jesus* could be a plausible alternative to *sola Scriptura*.

To Protestant ears, this may sound suspect. Isn't that what the Roman Catholic Church claimed for itself—to be the authorized interpreter of Scripture? Come to the Church and the Church will provide the fullness of truth, including the truth of Scripture and tradition (conceived of as the oral tradition passed down through apostolic succession), embodied in the formulations of ecumenical church councils. To the Catholic Christian, it's not "the Bible says … " but rather "the Church says … ."

What if the original intuition has always been the way forward? What if it's neither "the Church says" nor "the Bible says," but instead, "my rabbi says"? And the rabbi in view is not the magisterium of the Roman Catholic Church nor Martin Luther nor John Calvin nor Menno Simons. He is no one other than Jesus of Nazareth, who warned against calling anyone else "rabbi"[10]—perhaps because he planned to occupy that role in perpetuity. What if such a thing is only possible because he was, and would continue to be, *available as our rabbi still*?

The post-resurrection rabbi

Luke 24 serves as the bridge between two books attributed to Luke, sometimes referred to as Luke-Acts. In our Bibles, this is obscured by the placement of the Gospel of John between Luke and Acts. American New Testament scholar Luke Timothy Johnson says, "Virtually all contemporary scholars think that the Gospel [of Luke] and Acts were conceived and executed as a single literary enterprise which they have come to call Luke-Acts" (1).

---

10 "But you are not to be called rabbi, for you have one teacher, and you are all brethren. And call no man your father on earth, for you have one Father, who is in heaven. Neither be called masters, for you have one master, the Christ" (Mt. 23:8-10).

The Gospel of Luke takes us from the birth and childhood of Jesus through his public teaching and deeds, culminating in his death and resurrection. The book of Acts recounts the active leadership of Jesus through the Holy Spirit, made freely available from the day of Pentecost forward.

In Luke 24, two disciples walk from Jerusalem to the village of Emmaus on the evening of the day when rumors are circulating that Jesus had risen from the dead—the first Easter Sunday evening. Grieving and discouraged, they try to make sense of events that presently make no sense to them at all. As they converse, a stranger joins them, as happened frequently on such journeys. After all, no one wants to walk alone on the robber-infested routes between towns in Israel—safety in numbers.

The stranger inquires: What are they discussing so intently? What events have them so perplexed? They can't believe this new traveler hasn't heard about Jesus of Nazareth, who captured the affection of the Passover crowds, along with the opposition of some of their leaders, and eventually, the terrifying wrath of Rome.

"Then, beginning with Moses and all the prophets, he interpreted to them the things about himself in all the scriptures" (Lk. 24:7).

The stranger is doing what rabbis do: offering *midrash*, the act of interpreting and commenting on sacred text, often creatively stringing together texts from different parts of Scripture to build a coherent narrative (Kugel, *How to Read*, 13-14). In Part 2 of *Solus Jesus* we will offer an example of such an approach.

As they reach their destination, the two invite their companion to join them at the inn for the night. He complies. Seated for a meal, he blesses the bread and breaks it for them, and in that moment, they *recognize* the stranger as the Jesus they had known—and, simultaneously, he disappears from their sight. Later, in retrospect, they comment on their shared experience during the stranger's *midrash*: "Didn't our hearts burn within us, while he talked with us on the road and opened the Scriptures to us?"(Lk. 24:32).

Every resurrection appearance is not alike

This portion of Luke is part of a sub-genre within the Gospels called "resurrection appearances." For seven weeks after the resurrection, Jesus appears off and on to various groupings of disciples. During this period Jesus appeared in a transfigured bodily form: people could touch his body and feel something, witness him eat fish and so on. Such appearances are found in the Gospels of Matthew, John and Luke.[11]

The resurrection appearances selected by Matthew, John and Luke serve different purposes. Matthew confirms the authority of Jesus, which, as elsewhere in Matthew, is conferred on the disciples for the exercise of mission. John seems to use the appearances to support the authority of the apostles, especially after Peter's denial. The appearance on the road to Emmaus has a different concern than either of these—a concern that one might describe as *spirituality*. How is it that followers of Jesus can expect to experience him now that he is risen from the dead?

The resurrection appearance in Luke 24:13-35 differs from the resurrection appearances in Matthew and John (and the later appearance in Luke) in many respects. It doesn't focus attention on the apostles, the original 12 who had a special role within the community of disciples; instead, it features two unknown disciples. One is named Cleopas, but his identity (the name implies a man) is mentioned nowhere else in the New Testament. His companion remains unnamed, without so much as an assigned gender identity.

No significant instructions from the risen Lord are included for us—nothing like, "If you forgive the sins of any they are forgiven" (Jn. 20:23) or, "Go and make disciples of all

---

11 The resurrection appearance in the Gospel of Mark isn't well attested. It is not included in the earliest manuscripts of Mark and many scholars consider it a late addition.

nations" (Mt. 28:19). This is especially striking since Jesus had a lot to say to the two disciples during their lengthy walk.

Remarkably, the two are not startled, afraid or dumbstruck when Jesus draws close to them. Their interactions are rather ordinary—two people getting to know a newcomer on the road. Jesus remains unrecognized by the two until the very end of the episode. When he *is* finally recognized, he simultaneously disappears, so this might more properly be called a "resurrection *disappearance*."

It's not as though his identity is hidden at first, as was the case when Mary Magdalene mistook the risen Lord for "the gardener," only to quickly recognize him and continue the interaction (Jn. 20:14-17). No, his identity is hidden until the very end—and *just as soon as they recognize him*, he disappears! Rembrandt depicts the moment of recognition with a cloudy POOF!—like the smoke residue of a firecracker after it has exploded.

Unlike other resurrection appearances in the Gospels, this one is different in that the two disciples only become aware that it was Jesus himself communicating with them after the fact. That turns out to be very significant indeed because it means that the *conscious awareness* of someone-known-to-to-be-Jesus *happens* (is experienced) in the realm of memory—a realm that interacts, according to cognitive scientists, with functions of the imagination (Chi).

And that makes Luke 24 especially relevant to us, because this is the most common way that people experience Jesus today—through visions, dreams, impressions, mental images, inner promptings and voices, all involving the realm of imagination. In subsequent chapters, we will share contemporary examples of people experiencing Jesus in this way. This chapter offers an understanding of how these experiences relate to what we find in the New Testament, and especially in Luke-Acts.

How a risen Jesus might be known by the likes of us

Many scholars believe that Luke was either a companion of Paul (who is featured in the book of Acts) or was strongly influenced by Pauline Christianity. Paul, unlike the original 12 apostles, didn't know Jesus before his resurrection. In this respect, his experience of Jesus is (potentially) more like our experience of Jesus.

Paul's first encounter with Jesus also took place "on the road"; in this case, when he was traveling from Jerusalem to Damascus. Acts includes three distinct narrations of this experience with slight variations in detail. In all three, we learn that it began with a bright and enveloping light, followed by an unidentified voice saying, "Saul, Saul, why do you persecute me?" (9:1-19). In the first account, Luke reports that the traveling companions saw no one, but heard the voice. In the second telling, Paul is quoted as saying that the traveling companions saw the light but didn't hear the voice (22:9). The second and third versions mention that it took place at "midday," which may mean that it took place when the group had paused to say their midday prayers, as was customary. In the third telling, Paul refers to the experience as a "heavenly vision" (26:19). All of this suggests that we have an example of a mystical experience—something different than the classic resurrection appearances recorded in the Gospels.

The book of Acts is replete with people having an experience of Jesus mediated by the Holy Spirit, in what might be categorized as mystical experiences: dreams, visions, impressions and inner voices. These often happen during prayer, as when Peter had a vision while he was in a trance-like state during his midday prayers in Joppa (Acts 10:9-16).

Where the resurrection appearances recorded in the Gospels happened, at least in some sense, "out here" (with disciples touching Jesus's transformed body and watching as he ate fish), the experiences of Jesus mediated through the Spirit in Acts occur as something more like mystical experience. They occur in the mode of dream, vision, impression and inner voice. If the disciples see Jesus, they see him with what Paul referred to as "the eyes of the heart" (Eph. 1:8)—a realm of awareness that includes memory and/or imagination.

And while the two on the road to Emmaus walked with a stranger who was, in reality, the risen Lord, they only *experienced* conscious awareness of Jesus—recognizing their traveling companion as Jesus—using this same human capacity, "the eyes of the heart." They experienced Jesus using memory, a function of what we might call "inner awareness."

In this final chapter of Luke's Gospel, we are being prepared for the *kind of experience of Jesus* that will become commonplace in the sequel, the book of Acts. I think Luke wants us to see that the *nature of the experience* of the two disciples on the road to Emmaus is very much like the experience of those who are guided by Jesus through the mediation of the Holy Spirit, attested to in the book of Acts. Luke is inviting us to participate in something now available to us through the Spirit. The final chapter of the Gospel of Luke and the entire book of Acts convey a unified message: Jesus is now reliably and palpably, even if invisibly, present to us, to guide and empower us on our journey.

Jesus is our rabbi, still.

Jesus will be with us, though we may or may not be aware of his presence. The times of conscious awareness—*oh, this is Jesus near me, communicating with me*—will be sporadic, will come and go. These moments of conscious awareness will often take place in what we call the imagination—or, to use older language, "the eyes of the heart," the realm in which we "picture things." And these extraordinary moments of revelation will come sacramentally—that is, they will be conveyed through ordinary material means: a conversation with a stranger, a friend, or both; a discussion about the meaning of events or the meaning of Scripture; the breaking of bread and the blessing of wine in a meal shared with others.[12]

Jesus, Lord of Scripture

Martin Luther understood that Scripture didn't stand alone, to be interpreted willy-nilly. Luther emphasized that the Bible should be read through the lens of the Gospel message understood in light of *sole fide,* or justification by faith alone.[13] He argued for a Christ-centered reading of the Bible. He emphasized some portions of Scripture over others. We sometimes forget that Luther, regarded as the father of Protestant orthodoxy, took the liberty to dismiss (or at least de-emphasize) entire books of the Bible when he discerned that they bore scant resemblance to his understanding of the Gospel. He famously referred to the letter of James as an "epistle of straw" and held the book of Revelation in similar disregard (Gonzales, 48). All of this would embarrass later Protestants, who formalized his teachings into a new Protestant orthodoxy.

We are saying something different. Yes, Scripture is to be interpreted through the lens of the message of Jesus in Scripture. But Jesus also stands over and above Scripture and is present with us, not simply through Scripture, but by his own personal agency. He is present to us now, as a rabbi would have been present to disciples in the period of the apostolic writings. The Jewish experience of having the Law and the Prophets (the Bible) mediated to disciples through a rabbi isn't superseded by a new "Christian" approach to the Bible, in which Christians now have direct access to Scripture and function—in effect—as their own rabbis. As much as this appeals to our modern democratic ideals, this vision is an overreach on our part. It misses the fundamental reality of the

12 "….[Luke] provides a subtly shaded interpretation of the *mode* of Jesus's presence to humans after his resurrection: he can appear in the guise of a stranger on the road in the midst of human dialogue; he can be recognized in the ritual gestures of the community fellowship meal" (Johnson, 398).

13 For a discussion of the relationship between *sola Scriptura* and *sole fide* in Luther's thought, see Eire, 173-174.

resurrection: We have a rabbi who is with us, able to teach and to guide us, and as part of a larger whole of that leadership function, to mediate Scripture to us. And the "us" is important because we are not isolated individuals but members of a community—just as rabbis gathered students into communities and interacted with them in this communal context.

This means that we are as dependent on following our rabbi—which includes but isn't limited to receiving his reading of Scripture—as any disciples of any other rabbi of the period would be. The fundamental change has nothing to do with our dependence on a rabbi and everything to do with the ongoing life and new accessibility of one particular rabbi: Jesus of Nazareth.

This rabbi didn't simply *leave* the Bible to us; he continues to *interpret* the Bible for us. The Bible is only inspired, useful and helpful *in his hands*. We are not to be trusted with Scripture. He is.

Or, to put it another way: Jesus is Lord of the Bible in much the same way that he is Lord of the Sabbath.[14] As the Sabbath was made for the benefit of humankind and not humankind for the benefit of the Sabbath, so the Scripture was made for us and not us for the Scripture. Our rabbi is not simply a teacher of the Bible. He is also Lord *over* the Bible (Wilson, *Jesus Brand,* 149-150), and this is incredibly good news because his reading of the Bible is *for our benefit*. When we encounter readings of the Bible that, if followed, are harmful to others and ourselves, we are to step back and consult our rabbi.

Like so many rabbis before him, Jesus is a bold interpreter of the Bible. While operating very much *within* a tradition informed and shaped by the interpretation of others, he is unafraid to depart from traditional readings of Scripture. Thus, he expands the tradition, which is to say that the tradition Jesus is part of is a living tradition, and not a static one. Jesus is very much a *Jewish* rabbi in this respect.

---

14 "Then he said to them, 'The sabbath was made for humankind, and not humankind for the sabbath; so the Son of Man is lord even of the sabbath'" (Mk 2:27-28).

Our Jewish rabbi

My friend, Mark Kinzer, tells me that every Jewish soul was thought to be present at Mt. Sinai when God gave the Law to Moses. It is thought that each person is given a unique insight into the meaning of the law: a meaning not given to any other person. In this way, the law is a living, breathing word and the Jewish understanding of the law is dynamic, not static.

In the tradition of Jewish teachers before him, Jesus was capable of provocative readings of Scripture that seem to contravene previous readings. And he was unafraid to offer his provocative readings *provocatively*. Take, for example, his defense against accusations that, by claiming to be one with God, he is committing blasphemy—found in John 10 (the same chapter in which Jesus speaks of being a good shepherd whose voice is known by his sheep). Jesus says, "Is it not written in your law, 'I said, you are gods?' If those to whom the word of God came were called 'gods'—and the Scripture cannot be annulled—can you say that the one whom the Father has sanctified and sent into the world is blaspheming because I said, 'I am God's son'?" (Jn. 10:34-36).

In *The Jewish Gospels*, Daniel Boyarin, a preeminent Jewish Talmudic scholar, argues that there was a strong tradition based on the writings of the prophet Daniel, believing that the Messiah would be a second divine being who shared God's throne as God's son (Boyarin, 31-34). Jesus might have appealed less provocatively to this tradition. Instead, he appeals to Psalm 86, which speaks of God among "the gods," reflecting a more ancient strand in the Torah that either accepts the reality of many gods or is at least willing to adapt this language, perhaps as reference to angels.

Of course, we can't be sure how this line from Psalm 86 was understood at the time. Some suggest that Jesus was invoking a tradition whereby Israel entered a deathless state when they received the Law on Sinai (before losing it yet again, after worshipping the golden calf). We do know that by this time in

Israel's history, monotheism had been firmly established and was vigorously asserted in the face of the pagan occupation forces of Rome. However Jesus's response to the charge of blasphemy may have been understood, it was a provocative explanation at best. If it was meant to reassure his accusers that any charge of blasphemy was groundless, it failed.

Why did Jesus respond as he did? We don't know. We're left to pick up the pieces in a state of something very much like embarrassment at his use of Scripture. In modern English translations of Psalm 86, "gods" is placed in quotes, a contemporary convention that connotes "not really." But Jesus makes no such moves. All we can say is that rabbis felt free to offer interpretations of Scripture that were original and provocative—and that Christians follow such a rabbi.

We see this same approach to interpretation employed in the writings of Paul from time to time. In Galatians, for example, Paul asserts, without explanation, that Sarah and Hagar (Abraham's wife and Sarah's slave) represent two covenants: one from Mt. Sinai, the other from the heavenly Jerusalem. Modern Christians eschew allegorical interpretations and explain Paul's violation of the "no allegorical interpretations" rule by saying that he was operating within the sphere of his special "apostolic authority." That may be, but Paul was also operating, as was Jesus, in a longstanding rabbinic tradition that allowed for novel and original interpretations of many kinds.[15]

In particular, Jesus and Paul seemed not to be constrained by the idea that any given text could only admit of one "correct" meaning that trumped all others. The Jewish understanding is to regard Scripture as multivocal, not univocal—that is, the whole of Scripture includes many voices, and not all of the voices need to be in agreement with one another. Furthermore, any given text may admit of multiple and sometimes incompatible interpretations. And none of this

15 Paul makes a similar move in Gal. 3:16, offering a novel interpretation of the Hebrew word *seed*. The Jewish scholar Amy-Jill Levine offers a critical response to Paul's interpretation in *The Misunderstood Jew* (Levine, 79).

is viewed as a threat to Scripture's inspiration. If anything, it is a function of Scripture's inspiration.

Why does this make us so nervous?

If we are nervous about such an approach to Scripture, our fear may betray a lack of confidence that Jesus is actually available to us as Luke-Acts suggests that he is. Our fear may betray our doubt that Jesus is our rabbi still, in the same way that he was present to those disciples on the road to Emmaus—despite their confusion, their sorrow and their feeling of being abandoned by Jesus, of being left alone.

Perhaps Luke's resurrection appearance story is crafted to meet us in the middle of what may be, simply, the human condition. We often feel let down, abandoned and left to our own inadequate devices. We often feel confused about the meaning of events. Maybe this state we find ourselves in is precisely the condition that God, revealed in a Messiah like Jesus, is meant to address.

Like the disciples on the road to Emmaus, we, too—despite our disorientation—may not be left to fend for ourselves. We may, like them, be surrounded by a presence that we fail to recognize—until it dawns on us. We are not alone. God is with us, and the burden on God to guide is greater than the burden on us to get it right.

One of the most remarkable and suggestive aspects of the resurrection appearance of Jesus in Luke is what Luke decides not to include: the content of the extended interpretation of Scripture regarding the necessity of the Messiah's suffering and death, given by Jesus on the road to Emmaus. Why not, for heaven's sake, include us, the readers, in what Jesus told those two? The Church has been vigorously debating that very question—Why did the Messiah have to suffer and die?—for a very long time. A little more detail from Luke would have saved us a lot of time, contentious debate and uncertainty.

Either this was a gross omission or it wasn't the main point of this particular resurrection appearance. If Luke had included this material, we would have more of what we already have: more Scripture interpreting the Law and the Prophets. But Luke is after bigger game: not more Scripture, but more expectant faith that Jesus is our rabbi still.

One can imagine that the interpretation of Scripture that Jesus gave two Jewish disciples in the first century might differ from the interpretation of Scripture Jesus might give two Gentile disciples in the 21st century. God speaks to us in the language and modes of thought with which we are familiar. Scripture is, by definition, time and culture bound. It is written using the language and thought forms of the people to whom it was first given. We don't need more Scripture so much as a rabbi who, knowing us and knowing the world in which we live, can make better sense of Scripture for us.

If this sounds a little risky, it's because it is a little risky. In a privileged literate culture in which the text of sacred Scripture is widely available, it is easier for us to be assured of the avail- ability of Scripture than of the availability of Jesus as our rabbi. But in many cultures other than our own—and in sectors of our culture where literacy is not a given—*Jesus is more available than Scripture*. That, of course, can only be so if Jesus is truly risen from the dead and making his spirit available to all humans. That "if" signals the presence of inherent risk. There is no "proving" that proposition as one might attempt to prove a particular reading of the Bible as the only legitimate reading. There is only the possibility of trying it on for size and experimenting with it for one's self, with others.

For modern people like ourselves—reading a book, after all—this all seems more tenuous, more nerve-wracking than the notion that a book is available to us (and in the case of the Bible, a best-seller at that). But that is precisely the edge to faith: faith involves a childlike trust, a different sense than physical sight. Either Jesus is reliably present to us and dis- coverable by us or he is not. Either faith in Jesus is a means of knowing him or it is an illusion. Faith involves an embrace in the face of doubt, not an avoidance of risk.

Everything hinges not on our having the right knowledge system, but on whether or not Jesus really is our rabbi still.

2

Sola Scriptura and Power

Emily

EVERY SUNDAY AND Wednesday night in the late 1980s, my youth group friends and I played hide-and-seek in the fields and barn surrounding the rural church I attended in Indiana. We knew all the quality hiding places—the darkest corners of the barn, that little path in the woods nearby and the tall grass behind the main building. Just as we explored the physical terrain together, we also investigated spiritual and emotional landscapes—experimenting with prayer, Bible interpretation and figuring out how to navigate relationships with people we might not naturally be friends with outside of a religious gathering. We cultivated a space where I felt like I belonged.

I loved everything about church—the music, the friendships and the deep connection with Jesus that community nurtured in me. I loved church so much that I remember sitting in the back row with my friends one Sunday, thinking, "If I could serve God the rest of my life in some kind of vocational capacity, that would make me happy."

But I couldn't imagine being a pastor, because I'm female. My naïve response to that thought was, "I should become a pastor's wife."

It perplexes me now that the thought, "I should become a pastor's wife," didn't cause me to question my religious framework. I was a natural leader, even as a child, and an independent thinker. But, by repressing my desire to lead, I still had a way to fit in with my church group. It meant diminishing the fullness of my personal gifts and desires, but the pull of group acceptance was so strong—the good I felt I received from those bonds so powerful—that I let it dictate my life choices. In essence, I accepted a limited form of belonging because it allowed me to stay fully connected to my faith community.

It took me a further decade of spiritual wandering and study to arrive at a different view of women's roles in the Church. My first instinct, during college, was to opt out of faith altogether. Later, when I found I still had a spiritual itch to scratch, I discovered theologians I respected who advocated different perspectives on how to read Scripture—viewpoints that included respecting the full pastoral leadership of women. That, in turn, led me to a new openness to reading female theologians, which stretched my world further. Here were women writing about things I'd *felt* but not dared allow myself to linger on too long. Those voices were few, but they were powerful.

At the age of 30, I let myself say *I'm gay* out loud for the first time. I'd had loads of practice repressing feelings for the sake of social belonging, but this one finally bubbled up in a way I couldn't deny. And I was scared. Here, once again, a part of my *being* threatened my group standing—potentially in my family (though it turned out they were great), in my social circles, in my faith community and vocationally. By that time I was living overseas, serving as a missionary and "international pastor" for my church. I knew that coming out would potentially cost me everything, so I did nothing. For several years, I did nothing—until that became impossible.

During those years of knowing I was gay but feeling too afraid to come out, I searched for theological voices—others who might understand my predicament. I started tracking down writers who were not part of the elite white-straight-male-Western academy, who might understand the dynamic of having an essential part of yourself be seen as problematic. In my quest I found the company of the marginalized—people crying out for justice, demanding dignity for their full humanity and imagining a world where we accept and love others unconditionally. Writers like Ada María Isasi-Díaz, Traci C. West, Miguel A. De La Torre, Kelly Brown Douglas and Ivan Petrella sang to my heart. I also found books written by LGBTQ+ Christians, which gave me strength to own my story in the same way they'd learned to own theirs.

One fine evening in spring 2014, while attending a conference hosted by the church where I then worked as an assistant pastor, a friend grabbed my arm and said, "There's someone you've *got* to meet." I looked up and saw a sweet-looking woman in an army-green jacket with short brown hair, big green eyes and the widest smile, and thought, "Uh-oh, I'm in trouble. She's my type." I spoke to my wife for the first time that night.

I'll share more of the details later, but suffice it to say that my worst fears soon came true. I was, in fact, ejected from my faith community in a brutal and violating process after I started dating Rachel, and I lost a lot of friends. In many ways, it was worse than I imagined. However, I also saw and experienced some of the most courageous and powerful acts of love performed by allies and queer people alike. Many of them attend the church Ken and I now lead together. Beauty does come from ashes.

In looking over the narrative of my life, I see how profoundly I've been shaped by how others interpreted Scripture to me. And which voices interpreted it made a huge difference in both how I viewed myself and in the amount of life and joy I've been able to embrace. I'm the happiest I've ever been, and I don't think I could have arrived at this place without the voices speaking through the cracks of institutional American

Christianity, reminding me that I'm loved by God for all I am. I've come to realize the enormous power wielded by those upholding the status quo, especially those who refuse to be informed by those they perceive as "outsiders." I've also come to realize that I played a role in upholding their power over me by letting them dictate how I handled my vocation, my sexuality and my emotions—by letting their interpretations override the still, small voice inside of me.

No more.

The Oxford English Dictionary defines the word *resistance* as "the refusal to accept or comply with something." I now refuse to allow people who don't understand what it is to be female and gay dictate how I should live and follow Jesus. I refuse to silence or ignore the writings and teachings of those on the margins, especially people who experience life differently than I do (people of color, transgender people and those in the postcolonial world, for example). I refuse to tamp down my own feelings and desires for the sake of belonging or others' comfort. And, in my refusals, I've come into myself. At last, I've found my core. I've found peace and happiness, and I've found the strength to lead with integrity.

The power of institutionalized Christianity is real, it is pervasive and it is difficult to challenge. It manifests in myriad ways.

During the years I lived in western China, some fellow missionaries worked on how to talk about the Christian story with Tibetans, who are, by and large, Buddhist. (For a fuller view of how we see Christianity in relation to other religions, see Chapter 15.) Since a high percentage of Tibetans are illiterate, and thus couldn't read the Bible even if the entirety of Scripture were translated into their language (which it isn't), those missionaries condensed the biblical narrative into 12 three-minute oral stories. Those stories could then be memorized and passed around Tibetan communities like folklore.

A friend working on that project let me read the stories as they were translated into the local language. Some of the narratives communicated a questionable view of Scripture, and she hoped I could suggest a few changes—especially in the last one. The final story of the 12 summed up the book of Revelation, and it left the listener with the impression that the Christian hope climaxes with God destroying both the earth and anyone who didn't confess faith in Jesus in his or her lifetime. I grew up with that storyline—which is a distinctly American interpretation of Revelation—so I understood its roots, but have since come into a more hopeful (and less literal) interpretation.

I offered a rewrite. I'm not sure if they used it, but the experience highlighted my increasing awareness of the inherent power differential between storytellers and their audience. Those who hear a story depend on storytellers to accurately relay meaning and significance—especially if that story, like the Christian narrative, contains the richness of a tradition passed down for millennia.

Sola Scriptura privileges the literate

Creating, summarizing, translating, interpreting or distributing a story places one in a position of power over others. Those on the underside are often more aware of this dynamic, though some with more power are cognizant of it as well. In the 1920s, an American missionary to Nigeria wrote, "Ours is the opportunity to provide the only literature they will have for many years to come. Would it not thrill you to think that you controlled the reading matter of an entire tribe?" (Manarin, 169).

Humanity's spiritual stories are sacred, preserved and passed along as collective wisdom. The task of passing them along and interpreting them for the following generation is also sacred, but we don't often talk about the power dynamics at play in the process. Who gets to share and who gets to interpret? What criteria do we use to decide? By consolidating interpretive and communicative power into the hands of a few highly educated (and mostly Western) persons, we've effectively eliminated and erased the perspectives of the less powerful (De La Torre, *Reading the Bible*, 45).

It strikes me that educated, literate people—including myself—have the privilege of being seen as authoritative in matters of faith because we can better articulate our thoughts in writing. In many circles, my influence is somewhat negligible because I'm a woman, I'm gay and I don't hold a seminary degree. Many will disregard my perspective because of those factors. But I wrote this book, published it and had the funds and support to travel and live abroad, sharing my faith and bumbling into projects like the oral stories project described above. I have a greater chance of being "heard" and respected than, say, an illiterate woman in Ghana. Writers like Clara Sue Kidwell, Homer Noley, George Tinker and Ada María Isasi-Díaz challenge our norm (Kidwell et al., 27-28; Isasi-Díaz, 74-82). They posit that those who are illiterate can possess just as sophisticated and authentic an understanding of the Gospel as those who can read—and perhaps more so, because they often identify with the oppressed and outcast for whom Jesus's message was good news.

Back in the 1500s, when the Reformers based the primary authority of the Church on Scripture, they effectively placed the power of the Church story in the hands of those who were literate (Kalilombe, 452).[16] Around the time of the Reformation, literacy rates in Europe were low and, as you might expect, women lagged behind men.[17] As you can see in the chart below, literacy rates were less than 20 percent throughout the continent in the mid-16th century (Roser). Those who could read were the exception, not the rule.

---

16 By literate I mean those who can read and write. I acknowledge that there are different literacies such as music, math, media, technology, computer, information, digital, multicultural, cultural, visual, *etc.*

17 In 1630 in northern England, more than 30 percent of men were literate, while less than 10 percent of women could read.

Literacy Rates in Europe	1550	1750
Netherlands	12%	85%
Sweden	1%	48%
Germany	16%	38%
Great Britain	16%	54%
France	19%	29%
Italy	18%	23%

It's true that the Reformation helped catalyze a literacy movement, as churches came to believe that teaching congregants to read the Bible was imperative for their spiritual lives. Within 200 years, literacy rates increased dramatically in Europe and the United States. Even so, only 12 percent of the global population could read by 1820, some few decades after the Moravian revival in Germany sparked a global missionary movement. And in places with high literacy rates, there were remarkable differences between races and classes in the 19th century. In 1870, not long after the American Civil War, 80 percent of black people in the United States were illiterate compared to 11.5 percent of white people—a product of slavery and systemic racism.

Today, 17 percent of the world remains illiterate. That percentage may sound low, but when the world population is 7.4 billion, it represents over 1.2 billion people. In places like Guatemala, Haiti and sub-Saharan Africa, illiteracy remains high, ranging from 30 to 70 percent (Roser).[18]

18 In David Garrison's classic global church-planting book, *Church Planting Movements: How God is Redeeming a Lost World*, he is so reliant on biblical authority

The effect of *sola Scriptura* is to place the illiterate in a submissive position to the literate. Karl Barth saw the danger posed by this in the early 1930s, when he wrote the first volume of his *Church Dogmatics* series. He notes that our scriptural tradition began as oral proclamation of the Gospel. The written proclamation remains secondary to the spoken Gospel (Barth, 99).[19] He warns of "the constant danger that the Bible will be taken prisoner by the Church," and that it easily becomes the "Church's dialogue with itself" (103).[20] Ken and I fear that this is precisely what has happened. We gladly learn from those who spend their lives poring over Scripture and its meaning. We are not saying that we should dispose of theological elites, but only that theirs is not the only, or even the primary, lens through which we need to evaluate the effects of our Gospel narrative.

The fact remains: Those most likely to be literate and viewed as theologically sound in the last five centuries have

that he addresses the issue of widespread illiteracy in some cultures by saying it's the missionary's responsibility to transmit the Bible by any means necessary. In Chapter 11, he asks, "How do evangelicals, who are fundamentally a 'people of the book,' multiply among people who can not read and write?" He gives several options—memorization, audio-visual, storying, songs and using educated youth to teach. However, he neither addresses the power differential in such communications nor thinks to mention introducing believers to the living, risen Jesus known through the Holy Spirit.

19 Barth mentions that even the written word of God was first presented as oral testimony. "For a better understanding, one should note first what we have called the similarity as phenomena between Church proclamation and the second entity, which confronts it in the Church—namely, the Canon of Holy Scripture. This consists in the fact that in Holy Scripture, too, the writing is obviously not primary, but secondary. It is itself the deposit of what was once proclamation by human lips. In its form as Scripture, however, it does not seek to be a historical monument but rather a Church document, written proclamation" (99).

20 "Exegesis is always a combination of taking and giving, of reading out and reading in. Thus exegesis, without which the norm cannot assert itself as a norm, entails the constant danger that the Bible will be taken prisoner by the Church, that its own life will be absorbed into the life of the Church, that its free power will be transformed into the authority of the Church—in short, that it will lose its character as a norm magisterially confronting the Church. All exegesis can become predominantly interposition rather than exposition and to that degree it can fall back into the Church's dialogue with itself. Nor will one banish the danger, but only conjure it up properly and make it acute, by making correct exposition dependent on the judgment of a definitive and decisive teaching office in the Church or on the judgment of a historico-critical scholarship which comports itself with equal infallibility" (103).

been white, male, educated and Western. This means that the translation and interpretation of Scripture has largely been handled by the category of people with the most power in the world over the last 500 years. During the last several decades in particular, people who do not fit the above description began objecting to this—and for good reason (Sugirtharajah, 1-2).

But God privileges the marginalized

We know Christianity spreads fervently among the poor and oppressed, and has always done so (Jenkins, *Next Christendom*, 201).[21] It's not that God has been unable to use our current paradigm of power for his purposes—God has always worked with what she has.[22] But this paradigm remains demonstrably insufficient and limits the revelation we have of who Jesus is, including who he is to the poor and powerless. It means that the guardians of "truth" and "right theology" continue to be those with tremendous privilege in this world. It means that people who experience God outside of the proscribed boundaries easily get shoved aside. Their voices cannot be heard above the din of the institutional power upholding a Western, white, male, heteronormative interpretation of our faith (Kim, 116).[23]

Cuban theologian Ada María Isasi-Díaz talks about the vital importance of praxis in developing theology. By *praxis* she means reflective, liberative action—observing the very

21 Though it also thrives, at times, among middle and upper classes (Jenkins, *The New Faces of Christianity: Believing the Bible in the Global South*, 188).

22 Various aspects of the Trinity are referred to in both masculine and feminine terms throughout Scripture, so the authors have chosen to alternate between masculine and feminine pronouns when speaking of God. God incarnate as Jesus will be referred to as masculine, and God the Holy Spirit is most accurately feminine (or neuter in parts of the New Testament). So the Spirit is most often spoken of in feminine terms. God is both male and female; God is neither male nor female. God both transcends our human categories and paradoxically embodies them.

23 "While Asian immigrants experience marginality, it is a condition of oppression experienced by all people of color, including Native Americans, African Americans and Latino Americans ... Affirming the gifts and graces of our different cultures, we need to work together toward a prophetic intercultural future" (116).

real effects of theology in the lives of people, considering its outcomes carefully and allowing our conclusions to shape how we think and believe. To do so, we must consider the "on the ground" input from those impacted, and not treat those who aren't of the academy (or who aren't literate) as ignorant. Isasi-Díaz writes, "Women in general (but in particular poor women with little formal education, and even more so women whose first language is not English—as is the case with many Hispanic women) are commonly not considered quite capable of articulating what they think. Yes, many consider that Latinas' ability to think is, at best, limited. It is clear to see, then, why *mujerista* theology's claim that grassroots Hispanic women are 'organic intellectuals,' that their articulation of their religious understandings is an element of this theology is, in itself, a liberative praxis" (74).

She later describes how some poor and illiterate Hispanic women use theology to find meaning in their lives using unintentional methods that would make systematic theologians squirm (75-82, 151-153). But are these methods, when bearing the fruit of empowering the poor and communicating the Gospel, any less valid than traditional means of combing Scripture? If interpreting the stories of Jesus and his life, death and resurrection brings life abundant, then surely the Holy Spirit can make "organic intellectuals" of us all.

First Nations theologian and educator Richard Twiss points out that listening to marginalized voices generates fear in the established power centers. He writes, "It isn't unusual for influential church leaders to perceive any new movement as a threat to a 'genuine' expression of Christian faith. Because these new ideas often originate in the margins of power and end up outside the culturally-formed religious 'boxes' of these leaders, their authority as representatives of correct biblical truth is threatened. Their belief systems (or they often believe, God's perspective) are under attack" (36). Therefore, it is in the interest of the power elites to quell the perspectives of the disenfranchised.

Suppressing the voices of outsiders stands in stark contrast with all we know of the Bible and of Jesus. Jesus, who lived and ministered on the margins of his culture, embraced outsiders. He bounced into Jerusalem for festivals, but always back out again to take his message to those in the villages and in the hill country. Relatively powerless himself, Jesus critiqued those who held power in his day.

The voices or emotions of those with less power sometimes make those of us who have more privilege ill at ease—even those of us who are not academic elites. Sometimes their voices push against our cherished views of Jesus, the Church or of how to live. But oppressed people generated what became of our holy text. Men and women with little power recorded a shocking range of emotions and radical ideas. If we tune out the perspectives of the poor and the vulnerable, we misunderstand the Bible and its witness.

Think about it: The Bible is one of the few ancient texts in this world written by people who were not in a position of power. They were not history's winners. Normally, the powerful, the conquerors and the educated created the histories and narratives that supported their dominance. The Bible, on the other hand, is a collection of voices of those who were not, for the most part, dominant. Much of Scripture contains the stories of an exiled people. That's part of why Christianity is so often embraced by the less privileged— because they find themselves in the story and recognize it as good news.

The voices of the underdogs reverberate through our sacred Scripture in tones that are sometimes uncomfortable. They challenge the religious beliefs, traditions and interpretations held deeply by some in their day. Perhaps similar voices are the ones we need to listen to now.

We read through our cultural lenses

When I lived in Asia, a close colleague and friend of mine was from northeast India. He's a joyful man with a quick smile. At one point in our friendship we had a potentially serious misunderstanding that caused some awkwardness between us for a time. So I was surprised when he popped over to my apartment with an aloe plant after I got the worst sunburn of my life.

As I cracked the aloe and worked it onto my arms, he started talking about another friend of his, saying things like, "This guy I know communicated poorly with his American friend and it resulted in some confusion. Maybe his body language was confusing or maybe he said things in a way that didn't translate the same in her culture. What do you think?" So we talked about how wires get crossed when people of different cultures are close.

I decided to bring up the particular uncomfortable encounter we'd had a couple of weeks back. In my Midwestern American way, I was direct about it. My friend looked confused and squirmed in his chair. It took me a second, but then it hit me that we'd just talked about our own friendship. His "other friend" was him, and I was the American woman. We'd addressed our conflict indirectly, in the way many Asian cultures do. I said, "Ohhhhh … we just talked about it, didn't we?" He nodded, and we laughed. Then we moved on.

I lived overseas for the better part of four years and worked with people from several regions of the world. Even though I was trained to be aware of cultural styles—how people handle conflict, how we think about leadership, how we relate to time and so on—the sub-cultures in which I grew up were so powerfully ingrained in me that I sometimes didn't notice when they affected my communication—or my misinterpretation—of others. My American culture, my female culture, my Midwestern culture, my middle-class culture, my faith culture and my white culture, among others, became my default—just as your particular blend of cultures becomes yours (Hunting-ton, xv).

One of the most difficult parts of our discipleship path is untangling genuine Jesus-centered values from the values of our cultures. Every culture—even cultures trying to live out Jesus-shaped values—takes on baggage, because humans, being human, use culture to bolster our power and sense of belonging.

In *Invisible Influence: The Hidden Forces That Shape Behavior*, marketing professor Jonah Berger writes that we humans have a biological need for connection because without other humans, back in our hunter-gatherer days, we'd literally die alone. Our brains evolved a sophisticated mirroring system that helps us recognize our in-groups, so we feel safe and know we have teammates with whom we work to survive. We mimic the humans around us, creating cultures and sub-cultures that let us know who is part of "our tribe" and who will help and protect us. He says:

> *Mimicry facilitates social interactions because it generates rapport. Like a social glue, mimicry binds us and bonds us together. Rather than 'us versus them,' when someone behaves the same way we do, we start to see ourselves as more interconnected. Closer and more interdependent. All without even realizing it. If someone acts like us, or behaves sim-ilarly, we may infer that we have things in common or are part of the same tribe. Part of this may be driven by the association between similarity and kinship. Because we tend to imitate those around us, seeing someone doing the same thing we're doing may serve as a non-conscious signal that we are connected in some way. (40-41)*

Cultural forces exhibit such a strong evolutionary pull on us that we can be blind to how they cloud our interpreta-tions—both of interactions with people not like us as well as of Scripture (Lightsey, 43).[24] We wind up using the Bible to reinforce our own intuitive beliefs (C. Smith, 78).[25]

In *Transforming Culture: A Challenge for Christian Mission,* Sherwood Lingenfelter notes that church growth happens most quickly within homogenous groups,[26] so that creates environments ripe for groupthink. He cautions us that, when the Gospel remains disconnected from views outside one specific culture, it festers and grows sick (15-22).

Having a culturally homogenous church or network is not inherently unhealthy. There is an abundance of such faith communities around the world, and I've read stories from first-generation American immigrants talking about how, for example, attending their mostly Korean church was a lifeline—a reprieve from working and living as a minority in American society. Lingenfelter isn't discouraging highly contextualized churches so much as warning us about the tendency for groups of people with similar cultures and practices to discount outside voices that contradict strongly held beliefs.

Insularity breeds bad theology, so shaping church cultures rooted in humility is paramount. No one cluster of believers understands the Gospel on its own,[27] and our willingness to

---

24 "In fact, no reader of the text *enters* it *tabula rasa*. We enter the reading of the early Hebrews' context and first-century Palestine through the lens of our own 21st-century contexts, experiences and the traditions of our various cultures. To declare a pure, unbiased interpretation belies the arrogant attempt to sit as paragons of Christian virtue. Therefore, to maintain that scripture alone is infallible and the sole source for informing our practice of our faith and our theology is untenable for queer womanist theology" (Lightsey 43).

25 "In short, because many readers are first driven in interpretation by their personal, cultural and political *contexts*, the biblical texts actually often serve functionally even among biblicists as *pretexts* to legitimate predetermined beliefs and concerns, rather than as an independent authority as scriptural *text*" (C. Smith 78). Italics in original.

26 A popular, though somewhat simplistic, book in missionary circles encourages evangelists to "focus upon one specific people group" because "the Gospel will spread with the least barriers within a people group with common background and affinity to one another" (Sutter, 39). Also, see Garrison, 272-272.

27 "Most Christian workers have so overlearned their cultural values that they confuse them with the teaching of Scripture. They are blind to the passages of Scripture that contradict their point of view, and they are skilled in rationalizing their values through proof-texts from their Bible study. They read the indictments of the Pharisees in the

engage with people who think differently in order to discover truth together, as a global family, leads us toward Jesus and away from the faulty project of seeking certainty. Exerting some effort to learn from, and dialog with, people outside our religious and cultural bubbles is a worthwhile endeavor.

The Bible made impossible

In a broad sense, churches rooted in *sola Scriptura* that privilege literacy—and which take place within homogenous cultural and theological huddles—have impoverished the theology of the Church. This approach has also borne the fruit of extreme division.

In *The Bible Made Impossible: Why Biblicism is Not a Truly Evangelical Reading of Scripture,* Christian Smith offers a withering critique of the Protestant attempt to achieve unity through *sola Scriptura*. He calculates that if we consider just the top 17 disputable issues within Protestantism, and list the various answers that fall within Christian orthodoxy—*and* that can be backed up with Scripture—there are more than 5 million potential combinations of orthodox belief (24).

Things like:

1. Should women be pastors?
2. Is communion the *real* body and blood of Jesus, or is it symbolic?
3. Should people be baptized as infants or as adults?
4. How do we read the beginning of Genesis? As literal or metaphor?
5. What do we believe about hell?

Smith points out that *sola Scriptura* has resulted in 30,000 denominations, as church after church parted ways over this, that or the other—all the while insisting that their interpretation of the Bible was more authoritative than anyone else's.

New Testament as blind guides but would be loath to apply the same indictments to themselves and their ministries" (Lingenfelter, 172).

This certainty is rooted in the conviction that the Bible is "clear." He questions whether we're reading the Bible in a way it's not meant to be read. If the fruit of entrusting the authority of Scripture and its interpretation to (mostly) white, educated, Western, straight men has been 30,000 denominations in 500 years, then maybe we're missing the mark.

Smith's solution to countering biblicism is to read the Scriptures Christologically—thinking about everything in light of who Jesus *is*.[28] While he acknowledges that the revelation of the Gospel can be found outside the Bible, he squarely affirms the authority and power of Scripture.[29] Smith feels that all Scripture can be related to what "Christ testified to in Scripture and proclaimed in the church."[30] His anti-biblicist argument creates a significant challenge for literalists, but doesn't go as far as our proposal does. *Solus Jesus* says Christ is alive and an active agent moving in the world today, through the power and presence of the Holy Spirit. It's not just about the Jesus known in the Bible (or Scripture orally proclaimed), but also about the Jesus who personally speaks to the Church today through revelatory experiences (Mesters, 431-441).[31]

That means more than thinking in light of the Jesus recorded in the pages of the Bible as *sola Scriptura* (and the Anglican and Wesleyan discernment methods) implies.[32]

---

28 Thinking Christologically is also Lingenfelter's solution to church groupthink.

29 "Biblicism's limited perspective on revelation and static view of knowledge suggest that not only the heart of the Gospel but all of the Gospel's implications can and must be found only and explicitly in the Bible. It isn't so. To say that takes nothing away from the authority and power of scripture—quite the contrary. Biblicism, again, views the Bible as a kind of catalog or handbook in which complete information and instructions for right living can be found" (C. Smith, 170).

30 Smith, *ibid.*, 106, quoting (and agreeing with) Donald Bloesch.

31 Mesters has found this to be true among Brazilian churches. "In the course of these years, slowly, from within this renewed interest in the Bible, there grew up a new concept of *revelation* which is of great importance for an understanding of popular interpretation. In this, God did not only speak in the past; he continues to speak today!" (432, emphasis in original).

32 The Anglican tradition didn't adopt *sola Scriptura*, but it did privilege Scripture as an authority over reason and tradition. The effect, especially without a recognition of the role of experience (in the Anglican tradition) or the very limited understanding of experience (in the Wesleyan tradition), is similar to *sola Scriptura*.

It also means thinking in light of the Jesus with whom we have a relationship, the Jesus we experience in our lives. If Jesus is actually alive and is the head of the Church, then Jesus can still speak.[33]

When Jesus ascended into heaven, he didn't tell his disciples, "That's it—you're on your own now, equipped with the material about me that will eventually get written down and compiled into a canon in 300 years." No. Jesus said, "I have much more to say to you, more than you can now bear. But when the Spirit of truth comes, he will guide you into all the truth."[34]

Jesus doesn't say that Scripture will lead us into all truth, but rather the Holy Spirit—the Spirit who works *through* Scripture, but is also *not limited to* Scripture. If we're looking to be led into Truth (who is a person, not a set of propositions) then we are open to a dynamic connection with the Holy Spirit who leads us into greater relationship with the living Jesus, the embodiment of our God-Who-Is-Love, and who brings us life (De La Torre, 52).

For many, it can be a relief to admit that the Bible isn't always "clear"—that it's not a life manual filled with answers. The Bible doesn't directly address many questions about ethics or how to live. We can't look up "bioethics" or "cloning" or "IVF," or "semi-automatic weapons" or "cybersex," and find cut-and-dry answers. This drives us to wrestle with the text, individually as well as communally, within our various cultural contexts. That's where growth often happens—in asking questions and seeking God for answers. We might

---

33 "However, the doctrine of *sola scriptura*—the Bible as the unadulterated, inerrant, infallible word of God that contains 'those things which are necessary to be known, believed and observed, for salvation'—must be judged by each Christian generation for its capacity to speak truth to the conditions of its lives. Though doctrines have been derived from the Bible, doctrines are not necessarily the word of God" (Lightsey, 42).
34 Jn. 16:12-13a. Note the pronoun used for "Spirit" in Greek is neutral and could be translated either as *he* or *she*. For clarity, I retained the masculine pronoun for this verse. Also, I didn't want the Spirit to sound like the "female" part of God who takes orders from the "male" part of God, as picking out this one verse might imply!

come to different conclusions, but we can treat one another charitably in our quest.

The early Church didn't invoke *sola Scriptura*

The Church has resolved several major disputes in the so-called "ecumenical councils," named after the cities in which they were held: Nicea, Constantinople, Ephesus and Chalcedon. In these councils (spanning eight centuries), leaders from many places gathered to thrash out major questions like the divinity of Jesus, the Trinitarian nature of God and so on. But the very first such council took place in Jerusalem, and it was convened to resolve a fierce dispute about the inclusion of Gentiles within the burgeoning Jesus movement.

The controversy was precipitated by the rapid spread of the Gospel among Gentiles—first to Antioch, then the third largest city in the Roman Empire (modern day Antakya, Turkey) and from Antioch to several other cities in Asia Minor. This effort was spearheaded by the apostle Paul, who was working closely with Barnabas, an early leader in the Jerusalem Church.

The believers in Jerusalem were under intense pressure from both the Roman Empire and the non-Messianic Jews of Jerusalem (Bruce, 174). Stories of Gentile believers in Jesus mixing freely with Jewish believers, in violation of the prevailing interpretations of Torah, made things even worse for the beleaguered Messianic sect. The efforts of Paul and Barnabas to spread the Gospel among the Gentiles, aided by Paul's insistence that the Gentiles were not required to undergo circumcision or take on the obligations of Torah observance, came at a heavy cost to the Jerusalem Church. As a result, Paul and Barnabas got into a significant argument with the Jewish believers from Judah over this issue (Kinzer, 158).[35]

---

35 Kinzer's book argues that Jews, including followers of Yeshua, are still called to be faithful to Torah. Paul circumcised Timothy (whose father was Greek) himself (Acts 16: 3) when they headed to places with large numbers of Jews. But as an apostle to the

Eventually, Paul, Barnabas and some others went to Jerusalem to discuss the issue of circumcision with Church leaders. This assembly was called the Jerusalem Council, as described in Acts 15. Paul and Barnabas reported on the success of the Gentile mission, telling how people came to faith in Jesus with evidence of the Holy Spirit at work in their lives. This encouraged the leaders. However, some of the believers from the party of the Pharisees insisted the Gentiles be circumcised and keep the Law of Moses in order to belong to the faith.[36]

Peter got up before the Jerusalem Council and spoke, followed by Paul and Barnabas, and argued that "God, who knows the heart, *showed that he accepted [the Gentiles] by giving the Holy Spirit to them,* just as he did to us. He did not discriminate between us and them, for he purified their hearts by faith. Now then, why do you try to test God by putting on the necks of Gentiles a yoke that neither we nor our ancestors have been able to bear?" (Acts 15:8-10, emphasis mine).

This is crucial: There existed a prejudice against Gentiles backed up by both Scripture and tradition. Aside from a few hints in the prophets, the general reading of the Hebrew Scriptures up to that point did not envision Gentiles as part of God's people. Tradition certainly did not point that way, either. There's the odd Gentile here and there in the Old Testament (Ruth, Rahab, the weird story about Jonah preaching to

---

Gentiles with a calling to insist Gentiles be included in the family of God *as Gentiles,* he argued for full inclusion without adherence to Torah for the Gentiles (162-163).

36 Pharisees were trained in maintaining boundaries between faith insiders and outsiders; some apparently found relinquishing the impulse difficult. I have sympathy for them. Jews had no high regard, in that time, for Gentile morality, and a sincere concern for the ethics and reputation of this new movement manifested in their objections. Plus, severe persecution took place in and around Jerusalem. These early believers endured quite a lot of oppression and already had trouble justifying their faith in Jesus to their fellow Jews. And now they had to advocate for Gentiles? F.F. Bruce writes, "It was all very well for Barnabas and Paul to forge ahead with Gentile evangelization, but meanwhile, the Jerusalem leaders had to discharge their own responsibility to commend the Gospel to their fellow-Jews. The discharge of this responsibility would not be rendered any easier by reports that large numbers of Gentiles were entering the new fellowship on what must have seemed to be very easy terms" (174).

Gentiles in Ninevah), but the overall arc didn't appear to lean toward widespread incorporation.

Looking back from a later vantage point, people could see the arc actually was there but, at the time of the Jerusalem Council, Scripture and tradition pointed away from Gentile inclusion (especially *as Gentiles*, and not Torah-following converts). The only evidence that Peter, Barnabas and Paul provided the Jerusalem elders that God was indeed grafting the uncircumcised into the family of Abraham was evidence of their faith and the presence of the Holy Spirit.

Various means helped the leaders' discernment process, including an appeal to Scripture, an appeal to tradition and consideration of the impact "changing the policy" (so to speak) might have on the larger movement and on the persecuted believers in Jerusalem (Kinzer, 158-159).[37] However, we notice that *the Holy Spirit pulled each of these lines of thinking forward, past the objections.* Peter, James, Paul and Barnabas recognized that their understanding of Scripture, tradition and pastoral oversight could be reimagined when unexpected evidence of the Holy Spirit at work appeared. The spirit of Jesus led the leaders through their protestations, giving vision for an alternative perspective.

In the end, the leaders in Jerusalem placed very few requirements on the church at Antioch.[38]

Martin Luther and the other Reformation leaders acknowledged Jesus as the head of the Church, but they believed that the primary way to know about Jesus is through Scripture; and, as noted earlier in this chapter, Karl Barth added the proclamation of Scripture to the practice of highlighting scriptural authority (99). I think the Jerusalem Council belies this.

---

37 Rabbi Mark Kinzer rightly points out that James, the leader of the Church in Jerusalem, reached for a text from Amos 9 on the spot, interpreting it in light of the witness of the apostles ministering to Gentiles, as a matter of *halakhah*. Evidence of the Spirit pervaded the testimonies, illuminating Scripture for James so it could be understood anew.

38 When I look at the two requirements now, I chuckle a little, because Paul argued against them both in later writings. I can just imagine him being like, "This has been a long fight; I'll take what I can get."

Jesus is indeed the head of the Church, but the primary way to know Jesus is through a living relationship with the risen Lord, mediated by the Holy Spirit and manifesting in experience and evidence (fruit) of God's good realm. The primary way to know about Jesus is through Jesus.

The Spirit: an equal-opportunity advocate

At Antioch, the Spirit worked for those with less power and privilege in the church. Greeks may have had more privilege in the Roman Empire than Jews, but within the early Church, the Jewish leaders in Jerusalem clearly held the rule-making power, with authority to include or exclude and to interpret Scripture.

The Jerusalem Council could have used its authoritative power to build institutions upholding Jewish privilege within the faith. They could have appealed to various Scriptures and traditions to bolster their standing. They could have reacted in fear to the perceived threat of demographic shifts that could transfer church power to non-Jews. But they didn't give in to the temptations to use Scripture or culture as power. Instead, they appealed to Jesus through the Holy Spirit and were able to relinquish their privilege for the sake of the Gospel. And make no mistake: the very Gospel was at stake, at least if you believe the fervency with which Paul writes the letter to the Galatians and the letter to the Romans. The Gospel that Paul is talking about is a Gospel of encounter with the Messiah himself that is open to all.

Paul and the early Church leaders understood the Holy Spirit as the great equalizer.

Faith in Jesus (or the faithfulness of Jesus) made access to God available freely to everyone—no matter your race, ethnicity, class, sexual orientation, gender, ability, IQ, education, family background, marital status or ability to read and write. The Holy Spirit is available to all and is more than capable of leading us into Truth, who is a person with whom we have relationship. With the Holy Spirit, the effects of privilege are washed away. The apostle Paul described counting his advantages "as garbage" (Php. 3:8). The Gospel can be understood and practiced and shaped by fisherman and illiterate women (as first-century women likely were) as well as by trained rabbis like Paul. "There is neither Jew nor Gentile, neither slave nor free, nor is there male and female, for you are all one in Christ Jesus" (Ga. 3:28).

3

Questions of Authority

Ken

I FIRST SAW Haskell Stone sitting in a lawn chair in the backyard of a modest home in Detroit (where I grew up), teaching a group of then-young baby boomers drawn into the Jesus Movement of that era. He was smoking a cigarette in a holder like FDR used.

Many years later, Haskell lectured a group of pastors in a Wayne State University classroom. My classmates were concerned about the divisions in Christianity; Haskell had a different take. He said that he was impressed by the remarkable consensus around what C.S. Lewis called *Mere Christianity*. Christians dispute how the Bible is inspired, but it remains, singularly, "their book." Christians debate the proper form and mode of Holy Communion and baptism, but the vast majority do both. They differ on style of corporate worship, but all value and practice it. And they all relate these practices to one historical figure: Jesus of Nazareth, thought to be crucified, buried, then risen and ascended. They regard him as representing a God he called "Father," empowered by a Holy Spirit. This consensus held for two millennia among believers in vastly disparate cultures, despite sharp ecclesial divisions.

Haskell Stone had a characteristically Jewish take on what binds a community together, profoundly influenced by Jewish scholar Abraham Heschel. He said that the Jewish people are not united by a set of shared beliefs so much as by a set of shared concerns.

This creates a passionate, but non-anxious, approach to truth-seeking in a community.

As one Jewish friend told me, "For Jews, argument strengthens friendship. For Gentiles, argument threatens it."

In his lecture, Haskell described the approach to securing truth in Gentile-dominated Christianity. He said that Catholic Christians look to the teaching authority of the pope and bishops to guarantee an unsullied body of truth, while Protestants appeal to an inerrant or infallible Bible. Both are simply different forms of a self-contained system used to guarantee truth. Haskell offered his own take: "What if the only guarantee of truth is the Spirit of truth, given by Jesus?"

This is not such an outlandish possibility. If Jesus is alive after death, he could be expected to function as an active agent among those open to truth. His agency, it is believed by Christians, is mediated by the Holy Spirit, which has been (and continues to be) poured out "onto all people." Hence, his agency is near-at-hand. The Spirit of truth could indeed be an adequate cause for the preservation of a sufficient revelation of truth among his followers. *Solus Jesus*, rather than *sola Scriptura*, would be the slogan more in line with this reality.

The vexing question of who/what decides

Christians have tried to settle competing truth claims by appealing to various sources of authority that are regarded as criteria for determining what is true. In *sola Scriptura*, the Reformers privileged Scripture as the ruling, or sole infallible, truth-criterion. This claim was made in opposition to the Roman Catholic elevation of the teaching authority of the pope and bishops, or the Eastern Orthodox emphasis on the ecumenical councils of the first eight centuries.

The Protestant Reformers hoped that appeal to Scripture would resolve disputes and ensure the unity of the Church. It didn't work for the obvious reason: Faithful people disagree over how to interpret and apply Scripture. Since then, alternative proposals have been made. The Church of England offered its "middle way" between Catholicism and Protestantism: the "three-legged stool" of Scripture, tradition and reason.[39] Methodists, who emerged from the Church of England, added a fourth criterion: experience. This has been called the Wesleyan Quadrilateral: Scripture, tradition, reason and experience.[40]

All of these traditions would agree that ultimate authority is rooted in God. But each tradition offers its own proximate set of criteria to settle competing truth claims. This search-for-the-right-criteria project is concerned with the following sorts of questions: What sources do we use to determine who God is and what it is God wants? How are these sources related to one another? Which of these sources are privileged, relative to other sources? The attempt to provide answers to these questions has the same aim: to give those who apply the agreed-upon criteria the kind of shared certainty that resolves theological disputes.[41]

Judging by the fruit of this project, sometimes the magic works and sometimes it doesn't. When we apply the major criteria-options (Catholic, Eastern Orthodox, Anglican, Methodist) to the question, "Does God want us to help the poor?" each one confirms a resounding "Yes!" But for a long time, these truth systems buttressed the idea that slavery was a legitimate institution or that men are better suited to be leaders than women. With enough time-testing, we can see that each approach under-delivers on promised results.

---

39 Richard Hooker is credited with this formulation, though the term "three-legged stool" was coined later.

40 John Wesley was a Church of England priest who founded Methodism. The term "Wesleyan Quadrilateral" was coined by 20th-century Methodist scholar Albert C. Outler.

41 I am indebted to the work of William J. Abraham in *Canon and Criterion in Christian Theology* for understanding the philosophical framework underlying the treating of sources of authority as truth criterion. Abraham identifies *sola Scriptura* in the Reformation era as a quest for certainty: "Such a policy, they [the Reformers] thought, would lead to certainty in theological matters" (137).

Emily and I are tempted to offer a new take on which criteria, in which configuration, will work better. Maybe we're just a criterion or two shy of a more workable system, or perhaps we could adjust the privileging structure of the system. But really, are we that smart? Can we expect to solve a riddle our betters-in-faith couldn't?

Our approach is to step back from this project and to be content with asserting less, not more.

Why less may be more (sensible)

We can thrive without answering all the questions we can think to ask—even important questions, like, "How can we know for sure what God wants?" Children remind us that we can prosper without knowing many things, as long as we are looked after by adults who know more. Like children in relation to adults, our knowing is severely limited. We shouldn't be too certain of our knowing. Paul reflects this when he says to those who exhibited excess confidence in their knowledge, "For we know only in part" (1 Co. 13:8).

The broader context of his statement is significant. Paul is writing to a church troubled by those who boast of their knowledge. Paul frequently chides this excessive confidence claim, as when he says, "Knowledge puffs up but love builds up" (1 Co. 8:1). Let's look more closely at the immediate context for Paul's caution about the limits of our knowing:

> Love never ends. But as for prophecies, they will come to an end; as for tongues, they will cease; as for knowledge, it will come to an end. For we know only in part, and we prophesy only in part; but when the complete comes, the partial will come to an end. When I was a child, I spoke like a child, I thought like a child, I reasoned like a child; when I became an adult, I put an end to childish ways. For now we see in a mirror, dimly, but then we will see face to face. Now I know only in part; then I will

know fully, even as I have been fully known. And now faith, hope, and love abide, these three; and the greatest of these is love. (1 Co. 13:8-13)

Paul makes a subtle point here. He begins by asserting our incomplete knowledge, then he claims to have left behind his childish ways—as if to acknowledge that, as adults, we do know more than we did as children. But he doesn't follow this with an assertion that our adult knowledge is therefore complete. Instead, he reasserts his original thought: that now, even as mature adults, we still know only in part. That is, while we begin life as children and become adults, in relation to God, *we remain as children.* This is reflected in the fact that, like children, we are fully known by one who knows us better than we know ourselves. Just as children only later become adults, we, as children of God, will only later know fully as we are fully known.[42] Our remaining as children is *especially manifest* in our knowing, which is partial and childlike. Because our knowing is partial, there is always the possibility of growth in our knowing. Both implications of the childlike tendencies of our knowing are grounds for humility.

Jesus and the apostles repeatedly referred to his adult followers as children. Jesus even went so far as to say to adults, "Unless you change and become like children, you cannot enter the kingdom of heaven" (Mt. 18:3). Jesus enjoined us to regard God as he did, as "our father" (Mt. 6:9)—and elsewhere used maternal metaphors to refer to God's care for us (Mt. 23:37).

Our identity as "children of God" hearkens back to our origin story. There, in Eden, we are living in a garden, walking with God in the cool of the evening. At the center of the garden are two trees: the tree of life and the tree of the knowledge of good and evil. We are given all the fruit-bearing trees of the garden as food to eat, except the tree of the knowledge of good and evil. When we eat from the tree of

---

42 "Beloved, we are God's children now; it does not yet appear what we shall be, but we know that when he appears we shall be like him, for we shall see him as he is" (1 Jn. 3:2).

the knowledge of good and evil—seeking a wisdom that is God-like, or "grown up," in relation to God—our troubles begin.

This original scenario is too important to gloss over and we will develop it further in later chapters. But it pertains here. The two different projects are not labeled "good" and "evil;" instead, the two projects are labeled "tree of life" and "knowledge of good and evil." We are enjoined to choose life rather than knowledge of good and evil.

A young ruler approaches Jesus, calling him "good teacher." Jesus rejects the approach: "Why do you call me good? No one is good but God alone" (Lk. 18:17-19). This is such a counter-intuitive response. What could be wrong with characterizing Jesus as "good teacher"? The corrective makes more sense if Jesus is alluding to an original concern—not the choice between good and evil, but the choice between life and the knowledge of good and evil. Jesus calls us forward (not back) to a second version of childlike trust and innocence—what has been called a *second naïveté* (Wallace), by offering us fruit from the other tree at the center of the garden: the tree of life. Jesus is all about life—abundant life, eternal life.

Jesus often had disputes with those who thought faithfulness to God is about pursuing the knowledge of good and evil and distinguishing between the two based on knowledge. As they bring one moral test case after another to Jesus, for judgment, he offers his version of the warning against eating from the tree of the knowledge of good and evil: "Don't judge, leave it to God." It's not that the knowledge of good and evil is wrong, *per se*. But it is the *wrong project* for us to pursue. God is offering us something different than knowledge of good and evil. We are children in relation to God, and the thing we are to seek from God is life—the very thing Jesus offers us.

All to say, humility regarding our ability to know and the corresponding embrace of our childlike vulnerability is no peripheral concern. If there's anything we ought to be humble about—anything about which we should avoid excessive confidence—it is in regard to our ability to know.

Certainty: we'll be fine without it

We crave certainty, that's for sure. But in many realms, certainty is simply beyond us. Can we be certain, for example, that our dearest loved ones will never betray us? People do change over time. Unanticipated circumstances arise, leading to unexpected outcomes. So we can't be *certain* that our trusted loved ones will never betray us. But that lack of certainty doesn't have to cripple us. Every act of trust involves some measure of risk, and we can be confident enough to take the risk to trust. Whether or not we like to stare it in the face like that, we do it all the time.

To make my point a bit more painfully: Can we be *certain* that God, as we understand God, even exists? I wish I could honestly answer otherwise, but I think the answer is no. Certainty is a state of our consciousness—one that admits no doubt, no *un*-certainty. If we are mortal, limited, flawed creatures, it is sensible for us to admit that we might be wrong about even the things that we are most sure of.

But other states than certainty will do. Assurance will do. Conviction will do. Both of these terms are used by the translators of Hebrews 11:1: "Faith is the assurance of things hoped for, the conviction of things not seen." In *Proper Confidence: Faith, Doubt, and Certainty in Christian Discipleship*, Lesslie Newbigin, who spent 30 years as a missionary in India, describes certainty as a philosophical concern of early modernity—and not as something that pertains to the life of faith (66). When following Jesus, we can leave the quest for certainty to others.

I wonder if certainty is something we crave as a hedge against the fundamental condition of our creaturely nature: our contingency, our vulnerability. In 2012, I went to a therapist for help with anxiety. He walked me through a process called cognitive-behavioral therapy (CBT). This involves understanding how our brains process events. Our perceptions first pass through the limbic, or emotional, center, triggering our thoughts. These thoughts feel, to us, like rational thought unaffected by emotion (such as fear). Thus, we often experience anxiety as a "thought process," when in fact, it is triggered by an emotional response that precedes and shapes our initial "thoughts." CBT teaches us to step back from such thoughts, identify the feelings that may have triggered them and reassess their validity with further reflection.

One day, I talked with my therapist about anxiety over my wife's declining health (she was 60 at the time). He asked me, "What is your greatest fear about Nancy's health? Put it in concrete terms." Without hesitation, I replied, "I'm afraid that I'll come home one day and find her dead of a heart attack." It was a painful fear to state, let alone face.

My therapist didn't try to alleviate my anxiety by assuring me that this was unlikely. Instead, he asked, "Well, if that happened, what would you do?" For a long moment, I was speechless. He gently pressed me: "As painful as it would be, can you imagine that if your wife died suddenly like that, you could make it through—that you would be OK?" I thought of previous losses that I had been through—the death of my parents, in-laws and others. I thought about my sense of connection to God. I thought about my kids. I thought about hope in resurrection. Eventually, I responded, "Yes, I think I would be OK."

That was Thursday. On Sunday, I came home from work and discovered that my wife had died suddenly—of a heart attack, as it turned out. It was every bit as shocking and distressing and painful as you might imagine. For so many reasons, it felt like the worst thing possible. It felt that way for all of my children, and especially the youngest, who at age 19 was simply too young to lose her mom; and for me, married since age 18 to my best friend (and never having made a significant adult decision without her). And for our church, which at the time was on the cusp of a daring transition for an evangelical congregation—to full inclusion of LGBTQ+ people—it was the most destabilizing thing for an already anxious system. For months, I slept with the bedside light and radio on; the house felt so lonely, and I felt a cold terror lurking in the shadows. In some ways, it was much worse than I had anticipated. But with the help of family, friends and God, I came through it. I was OK. What got me through wasn't certainty. What got me through was *help* ... including the help I got in therapy, the assurance I had providentially "tried on for size" a few days earlier—that I would be OK.

In the realm of faith, we aren't offered certainty as a shield against vulnerability. Bad things happen even to the most fortunate people. We *are* vulnerable. But that's precisely what it means to be a child in relation to God: We are vulnerable. We don't have the resources to protect ourselves from every reasonable threat. After all our protective maneuvers, we are still exposed to risk. To proceed with sufficient assurance, we are left with trust in a higher power—a higher power who is committed to our ultimate good. Our shield is faith, or childlike trust.

If certainty regarding truth is offered to us through the Roman Catholic understanding of authority, or the approaches that characterize Eastern Orthodoxy, the Protestant Reformers, the Anglicans, Methodists and unspecified others, we may pick among these options or offer better ones that attempt an improved "truth criterion" approach.

But we offer a different approach—one less concerned for certainty and more willing to rest in a place of childlike trust: *solus Jesus*. This "less is more" approach doesn't leave us bereft of *help* in our pursuit of God, or in our response to God's pursuit of us. We're not adrift in a sea of subjectivity, alone. We have help—and help is what we need most, given our vulnerability.

Medicine for the soul

I grew up in the Episcopal Church during the presidency of Dwight Eisenhower, who called on Americans to attend church as a way to fight atheistic communism. Church attendance was seen as a patriotic duty, and while the effect may have been to swell the ranks, something about faith as a way to connect to God was lost in translation for me.

My experience of faith was tepid, and I left the church soon after being confirmed, at the age of 12. I returned to faith seven years later, as an anti-institutional "Jesus freak" of the early 1970s. I met some people whose lives were animated by their relationship with Jesus. I wanted what they wanted, because their wanting it seemed to give them more purpose, direction and joy in a tumultuous era. I read the Bible because they read the Bible to connect with God. I found that reading, and later meditating, on Scripture seemed to help me. I started to pray as I saw them praying; to gather with others to worship, sing, consider teaching and "break bread" (our informal language for Holy Communion). I happily surrendered to full-immersion baptism, to signify my newfound (or newly rediscovered) faith.

I continued along this path because it worked for me. With plenty of fits and starts, I had a growing sense of connection to God and, in the process, felt more connection to others, to myself and to the wider world. As expected, I wandered into several dead ends over many decades, accumulating my share of regrets and attendant opportunities to change course. But I never completely lost the scent that drew me back to what first attracted me—the goodness and beauty that I found in the "Jesus" way of doing God.

This experience of "catching faith in Jesus" is a rather usual way to become involved with God. Had my early Episcopal parish been more attractive (or I less dull to its charms), I might have known a similar sense of recurring connection and become a lifelong Episcopalian.

United Methodist scholar William Abraham offers an approach that makes sense of my experience of faith. He argues that Scripture, liturgy, sacraments and the "rule of faith" (later codified in the Apostles' Creed) were all part of a canon, or list, of materials to help people connect to God. They came to be listed in this way because the Church experienced their helpfulness. For this reason, they were regarded as "means of grace," or as "medicine for the soul," to "reconnect human agents with their divine source" (Abraham, *Canon*, 1).

Later, in response to various pressures, the Church began to regard these materials as sources of authority used to settle arguments and disputes—what Abraham calls "epistemic criteria (or norms)".[43] Abraham says that this later approach fits the realm of philosophy more than it fits the realm of faith (2). Faith is about connection, involvement and participation with the divine. Philosophy is about the justification of belief, rationality and settling disputes using accepted criteria for separating truth from falsehood.

To tease out the difference between Scripture as a criterion for truth and Scripture as a means of grace, ask yourself the question: "What's more important—that we have contact with Scripture (through whatever means) or that we regard Scripture as a criterion for determining what is true?" If you believe that God is an active agent who breathes in and through Scripture, it would be reasonable to answer: "It's more important that we have contact with Scripture, because if we do, we will encounter divine revelation, and this will exert its divine influence on us."

As the Church devoted more energy to the problem of generating criteria for truth that would settle disputes and offer confidence in our ability to know God's will, it was inevitable that varying approaches to the question of authority would emerge. The Roman Catholic Church privileged the pope (preeminent among the bishops) as the source of

---

43 The term "epistemic" refers to how we know what we know, so epistemic norms are sources of authority that a community agrees on to settle disputes about knowledge.

authority. The Eastern Orthodox privileged the early ecumenical councils as arbiters of truth. The Protestant Reformers
privileged Scripture alone, while the Anglicans added
Scripture interacting with tradition and reason. Still later, the
Methodists added experience to these three. The key is to see
that all these approaches are fundamentally *philosophical* in
nature: that is, they are attempting to answer the philosophical
question, "How can we know what we know to be true?"

Naturally, we're tempted to join the philosophical fray—to
pick and choose, revise and edit, subtract or add. But what if
William Abraham and his colleagues are on to something, and
by engaging in what is fundamentally a philosophical enterprise, we are, in fact, missing the more important point that
is proper in the realm of faith: connection, involvement and
participation with God?[44]

What if we took a more humble approach to our philosophical wrestling, acknowledging that the Holy Spirit gives
us Scripture, worship, sacraments, *etc.*, because God is a
physician prescribing medicine to a sick patient?[45]

To press it a bit farther: What if we have been given these
things *because we need them* and *not* so that we can have a
system that assures us of certainty regarding what we know or
as a way to settle our disagreements and disputes? This would
explain why faithful people can examine the same materials
and come up with such different answers to the philosophical
question, "What are the sources of authority that ensure
that we get things right?" Maybe the materials themselves

---

44 Abraham doesn't deny the validity or importance of attempting to answer the
philosophical questions, but argues that no one answer should be considered binding
on all. "All epistemological proposals, like papal infallibility, scriptural infallibility and
the Methodist Quadrilateral, should be treated as *midrash* [commentary], secondary
to the primary constitutive commitments of the Church as a whole. Hence we need
not give up our epistemological theories, but they do have to be decanonized if we are
to secure the unity of Christians. This is where the rub is going to come hard for many."
Earlier, Abraham—a Protestant himself—acknowledges that his approach "invites
Protestantism to a radical revision," and may be "post-Protestant at its core and cannot
be absorbed within Protestantism" (Abraham et. al., *Canonical Theism*, 7).

45 See Jason Vicker's chapter, "Medicine of the Holy Spirit: The Canonical Heritage of
the Church" in *Canonical Theism: A Proposal for Theology and the Church.*

were given for a different purpose than that, a more pressing purpose: to heal us, to reconnect us to God and as medicine for the soul—that is to say, *for our good*. Perhaps what we need to deal with the disagreements we have with one another regarding truth isn't definitive answers that we can all agree on, so much as the fruit of the Spirit: love, joy, peace, patience, kindness, goodness, faithfulness, gentleness and self-control.

How Jesus uses authority

James Edwards, American New Testament scholar and minister of the Presbyterian Church, summarizes the use of the most common New Testament Greek term for authority, *exousia*:

> *An overview of the 102 occurrences of exousia in the New Testament shows that it is used of God, Jesus and the authority conferred on the Church and/or disciples by the Gospel; also of Satan, spiritual powers and various forms of human authority. Exousia typically resides in or emanates from God or the supernatural realm. When it concerns human and earthly powers, it generally describes political, religious or military authorities. (220)*

For our good represents the aim, purpose and use of authority, in the hands of Jesus. According to Edwards, six of the nine occurrences of *exousia* in the Gospel of Mark refer to the authority of Jesus. Jesus teaches, and the common people are delighted and amazed at his authority. Jesus encounters a man afflicted with evil spirits and sets him free with the exercise of authority. He uses his authority to forgive the sins of a paralyzed man, simultaneously healing him. Jesus compares his authority to the authority of John to administer a baptism of repentance to all comers. Our encounter with God's authority as exercised by Jesus is *for our good*.

Jesus gives his authority to his disciples to be used for the same purpose: to heal the sick, cast out demons,[46] forgive sins and set captives free. Jesus uses his authority as Son of Man to declare that the Sabbath commands were given for the good of humans—and any interpretation or application of those commands that violates this principle are mistaken. This *for our good* principle seems to animate his interpretive key for reading the Bible: "Love your neighbor as yourself: This is the Law and the Prophets."

In *The Unity of the Bible: Unfolding God's Plan for Humanity*, Dan Fuller writes that the distinguishing mark of Israel's God, compared to the surrounding gods, is his determination to serve humanity (rather than his need to be served by humanity). Worshipers of the surrounding gods were thought to worship for the benefit of the gods, without concern for the impact on the worshipers. Israel's God is different. In Fuller's words, "Now the basic thrust of God's whole purpose in creation and redemption has become clear. It is that the earth might be filled with the glory of his desire to service people and, calling upon all his omniscience and omnipotence, to do them good with his whole heart and soul" (Fuller, 136). God's "mission statement" is found in the book of Jeremiah: "I will never stop doing them good ... I will rejoice to do them good" (32:40-41).[47]

Pause to consider a different emphasis

Before pressing out a bit further a "means of grace" approach, it's worth pausing to consider the difference between regarding things like Scripture, tradition, reason, *etc.* as "means of grace" versus regarding them as "sources of authority." Take Scripture as an example. William

---

46 If you're wondering what a "demon" *is*, the Bible seems not to answer that question directly. In Part 2, we will offer a perspective that understands evil at work among humans as a function of our reliance on the "scapegoat mechanism," and tied, in particular, to the work of accusation.

47 For a summary and interpretation of Fuller's work on a God who only seeks our good, see Dave Schmelzer's *Blue Ocean Faith* (46-55).

Abraham points out that when we regard Scripture as a source of authority, we implicitly mean "a criterion for truth," something that will settle disputing truth claims. Scripture functions, in that case, like the U.S. Constitution functions in American society: When there are certain disputes between citizens, they may seek to resolve them by appealing to law and seeking rulings about the application of the law to their situation from a judge, all of a which is founded on a guiding framework for law provided by the Constitution. Of course, there are different approaches to interpreting the Constitution, but the Constitution functions as a source of authority and one that is especially helpful for solving disputes.

This approach to Scripture is so ingrained in many of us (especially for those of us who live in the United States) that it's difficult to imagine a different way of relating to Scripture. But when we compare Scripture to a document like the U.S. Constitution, we can see that it doesn't seem to be written in the same way. There are portions of Scripture that share some qualities of the Constitution, but many parts of Scripture bear no resemblance to it whatsoever. These parts include long narrative stretches, letters written to address very particular situations in local congregations (situations that often remain opaque to us), apocalyptic literature that baffles most of us, folk-proverbs, erotic poetry and lyrics to songs whose music has been lost in the mists of time. One would have to say the vast majority of Scripture bears no resemblance to a document like the Constitution.

At the very least, we can say that Scripture *isn't as effective* as a source of authority in settling disputes as a document written like the U.S. Constitution. This troubles us, because we have a lot of disputes and we would all feel so much better if we had a document that we could use to settle them!

Here's a thought from a different direction: What if our well-being, as a community, isn't contingent on having a foolproof or even a highly effective system (at least in the short term) for settling disputes? Marriage therapists used to emphasize conflict resolution as a means of helping married couples—until research demonstrated that most couples who have long-lasting and satisfying relationships *never resolve their core disputes*. Instead, they learn to live with them. They learn to accept each other, warts and all (Gottman).

What if our greater need is to be connected to divine revelation? That is, our need to hear from God, to feel as God feels, to see what we couldn't see without help from a higher power than our own? Connection to divine revelation helps us connect with ourselves, with others, with the wide world and with God. It is a means of participation in the life generated by God.

Participation in the life generated by God might have many different effects on our disputes. In some cases, it might intensify them, creating more division. It might de-intensify many other disputes. It might resolve some disputes, but in many different ways—quickly, over a long time, easily, or with great difficulty. All of this would take place within the messy combination of the varied powers that influence us at any given time.

William Abraham argues that a "means of grace" approach isn't a new proposal, even if it now feels counterintuitive to many. Rather, it is closer to how materials like Scripture were regarded by the early Christian communities, situated as they were in close proximity to the traditions of Israel.

A five-bladed means-of-grace fan

We will not, then, offer yet another "sources of authority" proposal, assembling various criteria that, when applied, offer certainty that we are getting it right. Instead, we will take our cues from William Abraham and friends and shift our focus to a means of grace approach.[48]

We propose a five-bladed fan as a model for the kind of help we've been given by God to live a life more involved with

48 Abraham and his colleagues flesh out their own approach to the means of grace given to the Church in *Canonical Theism*.

God. We hope to offer nothing original. We're simply reflecting on two millennia of experience by those seeking to follow Jesus, wondering what it is that helps such people.

Picture a fan with five blades. The blades can be labeled (in alphabetical order): "Community," "Experience," "Practices," "Reason" and "Scripture." More could be added, but these five will do for our purpose. The blades are connected to each other and driven by the circle in the center, that represents the Holy  Spirit—or, if you prefer precision, the Trinitarian God, represented in Scripture as Father, Son and Spirit, all in irreducible relationship. Happily, if you like coherent metaphors, the Hebrew word for spirit, *ruach*, means "a disturbance of the air" and can be translated as "wind" or "spirit" or "breath." New Testament Greek has an analogous word, *pneuma*, which can be translated as "wind" or "spirit" or "breath."

Think of means of grace as the things necessary to sustain life on a recurring basis.

In a given day, we need several means of grace: food, air, water, shelter, warmth. (My older sister would add sunscreen, but let's keep it at five.) We can debate which of these is more important than the others, but clearly, no single item is sufficient to sustain life for long, and all are necessary. The absence of any is life-threatening, in time.

Remember: It's a fan, and so it only functions as a fan when rotating (not still, as pictured). So there's no "top blade" or "bottom blade," just a fan, moving the air, generating wind. Even distinguishing one blade from another isn't practical when the fan is moving. For that we have to stop the fan to inspect it, but what we inspect won't replicate the way the blades actually function in relation, always, to one another.

Community

There is no following Jesus apart from community. Even the very first disciples were called in pairs, ensuring there was never a community constituted by "me and Jesus." Knowing Jesus, then, is a communal enterprise—it means knowing Jesus in relation to others who become sisters and brothers in the process of following. The experiences we have are shaped by and shared with others. We share various spiritual practices with each other. When we use reason, we speak a language shared with others and we often "reason together," with others. And Scripture is something we engage in community, as "our book."

The community has a past, a present and a future, and it extends beyond death. So we are "surrounded by a cloud of witnesses," including those who have gone before us and are, in some sense, connected to us now. This means of grace includes what has historically been called "tradition"—the teaching passed on from one generation to the next. Part of this tradition is the revising of previously received tradition. But the revision is always done with regard for what others have understood before us.

Experience

Experience, at its most basic, is listed as a means of grace to recognize that everything that includes us, involves us. Everything we think, feel, perceive, do, or believe is mediated by our experience. There is no escape from our essential subjectivity, because the project is our involvement with God and God's involvement with us, and we are both, fundamentally, subjects—and not merely objects. Our experience shapes all the other means of grace, all mediated to us through experience.

Whereas the "experience" of the Wesleyan Quadrilateral has a narrow meaning,[49] we use the term "experience" in a broad sense. It refers to regard for the experience of others as mandated by the Golden Rule, and especially regard for the experience of the oppressed, which we are commanded to pay attention to because God does. Experience includes what can be known by the scientific method, especially in fields that study the experience of humans and of other of God's creatures. Experience refers to the wisdom that comes through what we might call "life experience," which includes feeling and thought. And experience refers to what humans can know through "subjective experience" of God.

To say that "God speaks," or "God reveals," in any meaningful sense is to say that God is able to speak or to reveal God's being, self, will, or ways to people like us. All of our perceptions of God are a function of our experience. In that sense, whether we know it or not, we choose to consider our experience because none of the means of grace happen apart from our experience of them happening.

Practices

Practices are not one-off occurrences but rather recurring events, routines and habits. Humans develop habits in order to be able to do helpful things with less effort. It takes some extra effort to establish a habit, but once it is set, the habit empowers us to do those things with less effort. Practices can refer to those habits of mind and body that have been found, by many, to involve us with God: sacraments like Holy Communion and baptism, regular worship, prayer, reading, memorizing, singing, studying or meditating on Scripture and observing the liturgical seasons (Advent, Christmas, Epiphany, Lent and so on).

Like so many human phenomena, we learn practices from others and pass them from one generation to the next. Most

49 The Wesleyan Quadrilateral refers to Scripture, tradition, reason and experience. By "experience," Wesley meant the experience of conversion.

"innovative practices" (a new way to pray or a new liturgy) are simply revisions of prior practices—so there is something profoundly conservative about them. We can think of practices going through a severe gauntlet of testing by communities—and the practices that endure through many generations are the ones that have been field-tested and then found to bear fruit. (We will consider such practices further in Chapter 14, "A Spirituality of Resistance: Pray and Act.")

Reason

"Come let us reason together, says the Lord," wrote the prophet Isaiah in the name of the Lord (Is. 1:18 RSV). It is assumed that we share our reasoning capacity with God. The universe is conceived of as "cosmos"—a word that means "a coherent whole," or a complex and orderly system (in contrast with a disorderly chaos). The Greek term "*logos*," which is applied to Jesus in the introduction to John's Gospel ("in the beginning was the word [*logos*], and the word was with God and the word was God"), includes what we mean by "reason."

While we share reason with God, it is also important that we remember that our version of reason can't be separated from us. In fact, we now know that what we experience as reason or rationality is powerfully influenced by our emotional responses.[50] Like human language, the rules of logic—which seem to be "objective"—were not handed down from God, even though they may be a reflection of likeness to God. They are the rules of *human* logic, conceived of and agreed to by humans.

Like the other means of grace, reason doesn't stand alone. We engage all the other means of grace with the help of our capacity to reason, to make sense of things and to be

---

50 In *The Righteous Mind: Why Good People Are Divided by Politics and Religion* Jonathan Haidt describes rationality as a rider guiding an elephant (emotions, intuitions, *etc.*). The rider senses where the elephant wants to go and finds a way to get him there (52-56).

intelligible rather than unintelligible—and we reflect on the means of grace using our reasoning capacity.

Scripture

You've probably noticed by now that this book is loaded with appeals to Scripture. Scripture exists because the people who became Israel (and those they came to influence) experienced certain writings as "means of grace"—that is, found them helpful in mediating connection to God, self, others and the wide world. People sing, pray, lament, rejoice, make sense of events, find comfort and rail against injustice with the words of Scripture. People die with the words of Scripture close at hand, on their lips or ringing in their ears. Long before the canon of Scripture was declared by religious leaders to be "authoritative," these writings were *recognized as helpful*.[51]

What one thinks about issues like the infallibility, inerrancy or authority of Scripture is less important than having contact with Scripture (directly or indirectly, through reading, hearing, song, telling) as a means to help and as an occasion for involvement with God. In that sense, Scripture is like food, air, water, shelter and warmth—it's less important what we think about these things than that we have contact with them. So important, in fact, that if we do that, we can function rather well with those other issues left unresolved.

Let's get personal with the truth

When we focus on Scripture, tradition, reason and the like, as sources of authority to guarantee our *correct grasp of truth*, we naturally come to view arguing for truth as a prime mark of our commitment to truth. We feel empowered, especially, to examine each other's truth statements in relation to a standard, offering criticism in relation to the standard—all in the guise of "speaking the truth in love." In so doing, we often

---

51 For a popular-level discussion of Scripture, including perspective on non-canonical writings, see *Jesus Brand Spirituality: He Wants His Religion Back* (Wilson, 131-173).

create an anxious environment regarding the truth within our communities.

In pursuit of this project, we may find ourselves distracted from Jesus, who frames truth in different terms. Jesus understands truth in personal terms—speaking of himself and the "Spirit of truth" as personal embodiments of Truth. Fundamentally, given the personal nature of God, Truth is a "someone," rather than a "something."

The aim in relation to Truth (understood as a person) is *involvement*. The major metaphors for engagement with Truth in the Gospels and the apostolic writings correspond to this aim. Truth is a vine and we are branches. Truth is a body and we are members. Truth is a community in which we participate.

Truth, thus understood, is akin to someone to be known— as a person is meant to be known. Persons—human beings in the image of God—are not to be mastered or used or wielded. They are to be approached in love, *under*stood (rather than *over*stood), respected, honored—given space to be and express themselves and to reveal themselves to others who receive that revelation.

Truth, coming to us in the form of a person, requires all our personal capacities to embrace: our senses, minds, hearts and bodies. That means we can feel with Truth as much as we can think with Truth. It means we can question Truth, argue with Truth and be angry at Truth, as much as we can agree with Truth because the proper response to Truth that presents as a person is *involvement*. It's only as we become involved with Truth in these personal ways that we are affected by Truth.

This approach to Truth comports with the repeated assurance of the risen Jesus when appearing to anxious disciples: "Don't be afraid!" When truth is an active agent interacting with us, knowing us, loving us and happily pursuing us, we're meant to relax a little. And that act of relaxing allows us to let down our guard—the same move that allows us to love and be loved by a trusted companion.

So maybe on the question of authority, asserting less is asserting more. If this is a form of naïveté, so be it. At least it's a *studied* naïveté, and one that corresponds to our status as children in relation to God.

Solus Jesus.

4

In Defense of Experience

Ken

I WAS MEDITATING on a text in the Gospels in which Jesus bids three disciples to join him on Mount Tabor. They fall into a sleepy, trance-like state, enveloped in light, when suddenly Moses and Elijah—the Lawgiver and the Prophet—appear in conversation with Jesus. Peter, stupefied, speaks: "Let us build a booth for each of you, right here, right now!" *A cloud descends and a voice from the cloud instructs,* "This is my son, listen to him," *and with that, Jesus was there, alone.*

The form of meditation involved placing myself in the scene, taking in the details and allowing what may happen to unfold. I was unusually absorbed, for once. I followed Jesus down a narrow path, listening to the crunching sound of the small stones beneath our feet. And then things became very quiet, as Jesus paused and turned back to say, "Why not write a letter to your congregation?"

The tone of voice was casual, not commanding: like a friend offering a suggestion, tossing it out for consideration. But in that moment, I knew what it was about, this communication from Jesus.

I had been agonizing—for months and months, stretching into years—over what to tell the church about my reluctance (now turned unwillingness) to enforce the traditional policies aimed at partnered LGBTQ+ people.[52] The cause of my distress? Getting to know LGBTQ+ people, whose lives didn't match the biblical texts that I had been told applied to them. They didn't have an "agenda" so much as an experience of suffering—something that my inherited theology had blinded me to. I hesitate to write their names even now, because the world is not yet a safe place for them.

I had written out my thoughts for myself and for a smaller circle of leaders, but the idea of writing to my congregation had never occurred to me. The casual tone of the words— "Why not write a letter to your congregation?"—contained its own rebuke. Why was I so afraid? Why not write such a letter—non-anxiously, as one might inform friends of some not-very-momentous news, of some new thoughts and perspectives gained from new experiences? Of course I could. Thus began the hardest thing I ever did.

A God who talks back

People talk to Jesus. All over the world, all the time, people are talking to Jesus. And sometimes—more often than we acknowledge—Jesus talks back.

That is, people have events within the life of their own minds that they interpret as communications from Jesus. These events can be characterized as auditory or visual impressions, words, pictures, visions, inner voices, thoughts they don't identify as their own, dreams, daydreams; lucid, vivid, wispy, ephemeral, startling, consoling, comforting, challenging, encouraging, stupefying, mundane or wondrous.

People also have a sense of companionship with Jesus, with or without words—just as an old couple might feel at ease in each other's company. Frightened and alone in a hospital room, in a prison cell, in a nursing home, at work or in the car, they might feel comforted and assured by a sense of divine

---

52 These policies include refusal to marry gay couples and limits on how LGBTQ+ people can serve.

presence. Or they might be urgently prompted by Jesus to call a friend who turns out to have just received bad news, or reminded by Jesus to turn off the stove.

In the Western world, we are embarrassed to speak of such things—and sometimes even to acknowledge them to ourselves. They don't *feel normal* to us, these experiences. If a doctor in the local emergency room were evaluating our mental status, we would be wise to keep any communications of this nature to ourselves.

Tanya Luhrmann, a psychological anthropologist at Stanford University, studied people who felt that Jesus communicated with them in this way. Her research is summarized in her book, *When God Talks Back: Understanding the American Evangelical Relationship with God.* Luhrmann found no correlation between having such experiences and mental illness (227), and attests to the surprising frequency with which people report phenomena that their brains interpret as communication from God (357).

The Pentecostal Socrates?

Socrates is widely regarded as the father and primary advocate of reason in philosophy. In *The Apology of Socrates,* Plato shows his teacher, Socrates, defending himself against the capital charge of leading the young of Athens astray with his ideas. Socrates appeals to his lifelong experience of hearing God's voice. It turns out that Socrates was an early Pentecostal of sorts—an aspect of his being that the tradition he founded tends, ironically, to marginalize.[53]

Listen to Socrates' defense of the sort of experience Tanya Luhrmann studied, and regards as more normal than marginal:

---

53 Perhaps it is fitting that it was my therapist, Daniel Greenberg, Ph.D, who pointed this out to me.

The reason for this [why Socrates doesn't advise Athenians on matters of state] is what you have often heard me say before on many occasions—that I am subject to a divine or supernatural experience, which Meletus [one of Socrates' accusers] saw fit to travesty in his indictment. It began in my early childhood—a sort of voice which comes to me— and when it comes, it always dissuades me from what I am proposing to do, and never urges me on. It is this that debars me from entering public life. (Plato, 17)

Later, Socrates adds:

This duty I have accepted, as I said, in obedience to God's commands, given in oracles and dreams and by every other way that other divine dispensation has ever impressed a duty upon man. (19)

Human beings have survived in a survival-of-the-fittest world by their wits—by their ability to interpret the sensory data streaming into their bodies in order to successfully navigate their environment. Another word for this is "experience," and it's what we have to go by. Communications of the sort Socrates bore witness to in his defense (as Plato tells it) include hearing and being guided by divine communication, described by Socrates as a "sort of voice." Luhrmann writes that her subjects who reported "hearing God's voice" are able to distinguish this phenomenon from the sensing of a variety of different voices in their heads. And they do so with the subtlety implicit in the phrase Socrates used—"sort of"—that is, they *think* it is different than hearing the voice of, say, their roommate, but they are not always sure. (Luhrmann, 227-266).

What if the Bible is not meant to replace or limit such communications, as it is meant to bear witness to a God who talks back? What if the Bible provides a record of people receiving communication from God to encourage the rest of us to do what they must have learned to do: discern the divine voice from the other voices in their heads?

If the reliability of communications of this sort cannot be regarded as plausibly normal, then *solus Jesus* is untenable. Let me suggest, though, that what happened to me—hearing a message that I took to be from Jesus—*is* normal. Which is not to say that these communications are as common as they might otherwise be. Christianity is still emerging from an experiential desert, after centuries of a rationalistic approach to faith that denigrates the role of experience. In fact, some argue that *sola Scriptura* implies a doctrine called "cessationism"—the concept that once the canon of Scripture was closed, God stopped (or ceased) all communication outside of Scripture.[54] This has taken its toll on all of us. When experience of such communication is regarded with suspicion—regarded as *abnormal,* in fact—it is muted or driven to the margins of our consciousness, treated as weird, embarrassing and not for "people like us." Such communications, when they occur, tend to be ignored and, hence, experienced less.

This marginalization of experience is *at odds* with the heart of Christian faith. If Jesus is risen from the dead, alive with active agency and eager to lead anyone willing to follow, why wouldn't he be accessibly present to us? Why wouldn't we trust experiences of contact with him? "He is and we can" is the *credo* of *solus Jesus*. What's more, we have no other choice. For better or worse, our experience is what we have to go by.

A personal knowing

All of this sounds frighteningly subjective, as opposed to reassuringly objective. So let's all take a deep breath and come to grips with the reality that Christianity is a form of personal knowledge. Whether there is any other form of knowledge available to humans is another question beyond my ken. But surely Christian faith is a form of personal knowing. That is,

---

54 For a discussion of cessationism, see *Are Miraculous Gifts for Today? Four Views* (Grudem, et al.).

it is a form of knowing that has to do with persons (us) being known by and knowing a personal being we call God. As the incarnation of God—God made flesh—Jesus is about nothing if he is not about a personal form of knowing. To know Jesus is to cast our nets into the sea of personal knowledge.

The form of knowing that corresponds to this realm is, by definition, experiential. We are the knowing subjects in the realm of personal knowledge. All of our knowing is mediated through the experience of our embodied brains, our consciousness, our sensory apparatus and our various and sundry capacities to perceive. Nothing registers *with* us that is not also registered *by* us. In that sense, all of our knowing is subjective.

I might have dismissed my experience of hearing, "Why not write a letter to your congregation?" I might have assumed it was a daydream and nothing more. But I didn't. I took it as a message from Jesus to me. That conclusion might be indefensible when subjected to the scrutiny of those who assume all such communications are spurious, but I didn't subject my decision to such scrutiny. I conferred with trusted friends, colleagues and confidants, and decided to "make my best call" about the message.

What did I have to evaluate the veracity of this experience? I had a lifetime of making little discernments about what is and what isn't reliable in my own stream of consciousness— the impulses, desires and voices in my mind—and of acting on those discernments, and seeing how those actions worked out. I had a lifetime of comparing notes with others seeking to do the same; a lifetime of considering the input of others, of accepting, ignoring or rejecting all or part of it; of trusting or distrusting the different voices of authority weighing in, and seeing how those little discernments worked out. Not a single bit of that process of sorting and sifting has taken place apart from my experience.

Reformation distrust of spiritual experience

Luther and Calvin assumed that Scripture spoke with such obvious clarity that it could function as the ultimate arbiter of disputed interpretations. They were doing their theology—as we all do it—on the fly. In particular, they were concerned about institutional authority claims that seemed insufficiently grounded, let alone harmful. *Sola Scriptura* functioned as a principle to liberate the Church from the oppression of these institutional claims.

The Roman Catholic Church used claims of miraculous events, associated with visions and religious experiences of saints and mystics, to buttress its assertion of all-encompass-ing authority. What was good for the goose, though—at least in this case—was not good for the gander. Rivals to Luther in the chaotic early years of the Reformation's unfolding in Germany made grandiose and apocalyptic appeals to special revelations from the Holy Spirit, provoking Luther's apoplectic condemnation of all such phenomena.[55] John Calvin, Luther's rival proponent of *sola Scriptura*, had, if anything, an even deeper distrust than Luther of spiritual experience, rooted in his view that matter and spirit were sharply divided (Eire, 317).

Dismissal of spiritual experience coincided with the emergence of the scientific revolution of the early modern period. Together, they constituted part of a much larger wave of disenchantment—the beginning of a shift. This shift went from a view of the world shot through with spirits, demons, angels, miracles and ghosts to one reduced to and explained by natural laws. The phenomena of this world could be observed, measured and—if enough data could be mined—predicted. That this approach solved vexing problems gave it a powerful momentum. Within the ferment of this tumultuous transition, the idea of a God communicating through a fixed, if inspired, vehicle like a text—a text that could be studied and,

---

55 "They boast of possessing the Spirit, more than the apostles, and yet for more than three years now they have secretly prowled about and flung their shit" (Eire, 194), is one of Luther's milder tirades.

in a sense, mastered, using a set of fixed principles—seemed a surer foundation.

The scientific revolution ground away. By the 19th century, science had thoroughly disenchanted our view of the world.[56] Suspicion of experience remained unchecked through the middle of the 20th century. The height of this suspicion can be seen in the virtual denial of experience—including the radical denial of the validity of human consciousness—that characterized behaviorism, a branch of knowledge that purported to decode the vagaries of human behavior.

And Pentecostalism's howling protest

The Pentecostal movement, exploding throughout the 20th century and into the new millennium, can be understood as a global protest against the dehumanizing disregard of what constitutes the essence of our humanity: our experience. Pentecostalism began in the lower economic strata of society and spread through the developing world. Its rise coincided with another revolution: the dawning of a "new physics," which introduced concepts intriguingly akin to the mysterious realm of faith and spirituality. The closed system of classical physics, in which certainty and predictability reigned, was challenged by new discoveries that suggested a more open-ended and mysterious dimension to physical reality. This led to a cautious new dialogue between science and religion, represented in works like *Quarks, Chaos & Christianity: Questions to Science and Religion* by John Polkinghorne, a theoretical physicist at Cambridge who became an Anglican priest and wrote on a

---

56 "Max Weber (1864-1920) was an intellectually capacious sociologist who became one of the most influential thinkers of the twentieth century. In 'Science as a Vocation,' a lecture written near the Great War in late 1917 and published in early 1919, he expressed a view about the relationship between science and religion that summed up a central thrust of nineteenth-century Western intellectual life, a view that would become increasingly widespread in the twentieth. According to Weber, 'intellectualist rationalization through science and scientifically oriented technology' means that 'fundamentally no mysterious incalculable powers are present that come into play, but one can—in principle—master all things by calculation" (Gregory, 25-26).

range of faith topics, including how the resurrection might be compatible with a new understanding of the physical world.

We now find ourselves in a swirling convergence of colliding forces. On the one hand, orthodox/classical theology had been forged in a pre-modern view of the world from which we've all moved on. Heaven is not literally "up there," just beyond the reach of the naked eye, as the ancients thought. Storybook depictions of the ascension of Jesus to such a place seem quaint, rather than compelling. All of it—life after death, virgin birth, resurrection, ascension—seemed thoroughly debunked by the findings of modern science. Meanwhile, reports of spiritual phenomena—especially from the developing world—abound, and we find ourselves craving such experiences as if they were an integral part of our humanity. We're also a century into the disruption of this older classical scientific worldview, a disruption initiated by the works of Plank, Heisenberg, Bohr, Einstein and others. These breakthroughs have been popularized through Star Trekian depictions of wormholes, time travel and spooky action at a distance, making us rethink the previous disregard of spiritual experience. It is no wonder, then, that we find ourselves in the midst of these colliding forces, both yearning for spiritual experience and deeply conflicted about it—feeling insecure, ill-equipped and yet hungry for more.

Our friend Tom Wassink, a research geneticist and psychiatrist at the University of Iowa, exemplifies a pilgrimage that many are taking in response to these historic cross-currents. Tom grew up in the center of Reformed Christianity in the United States, a member of First Reformed Church of Holland, Michigan. As a child of the Protestant Reformation, which cast a pall of suspicion over spiritual experience, Tom was drawn to the experiential dimension of charismatic Christianity. He developed a conflicted relationship with this form of faith, with its admixture of anti-intellectualism, powerful religious experience and magical thinking.

On the verge of giving up on the experiential dimension of his spiritual quest, Tom encountered the work of a Mennonite psychiatrist in the Chicago area: Karl Lehman, who had developed a healing prayer model that seemed to help people suffering from post-traumatic stress disorder (PTSD). Tom's clinical curiosity was piqued, because he worked with veterans suffering from PTSD.

The healing prayer method, called Immanuel Prayer, involved selecting a positive memory, focusing on it prayerfully and inviting Jesus to be present in the memory. Often, this yielded profound experiences of Jesus. Later—with a trained counselor—one might gently revisit traumatic memories, inviting Jesus to be present in these, as well. Through positive expectation, prayer and relaxed meditation, Tom experienced vivid and deeply affecting visions of Jesus present with him in both the pleasant and painful memories he opened up to this form of prayer.

It should be noted, however, that this renewed appreciation for a distinctly spiritual experience—impressions from the Spirit, such as Tom and many others have—shouldn't overshadow the importance of a more fundamental regard for the entire range of human experience, as a medium through which God speaks.

Yes, but whose experience?

I've been winding up to something that is more important than spiritual experience: a preferential regard for the experience of marginalized, oppressed and stigmatized people. In fact, this is the *intended effect* of the experience of the divine in the Scriptures generated by the people of Israel—so much so that the most intense spiritual experiences combined, without this effect actually generated, would amount to exactly nothing.

Jesus is compelled into public ministry by an experience of the Holy Spirit at his baptism—a deeply intimate experience

in which he is surrounded by the Spirit's presence (in the
form of a dove, alighting on him) and hears a voice speak
words of tender love to him. The Holy Spirit drives him into
the wilderness for weeks of prayer, fasting and more spiritual
experiences. Emerging from this vision-quest, his ministry
is marked by a *preferential regard* for the suffering of the
oppressed. The ailments and complaints of the powerful don't
seem to occupy his attention. Instead, he is drawn *preferen-
tially* to the suffering of the marginalized.

In *Reality, Grief, Hope: Three Urgent Prophetic Tasks*,
Old Testament scholar Walter Bruggemann tells how the
Hebrew prophets called out the powerful in Israel when they
allowed religious-ideological commitments to blind them to
the suffering of oppressed neighbors. As the elites of Israel
became dogmatically ideological about such matters as
Israel's chosenness, they were tempted to use this ideology to
close their ears to the marginalized. As might we all be. This
happened during the period when Israel became involved
in its own version of the extraction economy—centered in
Jerusalem, and maintained by the exploitation of the peasant
class, living in the surrounding countryside. Bruggemann
suggests that heavy taxation, exacted by the monarchy and
priestly classes to support an extravagant palace-temple
complex, brought segments of Judean society into a form of
serfdom—of economic slavery. The upper classes ignored the
suffering of the peasantry and justified this on the grounds
that they were upholding the religious system established by
Yahweh (Brueggemann, 8).

The Church, in its institutional expression, has been prone
to the same pitfall throughout history. Religious dogma has
been used to breed disregard for the experience of oppressed
neighbors—slaves, women and minorities. As the noisy
defense of orthodoxy intensifies, it often drowns out the voices
of the oppressed neighbors among us. Theological justifications of slavery trump the experience of slaves. Doctrinal
justifications of patriarchy trump the experience of the women

chafing under it. Interpretations of Scripture justifying the stigmatization of gay, lesbian, bisexual and transgender people trump the painful experiences of these members of the Church.

N.T. Wright's dismissal of experience

I was nervously preparing a paper for the Society of Vineyard Scholars, a paper that was in support of full inclusion of LGBTQ+ people. This was precursor to what I would later publish as, *A Letter to My Congregation*. A friend showed me a paper presented by my theological then-hero, N.T. Wright, titled, "Communion and Koinonia: Pauline Reflections on Tolerance and Boundaries." Wright's argument completely undermined my thesis—that Romans 14-15 provided a path to the full inclusion of LGBTQ+ people. Contrary to my proposal, Wright insisted that Paul's category in Romans 14-15, "disputable matters," could not provide guidance through this controversy. According to Wright, the interpretation of biblical texts addressing same-gender sex could never be regarded as a disputable matter in Paul's sense of the term. Wright asserted that keeping the Sabbath and eating meat sacrificed to idols (the probable "disputable matters" addressed in Romans) were "cultural (or ethnic) boundary markers," and not moral concerns, *per se.*

It nearly took my breath away—and my nerve. I was arguing that since keeping the Sabbath and eating meat sacrificed to idols would have been regarded as first-order moral concerns in their time,[57] the moral questions about same-gender sex in marriage relationships could plausibly be regarded as a "disputable matter." If the debate over the legitimacy of same-gender marriage could reasonably be regarded as a modern-day example of what Paul addressed in Rome,

---

57 Sabbath observance was commanded in the Ten Commandments, widely regarded as the foundation of Israel's moral code and adopted as such, by most Christians—until recently. Eating meat sacrificed to idols could credibly be viewed as participation in idolatry, another serious moral concern for Israel and for Gentile Christians.

then a policy of discrimination against LGBTQ+ people could be forbidden. In all my preceding research, I couldn't find a single scholar who explicitly applied Romans 14-15 to advocate for the full inclusion of LGBTQ+ people in the Christian community. When I presented my Romans 14-15 to one well known scholar, he did agree that it was sensible, but was not willing to state this publicly. I agonized, tempted to withdraw my paper entirely.

Then I remembered that my daughter, Maja Wilson, had written about the denial of experience in 20th-century behaviorism, with its concomitant harmful effects in much standard parenting advice of the 1950s. Her dissertation was titled *Writing Assessment's 'Debilitating Inheritance': Behaviorism's Dismissal of Experience* (University of New Hampshire). I reread Wright's paper, keeping an eye out for his treatment of experience.

This paragraph in Wright's paper stood out:

> *In order to have any serious discussion about ethical issues, we need to remind ourselves the whole time of the importance of Reason (along with, and obedient to Scripture and Tradition) as one strand of the classic threefold Anglican cord. The current fashion for substituting 'experience', which all too easily means 'feeling', or 'reported feeling', is simply not the same sort of thing. Experience matters, but it doesn't belong in an account of authority; put it there, and the whole notion of authority itself deconstructs before your very eyes.*

Wright was predisposed to dismiss experience when it challenged a teaching, buttressed for centuries by appeal to Scripture, tradition and reason. As a Christian heavily influenced by the renewalist sector of Christianity, I couldn't follow suit. My experience of Jesus—my sense of his leading in prayer, and in interior manifestations of the Holy Spirit over several years, on this very matter, had led me to listen—carefully, sympathetically—to the *experience* of sexual minorities, whom I had come to know and love. I could not dismiss their experience or mine.

Wright's paper, however, demonstrated no familiarity with or regard for the experience of queer people. Yet he feels free to weigh in on this debate—which has enormous implications for queer people—while admitting in the paper, "I am not an expert on current debates [regarding homosexuality]."

"Not an expert on current debates!? Then why weigh in on such a consequential subject with your considerable scholarly prestige?" I thought. Instead, Wright cites his reliance on two sources. The first is *The Moral Vision of the New Testament*, by Richard Hays—who refers to the disagreement over homosexuality within the Methodist Church as one that calls for tolerance, using the logic of Romans 14-15 (but without citing it explicitly).[58] The other is *The Bible and Homosexual Practice: Texts and Hermeneutics*, by Robert Gagnon—a book that rivals Wright's paper in ignoring the experience of gay people while condemning them.

Wright makes other rhetorical moves to support his disregard for experience. Consider Wright's rhetoric, with my commentary bracketed: "*The current fashion* [a dismissive term] *for substituting 'experience'* [so now to regard experience is to substitute it for Scripture, tradition or reason, rather than interacting with these with experience in view] *which all too easily means 'feeling'* [and experience is reduced to feeling] *or 'reported feeling'* [even more suspect]."

There is one important exception to Wright's dismissal of experience. Wright pays careful attention to the hurt feelings

58 In *The Moral Vision of the New Testament*, Hays writes (regarding homosexuality): "This means that for the foreseeable future we must find ways to live within the church in a situation of serious moral disagreement while still respecting one another as brothers and sisters in Christ ... Just as there are serious Christians who in good conscience believe in just war theory, so there are serious Christians who believe that same-sex erotic activity is consonant with God's will. For the reasons set forth in this book, I think that both groups are wrong, but in both cases, the questions are so difficult that we should receive one another as brothers and sisters in Christ and work toward adjudicating our differences through reflecting on the witness of Scripture" (400-401). Here, Hays is using the logic of Romans 14-15 without citing it explicitly.

of those who have to suffer the suggestion that their convictions may be fueled by a non-rational, disgusted reaction to same-gender sex.[59]

One suspects he has his own feelings in mind. Wright doesn't consider the possibility that what we often uncritically regard as "reason" may simply be the rationalizations we generate to buttress our positions shaped by vested interests—and that this could affect traditional as well as revisionist readings of Scripture on homosexuality.[60]

Scripture warns against ignoring what God regards

Scripture itself emphasizes the importance of paying attention to the experiences of oppressed minorities. The God of the Bible, in direct contrast with the divinities of archaic myth, is known for regard for the voice of the victim—from Abel to Hagar; from the people of Israel under Egyptian bondage to Job; from Jesus to the harassed followers of Jesus, in the early Jesus movement. Yahweh, as James Kugel says, is the God who hears the cry of the victim (109-136), which can only mean that God *regards the experience* of oppressed minorities. Their voices are like the anguished voice of Abel, scapegoated and murdered by his brother, Cain—when he cried out to God from the ground, and God did not dismiss it. "Because the needy are oppressed and the poor cry out in misery, I will rise up, says the Lord, and give them the help

---

59 The portion of the paper in question reads: "We have allowed ourselves to say 'I feel' when we mean 'I think', collapsing serious thought into knee-jerk reactions. We have become tolerant of everything except intolerance, about which we ourselves are extremely intolerant. If someone thinks through an issue and, irrespective of his or her feelings on the subject, reaches a considered judgment that doing X is right and doing Y is wrong, they no sooner come out and say so than someone else will accuse them of phobia. If someone says stealing is wrong, we expect someone else to say, 'You only say that because you're kleptophobic.'" Notice how Wright reduces homophobia, a well-attested phenomenon, to the absurdly unattested "kleptophobia," and how he equates feeling with "knee-jerk reactions"—using a term for a mere reflex to diminish regard for feeling.

60 For an understanding of the brain's tendency to find rationalizations for such inclinations, see *The Righteous Mind* by Jonathan Haidt, Part 1: Intuitions Come First, Strategic Reasoning Second.

they long for" (Psalm 12: 5). Emily expands on this theme in
Chapter 6, "God of the Victim."

What's more, Scripture warns against *using Scripture* to
disregard the voices of suffering people. The New Testament
places this at the center of its teaching. Jesus summarizes his
Sermon on the Mount by saying, "In everything, do to others
as you would have them do to you; for this is the Law and the
Prophets" (Mt. 7:12). He follows this with the admonition
to "enter through the narrow gate" as if the practice of this
demanding love is the narrow gate that leads to life, rather
than to destruction (Mt 7: 13-14).

This saying echoes one repeated by Jesus and the apostles
in other places—various versions of "Love your neighbor as
yourself, for this is the Law and the Prophets" (Mt. 22: 38-40,
Mk. 12:31, Ro. 13: 8-10, Gal. 5:14, Jm. 2:8).[61]

Acting in accord with "the Law and the Prophets" (the New
Testament term for "the Bible") justified the persecution of
Jesus and his followers. Saul of Tarsus harassed his fellow Jews
out of devotion to Scripture. This danger, from the hands of
Bible people, was seared into the consciousness of the early
Jesus movement. It's no wonder that love of neighbor (a love
that meant paying attention to the experience of the neighbor)
was the distinctive mark of the Jesus movement's *approach to
Scripture*.

The version of this saying in the Sermon on the Mount
emphasizes the need to *empathetically regard the experience*
of the other. "Do unto others as you would have them do
unto you" calls us to measure our own actions by first placing
ourselves in the position of others—the skill we call empathy.

Where disregard for the experience of the neighbor is
defended by appeal to Scripture, the fruit is often bitter. In
Luther's Germany, the peasants rebelled against the oppression

---

61 The version in Matthew 22 pairs "love of neighbor" with "love of God," while
the "golden rule" of Matthew 7 and the "royal law" of James 2 simply refer to "love of
neighbor." This is mirrored in Galatians 5: 14, "For the entire law is fulfilled in keeping
this one command: Love your neighbor as yourself." The effect is to emphasize the
importance of love of neighbor for those prone to emphasize love of God.

of German landlords. These peasant demands seem moderate by comparison with the demands of the American Colonists. Luther was incensed. He called for the peasants to be slaughtered. "Let everyone who can smite, slay and stab … If you die in doing it, well for you! A more blessed death can never be yours, for you die in obeying the divine Word and commandment in Romans 13," he wrote. Historian Carlos Eire reports, "the landlords did precisely as Luther suggested, stabbing, smiting and slaying about seventy thousand to one hundred thousand rebels, most of them peasants" (203-209).

John Wesley's *Thoughts Upon Slavery*

John Wesley, founder of Methodism, eventually spoke out forcefully against slavery in his tract, *Thoughts Upon Slavery*—a brilliant prophetic screed. Wesley is credited with adding experience to the "three-legged stool" of Scripture, tradition and reason. Methodist scholar Albert Outler—who coined the term "Wesleyan Quadrilateral," referring to Scripture, tradition, reason *and* experience as tools for theological reflection—argues that Wesley understood experience in a narrow sense. According to Outler, Wesley meant, specifically, the confirming witness of the Holy Spirit in conversion and assurance of the forgiveness of sins (Oden, et. al., 24-25).

Once you recover from the sheer force of Wesley's words, it's fascinating to consider how Wesley composed his theological reflection regarding slavery. To put it more specifically: How did Wesley appeal to Scripture, tradition, reason and experience? Let's take them in reverse order.

The experience in which Wesley grounded his appeal was much broader than the witness of the Holy Spirit in the believer's heart, regarding conversion or the assurance of forgiveness. He relies heavily on the experience of others when regarding the gruesome brutality of slavery: newspaper reports; laws allowing and requiring mistreatment of slaves; historical data from the African cultures from which people were taken as slaves; and, throughout, Wesley's own intense emotional responses to all of this. One would have to say that *Thoughts Upon Slavery* is primarily grounded in appeal to experience— broadly defined, and not narrowly defined, as in "orthodox" understandings of the Wesleyan Quadrilateral.

It is difficult to discern *any* appeal to Christian tradition in *Thoughts Upon Slavery*, and this is understandable given the preponderance of support for (or at least tolerance of) the institution of slavery in the Christian tradition.

Wesley also appeals to reason throughout, defining terms, marshalling arguments and wielding the rules of logic to make his case against slavery.

Most telling, though, is Wesley's appeal to Scripture. He includes, of course, appeals to the Golden Rule: the command to love our neighbors, injunctions to show mercy and threats of divine punishment for those who do violence to others. But despite his characteristic thoroughness in refuting the common justifications of slavery in his day, Wesley is strangely silent regarding what would have been the primary Christian justification for slavery: the many biblical texts that support slavery and the absence of texts condemning it. This is especially noteworthy in light of the fact that Wesley was unflinching in his condemnation of the Church's complicity with slavery. But regarding the scriptural case made by many Christians in support of slavery (a compelling case, given the texts marshaled in its making, and one that Wesley himself accepted earlier in his life): not a word from Wesley.

One suspects that the Wesleyan Quadrilateral failed Wesley as an adequate tool for discerning God's will regarding slavery. In *Thoughts Upon Slavery,* Wesley moved beyond the confines of his own understanding of the role of experience and its relationship to Scripture, tradition and reason, in condemning what he knew in his heart to be wrong.

Can we listen to God apart from experience?

When I was deep into my reassessment of the traditional condemnation of homosexuality and its attendant insistence on stigmatizing practices aimed at LGBTQ+ people, I reached a point where I could no longer ignore the suffering of sexual minorities at the hands of the Church. I realized that I could not, in good conscience, implement these harmful policies in my pastoral capacity, *even if* Scripture seemed to support such policies. I was prepared to be wrong, to violate the plain sense of Scripture if need be, and to answer to God for that—but *I could not deny my experience.*

Counterintuitively, for one who was, at the time, immersed in anxious evangelicalism, I felt that Jesus was *with me* in that frightening space. I was able to ignore my religious fear and proceed. In effect, only my regard for experience had the power to wrench me from the reading of Scripture on which my good standing within my evangelical denomination depended. Only my regard for experience moved me to employ reason to critique the ways in which this reading was employed to harm LGBTQ+ people. Only my regard for experience allowed me to conclude that the tradition of the Church, regarding homosexuality, was wrong—that it was based on a faulty interpretation of Scripture, and that a better interpretation was needed.

Eventually, I concluded that Scripture is most likely silent regarding the moral questions behind the marriage and ordination of gay people. (Though Scripture is not silent about the danger of using Scripture to harm people.) I concluded that the prohibitions of Scripture did not properly apply to the people I knew. To argue from silence, given the assumption within evangelicalism that Scripture *must surely speak clearly* on such matters, is to go out on a limb that extends beyond the boundaries of present-day evangelicalism. In the end, though, I couldn't deny my experience—of the suffering of LGBTQ+ people, of the validity of my responses to that suffering, and of my sense of the leading of Jesus.

Mystical *midrash* on Mount Tabor

Which brings us full circle to the voice from the cloud on Mount Tabor.

The disciples were excited to see Jesus in the company of Moses, the Lawgiver, and Elijah, the preeminent Hebrew Prophet—who, together, personified "the Law and the Prophets." Peter and the others may have been enamored by the enhanced prestige that would accrue to their master (and, by association, to themselves) by this visitation. They would want others to witness what they were witnessing. But this moment didn't signify the return of Moses and Elijah to the present-day situation; instead, it was a mystical interaction involving Moses and Elijah with Jesus, an unveiling for the disciples of that interaction. The attempt to enshrine the moment would have misrepresented its significance. The voice from the cloud would have none of it: "This is my son, my chosen, listen to him." This is followed by: "When the voice had spoken, Jesus was found alone." Or, in the more emphatic language of Matthew: "And when they looked up, they saw no one but *Jesus Himself alone*" (Mt. 17:8 NASB).

The point here is not to dismiss Moses and Elijah. Jesus is portrayed in the Gospels as relying on the instruction of Moses and the prophets. He is a Jewish rabbi engaged in *midrash*—the ongoing process of interpreting Torah (a task in which the prophets of Israel were also engaged). In fact, our first view of the young Jesus in Luke shows him conversing with his elders in the Temple—listening, asking questions and offering his own answers (Lk. 2:46-48). The Mount Tabor exchange can be understood as a mystical example of *midrash* with Moses and Elijah, enabled by a temporary tear in the fabric of space-time.

The Jewish people do not regard Torah as a static or fixed revelation, concerning which the task is simply to uncover what it meant to Moses and to the people to whom it was first given. Torah is a living revelation. The process of *midrash* is undertaken, in a sense, by every Jewish person seeking to understand, interpret and apply its instruction as history unfolds, offering new experiences.

On Mount Tabor, then, we can imagine Moses, Elijah and Jesus conversing with each other—questioning, answering, learning and instructing, as the groggy-with-sleep disciples listen in a dream-like state (Lk. 9:32).[62] The voice from the cloud startles them awake, saying, "This is my son, my chosen, listen to him!" Jesus is reaffirmed as their rabbi. He is a rabbi who has been informed by Moses and the Prophets (and, in this appearance, in turn informs them). But he is there with his disciples in their *present* experience, in a way that Moses and Elijah cannot be.

If he is our rabbi still, then the message to them pertains to us as well: *solus Jesus*—listen to him.

---

62 As Luke, alone among the synoptic Gospel writers—characteristically attuned to the subtleties of mystical encounters—reports.

5

The Age of the Spirit

Emily

THIRTEEN YEARS AGO, when I was 27, I attended a conference hosted by my former church denomination. Our national director spoke the final night of the event, and at the end of his sermon, invited anyone under the age of 30 to approach the stage so that he could pray over us. I, along with several dozen other young people, walked toward the front of the auditorium.

As he prayed, something peculiar took place inside my body. I began shaking and crying and felt like I couldn't stand up. I dropped to my knees and, as I started to pray aloud myself, I realized that the words were not English words. I'd encountered glossolalia (speaking in tongues), having grown up in a charismatic Christian tradition, but this occurrence surprised me because it sounded different than the prior times I'd experienced it in my life.

As I prayed in this new tongue, I heard a recurring English phrase in my head: "You will see Tibet. You will see Tibet. You will see Tibet." I pictured an elderly woman crouched on the side of a mountain. I began to pray for this woman, sensing that God held her in high esteem—the Almighty honored this woman's faithfulness, love and hope.

Here's the unusual thing: I prayed in English in my mind while foreign-to-me words continued coming out of my mouth, almost as though I were internally translating my own sentences as I went along. Whether or not that was the case I will never know; regardless, I entered a state of what I might describe as deep meditation.

This went on for some time—an hour, maybe? Time evaporates in that prayer condition. When it stopped—or when I stopped?—I remember thinking, "OK, either that was one of the most real things I've ever experienced or I'm losing my grip on reality. Maybe I'm caught up in an ecstatic spiritual state because of the suggestive environment. God, if you're there, could you let me know if this was real?"

The same voice I'd heard in my head as I prayed—the one saying, "You will see Tibet"—said, "See that young woman over there? Go and pray for her brother. His name is Jeremy." That made me nervous; it was so specific! What if I asked the woman if I could pray for her brother Jeremy, and I was wrong?

I took the risk because I needed to know. I approached her and told her that God had (maybe?) asked me to pray for her brother, Jeremy. It turned out that the woman had a brother-in-law named Jeremy, who was in jail. We prayed for him together, and I made note of what happened that night because it felt like a signpost in my life; it felt like God had spoken to me.

The modern Pentecostal infusion

I'm not alone in holding onto a mystical experience. In the previous chapter, Ken described the 20th-century explosion of the Pentecostal movement as a global protest against a dehumanizing disregard of experience.

And explode it did. A flurry of revivals kicked off the turn of the century as people witnessed powerful encounters with the Holy Spirit, especially glossolalia, physical healing, visions and prophecies.[63] For many, the Azusa Street Revival in Los

---

63 Revivals included, but were not limited to, the Welsh Revival (1904-1905), the Mukti Revival in India (1905), the Azusa Street Revival in Los Angeles (1906), the Korean Revival in Pyongyang (1907) and the Chinese Revival (1908).

Angeles in 1906 marks the birth of global Pentecostalism, because of both the scope and longevity of that revival's influence (Robeck, 314).

The person credited with sparking the Azusa Street Revival is William Seymour, a man born to former slaves in the bayous of Louisiana. Cecil Robeck writes that Seymour "undoubtedly heard appeals to dreams and visions within Louisiana's African-American community," and was "aware that similar things were frequently invoked in the 'Hoodoo' tradition" (33). His absorption of the spirituality of bayou cultures shaped his openness to such phenomena.

William Seymour first embraced Christianity for himself when he moved to Indianapolis for work in the late 1800s. While there, he worshipped in an African Methodist Episcopal Church, in addition to attending services held by the Evening Light Saints, a "radical holiness group" (Robeck, 29). Both congregations were rooted in the Wesleyan holiness tradition and, as such, Seymour understood his spiritual formation as being saved (having a personal conversion experience), followed by being purified—or sanctified—by God. Like others shaped by holiness movements, he viewed sanctification as an instant event, taking place after conversion, rather than as a lifelong process (Anderson, 146). This framework seems to have held throughout his life.

That said, two important aspects of Seymour's time in Indianapolis stand out as important indicators of his willingness to challenge status quo holiness theology. First, despite his African Methodist Episcopal Church's stance on "the gifts of the Holy Spirit" (that they ceased to exist in the decades following Jesus's life on earth), Seymour privately nursed an interest in the supernatural. Second, the Evening Light Saints he associated with encouraged gifted women to preach and maintained a racially mixed congregation—a rarity in that time and place (Robeck, 29-30).

Following his stint in Indiana, Seymour spent time briefly in both Cincinnati and Houston. While in Texas he met the

Rev. Charles F. Parham, a man preaching that the gifts of the Spirit are available to all. Parham ran a Bible school in Topeka, Kansas, in which Seymour eventually enrolled. Jim Crow laws dictated that black students could not be taught in the same classroom as white students, so Parham asked Seymour to sit outside the door and listen to lectures from the hallway (Robeck, 48). In spite of the humiliation of segregation and the racist theologies taught at the school,[64] Seymour absorbed the parts of Parham's teaching that affirmed the role of the Holy Spirit in guiding and empowering believers through dreams, visions, prophecies, healings and tongues.

One month into his classes, Seymour was offered a pastorate in Los Angeles, replacing a woman (Julia Hutchins) who felt called to serve God in Liberia. He accepted and, in February of 1906, moved west and took up his post. However, Julia Hutchins listened to Seymour's first teachings at the church and deemed his views on speaking in tongues heretical. Instead of supporting his call to the church, she locked him out of the building the following Sunday.

Undeterred, Seymour moved in with new friends and began holding prayer meetings in their home. The gatherings grew, and after a few weeks of fervent prayer and fasting, Edward Lee—the owner of the home—"fell to the floor and spoke with tongues" when Seymour; Lee's wife, Mattie; and a woman named Lucy Farrow laid hands on him (Robeck, 67). As Edward shared his testimony with those gathered that evening, the Spirit came on the group and they also spoke in tongues and prophesied. Word got out, and soon the house and lawn were unable to contain the number of attendees coming to worship each night. The meetings then moved to a building on Azusa Street—an unused, dilapidated former stable owned by the First African Methodist Episcopal Church, who rented it to Seymour and his friends.

---

64 "[Parham] believed that the United States had been intended by God to become a nation for whites, just as Africa was intended to be a continent set apart by God for those with black skin" (Robeck, 48).

For the next two years, people came from all over the world to participate in the revival, including a large number of pastors and evangelists. In his research, Robeck collected the names of as many visitors to Azusa as possible, and says that nearly 1 in 3 were vocational clergy or missionaries (82). Not unlike the Toronto Blessing, a charismatic revival of the 1990s, the large number of Church leaders in attendance meant the influence of the outpouring of the Spirit affected congregations and believers around the world.[65]

In *The Age of the Spirit: How the Ghost of an Ancient Controversy is Shaping the Church,* Phyllis Tickle and Jon Sweeney offer this assessment of the Azusa Street Revival:

> *No human agency could have created what happened in 1906 in Los Angeles, nor could any human agency have either contained or interrupted it. What roared out of William Seymour's re-consecrated stable was a Presence; and what that Presence brought, among other things, was freedom—the freedom to think and to know the Holy in an unfettered, unmediated way that was frightening and exhilarating and soul-sustaining all at the same time. (146)*

Along with Tickle, Sweeney and others, we agree that this seems to have been a turning point,[66] as the authority of the global Church began shifting from Scripture back to the living, revelatory Trinitarian godhead most especially mediated by the Paraclete (Cox, *Future of Faith*, 224).[67] The process was

65 The Toronto Blessing was a large Pentecostal revival which took place between 1994-1996. "News of God's visitation quickly spread, and by May 1995 more than 700,000 people from around the world had attended meetings there" (Flinchbaugh).

66 Tickle and Sweeney advocate a view first put forth by Joachim of Fiore, suggesting that history moves through different "ages," or epochs, based on the Trinity: the age of the Father, the age of the Son and the age of the Spirit, the latter of which they believe began around the turn of the 20th century. I don't ascribe to that framework, but find Tickle and Sweeney's work helpful for understanding the shifting source of authority within the global Church (Tickle and Sweeney, 111).

67 "The wind of the Spirit is blowing. One indication is the upheaval that is shaking and renewing Christianity. Faith, rather than beliefs, is once again becoming its

and is messy, and remains incomplete.[68]

Solus Jesus requires access to the Spirit

Ken and I advocate *solus Jesus* since the apostle Paul speaks of Jesus as the head of the Church, but doing so inherently means we speak of the entire Trinity.[69] The authority of the Church (and all authority in heaven and on earth) may belong to the Son, but it is the Spirit of God released on earth who works in forming and shaping the Church (Vanhoozer, 164).[70] Jesus is a living agency and the Spirit is the way Jesus leads us.

> *I have much more to say to you, more than you can now bear. But when he, the Spirit of truth, comes, he will guide you into all the truth. He will not speak on his own; he will speak only what he hears, and he will tell you what is yet to come. He will glorify me because it is from me that he will receive what he will make known to you. All that belongs to the Father is mine. That is why I said the Spirit will receive from me what he will make known to you. (Jn 16:12-15)[71]*

Solus Jesus requires the guidance of the living God, tangible and accessible to all, making known the ways of love to us

---

defining quality, and this reclaims what faith meant during its earliest years. I have described how that primal impetus was nearly suffocated by creeds, hierarchies and the disastrous merger of the Church with the empire. But I have also highlighted how a newly global Christianity, enlivened by a multiplicity of cultures and yearning for the realization of God's reign of *shalom*, is finding its soul again. All the signs suggest we are poised to enter a new Age of the Spirit and that the future will be a future of faith." (Cox, *The Future of Faith*, 224)

68 Hence our submission of *solus Jesus* as a proposed post-Protestant slogan—an attempt to help along this massive undertaking in the small way in which we feel called.

69 Eph. 1:22, 5:23; 1 Cor. 11:3; Col. 1:18, 2:10

70 Mt. 28:18

71 Note that the pronoun used for "spirit" in Greek is "neuter," and could be translated either as *he or she*. I didn't want the Spirit to sound like the "female" part of God who takes orders from the "male" part of God, as picking out this one verse might imply. So, for clarity, I retained the masculine pronoun for this verse.

humans. The *Presence* at work at Azusa Street, described by
Tickle and Sweeney, became part of our collective spiritual
heritage on Pentecost—when "a sound like the blowing of a
violent wind came from heaven and filled the whole house."
This outpouring of the Spirit empowered the disciples as they
dispersed from Jerusalem to share their good news with the
known world. At the Azusa Street Revival in 1906, a similar
spiritual force sparked yet another worldwide movement.
It's not that the Spirit was inactive between-time—certainly
not—but occasionally, a massive infusion of God's presence is
needed to blow open our preconceived theological constructs.
We've been undergoing one of those massive infusions for over
one hundred years.

At the time of writing, Pentecostalism is the fastest-growing
religious movement on earth. Mystics and others recorded
ecstatic experiences of the Spirit throughout history—this
aspect of Christian faith never disappeared from the
landscape. But the early 20th-century revivals catalyzed the
renewalist energy presently circling the globe. The idea that
the Spirit actively guides humans on a daily basis is alive and
well in faith communities worldwide—from house churches
in the poorest regions of East Africa to affluent Korean mega-
churches. The non-Western world is alight with charismatic
experiences, and has been so since Azusa.

The Pentecostal movement looks to continue its tremendous growth for decades to come. Philip Jenkins, who wrote
about this trend more than 10 years ago in his book *The Next
Christendom: the Coming of Global Christianity*, outlined
the characteristics and growth patterns of churches in what
he calls the global South: South America, Asia and Africa.[72]
Harvey Cox wrote similarly, a decade prior, in *Fire From
Heaven: The Rise of Pentecostal Spirituality and the Reshaping
of Religion in the Twenty-first Century.*

---

72 His updated 2011 version of the same book underscores the same growth patterns
of Christianity in the global South.

The Center for the Study of Global Christianity at Gordon-Conwell Theological Seminary states that there were 582 million charismatic/Pentecostal Christians in the world in the year 2000; by 2025, that number is set to rise to over 800 million. A recent collaboration by a sociologist from Biola University and a researcher from the University of Southern California suggests the rise of a related form of Christianity—what they call Independent Network Charismatic (INC) Christianity—is the fastest-growing Christian movement in both the global South and the West (Christerson and Flory, 2).

Many Western Christians view Pentecostalism with caution—myself included, to some degree. But I also view it with hope.

I identify as a Pentecostal—but a self-critical one who finds aspects of this branch of Christianity deeply offensive. As a happily married lesbian pastor, I find the homophobic aspects of Pentecostalism personally diminishing of both my humanity and my calling.[73] But I still hold to personal experiences like the one I described at the beginning of the chapter, and find it difficult to dismiss the numerous occasions when it seemed like God—or some*thing*, some*one*—helped, comforted, healed and/or navigated me or someone I know. The Spirit is real in my life. Plus, dismissing charismatic expressions of faith would disregard the daily encounters experienced by some of the poorest and least powerful people in the world.[74] That feels patronizing.

It might seem surprising that a lesbian pastor would embrace Pentecostalism, with its still-present tendencies toward social conservatism and holiness movement under-tones. However, I'm not *too* bothered by the theological differences, as there are many streams of Pentecostalism and their various theologies continue developing. First, let me

---

73 Not all Pentecostals exclude LGBTQ+ people from the full life of the church.
74 "At least for the foreseeable future, members of a Southern-dominated church are likely to be among the poorer people on the planet, in marked contrast to those in the older, Western-dominated church" (Jenkins, *The Next Christendom: The Coming of Global Christianity,* 7).

share two things that give me pause about Pentecostalism, and then describe how I have come to make meaning of what seems to be a move of God.

Co-opting the early impulses of Pentecostalism

Early Pentecostalism's initial impulses were toward radical inclusion and pacifism—which might surprise the contemporary reader. However, within two decades, Pentecostalism uncritically adopted theologies shaped by increased social, political and institutional power acquired after its early years. The original Pentecostal instincts of expansive inclusivity and non-violence dissipated, obscuring the beauty of what the Spirit revealed in the first few years.

While William Seymour's spiritual formation matured in the context of the Wesleyan and Nazarene holiness traditions, he displayed openness to resisting restrictive biblical interpretations when they undermined what he saw the Spirit doing. When it seemed like "clear biblical instruction" contradicted his lived experience, Seymour chose the latter as a matter of pastoral praxis.

A good many aspects of the Azusa meetings defied holiness movement norms. Services crossed racial, gender and socio-economic classes in ways seldom seen in America then or now. Those who were so often excluded from preaching—women, the uneducated, the poor—found freedom to exercise their gifts. From the onset, Seymour's leadership team drew from people of various races and ethnicities (Robeck, 14):

> *Where [Seymour] differed from many holiness leaders was in the way he lived out his belief in the equality of every person who gathered for worship at his mission … he allowed his people to express themselves even when he disagreed with them. It did not matter if they were old or young, rich or poor, black or white, male or female, lay or clergy. Seymour took them all seriously and thereby*

empowered them within the space he seemed to enlarge just for them. (92)

Even today, Pentecostals often bless female leaders, pastors and preachers. But early on, in the late 1910s and 1920s, the American portion of the movement split along racial lines (Yong, 73).[75] The Church of God in Christ became the predominantly black arm of Pentecostalism, and the Assemblies of God became the predominantly white arm.[76]

The first two decades of Pentecostalism also saw practitioners reject violence, including killing in war. However, World War II affected the hardly-yet-formed Pentecostal belief system in ways that distorted its earliest instincts.

In the foreword to *Pentecostal Pacifism: The Origin, Development, and Rejection of Pacific Belief Among the Pentecostals,* John Howard Yoder writes:

> *Pentecostalism's changes have become a classical specimen of the 'sect cycle,' making within barely two generations some fundamental accommodations to establishment like those which took early Christianity centuries. The prima facie biblicism did not mature into a solid ethical hermeneutic. The prophetic discernment of the evils of social stratification yielded with astonishing ease to personal prosperity and institutional respectability. (iii-iv)[77]*

In other words, early acquiescence to existing power structures—both the military and class privilege—dulled

---

75 "Nevertheless, the social forces of segregation and racism were too strong for even those filled with the Spirit. By mid-1920s, segregated denominations were emerging: most whites found that the 'three strikes' of being black, poor and pentecostal were too much to handle" (Yong, 73). Also, William Seymour largely blamed the white congregants for the divisions and described the Holy Spirit as "grieved" over the tension (Robeck, 317).

76 The latter has, more recently, become increasingly diverse, drawing especially from the Latinx population.

77 The irony of John Howard Yoder writing about ethics, social stratification and institutional respectability is not lost on me—though I think his point still stands.

Pentecostalism's revivalistic shine in the United States and lessened its capacity for a coherent ethic (which it still lacks). Pacifism gave way to militarism, and concern for the gap between rich and poor gave way to "name-it-and-claim-it" theologies blessing and sanctifying the pursuit of power and wealth.

Jay Beaman, the author of *Pentecostal Pacificism*, gives three reasons Pentecostalism changed in its early decades. First, while the Azusa Street Revival took place largely among the poor, Pentecostals found themselves swept into a spiral of upward social mobility during and after World War II, as their influence entered the mainstream. This led them to accept beliefs initially missing from their theology. Second, the number of Pentecostals who served in World War II and the establishment of Pentecostal army chaplains (34 chaplains by 1944) meant that, "It would only be a matter of time before they would write a biblical justification of the work of a soldier" (Beaman, 111). Finally, its entwinement with evangelical institutions—namely, its membership in the National Association of Evangelicals in 1942—affected the Assemblies of God's former pacifist stance. "It is significant that in the same year the Assemblies of God joined the National Association of Evangelicals, the Assemblies of God also reviewed the adequacy of their statement on military service" (Beaman, 112).

Pentecostalism's conflicted relationship to evangelicalism

Pentecostalism's relationship with evangelicalism, and the biblicism[78] infecting that branch of American faith throughout the 20th century, is symptomatic of its inability to decide whether the Bible informs experience or vice versa—a classic chicken-or-egg conundrum.[79] In *To the Ends of the Earth:*

---

78 Literalist interpretation of Scripture adopted by fundamentalists.
79 I like what Beaman writes in his brief conclusion: "Pentecostals need to ponder whether they can long maintain their distinctive views about the Church and the Holy Spirit, while conforming to mainstream Evangelical socio-religious views" (123).

Pentecostalism and the Transformation of World Christianity,
Allan Anderson says, " … pentecostals have two reciprocal
sources of authority held in tension: reading the Bible affects
praxis, and the experiences that follow influence the understanding of the Bible" (122).

The conflicted connection between Pentecostalism and the
fundamentalism-evangelicalism[80] from which it emerged is
important to understand. On the one hand, early Pentecostals
maintained the biblical literalism of the holiness movements
they evolved out of, but, ironically, the fundamentalists
disavowed them. People like William Seymour said, "Look!
The Bible shows Jesus's disciples healing people, so we should
be able to heal people too! The Bible talks about people
speaking in tongues. We should be able to speak in tongues
too!" The non-pentecostal fundamentalists were uncharac-
teristically *non-literal* in their interpretation of supernatural
phenomenon. They had adopted the doctrine of "cessationism,"
which said things like miracles, healing and gifts of the Spirit
like prophecy and speaking in tongues ceased once the New
Testament canon was completed. The Pentecostals simply
applied fundamentalist literalism beyond where the fundamentalists' comfort level allowed, and that discomfort is what
led the fundamentalists to wash their hands of the Pentecostals (Kyle 145).[81]

One might say the fundamentalists read the situation
correctly—Pentecostals wanted to claim the authority of the
Bible inherited by their forebears, yet so often acted in ways

---

80 Evangelicalism attempted to distinguish itself from Fundamentalism in the decades
after Azusa Street. Fuller Theological Seminary, where I took a few graduate classes,
was established to be the anti-biblicist, pro-intellectual evangelical training ground
in 1947. However, in spite of this attempt and other similar moves to differentiate
between the two streams, both fundamentalism and modern evangelicalism now
largely share a literalist view of Scripture (with a few exceptions in the evangelical
camp, who one could argue are outside modern evangelicalism but for whom retaining
that label remains an important identity marker).

81 "Before the 1940s, the fundamentalists took a very dim view of Pentecostalism …
At their 1928 convention, American fundamentalists condemned Pentecostalism as
fanatical and unscriptural, regarding it as 'a real menace to the churches and a real
injury to the same testimony of Fundamental Christians'" (Kyle, 145).

contradicting traditional fundamentalist interpretations of Scripture when it seemed the Spirit led them to do so. They were not *bona fide* fundamentalists, but were still too steeped in their pre-existing theological framework to understand why not.

The early Pentecostals even went beyond the tenants of *sola Scriptura* when they paid more heed to what they discerned as "moves of the Spirit" than to traditional Reformed inter-pretations. As Ken discussed in Chapter 3, the project of *sola Scriptura* was to lead Protestants into greater certainty about their beliefs, and here the Spirit was shaking up that delusion of certainty—a function of the modern need to control. So long as we deceive ourselves into thinking we can master the Bible and its "clear" instructions for how to live, we can hold tight to the illusion of control (and thereby, power). But the spiritual manifestations and leadings of Pentecostalism prove uncontrollable—we can't constrain or regulate the Holy Spirit and her leadings.

Perhaps the controlling inclinations of *sola Scriptura* are so ingrained in the Western Protestant imagination that it's taken this monumental move of the Spirit to dislodge our idolization of the Bible, beckoning us to view the fullness of what God is doing in our time. The question is: Will Pentecostals continue to be co-opted by adherents to *sola Scriptura*, or will they lean into the gift they've given Christianity?

Pentecostalism's misuse of power

My second reservation about the Pentecostal movement is the widespread abuse and exploitation of the vulnerable that is found in some segments.

About 10 years ago, I visited a Pentecostal revival center in Florida. A preacher was said to have a gift of healing, so believers from all over the world gathered to hear him teach and have him pray over them.

The event, held in a local arena, made me cringe for a few reasons. First, the services centered on the faith healer, who was loud, showy and attention-seeking. While he invited everyone in the arena to pray for those near them—ostensibly indicating a theology that says anyone can participate in the healing acts of God—the whole affair actually focused on him. He was a young, white, straight married man from North America who seemed to soak up the acclaim. I later learned he was secretly having an affair with a woman on his staff, which aptly summed up this man's confusion regarding how power should be handled.

Second, I saw what I considered to be abusive practices. The preacher implied that people would get healed from whatever ailed them if they only had enough faith. This led to attendees surrounding and praying for people in wheelchairs— literally lifting the differently abled men and women from their chairs in attempts to help them walk. None were able to, even after prayer. Perhaps those who made the trip welcomed the aggressive prayer tactics, but watching them encircled by eager participants who were *certain* God would heal our brothers and sisters in wheelchairs because the prophet declared it so—I flinched.

Later, I saw a woman on the side of the stadium near the hallway, crying and writhing on the floor as another woman stood over her, speaking loudly in what I assumed to be glossolalia (tongues) while occasionally saying in English, "I cast you out of this woman, demon, in Jesus's name!" I almost intervened on behalf of the woman on the floor; I wish now I had done so. I have no idea who the crying woman was or what caused the woman "praying" for her to think she had a demon manifesting, but the woman on the floor could have had a mental illness, or Tourette Syndrome, or severe trauma—or any other number of things where this kind of "prayer" could do lasting damage. I was taken aback by what I interpreted as a misguided disregard of compassion—both in that the position the crying woman was in, on the floor, was

very public (and quite probably humiliating), and in the lack
of care in thinking through possible mental health issues or
trauma-related responses.

These kinds of abuses are the reasons people *rightly* run
screaming from some Pentecostal meetings. We are responsible to protect the vulnerable in any situation. That's part of
loving our neighbor. Some people experience healing of their
physical illnesses—I know of too many accounts to think I
can deny it. But the vast majority do not get healed in this
age. Lifting people from wheelchairs to claim their healing
demeans our brothers and sisters who traverse the earth
differently than most of us. If our theology exploits the most
vulnerable in the room, we should table what we're doing.[82]

Spiritual abuse is real and pervasive. In communities where
gifts of healing and prophecy are taken seriously, we must
take the gift of discernment as seriously as the "flashier" gifts.
When I worked with missionaries overseas, I often observed
spiritual manipulation based on perceived "spiritual power."
People would claim to "have a word" for someone, or to have
"heard from God" about what a mission team (or individual member) was supposed to do, with little to no pastoral
guidance. If the prophetic word was given loudly and with
many tears, it "must be from the Spirit."

One woman, a self-appointed apostle and prophet from
New Zealand, traveled to China with her spouse and a friend
to hold prayer meetings with missionaries. Her two companions walked behind her to "carry her robe of anointing
in the Spirit" and to protect her from demonic attacks with a
"spiritual shield." Of course, no one could see either the robe or
the shield these men pretended to hold and, to my mind, the
makings of a cult were in the works. But other missionaries
listened to this woman and took her "prophecies" to heart,

---

82 And note that I do not think people who use wheelchairs to get around are
inherently vulnerable, but rather that they become so in a room filled with people
either 1) eager to see a healing that will confound those doing the praying; or 2) filled
with such overwhelming compassion that it causes those praying to break boundaries
of culturally defined decency.

because she was somewhat magnetic in her teaching style—a masterful manipulator.

The gift of prophecy can be tremendously encouraging—in 1 Cor. 14, the apostle Paul tells us to desire it more than any other spiritual gift. However, leaning into those with discernment and pastoral gifts as much as we honor more showy gifts like prophecy is essential to maintaining balance and health in our faith communities. Otherwise perceived power goes unchecked, and that always goes badly.

The misuse of power is so pervasive in some Pentecostal circles that it has become theologically justified. Over the years, I became acquainted with two charismatic theologies: one called "The Seven Mountain Mandate,"[83] and the other, "Dominion Theology."[84] The reader may have never heard of these, but understanding them will help make sense of the American evangelical embrace of Donald Trump.[85]

Dominion Theology is a belief claiming that, since God gave Adam dominion over the earth in Genesis, we Christians should seek to dominate the world in the name of establishing the kingdom of God. "Seven mountains" refers to the thinking that seven major areas of human life need such Christian influence: education, religion, family, business, government/military, arts/entertainment and media. Brad Christerson and Richard Flory write, "This model of social transformation is clearly top-down or 'trickle down' model" (98). In other words, the more powerful and influential one becomes, the more social transformation one affects. It follows, then, that God blesses the pursuit of power in followers willing to use

---

83 The "Seven Mountain Mandate" is sometimes called "seven pillars," or "seven spheres." It was originally called "seven spheres," based on a shared vision between Loren Cunningham (founder of Youth With a Mission), Bill Bright (founder of Campus Crusade for Christ) and Francis Schaeffer.
http://www.7culturalmountains.org
84 Dominion theology is part of C. Peter Wagner's Kingdom Now Theology and informs those who are part of the New Apostolic Reformation movement.
85 Certainly not all evangelicals consider themselves Pentecostals, but many evangelicals have embraced "The Seven Mountain Mandate" as a missional tactic.

their authority to further an often-narrow interpretation of godliness in a given field.[86]

The objective of influencing one or more of these "mountains" caused many evangelicals and Pentecostals to turn their heads away from the distasteful behavior of a number of top politicians in the last few years. The pursuit of power and influence trumped protecting the human dignity of the vulnerable: undocumented immigrants, DREAMers (DACA recipients), women, the poor and uninsured, those who are differently abled, African-Americans and the LGBTQ+ community (especially transgender persons), among others. The alarm bells were drowned out because power has become a sacred entitlement in this religious subculture.[87]

The pursuit of power hinders the work of God. It distorted Pentecostalism's early instincts of inclusion and pacifism, and power continues tempting people to misuse their gifts to gain the praise and acquiescence of others.

Is Pentecostalism evolving beyond these problems?

Despite my concerns, I still believe the Pentecostal movement is of God.

First, the lightning-quick pace of its spread is nothing short of miraculous; it flourishes among the poor and outcast. It exhibits the fruit of vibrantly connecting people to Jesus. Widespread and credible reports of healings and other miracles abound. And Pentecostalism exhibits cultural diversity second only to the Roman Catholic Church, which has been heavily influenced by the charismatic movement in the majority world (Jenkins, *The Next Christendom,* 7).

86 To be fair, some who embrace "The Seven Mountain Mandate" caution against pursuing self-seeking goals. But often the counsel sounds convoluted and reveals a tortured relationship with power. As an example: http://www.ihopnetwork.com/index.php/2016/05/11/seven-mountains-analyzed

87 A group of Church scholars called Independent Network Charismatic (INC) Christians embrace Dominion Theology and the seven mountains of influence. They are the fastest-growing faith sect in both the United States and the world, with outsized global influence due to innovations in how they operate and finance themselves (Christerson and Flory 2).

Second, I am encouraged that the theologies of Pentecostalism are not set. The fast-moving evolution of the theologies of the global South means they are like new wine still in the process of aging. Admittedly, much of the non-Western world inherited various versions of Christianity with roots firmly set in *sola Scriptura*, traditional social norms and colonialist power structures bequeathed by Western missionaries. However, those beliefs seem to be pliable as Christians around the world grapple with the Gospel mandate in their own contexts, throwing out what does not seem to be of God. "Social and political issues among Pentecostals will continue to be debated, and in such a fast-moving and changing movement it is difficult to draw precise conclusions. In fact, as Joel Robbins has pointed out after surveying the literature, 'the way Pentecostalism shapes political attitudes and practices is at this point utterly inconclusive'" (qtd. in Anderson, 141).

Philip Jenkins notes the reluctance of Western Christians to embrace the Pentecostal movement because much of Christianity in the global South remains focused on individual salvation and espouses a more traditional, or socially conservative, brand of the faith (Jenkins, *The Next Christendom: The Coming of Global Christianity*, 8). However, he made that observation in the 2001 publication of his book, musing that it would remain to be seen whether or not Western influence would prevent Southern churches from contextualizing and adapting. By the 2011 update of the book, enough change had taken place for Jenkins to observe that contextualization had indeed begun:

> *Looking at Southern Christianities gives a surprising new perspective on some other things that might seem to be very familiar. Perhaps the most striking example is how the newer churches can read the Bible in a way that makes that Christianity look like a wholly different religion than the faith of prosperous advanced societies of Europe or*

> *North America. We have already seen that many*
> *global South churches are quite at home with bib-*
> *lical notions of the supernatural, with ideas such*
> *as dreams and prophecy. Just as relevant in their*
> *eyes are that book's core social and political themes,*
> *themes of martyrdom, oppression and exile. In*
> *the present day, it may be that it is only in the*
> *newer churches that the Bible can be read with*
> *any authenticity and immediacy, and that the Old*
> *Christendom should listen attentively to Southern*
> *voices. (273)*

So while there has been hair-splitting in the United States over where the authority lies for the Pentecostal Church—the Bible or spiritual revelation—we are starting to see the balance tip in the latter direction overseas. While most Protestants embrace the Bible as the sole or final authority, Pentecostals "rely on direct spiritual revelations that supplement or even replace biblical authority" (Jenkins, *The Next Christendom: The Coming of Global Christianity*, 80).

As a gay woman, I have concerns with participating in faith communities where I am not able to exercise the full range of my gifts or enjoy the blessing of my (very joyous!) marriage. I embrace my Pentecostal heritage, doing what I can to bear witness to my experience and contributing to moving the needle forward while working within a realm of the Church that celebrates my full humanity. I don't want to give the impression that, just because Pentecostal theologies are changing and we need to wait and see where things land, people should stay in faith communities that hurt them. I would encourage the opposite. But I also do not want to pass judgment on a global phenomenon that bears the marks of God. It still remains to be seen how the whole will form, but as the authority of the Pentecostal Church continues shifting from *sola Scriptura*—with its attendant biblicism—to the leading of the living, revelatory Spirit, my hope remains that the Church will be more and better equipped to love all people without reservation.

The Spirit moves within and beyond our theological constructs

When I lived in western China, I studied the Amdo Tibetan language with a private tutor, a young Buddhist man. We attended the local university together and got to know each other, going over flashcards and rehearsing simple conversations. One morning, he told me about a vision he'd had while he was meditating. In the vision, a man dressed in white handed him a ball of light. "I think this man was Jesus," he said to me. It was the first of many such conversations we had, as he continued having visions and dreams that included both Christian and Buddhist symbols.

People unfamiliar with the Christian faith surely can access the divine spirit of love, even if they call it by another name. Spiritual experiences—such as revelatory visions, dreams and ecstatic prayer—occur in many religions. Perhaps this human capacity is from the God who *is* love—a way the divine relates with us, regardless of our context, even if none of us fully understands it. This spirit of love is less concerned with our theology than it is with relationship.

In the New Testament, we read:

> *The Son is the image of the invisible God, the first-born over all creation. For in him all things were created: things in heaven and on earth, visible and invisible, whether thrones or powers or rulers or authorities; all things have been created through him and for him. He is before all things, and **in him all things hold together** [emphasis added].* (Col. 1:15-17)

We enter mystical territory here, but the apostle Paul attempts to describe how all things are *in* Jesus—the entire

human race included, not just Christians. Informed by a
Christian perspective and imagination—because it's the
tradition in which I am steeped and which also informed
the apostle Paul—all humanity is part of the Trinitarian
godhead through Jesus, and thus can access the unity, love and
communion of the godhead unhindered. The Holy Spirit has
been sent into the world to show us that we are held in Jesus
by grace, that we are completely loved by this triune God, and
that we have access to the divine power and presence of the
God who is love, accorded to us as adopted children of a holy
triune community of persons.

Each of us may have a different understanding of what this
means, and it's the Holy Spirit's job to lead us into ever-greater
understanding.[88] Some Christians do not fully understand the
implications of this reality. Some who are not Christians nevertheless intuit the grace, love and inclusion they are part of
because the Spirit has revealed the nature of God to them by
whatever means available, and they live their lives accordingly.
Jesus describes this dynamic in the parable of the sheep and
the goats in Matthew 25, where people who do not recognize
him are called righteous because of actions that indicate
compassionate hearts.[89]

What it comes down to is this: The Holy Spirit moves
where it will, on whom it will, doing what it will, regardless
of our theological constructs. It is not containable, controlla-
ble or predictable. It is wind, it is fire, it is water, it is breath.
It is a river flowing out of the heart of God and into the
world. Is there a way to live with the immanent messiness of
humans interacting with God unfettered, without trying to

---

88 "Upon the homecoming [ascension] of the incarnate Son, with the human race
gathered in his arms, the Spirit of adoption was unleashed upon the world with the
singular mission of leading us to *know* the truth" (Kruger, 56).

89 Also, Mt. 7:21-23 describes those who know the name of Jesus but who are not
acting out of their god-nature. "Not everyone who says to me, 'Lord, Lord,' will enter
the kingdom of heaven, but only the one who does the will of my Father who is in
heaven. Many will say to me on that day, 'Lord, Lord, did we not prophesy in your
name and in your name drive out demons and in your name perform many miracles?'
Then I will tell them plainly, 'I never knew you. Away from me, you evildoers!'"

intellectually control the narrative of how and when and on whom the Spirit moves? "The wind blows wherever it pleases. You hear its sound, but you cannot tell where it comes from or where it is going. So it is with everyone born of the Spirit" (Jn. 3:8).

Emergence theory: a new way to imagine the Spirit at work

The Church in the West doesn't have a great imagination for how to envision the work of the Holy Spirit—perhaps because faith is so messy, and we prefer predictability and order. The Spirit brings order, but of her own kind and always out of chaos.[90] How can we speak effectively about how disparate (and often untidy) things like revivals, prayer and gifts of the Spirit affect the coming of God's good realm? In many ways, science and mathematics have done a better job helping postmodern people[91] understand complex systems, and I suggest we adapt insights from these fields to help us think more clearly about faith.

A couple years back, my friend Andrea (who has a background in mathematics) started talking to me about emergence theory, and how it helped her better comprehend her spirituality and increase her ability to visualize the global Church.[92] Intrigued, I bought a book on emergence theory and found that it opened my imagination, as well.

In a nutshell, emergence theorists study seemingly chaotic systems that have underlying organizational structures. The weather is one example: Weather systems appear disorderly, yet there are underlying patterns discernible through careful and long-term observation. The ways cities develop is another example of an emergence system. The initial formation of

---

90 Phyllis Tickle and Jon Sweeney have a marvelous, short chapter about the Spirit as the agency of change in the world. The Spirit is the aspect of God "about movement/disruption and change/transformation" (117).

91 or post-postmoderns, or post-post-postmoderns ... wherever we are now!

92 Listening to her describe emergence theory reminded me of a book I read in my 20s called *Chaos: Making a New Science*, in which the author talks about how seemingly chaotic systems ultimately have underlying patterns.

cities seems chaotic and random but, over time, the arrange-
ment of neighborhoods and businesses becomes surprisingly
predictable. The authors of *Emergence: The Connected Lives
of Ants, Brains, Cities, and Software* say people and organizational structures seem to "spontaneously organize" into "a
pattern with multiple, clearly separated business centers." As
they organize, it's possible to forecast where the city's future
shopping districts, business centers, poverty or wealth centers
and so on will pop up, based on how current people and
businesses interact (S. Johnson, 101-113).

After college, I worked for Borders Group, where I wrote
press releases about the company's new store openings. At the
time, the now-bankrupt Borders Books and Music stores were
expanding at a rate of 35-50 stores per year. Borders stores
found synergy with other big-box retailers drawing from a
similar customer base: you likely found a Bed Bath & Beyond
near a Borders store, or an Old Navy, a Whole Foods or a
Best Buy in the same strip mall. Having a Bed Bath & Beyond
nearby amplified foot traffic into the bookstore because similar
types of people with comparable income levels shopped at
both stores.

If you simply looked at a city map that didn't indicate
where businesses were located, you could not predict where
Borders might locate a store. But if the map indicated where,
say, a Bed Bath & Beyond was located, you could predict
where a bookstore might flourish, based on a piece of local
information. "Local information can lead to global wisdom,"
(S. Johnson, *Emergence: The Connected Lives of Ants, Brains,
Cities, and Software*, 79).

Segments of cities solidify and remain part of its lasting
structure. In Florence, Italy, the gold district is located in the
same place it was situated hundreds of years ago and will
remain there for the foreseeable future. Similarly, it is likely
that Chinatown, in New York City, will continue to welcome
Chinese immigrants. Individuals can act randomly—not
all Chinese immigrants in New York City will move to

Chinatown—but enough will fit the larger pattern that we can confidently assert an underlying trend. Once there is enough "local information" about a part of the complex system, global conclusions can be drawn as to the lasting structure of the system.

It is rare for complex systems to experience noteworthy underlying change. In order for complex systems to significantly reshape themselves—like Chinatown relocating to a different area of New York City or dissolving altogether— there must be *an exceptional change in the system's energy*. A few hundred years ago, villages and agrarian fields populated Europe and looked to do so for the foreseeable future—until major technological advances took place, making it more likely that cities would arise. In relatively short order, the Industrial Revolution spurred the growth of numerous urban metropolises. Technology provided such a significant energy change that it completely reorganized the way people lived and worked. Something of that magnitude could happen to alter New York City's neighborhood map—say, a natural disaster or a dramatic change in immigration patterns. It's unlikely in the immediate future, but possible.

The global Church is also a complex system. It appears chaotic and fractured at times—especially when you consider its various and sundry factions worldwide— but underneath the disarray lies an ancient framework that is both somewhat predictable and difficult to change. Like all complex systems, major redesigns to the foundational structure only come when there's a surge in new energy that alters the fundamental organization of the whole. Perhaps the Holy Spirit is the energy our triune God uses to shape and form the Church more closely to what God hopes we can become, when we've become stuck in a particular pattern. Maybe events like the Azusa Revival and the present Pentecostal movement are symptomatic of a global shift in how the Church will behave going forward, catalyzed by a God-given insertion of energy into the system.

The advantages of an emergence-informed view of God

Emergence theory helped me process my faith in three ways.

First, I find it helpful that, in emergence theory, local choices affect global patterns. What if that's the genius of "love your neighbor as yourself"? Sometimes we Christians want to tackle enormous systemic problems, but it can be overwhelming. What if we can best affect large-scale change by caring for the people in close proximity to us?

My friend Caleb Brokaw, who died of lung cancer a few years back, once said that he didn't want to be known for being successful or for doing "great" things—he'd rather be known for shoveling his neighbor's sidewalk when it snowed. If all 2.3 billion Christians in the world (Hackett and McClendon) spent their days and nights contemplating how to *really* love their actual neighbors—how to treat them the way they, themselves, want to be treated—this world would be transformed. Even 10 percent of 2.3 billion could affect large-scale change. Jesus's strategy appears mathematically sound, not to mention practical. As the authors of *Emergence* put it,

> *Local turns out to be the key term in understanding the power of swarm logic. We see emergent behavior in systems like ant colonies when the individual agents in the system pay attention to their immediate neighbors rather than wait for orders from above. They think locally and act locally, but their collective action produces global behavior. (74)*

Second, emergence theory tells me that I have many choices and potential paths in this life. As a pastor, I've spoken with people who are frightened that they've either missed or will miss "God perfect plan" for their life. A lot of angst could be relieved by seeing the world as a complex and open system. God is with us and can help us navigate our way in life, but our well-being and our faithfulness to God doesn't hinge on following one specific "plan" that we might easily overlook, ignore or reject (Pinnock, *The Openness of God: A Biblical Challenge to the Traditional Understanding of God,* 162-168).[93]

Finally, the idea that well-established patterns in complex systems often don't alter without a major change in energy helps me imagine how revivals and prayer work. When the Church, as a complex system, gets stuck in a pattern that hinders its growth and effectiveness, an influx of the Spirit is needed to disrupt the old ways of thinking and open our hearts to new possibilities.

Larger infusions of the Spirit empower us for ongoing intimacy with God (that can be maintained) and for long-term justice work. But while revivals feel great—they energize and renew the faithful—when we keep going back to an old well trying to find new water, we miss the reason we initially took a drink. We hydrated to get to work. Revival is not a state we seek to keep the Church in; it is an energizing experience in which we partake in order to revitalize and get new direction from God.[94]

By envisioning the Church as a complex system and the Holy Spirit as both our guide through it and the energy of change, I think we offer more compelling reasons for embracing both the gifts of the Spirit and prayer in general. The far-reaching Pentecostal movement has the feel of a move of God, sent to shake up the system. Only such a move could help us transition into an age in which we break free from *sola Scriptura's* constraints and embrace a more life-giving spirituality.

---

93 Open theism, an evolution of Arminian (as opposed to Calvinist) thought, compliments emergence theory in the theological realm. Clark Pinnock, John Sanders, Gregory Boyd and Roger Olson are theologians associated with pressing out open theist thinking.

94 "I have also come to realize that revival is not the normal state of affairs, nor is it intended to be so. Those of us who appreciate the role that revival plays often miss this. At the core of the term 'revival' is the Latin root *viv*—'life.' That is what revival does: it brings life into life-less situations or people. And the prefix *re* indicates something being done *again.*" (Robeck, 322)

The impulses of the age of the Spirit pull us toward greater openness to others, greater equality within the Church, justice, humility, pacifism and the laying down of power, which were all part of the original ethos of Pentecostalism. The current embrace of violence, of exploiting the vulnerable for self-serving ends and of holding onto biblicism—using a patchwork of Scriptures to justify gaining power—among much of American Pentecostalism belies its roots. We in the West should watch, wait and learn from the Church in the global South, as it adapts charismatic faith and allows it to shape their theologies and practices. I have faith that the Holy Spirit will continue shaking the unhelpful aspects out of our collective theologies. While Ken and I embrace Pentecostalism and this age of the Spirit, we don't do it uncritically; rather, we watch and wait patiently, discerning through the best lenses we have, as Christianity morphs and adapts.

The theology of resistance we propose in Part 2 directly combats our human instinct to acquire power and provokes us to either share it or lay it down for the sake of others. When Christians adopt interpretations of Scripture and of the meaning of the cross that are based on a God who embraces violence, we naturally pursue power that justifies doing violence to others (Douglas, 59-70).[95]

Whether we *pursue* power or *lay down* power in the name of Jesus makes all the difference in our witness. The Church's increasing revelation—that we worship a God who stands with the vulnerable of the world—encourages us, and as we grow in our collective understanding of the Gospel, our interpretive lenses for our experiences will shift.

Things are already shifting.

---

95 "While the cross in and of itself may not precipitate deadly terror, the cross invested with power does" (69).

Vision of a Tibetan woman realized?

When God told me I would see Tibet and allowed me to have a vision of an elderly woman in the mountains, I never understood this prayer experience as containing a directive from God; rather, I viewed it as more akin to an invitation. My vision contained a glimpse of a path that *could happen*, but was not inevitable. I also noted that the voice I heard in my head didn't say, "Go to Tibet as soon as possible," or "Go find that old woman on the hill you saw while praying," or even "Go convert that woman to faith in Jesus." No, the voice told me I would *see* Tibet. That's all. I try to be cautious in not reading more into my experiences than is there.

I did see Tibet and I believe I met the woman in my vision two weeks before I moved back to America. A part of me still dismissed the idea that the person I saw in my mind's eye could be real; I thought she might be metaphorical. However, when I saw an elderly woman in a monastery in the mountains, something in me knew this was *her*.

I met the woman in a village high in the Himalayas. Along with a few friends, I visited this village, which was built around a large Tibetan Buddhist monastery where few Westerners visit. Tibetan Buddhists believe that humans gain karma and spread blessings with certain actions—including the spinning of prayer wheels, called Mani wheels—that contain strips of prayers. Prayer wheels can be small, handheld items, or larger canisters that take the energy of one's entire body to spin. Medium-sized ones often line the outer boundary of monasteries, where dozens of prayer wheels stand in a row, as was the case with the sacred space in this particular village in the mountains. The monastery was a mile in circumference and the faithful walk around the many buildings in a clockwise circle, spinning wheels as they make their rounds. Some people wear special gloves to keep their hands from blistering.

My friends and I took a leisurely stroll around the village and monastery, pausing to eat *momos* (dumplings filled with yak meat) and chat with various locals. We came upon three elderly women sitting on a bench alongside the red wall of one of the temples, one of whom was older than the rest—probably in her mid-to-late 80s. My insides stirred and I asked a friend (who spoke better Tibetan and understood the specific local dialect) if she could help me communicate with the woman, who was waving and smiling at us foreigners (Americans, Indians and Romanians).[96]

The old woman directed me to sit beside her, and we exchanged niceties. What's your name? Where are you from? Do you have children? She held a Mani wheel and was taking a break from walking around the monastery with her two friends, who watched us with amusement.

Since she clearly was a woman of prayer, I asked her if I could pray with her. She said yes, so I asked if I could put my hand on her shoulder. Then, sitting beside her, I prayed aloud for God to bless her, and for whatever else came into my mind. She started crying; then she was shaking and crying. I prayed in my prayer language, figuring she wouldn't know the difference, and that way, the Holy Spirit could intercede in whatever way might be most effective. As I prayed and she cried, she also began praying out loud. I have no idea what she said—whether she was praying for me in return, or for something going on in her own life, or general expressions of joy and blessing—but what I do know is in that space there was a meeting between two souls I've rarely felt in my life. I don't mean to romanticize the situation, but I struggle to find words to describe the spiritual connection that took place between us and the energy that flowed in that interaction. It was as though we were praying as one, only in two languages.

The experience was as profound to me as when I'd had the original vision of the woman, years before. I hope she felt

---

96 There are three Tibetan languages (Central, Amdo and Kham) and several dialects within those language groups.

as blessed and loved by God as I did, perceiving that God honored two women seeking truth and light and love that day, by giving us a glimpse through the mysterious liminal threshold where humans meet the divine.

We now live in the age of the Holy Spirit, a time in our collective spiritual history when God's Spirit, unleashed into the world with unprecedented power, roams and romances those desperately seeking unfettered connection with both God and humankind. For all the mess and misappropriation of Jesus's name, we still hold that the Holy Spirit works in this complex system we inhabit and that this Spirit is working for our good.

Part 2:
A Theology of Resistance

After offering *solus Jesus* as an alternative to *sola Scriptura* in Part 1, we address the inevitable question, "Which Jesus?" Our answer, informed by the insights of Dietrich Bonhoeffer, René Girard, and others, is the God of the victim—Jesus revealed through the lens of scapegoat theory. We regard this as a "theology of resistance," grounded in the Gospel demand to resist our tendency toward rivalry, which drives our scapegoating ways. This calls for a radical embrace of the empowering of Spirit available in Jesus.

Throughout these chapters, we speak from our distinct vantage points—Emily as a queer woman deeply affected by religious exclusion, and Ken as a straight man who had his own taste of exclusion when he became an ally of sexual minorities.

God of the Victim

Emily

A FEW YEARS back—after I'd fully come out to myself concerning my sexual orientation, and while I still pastored a church grappling with how to be fully inclusive of sexual minorities—I decided not to date until our staff completed the three-year change process we had committed to working through together. We hoped our congregation could embrace theological tension while becoming fully accepting of the LGBTQ+ community.[97]

In that stressful interval, as a single, gay woman in my mid-30s, I navigated the murky waters between hope and pain. I hoped God would open our congregation's heart to receive a greater revelation of her love for all humanity, and I yearned to help shape a community capable of living in the midst of disagreement and in a way that would be safe for LGBTQ+ congregants. To create such a space, everyone—both conservative and progressive—would need to relinquish their inclination to judge the "other," and the community would have to remove barriers (based solely on sexual orientation) regarding both leadership service (all the way up through senior pastor) and marriage.

---

97 See Ken Wilson's book, *A Letter to My Congregation: An evangelical pastor's path to embracing people who are gay, lesbian, bisexual, and transgender into the company of Jesus, 2nd edition* for additional reading on how he proposed to manage the tension based on Romans 14-15.

However, longing for that ideal cost me personally. I, along with other staff members, held conversation after conversation with our 60 or so church leaders to think through, together, what it might mean to be an inclusive community. Being gay and listening to people unpack their reservations about LGBTQ+ inclusion was intensely distressing. My gayness was hidden from most, so no one held back. Some talks left me praising God for the beauty of unconditional love; others left me in tears. The latter tore at my dignity and my humanity.

I remember one particular conversation with a couple who had met in a class I taught at the church and married soon afterward. I had a particular fondness for them because I had watched them fall in love. I went to their house and ate dinner, listening throughout the meal to their objections to full gay inclusion in the Church. We talked about different interpretations of the Scripture, we discussed what it means to discern issues as a community of faith and we chatted about the tragic effects of the traditional posture of exclusion and the need to rethink the Christian response to LGBTQ+ people in light of the general (and rightful) disaffection gay people have with the Church. We specifically talked about the astronomical queer teen suicide rate and the Church's culpability in contributing to that number. Yet they could not get past the six "clobber verses" in the Bible, and I felt their heartbreak when they told me they needed to leave the Church. I cried with them and we prayed together, with me blessing their path. But I cried harder on the drive home, feeling their rejection on a deeply personal level that was invisible to them at the time. Soon after, I realized I could not carry on with these talks without doing irreparable damage to myself. I needed God to speak to me about what to do.

Lenten longings

If a time exists in the Church calendar conducive to desperately crying out to God from your inmost, it is Lent. During
Lent, we Christians spend six weeks preparing ourselves to
observe the life, death and resurrection of Jesus by fasting
and praying in the way Jesus did when he spent 40 days in the
desert, at the beginning of his ministry. The ritual practice
of recognizing our mortality on Ash Wednesday marks the
beginning of the liturgical season.

During Lent, our church employs several prayer disciplines
designed for spiritual growth. For one such practice, we
choose something important to us and ask God to move in
that area of our life every single day. We don't petition God
because we think he is a slot machine—if we put coins in the
slot and pull the lever often enough, we'll hit the jackpot. We
do it to practice vulnerability and intimacy with Jesus.

For Lent that year, I participated in the practice and asked
God for something every day, leading up to Easter. I don't
remember what it was, though, because it wasn't what I really
wanted. I still found being completely honest with Jesus risky,
and I couldn't quite trust God with what my heart desired.
My heart cried out for a wife. The Bible talks about how it
isn't good for the human to be alone, and I understood in my
bones the nearly universal longing to join my life to someone
else's more intimately.

I grew up in a large city, I spent time overseas and I've
lived much of my adult life in a university town; in all of these
environments, people come and go. They move for jobs or for
school, and it's common for people to live away from family,
as I do. As friend after friend moved away or got married
during my 20s and early 30s, I spent my nights alone, yearning
to find someone who could make me laugh and with whom I
could build a life. Everyone deserves to love and be loved; our
faith tradition knows it is not good for it to be otherwise.

In the midst of helping lead the tumultuous and anxi-ety-ridden church system I found myself in, my distress hit its peak just after Easter. I found myself alone in the church one Saturday and fell on my knees in the sanctuary, asking God what I needed to do. Should I resign? Should I apply to a different seminary and change denominations?[98] Should I go back to working in the business world? Or should I stay? If I leave, what am I modeling for our gay congregants (we counted about 40 LGBTQ+ church attendees at that time)? What am I modeling for women and girls? What do *you* want for this church, Lord? So many questions gnawed at my heart. I picked up a guitar and sang out in the auditorium-like room, worshipping and waiting. My head told me one thing, my heart said another, but I wanted—no, I *needed*—a word directly from Jesus.

"Ask me for what you really want." That's what I thought I heard God say to me that afternoon. Very simply: "Ask me for what you really want." I felt invited to share my innermost desires with God, and to entrust Jesus with my deepest longings and fears. I felt God telling me not to be afraid.

I started a second 40-day prayer discipline, only this time voicing my sincere request. I hoped to not only share my heartache with God, but to receive some kind of additional direction, so I took copious notes of my prayer experiences each day. A certain richness entered my petitions, and God's nearness and comfort blanketed me as I spoke my wants and needs aloud to him each day.

During the second week of my intentional praying, I spoke to God in a private room in a home where I lived communally. As I stretched out on the ground I sensed the communion of saints gathered around me: praying for me, laying hands on me, bearing my burdens. I had a mystical sense that bearing one another's burdens was something which could be done beyond time and space, as if those who suffered before me could carry my fears before the presence of Jesus on my behalf.

---

98 At the time I was pursuing an M.A. through Fuller Theological Seminary.

Then I sensed that Saint Peter himself placed his hand on my forehead. In all my years of praying, I'd never once imagined an ancient apostle praying for me.

I continued talking to God, and in that moment remembered my Tibetan name. When I lived in China, I'd stayed at a Tibetan Buddhist monastery for a short time. I asked the women there to give me a name, and the one they gifted me with means "white woman in whom there are buried treasures." As I thought of my name and pictured the saints praying for and with me, it felt like I was finally prepared for the *next thing*, however or whenever the *next thing* unfolded. The buried treasure God forged within me over the years would provide strength and wisdom for the road ahead. I still didn't know what to do, but I was poised and alert, anticipating God's move.

One week later I met my wife. She waltzed into the very church where I served to attend a conference and promote her soon-to-be-published book.[99] A dear friend grabbed my hand and said, "There's someone you've *got* to meet." They were right. My wife, Rachel, is a gift from God and the answer to my heart's prayer—and, it was pretty much love at first sight (which I didn't think I believed in).

Our budding relationship quickly catalyzed a process whereby Ken and I became the scapegoats of our church community. I was publicly outed while in the process of coming out to various circles, including my family and the people at the church who didn't already know my orientation. After a long and painful process, in which I had to give an account from the pulpit for two packed services and weather a three-month series of brutal all-church "open mic nights" concerning the topic, our board of directors reluctantly asked me to resign from my pastorship for being in a relationship with Rachel—and they asked Ken to resign for not firing me.[100]

---

99 Murr, Rachel. *Unnatural: Spiritual Resiliency in Queer Christian Women*. Wipf and Stock Publishers, 2014.
100 Though I think he technically quit first, in protest.

A piece of my idealism died a hard death as I both observed and experienced the public shaming of sexual minorities in our faith community, through their condemnation of my relationship and call for me to step back from pastoring. But not all of my "may your kingdom come here and now" hope died—because, as we know, resurrection follows death.

Looking back, I believe that God prepared me for the months-long process of my firing and allowed it to happen in order to birth a new community of faith that is fully inclusive and safe for all people. As I consider my time in prayer with the great cloud of witnesses, and with Saint Peter in particular, I regard it as God letting me know I wouldn't be alone in what was about to happen to me. I felt comradeship with the ages; so many others before me faced exile, trauma and even death witnessing to the experience of Jesus in their lives. I encountered the first two—trauma and exile from my faith community—in testifying to God's goodness to me.

I'm also convinced that God provided me with tools to grasp the social dynamics of the community I led as they unfolded: the very same dynamics of the scapegoating ritual his son, Jesus, faced before he carried his own cross to Golgotha. I came across authors who helped me better decipher the good news from the standpoint of the oppressed, and I felt encouragement in knowing I wasn't the first pilgrim to traverse such territory. The Gospel came alive as my own humiliation unfolded, and my appreciation of Jesus and what he endured matured, even as I felt the intense nearness of his presence. I follow a God who led the way through brutal terrain by showing me how to lay down power—and he was, indeed, with me always, standing by my side as I did my best to pastor a church surrounding me (and Ken) with torches and indictments.

This unique reading of the biblical narrative I discovered is what Ken and I unpack in the following chapters, based largely on the works of Dr. René Girard and those theologians working on applying his theory to our theological practices.

My understanding of the Gospel and of what Jesus did by his life, death and resurrection changed in reading Girard, and Ken and I hope what we learned will be of use to you, our readers, as well.

A view from the margins

Before we can successfully dive into Girard, which we will do in the next chapter, we must start by talking about the last becoming first, and the first becoming last.

I'm persuaded that we don't understand Jesus until we more fully comprehend his suffering. In this, I'm not talking about interpreting it romantically, as popular worship song lyrics lead us to do (e.g., "Like a rose trampled on the ground, you took the fall and thought of me above all"), but rather understanding Jesus's afflictions as a present roadmap to our own sure suffering, both individually and corporately. His beckoning us to pick up our crosses and follow his way forewarns us to expect our own wounds and scars as we open wide the embrace of God to all humankind. *Sola Scriptura*'s impoverishment manifests in part because those interpreting Scripture for us in recent times have suffered very little.[101]

Who best understands the suffering messiah? It should be obvious that the oppressed, the poor, the dispossessed, the outcasts, those in ill health and the second-class citizens of the world have greater insight into the salvific work of God—just as they did when Jesus traversed the earth, as a human.[102] They recognize Jesus and what he did more readily than do those with power. Discovering deeper Gospel wisdom requires that we turn to the people compelled to use *theology as survival*.[103]

When we neglect the perspectives of the downtrodden, the likelihood of Scripture distortion rises exponentially.

---

101 See Chapter 3
102 "For made clear through Jesus is that the power of the incarnate God is best reflected in the condition of those rendered powerless. It is reflected through the crucified class of people" (Douglas, 97). See also: (Kim, 115-116) and (Tamez, 13-26).
103 as Fr. James Alison so eloquently puts it.

Nearly the entire Bible is written from the perspective
of the persecuted. If we haven't experienced persecution
ourselves—whether as a community outcast, by experiencing
the consequences of standing with community outcasts or by
being part of a minority community—then we do not have
a full understanding of Jesus and what he did on the cross.
When Ken and I say *solus Jesus*, we mean the Jesus whose
friends turned on him, who was falsely accused, who was
mocked, who was called a blasphemer and who was killed for
his radical embrace of the oppressed.

Being publicly outed and fired produced real trauma for
me, which required therapy and a long process of learning to
forgive those who did me harm. I know the difficulty of my
own road, and I didn't face a fraction of what many scapegoats
throughout time faced. Reading African-American theologians' perspectives on the cross and on the Gospel—given
the long history of white supremacy, slavery, lynching, Jim
Crow and the continuing mistreatment of black bodies in
our society—provided additional substance to the Girardian
framework I had discovered. *The Cross and the Lynching Tree*
by James H. Cone and *What's Faith Got to Do with It?: Black
Bodies/Christian Souls* by Kelly Brown Douglas are accessible
for broad audiences and should be read far and wide in faith
circles. Black theologians in the U.S., both academic and lay,
understand the cross in a way few white people understand it.
These writers understand the need to resist the power structures that place unbearable burdens on people. I learned from
them how white supremacy and power became entangled in
our shared American culture and in the strands of Christianity
practiced through much of the country. I'm ashamed I did not
read more theology from the margins sooner than I did.

And false claims to victimhood

When our interpretive theology flows primarily from
sources with greater social power (i.e., white, educated,

straight, men … often tenured and/or with the word *pastor* before their name), it untethers from the stories that moor it. When this is pointed out, those with systemic power are tempted to begin imagining *themselves* as victims.

Paulo Freire talks about how privileged people regard any lessening of their power as persecution, and they capitalize on it and gain credibility within their circles.[104] Those possessing power consider any decline of their power as mistreatment, even when they still control most of the leverage in cultural systems (58).

For example, there was a time when a person could either insinuate or outright declare in public that being gay is a sin and LGBTQ+ people shouldn't have the same rights as other citizens, and the person saying such things could expect everyone in the room to agree with them (even if tacitly). Today, the LGBTQ+ community claims modest—if tenuous—gains in civil rights, so when someone declares they do not believe that LGBTQ+ people should have equal legal protections and access to services, more friends, family and colleagues of queer people disagree and feel emboldened to state—even argue—their opposition in front of others.

The person saying that homosexuality is sinful experiences the pushback as persecution, even though such dissent harms none of their rights while LGBTQ+ peoples' rights remain sub-par and tenuous. LGBTQ+ people can still, in some

---

104 "But even when the contradiction is resolved authentically by a new situation established by the liberated laborers, the former oppressors do not feel liberated. On the contrary, *they genuinely consider themselves to be oppressed. Conditioned by the experience of oppressing others, any situation other than their former seems to them like oppression.* Formerly, they could eat, dress, wear shoes, be educated, travel and hear Beethoven; while millions did not eat, had no clothes or shoes, neither studied nor traveled, much less listened to Beethoven. Any restriction on this way of life, in the name of the rights of the community, appears to the former oppressors as a profound violation of their individual rights—although they had no respect for the millions who suffered and died of hunger, pain, sorrow and despair. For the oppressors, 'human beings' refers only to themselves; other people are 'things.' For the oppressors, there exists only one right: their right to live in peace, over against the right, not always even recognized, but simply conceded, of the oppressed to survival. And they make this concession only because the existence of the oppressed is necessary to their own existence" (Freire, 58, emphasis mine).

states (including mine) be legally fired for their sexuality and discriminated against for housing, adoption, medical care and other services where there are no prohibitions on straight and/or cisgender people based on their orientation or gender identity. The plethora of stances toward LGBTQ+ people viewed as legitimate increased as queers gained enough safety and power to share their perspectives and experiences of life. Just because this community feels somewhat encouraged in being open about their lives and pursuing justice when treated inequitably does not mean it is equivalent in power and influence in our culture and/or political system. Nowhere near.

I personally knew two men shot and killed for their faith in Jesus at separate times and in separate places—one Kashmiri and one Somali. I worshipped with underground Christian communities on two continents and know of women taken to police stations and tortured for their belief in Jesus. I know believers whose homes were burned down, who lost their jobs and who fled their villages for their lives. When a storekeeper in America claims "Christian" victimhood for refusing to sell cake or flowers to gay people, I feel infuriated on behalf of my friends who have truly suffered.

Those storekeepers lose zero credibility among circles they care about and their "stand" costs them nothing other than disapproval from people whose opinions for which they care nothing; in fact, these "defenders of the faith" become heroes in their social groups. They win the approval of their in-group while treating their out-group with contempt. If there's anything we learn from Jesus, it's that we need to treat our out-groups with love and acceptance. People who say they follow Jesus but who treat Muslims, immigrants (undocumented and otherwise), women, people of color, Native Americans, LGBTQ+ people (most especially transgender people) and others as second-class citizens—both in the sociopolitical sphere as well as in the faith sphere—while winning accolades from their friends *neglect the heart of the message of Jesus.*

We dishonor our brothers and sisters who suffer intensely when we, who practice our faith openly in a pluralistic society, claim victimhood. And we disrespect those who live on the margins of our own culture when we claim they have a nefarious agenda and when we, ourselves, have the power to exclude them. Instead, listen. Without glamorizing poverty and distress, we must pay attention to those who are tyrannized for simply existing and refocus our theology accordingly.

The book of James contains a startling warning for the powerful. Instead of twisting their situation so they convince themselves and others that they are victims, they should "take pride in their humiliation."

> *Believers in humble circumstances ought to take pride in their high position. But the rich should take pride in their humiliation—since they will pass away like a wild flower. For the sun rises with scorching heat and withers the plant; its blossom falls and its beauty is destroyed. In the same way, the rich will fade away even while they go about their business. Blessed is the one who perseveres under trial because, having stood the test, that person will receive the crown of life that the Lord has promised to those who love him.*[105]

Again, we do not understand the Gospel until we know intimately the suffering and humiliation of Christ. We do not comprehend the message of Jesus until we grasp the effects of our actions on the poor, outcast and oppressed, which means listening without dismissing or prejudging their views as uninformed, less spiritual or demonic.

One of liberation theology's trailblazing theologians, Hugo Assmann, said, in 1973: "Any kind of Christian theology today, even in the rich and dominant countries, which does not have as its starting point the historic situation of dependence and domination of 2/3 of humankind, with its 30 million dead

---

105 Jm. 1:9-12

of hunger and malnutrition, will not be able to position and concretize historically its fundamental themes. Its questions will not be the real questions" (qtd. in Petrella, 40). This is as pertinent a quote today as it was then, since we continue on in our negligence of the real questions, as the American Church hyper-focuses on who's in and who's out of their in-groups, sweeping aside larger issues of injustice and systemic oppression. The voices of the marginalized wail at us from the four corners. If we know anything of God, it's that God hears their cries (Kugel, 109-136). We'd best pay heed as well.

Introducing Dietrich Bonhoeffer

Many who read this book likely have a significant amount of privilege, though some more than others. I'm queer and female, but I'm also white, educated, middle class and American—and make no mistake, my whiteness counts for a lot. Is there hope that those who carry more power in this world can grasp the Gospel in the same way as those named in the Sermon on the Mount? Can we repent of oppressing others and work for a systemic change that values all humans? Can we learn to join with and support others resisting oppression? I think we can, and I think a good person to point out how is Dietrich Bonhoeffer.

A few years back I picked up a copy of his book, *The Cost of Discipleship,* and discovered, like so many before me, the profundity of his work on cheap grace versus costly grace.[106] I went on to read his book *Life Together,* but didn't know much about the man himself other than that he stood against Hitler and eventually died in a concentration camp. To remedy my knowledge gap I ordered Charles Marsh's biography of

---

106 Bonhoeffer defines cheap graces as "grace without discipleship, grace without the cross, grace without Jesus Christ, living and incarnate." He defines costly grace as "the treasure hidden in the field ... the Gospel which must be *sought* again and again, the gift which must be *asked* for, the door at which a man must *knock.* Such grace is *costly* because it calls us to follow, and it is *grace* because it calls us to follow *Jesus Christ.* It is costly because it costs a man his life, and it is grace because it gives a man the only true life" (45, emphasis in original).

him, curious about Bonhoeffer's insights into the meshing of German nationalism with the Protestant Church of the 1920s and 1930s, and how he grew into his thinking on costly grace.

After reading a few chapters of the biography, I found myself surprised at the theologian's strikingly affluent upbringing. As Marsh laid out Bonhoeffer's childhood privileges, I wondered how this highly educated, upper-middle-class man—who constantly wrote home asking his parents for money (for clothing, tennis rackets and travel)—wound up writing about the high price of sacrificial love and dying in a Nazi concentration camp. Hitler personally ordered Bonhoeffer's death for speaking out against the evils of the national socialist regime and its white supremacist philosophy (and theology). Not only did he name the harm done by the Nazis, but he tirelessly fought against the poor theology that led to the German Church largely supporting, even cheerleading, the Third Reich.

Most Christians like to believe that they would have been like Bonhoeffer in the face of Nazi fascism, fighting theological heresies and embracing the tenets of Christian love, hospitality and justice for all people. Yet the truth is that he stood nearly alone, and none of us can assume our own heroism given the same circumstances. Most of Bonhoeffer's seminary students, professorial colleagues and fellow pastors in Germany embraced a warped theology that allowed them to justify collusion with the Nazi state. Had theology been centered on and grounded in Jesus's life, death and resurrection—and had it not been entwined with anti-Semitic racial philosophies—perhaps the nationalistic tide in interwar Germany could have been staved.

Theology matters. How we view Jesus matters. How we practice our faith, and with whom we practice it, matters. Marsh writes, "Faced with the ruins of German Protestantism, he [Bonhoeffer] could not have understood more clearly that the way Christians imagine Jesus Christ determines the totality of their worldview" (171).

How did Bonhoeffer become the Bonhoeffer we know?

So how did Bonhoeffer come to understand Jesus differently than his contemporaries? How did he come to such distinct conclusions about the Gospel, leading him to declare the German Church heretical? Can his life offer clues as to how to remain faithful to Jesus and his call to care for the poor and the outcast? I think it can.

Three pivotal aspects of Bonhoeffer's life stand out to me as distinctly informing and shaping his faith. First, studying in New York City allowed him to interact with African-American churches and learn from theologies developed on the margins of society. Second, the influence of Catholic monastic practices on his personal spiritual life helped him form an intimate, experiential relationship with Jesus. And third, it seems he was a minority himself. Though he never spoke explicitly about his sexual orientation, Marsh makes a solid case—based on previously unreleased and unstudied letters and other personal documents—that Bonhoeffer was gay.

In the late 1920s, young Bonhoeffer preached the same nationalistic theology expatiated by most of the German Church during Hitler's reign the following decade—the same damaging rhetoric which led to the Holocaust. (He, of course, came to regret this later.) However, in 1930, Bonhoeffer spent a year doing post-graduate studies at Union Theological Seminary in New York City. While there, he took classes with Reinhold Niebuhr, who pointedly told him, "In making grace as transcendent as you do, I don't see how you can ascribe any ethical significance to it. Obedience to the will of God may be a religious experience, but it is not an ethical one until it issues in actions which can be socially valued" (qtd. in Marsh, 107). In other words, the Gospel has to translate into good news for people in the here and now, in tangible ways that benefit humans.

This ongoing conversation with Niebuhr catalyzed a pilgrimage of sorts for Bonhoeffer, who spent the next few months worshipping and serving at the Abyssinian Baptist Church in Harlem. There, Dietrich learned from the Rev. Adam Clayton Powell Sr., the lead pastor, and his fellow congregants about both the plight of African-Americans in the United States and different theological perspectives proceeding from those vantage points.[107]

Bonhoeffer then drove to Mexico with a friend and meandered through the Jim Crow South on his way back to the East Coast. As he did, his eyes opened to the vast inequalities evident between blacks and whites in America, the cultural ramifications of those disparities, and how African-Americans—out of need, for their very survival—forged new theological canals down which the river of life could flow. As Bonhoeffer observed his surroundings and tried integrating it with his beliefs, he slowly recognized the social justice-shaped hole in early 20th-century German theology. He spent the rest of his life trying to repair that breach; hence, his writings on costly grace. Bonhoeffer's heart changed when faced with the Gospel as considered from the vantage point of the poor and powerless worshipping on the margins of society.

Second, early in his undergraduate studies, Bonhoeffer sojourned to Italy for a few months, where he visited cathedrals and monasteries and attended mass in various locations, including St. Peter's Basilica in Vatican City. The teenaged Bonhoeffer seemed taken by the prayer rituals and aesthetics of Roman Catholicism, and this fascination only grew when he later pastored a church in Barcelona for a year. Toward the end of his life, he lived and taught in a Bavarian monastery at the start of World War II.

In the early 1930s, after returning from America and finishing his tenure as a rector at two Lutheran churches in East London, Bonhoeffer travelled around England, visiting non-Catholic neo-monastic communities. He learned from

---

107 A good resource for this aspect of Bonhoeffer's journey is *Bonhoeffer's Black Jesus: Harlem Renaissance Theology and an Ethic of Resistance* by Reggie L. Williams.

them so that he could return to Germany to set up a neo-monastic Lutheran seminary centered on the values of the
Sermon on the Mount. His community, called Finkenwalde,
educated and trained pastors of the Confessing Church, a
small branch of the Church resisting Hitler's reign.

Part of the regiment at the seminary he founded required
daily silence, during which students listened for the voice
of Jesus. They also practiced a form of the offices, *imitatio
Christi* and *lectio divina*. "Dissent and resistance, they were
taught, required spiritual nourishment: prayer, Bible study and
meditation on the essential matters to expand the moral imagination … By design, each day would begin and end in quiet
meditation. The brethren would rise and proceed in silence
to the dining rooms for prayers; there, in the early morning
light, they would sit until God had spoken some word for the
day into their hearts—or until a half hour had passed" (Marsh,
232). Bonhoeffer gladly borrowed time-honored spiritual
disciplines from the Catholic mystics to prepare his students
for the coming troubles. He knew they needed a prayerful
foundation, a life-giving connection with the risen Jesus, to
effectively lead congregations in resisting Nazi policies (304).[108]

As Ken and I argued in Part 1, a commitment to relationship with Jesus—mediated by the Holy Spirit and shaped
by spiritual practices and rhythms—proves vital to the
formation of the Gospel as understood by followers of this
way. Combined with a theology of the marginalized, mystical
connection with God fanned the flame of Bonhoeffer's conviction and courage. In Chapter 14 we'll explore spiritual habits
in more depth, because they're such an important characteristic of *solus Jesus*.

The third aspect of Bonhoeffer's life—which perhaps
proved important to his spiritual shaping—is his sexual orientation. Marsh makes a compelling case for his queerness,
and his access to vast troves of previously unavailable primary

---

108 More than half of Bonhoeffer's students died in the war. Hitler called up clergy for
active duty early on (eliminating conscientious objector status) to effectively curtail
their influence.

source material provided the foundation for his assessment (Stanley).[109]

In an interview with Tiffany Stanley, Marsh says:

> *What I had that scholars didn't have, and do now, is the body of letters that Bonhoeffer and Eberhard [Bethge] exchanged. They wrote when they were apart during those seven years of their partnership. To be sure, I was intrigued when I found in those archives in Berlin a statement from a joint bank account. I did not realize that their partnership had that kind of formality about it as well. So Bonhoeffer and Eberhard began giving gifts together as a pair, Christmas presents and the like. They traveled and shared a room. They were soul mates of a sort. Bethge never reciprocated the intensity of Bonhoeffer's affections. I don't think Eberhard was gay; I simply don't have any reason at all to think that. I think that Bonhoeffer's love of Eberhard was one that he, Bonhoeffer, wanted to define as a kind of spiritual marriage, but Bonhoeffer's love of Eberhard was also deeply romantic.*

We don't know how Bonhoeffer processed this element of himself or how he felt about it, but it's reasonable to assume his awareness of his sexuality by the content of these letters and writings.

Being gay myself, my ears perked up when I first read about Bonhoeffer's orientation. Embracing and re-embracing the

---

109 Additionally, Tiffany Stanley, interviewing Marsh, quotes him as saying, "… I had access to just a treasure of newly obtained documents through the library in Berlin, the *Staatsbibliothek*, and the documents appearing in published form in the *Dietrich Bonhoeffer Werke*, which is now translated into English. The translation was just completed this past fall, the 16-volume, complete writings of Bonhoeffer. This is someone who died when he was 39 years old and whose complete writings come to well over 10,000 pages. As a discipline and in terms of my own creative process, I took all the biographies, including Bethge's, and I hid them away and made myself, or told myself, I wouldn't look at any biographical writing until I finished with my complete draft of my book, using only the primary materials and documents."

Christian faith took a lot of work for me, and in the process
God performed a series of surgeries on my approach to
understanding what Christ did on the cross, ultimately giving
me greater strength and confidence in the stories we tell
about who God is and why it matters. So naturally, I wonder
if Bonhoeffer wrestled with similar ideas—and if, in fact, his
compassion on himself led to greater empathy for others, as I
believe it has for me.

Loving our enemies

Lack of empathy toward Jewish people, and toward those
who were otherwise outsiders (non-Aryans, differently abled,
gay, *etc.*), played a huge role in allowing Hitler's regime to
destroy so many human lives. Empathy enables us to love even
our enemies. If there's one, single startling feature of Christianity, it's the faith's insistence on its adherents loving their
enemies.

Anyone can treat their in-groups with kindness. Even Nazis
and their supporters brought each other casseroles when they
were sick. "If you love those who love you, what reward will
you get? Are not even the tax collectors doing that? And if you
greet only your own people, what are you doing more than
others? Do not even pagans do that? Be perfect, therefore, as
your heavenly Father is perfect."[110] So often Christians treat
other Christians compassionately; gallantly, even. They're
"good people." Yet Jesus says that anyone can treat their own
well. It's those who treat their out-groups and their enemies
as they do themselves who do the true work of God. That
does not mean simply being nice to those outside our "tribe,"
smiling and saying kind things, but actually treating them
as we treat ourselves. Adopting welcoming language for our
friends on the streets, for the LGBTQ+ community or for
families with a single parent—but then placing restrictions on
their leadership opportunities in our churches, based solely on
<u>one of these</u> features—shames people.

110 Mt. 5:46-48

I think Bonhoeffer's story contains both warnings as well as spiritual gems. The story of the early 20th-century German Church cautions us against allowing only the powerful to shape our theology. We must swim against the tide and educate ourselves by reading, listening to and learning from those whose eyes more keenly perceive injustices. Bonhoeffer broke out of his privileged circle by listening to and studying a spirituality developed on the margins of culture and faith.

I am white and American, but I am also female and queer. Ken is a straight, white, American male, but he sacrificed his job and the faith community he led and built over the course of 40 years, for the sake of embracing a traditionally shunned group. While we both still have much to learn from fellow travelers in various parts of the world, we believe that we have something to offer from our own journeys, since our experiences of faith have been costly and sometimes, frankly, brutal. Our hope is that the next few chapters contribute to the plethora of Christian material emerging from marginalized outposts of Jesus followers, and that it sparks others' interest in diving deeper into the theological waters to flesh out the ideas we propose.

What we offer is a developing theology based on Dr. René Girard's theory of scapegoating and apply it in a way we hope further elucidates the Gospel for us all. Girard himself was a straight, white, male French scholar, but the man currently integrating Girard's theories most thoroughly with theology is a queer, British, Catholic priest named Father James Alison. I discovered Girard's work before I learned of Fr. Alison's scholarship and intuitively recognized the value of Girard's framework, but Fr. Alison and the many other marginalized theologians and pastors we've read put more pieces into place for both Ken and me. Additionally, since we actively pastor a beautiful church community, we get to analyze how the theologies we're grappling with play out in the lives of our congregants. If theology doesn't bring life to people and bring them into greater connection with the divine, then we need to rethink our theology. And, being Christian, our theology centers on Jesus.

When Ken and I talk about *solus Jesus*, the natural question is, "Which Jesus?" Our answer is: the Jesus of the oppressed, the disinherited, the marginalized, the poor and the outcast. This book is but one voice of many, but perhaps this queer perspective on Girard, Jesus and the witnesses of Scripture will be of as much help for you as it has been for us. We pray this is so.

7

Scapegoat Theory: Unlocking a Better Story

Emily

ABOUT 15 YEARS ago, when I was in my mid-20s, one of my roommates in Ann Arbor hailed from East Asia. He described himself as Buddhist by tradition and atheist by conviction. One night, I gathered from our conversation that he was genuinely curious about my Christian faith. Not curious in a seeking-faith-for-himself kind of way, but in an oh-it's-interesting-you-think-that sort of way. The idea of how God killing his own son did anything at all for humans especially intrigued him. "Why," he asked me, "does that story make sense?"

Perhaps like some of you, I grew up with a substitutionary atonement view of the cross. In a nutshell, substitutionary atonement says: God created humans to be perfect in the Garden of Eden, but humans disobeyed God, thereby bringing sin and death into the world. All of humanity, then, deserves punishment because our sin made us unworthy to be in God's presence. To resolve this, God killed his own innocent son in our place; we deserve the punishment, but he took it on himself instead.

I'd rejected that view by the time I spoke with this roommate because of all the questions many rational people ask, like the ones my roommate asked: "What does it say about God that he murdered his own innocent son? How does a wrong—murdering an innocent—make a right? How does that make God *good*? He sounds scary and abusive! I wouldn't want him to be my dad."

I'd abandoned that childhood narrative and was armed with the work of N.T. Wright and a newly embraced *Christus Victor* (or Christ, the Victor) view of atonement.[111]

The *Christus Victor* view of atonement says that God created humans to be perfect, but humans disobeyed God (same as before)—only this time, Satan somehow kidnapped or enslaved humanity. God then sent his son, Jesus, to earth as a blood ransom to be paid to our captor, in return for our freedom. God ransomed us; he bought us back from Satan because he loves us and wants us to be liberated from the effects of both evil and death. With his resurrection, Jesus gave us a sort of "do-over" in regards to creation since we messed it up the first time—only this time, we get to be part of the re-creating, helping God remake the world. Christ was victorious in renewing all things through his crucifixion and resurrection, hence *Christus Victor*.[112]

I talked about this with my roommate and he asked a lot of good questions. To begin, he didn't buy into the idea that humans need rescuing. He figured that evolution was working out the kinks as necessary for life to continue. He also didn't believe in Satan. I understand that term differently now than I did then (and I'll touch on that in Chapter 9), but at the time

---

111 *Christus Victor* is sometimes called Ransom Theory.

112 Clearly, I'm simplifying atonement theories. I found Tony Jones's book, *A Better Atonement: Beyond the Depraved Doctrine of Original Sin*, to be a helpful overview of the various atonement theories that is highly accessible for those seeking a less academic summary. For a thorough treatment of *Christus Victor*, see Wright, N.T., *The Resurrection of the Son of God*. For a penal substitutionary atonement response, see Piper, John, *The Future of Justification: A Response to N.T. Wright*.

I pictured Satan as the literal lead being among all evil beings. My friend said something like, "OK, so you believe this being I don't believe exists enslaved humanity. First, how could you even know that happened? Second, if this God is so powerful, why would he pay ransom to a captor? You don't pay ransom to kidnappers, it only emboldens them! If he's so powerful, why did he not just rescue you without allowing his son to die? And why is his son—in human form, no less—the payment? How does that work? Why does innocent blood buy freedom?"

I couldn't answer in ways that felt intellectually sound or honest. I realized that understanding Jesus in this way requires people to swallow several ideas at once if it is to make any sense. Even then, it doesn't *entirely* make sense. What's compelling in this story for people like my friend?

It jarred me, realizing that my understanding of the Gospel was incomprehensible. I rationalized that the divine is mysterious and I may never understand why that kind of spiritual transaction needed to take place or how it worked. I could sit in the discomfort of feeling like my life didn't adhere to a coherent story (that's faith, right?), but I could not rest.

Introducing René Girard and the scapegoat theory lens

Over the years, I've thought deeply about our Christian story and what it means from the point of view of people who don't have anything invested in upholding it. As a lover of Scripture, it bothered me that I felt as though I was missing the nub of it—like a word on the tip of my tongue.

Then I took a class on postmodern film and theology at Fuller Seminary, where I was introduced to the work of René Girard.

There are many lenses that help us make sense of the biblical narrative as a whole. We can read the narrative through the lens of physical and metaphorical exile (from the Garden of Eden, the Promised Land, from others or from God). We can read it through the lens of understanding the world as God's temple, in the process of being restored and reinstating humans as his priests to "tend and till" the earth (Beale, 5-31). We can read the Bible as subverting an empire, with God seeking an alternative reign of peace and justice. All of these, and many more, are valid and helpful. We propose that Girard provides yet another lens, only it's the *single most helpful lens* we've come across—especially in regard to the death and resurrection of Jesus.

In this chapter I will introduce you to the basics of Girardian theory and then apply it to the story of Joseph in the Torah. I'll do my best to simplify his theory, and then Ken and I will work out the broader theological implications over the next five chapters. I hope you find the payoff to be as rewarding as we have found it.

To begin, Girard was a literary critic, anthropologist, historian and social science philosopher who finished his career at Stanford University. He was born in France in 1923 and died in 2015. Having studied ancient and modern literature from around the world early in his career, and having studied history, Girard noticed a particular pattern that seemed to describe and explain cycles of human violence.

It all begins with mimetic desire

First, Girard said that all violence begins with *mimetic desire*. Mimetic simply means *imitative*. Girard observed that, like other mammals (and especially our fellow primates), we humans learn from each other by imitation. If you were sitting across from me, facing me, and I lifted up my arm, your brain would send signals as if your body were lifting up its arm as well. Just watching me, your brain's "mirroring system" would activate as though you were also raising your arm.[113] Luckily, our brains have overriding mechanisms that keep us from

---

113 There is debate in the scientific community in regards to mirror neurons. They seem to function in multiple ways that could have helped humans develop evolutionarily. I write about the mirror system understanding—and hoping—that scientists will continue to better understand what these various neurons do and how they function in regards to human relationships.

copying each other's movements all day long. But even if these overriding mechanisms keep our bodies from involuntarily moving around, our brains still act like what they see. This system helps babies and children learn how to be in the world. Their brains learn to smile by watching us smile; they build neural pathways that help them learn to walk by watching us walk.

Sometimes mimicry happens just in our brains, as described above, but other times our bodies do, in fact, mirror the body language of those with whom we associate in a way that signals to others that we—consciously or subconsciously— want to affiliate with them. In his book, *Invisible Influence: The Hidden Forces that Shape Behavior*, Jonah Berger says, "Mimicry facilitates social interactions because it generates rapport … In fact, the only time we don't mimic others is when we don't want to affiliate with them."

Berger details a fascinating study in which researchers watched participants negotiate business deals. Participants who were instructed to deliberately mimic the body language of their counterparts were five times more likely to close a deal as those who deliberately did *not* mimic their body language. He reports that, "People who are satisfied in their current romantic relationship, for example, were less likely to mimic attractive members of the opposite sex. Only when we don't want to connect with others do we break from this default tendency." Berger further notes that people feel rejected when others don't imitate them, and hormones associated with belonging spike (40-41).

Forming neural pathways, connecting with others and establishing safe social ties are crucial aspects of our evolutionary development. Our imitative capacity is key to our surviving and thriving as a species. However, unlike other imitative species, we humans have a more highly developed capacity for imitation. Not only do we have the ability to imitate the external gestures and actions of others, but also to imitate others' *internal states*. We're especially adept at imitating the desires of others.[114]

Girard would say that all humans have desire, and all desire is—at least in part—imitative. I may find myself wanting a new watch when I notice you wanting a new watch. The entire advertising and marketing industry is built around this idea.

Mimetic desire isn't in and of itself harmful—it's essential to our ability to learn and connect and survive as a species. But it can become detrimental in two ways. First, it can become harmful if we take on someone else's *destructive* desire. For example, if a Wall Street trader finds they have a growing desire for more money—whatever the risk—because their peers desire more money, that could lead to destructive and/or unethical behaviors. Taking on someone else's destructive desire can not only harm us, but also cause us to lose our bearing on what's actually important to us as individuals.

Imitation fuels envy and rivalry

Second, mimetic desire becomes toxic if it leads to envy and rivalry.

When more than one person desires the same object, and both can't have the object (or think they can't both have the object), rivalries begin. This dynamic comprises the major plot point of most of the stories we tell in our culture. In nearly every romantic comedy, two people vie for the affections of a particular beloved man or woman. While violence in a romantic comedy differs from violence in battle-ridden movies, the emotional pain of the rejected love interest serves as the collateral damage. Uncontrolled rivalries inevitably lead to some form of harm being done to another.

---

114 In *Jesus the Forgiving Victim: Listening for the Unheard Voice: An Introduction to Christianity for Adults,* James Alison describes how humans are wired to imitate desire even more than actions. Interestingly, if we make a mistake showing a young child how, for example, to put a plastic ring on a stick (meaning we miss the stick!), they will imitate our intention—not the mistake. Science corroborates that we mimic one another's desire more than each other's actions (24-25).

Sometimes, rivalrous feelings are one-sided. Imagine that two friends who work together want the same promotion, but both can't have it. Unexpectedly, one of them starts speaking poorly of the other in front of executives so as to elevate themselves over their rival. The one being torn down may not even know the rivalry exists.[115]

Consider the current political situation in the United States. Two major parties vie for power. The desire of each party fuels the desire of the other as they mimic one another in their quest for dominance, each doing as the other does. (Remember how one party decried the use of executive orders and then, when they gained power, immediately made use of them?) Their mimicking one another doesn't inherently need to be toxic, but it has become so because envy and rivalry for power ripened in an environment hospitable for destructive imitative desire. Girard warns us where such rivalries lead.

As the rivals contend for the desired object, the object itself (power, money and so on) becomes less important than dominating the rival (Girard, *Violence and the Sacred*, 145-146). The two rivals become increasingly obsessed with one another, each mimicking the other in their quest to overcome (Warren, 35). The desire to win begins to trump the longing for the desired object.

According to Girard, once envy and rivalry enter a social system, there is increased group anxiety and tension.[116] If this tension builds enough, it hits a tipping point and turns to violence, with members of the group turning on one another. With his anthropologist hat on, Girard postulates that the very earliest human groups frequently succumbed to such violence.

---

115 "The rivalry may exist purely in the mind of one party, unreciprocated by the hated other ..." (Warren, 33).

116 The social system can be any group of people: within a family, a company, a church, a team, a nation, *etc.*

Relieving group tension: accuse a scapegoat

Stay with me here, because we're coming to the crux of it!

Humans discovered a mechanism over time, says Girard, that prevents full-scale violence from breaking out. To save their communities from self-implosion, the group members identified a scapegoat on which to project their collective anxiety, envy and rivalry. The scapegoat could be an individual or a group of people who are singled out for being different. We present-day humans inherited this tool—identifying a scapegoat on which to project our rivalries—in order to protect the survival of our social groups. It's important to keep in mind, though, that the scapegoat mechanism is largely unconscious. We now use the term "scapegoat" to refer to innocent victims thought to be guilty. But the members of the group who turn on a scapegoat don't view the victim as innocent; instead, they view the scapegoated individual or group as guilty of the crimes of which they are accused (Girard, *Oedipus Unbound*, 110).[117]

The difference(s) a group identifies to mark a scapegoat can be *anything*. It can be sexual orientation, race, stuttering, the kid with the uncool hair, being an immigrant, being differently abled—anything that makes a person or group of people *other*.[118] It could even be that they are part of the 1 percent; the rich and powerful, rulers and royalty and celebrities, are just as vulnerable to becoming scapegoats as anyone in a group (Warren, 113-119; Girard, *The Scapegoat*, 18-19).

---

117 "During great disasters, irrational mobs turn violent against victims they regard as guilty even though they cannot be responsible for vast social catastrophes. Through its recourse to arbitrary violence, the helpless population manages to forget its helplessness in the face of uncontrollable events. When we understand this, we see that the victims are scapegoats" (110).

118 Speaking of the United States in particular, Walter Brueggemann writes: "And yet there are important indications of despair among us, not least the amorphous anxiety that recognizes in inchoate ways that the old world in which we have felt comfortable, safe and in control is slipping through our fingers. That anxiety is variously directed against Muslims, immigrants or gays, as though any of these populations were the cause or agent of our world loss" (113).

Once a scapegoat is identified, the larger group succumbs to a form of mob mentality and falsely accuses the scapegoat of a taboo crime, in order to dehumanize them. Mark Heim writes, "To forestall any motive for revenge and to maintain the unanimity of the persecutors there must be unassailable justification for the sacrifice of the individuals in question. Therefore it is predictable, Girard maintains, that these individuals will be charged with violating the community's most extreme taboos" (44).

For example, in the 2016 U.S. presidential campaign, Donald Trump tried (with mixed success) to make scapegoats of several groups.[119] Two prime examples include undocumented Mexican immigrants and legal Syrian Muslim refugees.

Trump accused undocumented Mexican immigrants of being rapists (Lee) and Muslim refugees of being terrorists infiltrating our country (Tanfani). Rape and terrorism: two taboo crimes. The narratives can then serve to make these groups *other* so we do not feel bad when we eventually put measures in place to purge *them* from *us*. By the time we implement such policies, *they* are no longer *us* ... *they* are mostly rapists and terrorists—and we have to protect ourselves, right? This kind of thinking justifies policies like building a wall along the Mexican border, halting Syrian refugee intake, banning travel to the U.S. from specified Muslim countries, aggressive enforcement tactics by Immigration and Customs Enforcement (ICE), separating children from their parents at the border and pardoning an unpopular sheriff who defied the Bill of Rights by illegally detaining people of color in Arizona and mistreating and torturing them (Robinson).

Immigrants are no more prone to illegal activity than the general population (Green; Ewing). However, 1 in 5 adult women in the United States is a victim of rape or attempted

---

119 Not to mention the other groups he's subsequently tried to scapegoat during his presidency, including but not limited to: transgender people, the media, those protesting his policies, the FBI, various members of his staff and/or congress, *etc.*

rape—not by undocumented Mexican immigrants, but by American citizens, and often someone the woman knows. And almost half of all American women have been victims of other types of sexual violence, including unwanted sexual contact and sexual coercion (Basile).

Similarly, the vast majority of terrorist attacks and mass murders carried out in our country are carried out by white American men. Not Muslims. Not immigrants. Not refugees. There are, of course, exceptions: 9/11 is a significant one. However, the FBI reports that 94 percent of terrorist attacks in the U.S. between 1980 and 2005 were committed by non-Muslims (Federal Bureau of Investigation Counterterrorism Division, 57-66).[120]

Homegrown Americans are the rapists and terrorists; *we are a very violent people.* When we succumb to the mob mentality of scapegoating, we project *our* violence onto *them.* *They* carry our sins. *They* become the violent ones, instead of *us.* The psychological projection relieves us of guilty feelings and of having to figure out, together, why our society is so violent and what kind of difficult emotional and spiritual work we need to do to solve the actual issues. We direct our collective energy toward a scapegoat because the process of examining our awful feelings of guilt and shame seem overwhelming and uncontrollable. It feels better fixating on something we perceive we can manage. "Managing" immi-gration policies feels easier than trying to "manage" our own violence, fear and rivalries.

Scapegoating dynamics and false accusations can take place in families, too. In family systems, the person labeled the "black sheep" serves as the scapegoat for the family. Sometimes the kid who gets picked on in school serves as the class scapegoat. In the case of the larger Church today, LGBTQ+

120 See pp. 57-66 for 1980-2005 terrorism list. Also, this quote on p. 29: "The preceding summary of terrorism-related events and investigations offers a picture of the FBI's response to domestic and international terrorism from 2002 through 2005. *In keeping with a longstanding trend, domestic extremists carried out the majority of terrorist incidents during this period.* Twenty-three of the 24 recorded terrorist incidents were perpetrated by domestic terrorists" (emphasis mine).

people (and especially our transgender friends) often carry our communal burden. A scapegoat does not have to die or be sent away to serve the purpose of carrying collective sin.

Unifying the community into a mob

Girard tells us that the projection of sin and anxiety onto the scapegoat has the effect of unifying the group (which he sometimes refers to as a mob) against the scapegoat and relieving the group's anxiety about its own corporate sins. It even unifies people who would normally defend the scapegoat.

This is a key point: The idea that *if anxiety and tension within a group is high enough, people will coalesce against a vulnerable person or group of people.* When it happens, mob amalgamation around a scapegoat(s) often takes the form of silence.

David Gushee, Distinguished University Professor of Christian Ethics and Director of the Center for Faith and Public Life at Mercer University, wrote his dissertation on the people who helped rescue Jews during the Holocaust, later publishing it as *Righteous Gentiles of the Holocaust: Genocide and Moral Obligation*. He found that less than 1 percent of the non-Jewish population helped Jewish people during World War II (Gushee, *Righteous Gentiles of the Holocaust: Genocide and Moral Obligation*, 80). And lest we pat ourselves on the back (if we identify as Jesus followers), only about 12 percent of that less than 1 percent said that they were compelled by a sense of "Christian duty"; *non-Christians were more likely than Christians to help Jews* (Henry, 151). It's not that the other 99 percent of people picked up stones or personally carted Jewish people to concentration camps. The vast majority of people remained silent so as not to attract the attention of Nazi authorities. Even sympathetic people turned Jews away from their homes out of fear for their own lives or the lives of their families. There was no public outcry after *Kristallnacht*, the "Night of Broken Glass,"[121] when the paramilitary Nazi

121 *Kristallnacht* took place November 9-10, 1938.

storm-trooper forces murdered dozens of Jews; burned more than 1,000 synagogues; ransacked Jewish hospitals, businesses and homes; and saw more than 30,000 Jews sent to concentration camps—all in one night.[122]

Similarly, after four girls were killed when white supremacists bombed the 16th Street Baptist Church in Birmingham, Ala., in 1963, African-Americans noted the relative silence of the majority of white Christians. In a conversation with Reinhold Neibuhr, James Baldwin says, "I don't suppose that ... all the white people in Birmingham are monstrous people. But they're mainly silent people, you know. And that is a crime in itself" (qtd. in Cone, 55). Martin Luther King Jr. took on the passivity of the white pastors in midst of the civil rights movement in *Letter From Birmingham Jail*.[123]

This silence happens on a smaller scale in other situations, but the basic premise is the same. Groups of people remain silent in the face of injustices, or else they express their sympathy for the persecuted but persist in their unwillingness to sacrifice themselves on behalf of the scapegoat(s).

The galling pretense of 'ally theater'

I learned a term from people of color describing this very dynamic: *ally theater*. Ally theater occurs when people who describe themselves as allies are not willing to lay down their own privileges on behalf of the oppressed. They merely *act out* the part of being an ally, without being willing to suffer consequences.

For example, you see someone suffering discrimination at work because of their race or gender, and that person quits—frustrated and exhausted. You go to the person and affirm their feelings, telling them that you see the poor treatment

122 "There were isolated cases of neighbors and friends showing solidarity with those being persecuted and trying to help them, but they were the exceptions. As a rule, people expressed sympathy with the victims and outrage at the perpetrators only in private ... Nowhere was there vocal public protest, not even within the churches, as might have been expected (Volker, 676)."
123 Widely available free online.

occurring; you support them and you will stand with them. However, you choose to say nothing to superiors about your observations, out of fear of drawing attention to yourself. In this way you participate in ally theater, like a thespian performing a "supportive friend" role so that you can feel good about yourself; but in reality, your silence bolsters a system that perpetuates injustice and causes your colleague to view you as a fraud. Let your "yes" be "yes" and your "no" be "no."[124] It is better to say nothing to your friend about supporting them than pretend to be an ally.

I personally experienced this dynamic when I was outed and fired for being a gay pastor. Some church members and fellow staff members claimed full support for gay marriage and LGBTQ+ ordination, yet when faced with the possibility of real cost to themselves, they chose to blend into the crowd and say nothing. Some were concerned that they would lose their own church jobs or related financial benefits; others were concerned with losing friends or causing tension with conservative family members; still others were intensely conflict-averse and wanted "everyone to get along." A small handful saw opportunities for job openings or promotions, with Ken and me out of the way. The perniciousness of silence infects groups as people look to preserve their own interests—even if that interest is simply maintaining the status quo. People often want it both ways—they want to say that they support the oppressed, but they don't want it to cost them anything tangible. Our own faith highlights that standing with marginalized people means we pick up our crosses; to expect otherwise exposes a deep misunderstanding of the Gospel.

Desmond Tutu writes, "If you are neutral in situations of injustice, you have chosen the side of the oppressor. If an elephant has its foot on the tail of a mouse and you say that you are neutral, the mouse will not appreciate your neutrality" (qtd. in R. Brown, 19). We'll explore this more in the next two chapters, but keep in mind that the vast majority of crowds

---

124 Mt. 5:37

unify around persecuting a scapegoat—and they do so by not speaking out, and standing by as the violence takes place.

The temporary relief of expelling a scapegoat

Once a scapegoat is fully identified and carrying the projected anxiety, shame and collective sin of the group, it is bullied, exiled, isolated, fired, incarcerated, killed and/or deported. Girard tells us that this sacrificial system works surprisingly well for achieving group harmony. Oppressing, beating up and/or getting rid of a scapegoat does bring temporary calm and unity to an anxious group. If the scapegoat is actually exiled or killed—when the process plays all the way out—the relief of having the scapegoat gone is so strong that the person or people who were once accused of being so horrible (and bringing terrible calamity on the group) are often thought of more kindly by those who did them violence. A mysterious peace descends on the group; the exiled or murdered scapegoat is then remembered in nostalgic terms, even eliciting pity.

The feeling of relief is so strong that ancient people often deified their scapegoats. According to Girard, many old stories of the founding of cities (like the tale of Remus and Romulus founding Rome), and of gods and goddesses, may have found their origin in a scapegoating event (Girard, *The Scapegoat*, 76-99).

After the scapegoat is gone, no one in the mob feels personally responsible for what they did. The guilt becomes dispersed because so many people activated the social mechanism, together. No one owns the consequences because everyone did it. As Sandra Schneiders says:

> As antagonism toward the scapegoat spreads through the crowd it becomes a mob, a single collectivity moved by motives for which no one is responsible, at least until the next morning when some individuals begin to wonder how they ever

could have participated in "what happened" (not "what we did") last night. But the renewed peace that miraculously descends on the group now that the victim is gone proves that the destruction of the scapegoat was something that "needed to happen." (Schneiders)

The scapegoat will not usually receive an apology from anyone in the mob. If someone does apologize after the fact, it is the rare occurrence.

Scapegoating ultimately makes groups potentially unsafe for everyone. Once a group sacrifices a scapegoat to relieve collective unease, they will eventually have to find another, because scapegoating does not address the roots of the underlying tension. In the end, scapegoating achieves a false peace at the expense of the vulnerable.

To recap, Girard's theory of scapegoating says:

- All desire is mimetic, or imitative.
- When we desire the same thing someone else desires, envy and rivalry can develop.
- Unbridled rivalry results in group anxiety/tension.
- When group anxiety reaches a tipping point, violence erupts and the group turns on itself.
- To prevent group violence, a scapegoat (an individual or group of individuals) is identified, onto which the larger group projects its own sins.
- The scapegoat is falsely accused of a taboo crime and dehumanized.
- The scapegoat is bullied, exiled, isolated, fired, incarcerated, killed and/or deported.
- A false peace descends on the group, and the group both creates myths justifying the violence and disperses responsibility for said violence, so no one claims responsibility for "what happened."
- The cycle repeats, to manage group tension and maintain a false sense of stability.

The Bible gives voice to scapegoats

René Girard identified this pervasive cycle of violence in human literature, history and myth—and *then* noticed that the Bible does something unique. The Bible seems to unmask the system of violence and offer ways to counter it and break it (Kaplan, 40).[125]

The first way the Bible unmasks the cycle of violence is by listening to the voices of the human scapegoats; they tell the stories of God, passed down to us over thousands of years. The Bible is one of the few ancient texts in this world written by people who were not in power. The Jewish people have been almost perpetual scapegoats throughout history. It's a truism that the powerful write most of history: victors in war, the educated, the literate—people (consciously or subconsciously) creating narratives supporting their dominance. The Bible, on the other hand, remains a beautiful collection of voices of people who, for the most part, were not dominant. Historically, Christianity has appealed to the underprivileged for this reason.

The Bible humanizes scapegoats and reveals the guilt of the mob sacrificing them—something no other ancient text does so clearly.[126] Scripture allows us to see the effects of scapegoating on biblical figures like Abel, Hagar, Joseph, Job, David, Jeremiah, Daniel, Stephen and Jesus. We see the trauma and dehumanization the dynamic causes. We see the guilt of the perpetrators, both the ringleaders and the mobs that form around them, in a way no other literature preceding it does.

The Bible models how to counter the scapegoating mechanism. We must humanize scapegoats the way the Bible humanizes them. We must give voice to the oppressed and name the scapegoaters as guilty, calling people to repentance.

125 Seeing this pattern, Girard became an adult convert to Christianity, joining the Roman Catholic Church.

126 "The myths always condemn all victims, who are isolated and overwhelmed. They are the work of agitated crowds that are incapable of identifying and criticizing their own tendency to expel and murder those who cannot defend themselves ..." (Girard, *I See Satan Fall Like Lightning*, 110).

The Bible sheds light on a process that routinely remains hidden from general awareness, so that we can change our own scapegoating ways.

The Joseph story: a scapegoating primer

While elements of the unveiling of this mechanism exist from the very beginning of Genesis, the story of Joseph, spanning chapters 37-50, provides the most poignant and thorough revelation of the entirety of the scapegoating dynamic in that book.

When we meet Joseph, he's 17 years old. We're told that:

> *Israel [Jacob's other name] loved Joseph more than any of his other sons, because he had been born to him in his old age; and he made an ornate robe for him. When his brothers saw that their father loved him more than any of them, they hated him and could not speak a kind word to him. (Gn. 37:3-4)*

Joseph's younger brother, Benjamin, was born seven years after Joseph; surely he would be the son of Jacob's old age. Why wasn't Benjamin, then, loved the most? And why would being born to a man in his old age make a son more lovable than his older siblings?

Leon Kass, a bioethics professor at the University of Chicago who uses Genesis to teach ethics, suggests the phrase "born to him in his old age" means Jacob loved Joseph best because he saw him as the solution to a problem arising from Jacob's old age—the problem of who would lead the family and carry the ancestral blessing after he died (515). The eldest brother, Reuben, slept with one of his father's wives, so Jacob did not view Reuben as his primary heir. The next two sons, Simeon and Levi, were particularly violent and were therefore disqualified (Gn. 34:25).

But then there is Joseph. He appears full of himself, yet shows promising signs of leadership.

Jacob gives Joseph the famous "coat of many colors," likely a unisex garment worn by well-to-do virgins (Alter, *The Five Books: A Translation with Commentary*, 207). "Now Israel loved Joseph more than any of his other sons, because he had been born to him in his old age; and he made an ornate robe for him." Notice the semicolon in the middle of that sentence. *Linguistically* the tunic links to Joseph as the favorite; *symbolically* the robe links to succession. It encompasses the blessing Jacob stole from Esau and, now, confers on his 11th son as a mantle of leadership. Joseph's brothers know it, and they hate him; they desire that coat and despise it on Joseph.

As if that weren't enough, Joseph makes things even worse for himself by relaying two dreams to his brothers. In his dreams, Joseph's family bows down to him, spurring his older siblings to spit out, "Do you intend to reign over us? Will you actually rule us?" (Gn. 37:8). In doing so, they voice their deepest fear and resentment.

One day, while Joseph's older brothers tend animals in the pastures, they see Joseph walking toward them and decide to murder him. After a disagreement, they resolve not to kill him, but instead to throw him into an empty water pit. They strip Joseph of his robe—his symbolic cloak of leadership—and fling him into the cistern. Later, his brother, Judah, suggests they sell Joseph to traders traveling to Egypt, for 20 pieces of silver—which they do. Afterward, they slaughter a goat and dip the ornate robe in its blood, telling their father that a wild animal killed his favorite son—as if to say, "This is what we think of you designating our younger brother as the family leader."

We have in this story the elements of a Girardian cycle of violence. First, the brothers desire the love of their father and feel envious of the special preference given Joseph. With an inheritance at stake, their jealousy of Joseph's cloak—and all it signifies—drives them to treat him as a rival. Their enmity heightened preexisting relational tensions within the family, exacerbated by Joseph himself when he shared his dreams of grandeur. Because of their envy and the family tension it produced, the brothers decide to turn on Joseph. They (perhaps falsely) accuse him of intending to reign over them. We don't know if Joseph *intended* to reign and rule over them; he simply recounted his dreams. Jacob, their father, likely intended that, but we don't know about Joseph.

Girard points out that false accusations made by a group are usually true of the mob itself. People project their own evil intentions onto the designated scapegoat. The brothers accused Joseph of wanting to dominate them when they, in fact, overpowered him.

Humanizing the dehumanized scapegoat

This narrative diverges from other pieces of ancient literature in that the story continues after the scapegoat is eliminated, and it continues from the point of view of the scapegoat (Joseph) and not from the perspective of the mob (his brothers). We're allowed to see the impact of the violence on Joseph's life. From the point of his expulsion onward, the narrative takes him from being a somewhat arrogant, two-dimensional teenage character to a complex, three-dimensional man; the Bible humanizes the scapegoat.

First, the story allows its audience a glimpse of Joseph's life as a slave in an Egyptian household, and we empathize with the injustice done to him. Joseph lands in jail, and we then become privy to the impact his jail time had on him. Next, we watch Joseph come into favor with the ruler of Egypt, and we observe how he came to be second-in-command of the kingdom. In his new role, Joseph oversees the selling of grain to surrounding nations during a long famine. As he supervises the operation, he again meets his brothers, who come to Egypt to buy grain for their families.

Understandably, Joseph does not trust his brothers—who abused and rejected him—and so does not reveal his identity. At this point we're told, for the first time in the story, the harrowing details of what it was like for Joseph to have been sold by his brothers: how distressed he became and how he pleaded for his life (Gn. 42:21). We, as readers or listeners, gain an account of what the scapegoating process was like for the victim. It frightened him, harmed him and devastated him.

Joseph designs two tests meant to determine whether his brothers are safe for him and if they regretted having sold him to Egypt. In the final test, he slips his personal drinking and divination cup into Benjamin's sack of grain, before the brothers head back home to Canaan. Benjamin is the youngest brother; he and Joseph shared the same mother, and Benjamin was not present when his older brothers plotted against Joseph. He is innocent of conspiring against Joseph and innocent of stealing his cup.

Yet Joseph sets up Benjamin to be accused of just that: stealing. On Joseph's command, his servants chase down the brothers and search their sacks. Of course, the servants find Joseph's personal cup in Benjamin's sack, and the brothers are brought back to the court of Joseph.

Joseph tells his brothers that he will take Benjamin as a slave, as punishment for stealing his cup. This is the test: One of Rachel's sons still lives—Benjamin—who is probably the favorite of their father, since he thinks Joseph is dead and because he loved Rachel, Joseph and Benjamin's mother, the best of all his wives. Will the older brothers turn Benjamin over to slavery in Egypt? Will they scapegoat him? Do they want to be rid of Benjamin like they were rid of Joseph? Joseph is giving them an easy opportunity to turn both of Rachel's sons over to slavery in Egypt. Just as trauma victims often re-experience their trauma, Joseph replays what happened to him—only with Benjamin in the role of scapegoat.

The framework of the story allows us to see the parallels. Instead of selling off Benjamin, like they did Joseph, the brothers show compassion on their father (who they said would probably die of grief) and compassion on their youngest brother (who did nothing wrong). Judah (whose idea it was to sell Joseph into slavery) offers himself in Benjamin's place (Gn. 44:33).

Whether Joseph is ready for it or not, Judah's act undoes Joseph, because he realizes they won't scapegoat Benjamin the way they scapegoated him. In a frenzy, Joseph orders all of his attendants to leave him with his brothers. "Have everyone leave my presence!" he shouts. Then the text says he wept so loudly that everyone in his house heard him, and the Pharaoh's household was told about it (Gn. 45:1-2).

All the years of pain, isolation, terror and anger unraveled as he cried, "I am Joseph! Is my father still living?" His brothers froze, utterly terrified of what he could do to them (Gn. 45:3) (which is probably the position Joseph needed them in, in order to reveal himself safely).

The narrative reveals the injustice of scapegoating; It shows the pain this cycle of violence caused Joseph, the victim. He wails and wails. He cries six times in the last seven chapters of Genesis, as decades of pain well up.

Scripture also unveils the innocence and humanity of the scapegoat (Girard, *Oedipus Unbound,* 111).[127] If we didn't entirely see it before, when Joseph was accused of intending to rule and reign over his brothers, we definitely see the innocence of the scapegoat when Joseph sets up Benjamin in order to test his brothers. Benjamin was not guilty of the accusation against him.

We also note that Judah, the brother who orchestrates Joseph's sale into slavery, redeems his family. He no longer schemes with the scapegoating mob to be rid of a younger brother because of rivalry, but instead offers himself in Benjamin's place. How astonishing it is that Scripture begins to hint that the universal cycle of violence can be broken or changed.

---

127 "At every turn, the biblical story ridicules the nonsensical evidence against the scapegoat which we have in mythology and replaces it with arguments favorable to the victim. The repudiated mythology is repudiated as a lie. Each time Joseph becomes a victim, either of his brothers or of the Egyptians, the accusations against him are shown to be delusions arising from envy and hatred. So we have both the account given by the brothers to the father and the exposé of that account." (Girard, *Oedipus Unbound,* 111)

Stories like this both reveal the injustice of the expulsion
of the scapegoat and demonstrate that perpetrators have
the ability to repent (Girard, *I See Satan Fall Like Lightning,*
112-113).

Unmasking the mob

The story of Joseph is the first in the Bible revealing the
role and social dynamics of the mob in the Girardian cycle.[128]
We never observe the brothers apologize to Joseph for the
harm they caused him. After Jacob dies, they do send word to
Joseph, saying, "Our father's final deathbed request was that
you forgive us" (Gn. 50:17), but this would be a very indirect
apology. Joseph's brothers do not come out and say, "We
harmed you terribly and we're sorry."

The absence of a direct apology could be cultural. However,
it lines up with what Girard notices about mob dynamics in
other stories. The mob will not, on the whole, take responsibility for their actions. They talk about "that terrible thing
that happened," but never about "that terrible thing we did,"
or "that terrible thing I took part in." When a group acts out
against a scapegoat or scapegoats, they disperse the guilt so
they never have to personally own it (Schneiders). This is a
hindrance to reconciliation; we will talk more about the idea
of needing to own our part in the mob in order for reconciliation to take place in Chapters 9-11.

From a Christian perspective, such stories in the Hebrew
Scriptures lead into the story of Jesus. They help us understand the prophetic tradition in which Jesus saw himself.

In *The Prophetic Law: Essays in Judaism, Girardianism,
Literary Studies, and the Ethical,* Jewish scholar Sandor
Goodhart indicates that the full revelation of the scapegoating
process is present within the Hebrew Scriptures, without
requiring the New Testament. I believe him, but am limited

---

128 Envy, rivalry and violence also can be found in the other brother stories in
Genesis: between Cain and Abel, Isaac and Ishmael (and Sarah and Hagar particularly),
and Jacob and Esau.

in my ability to speak authoritatively about that tradition and recognize that I have particular interpretive blinders, given my Christian heritage. As a Christian, I understand the full revelation of God through Jesus, but acknowledge that I have much to learn. We now turn to the story of this first-century rabbi, locating Jesus in the larger account of the biblical scapegoats and exploring the implications of his life on that narrative.

8

Jesus Through the Lens of René Girard

Emily

THE WEEK BEFORE I came out to my congregation from
the pulpit, I came down with a nasty respiratory bug. The
emotional stress of being outed weakened my immune system,
and I found myself slogging through the beginnings of a
months-long, traumatic church split with a 103-degree fever.
Crisis management already requires your all, but as I sat in
a hotel lobby talking to a pastor colleague from Manhattan—
who had flown into Ann Arbor to provide counsel and
support—I wasn't sure I could muster the energy needed
to adequately lead. While I cried, Charles gently said to me,
"You don't have to come out publicly. However, if you decide
against it, know that your story will be told *for* you, and it will
probably not be charitable. In the long run, I think it will be
worse for both you and the other queer people in the church."

My heart knew he was right. The Holy Spirit had led me
to study René Girard's work the previous few months, and
I understood full well the role I needed to play in testifying.
I, the scapegoat, needed to be humanized. Only in owning
my story and journey with Jesus could I hope to lead people
through the messiness of intense disagreement with integrity.
I'd felt the presence of Jesus throughout my entire life, and

now was the time to trust the *realness* of it. If I had been
hearing Jesus as I thought, then the Spirit would continue
guiding me.

I also knew people would be upset about my speaking.
Anxious groups try to silence scapegoats because when the
vulnerable speak, they expose the violent process leading
to their removal. They talk about how lonely and afraid
they feel, and they talk about the harm done—physically,
emotionally, psychologically and spiritually. The revelation
of the humanness of the victim(s) wipes away the salve
the mob slathers on themselves to make them feel justified
and innocent in getting rid of the scapegoat. It's easy to fire
the "gay pastor," but less easy to fire *Emily*, the woman we've
known for 15 years who is openly sharing her heart with us.

As expected, when people discovered that our board of
directors had asked me to tell my story publicly, a small
cadre of congregants—past and present—barraged the board
with letters and emails. "You'll further divide the church if
Emily talks," they said. "She should not be allowed to give a
public account." Groups organize around their most anxious
members, and I feared that the pressure might sway the
original decision. As it happened, it didn't: I was able to give
voice to my story, speaking as one of the many vulnerable
LGBTQ+ Christians witnessing the pain of communal accusation. I chose to keep my talk off the internet for a time, so as to
shield the congregation from any wider attention from press
or other churches in our denomination. I felt responsible to
tend that specific group of people, and becoming a symbolic
figurehead in a wider national conversation didn't feel helpful
in my particular circumstance.

A week later, on September 14, 2014, I prepared to
stand before nearly 1,000 people. I felt like the lamb I was—
groomed for slaughter. A peculiar peace surrounded me
that morning—an indescribable comfort of the Spirit—that
seemed inconsistent with the anguish that had overwhelmed
me the week prior. Instead of wrestling against the injustice

of being outed, coupled with the fear of having my personal life spewed all over the altar, that morning I surrendered, knowing that the company of Jesus and the saints would help me stand and testify. In fact, it felt like an honor.

When I look back on the sermon I gave that morning—to a standing ovation—I feel somewhat embarrassed by the conciliatory tone.[129] It was the right sermon to give at that time, but entreating for my belonging feels small from this vantage point. I am a child of God, known by him and dearly beloved. It makes me sad to think that a group of believers drove me to beseech my right to exist in community as God created me. I asked them twice: "Will you accept me?"

Picturing myself standing on that stage reminds me of when a girl in middle school pulled my hair so hard in the lunch line that I fell to my knees, begging her to stop. Why must the oppressed plead for basic kindness? When Colin Kaepernick took a knee, respectfully asking police to stop harassing and killing unarmed black men in disproportionate numbers, much of white America responded with "Shut up and stand up. I can pull your hair as hard as I deem necessary." Before I preached that morning, I also dropped to my knees in my office at the church, lighting candles and praying that God would use my story to expand our understanding of the wideness and depth of the family of faith.

That day, I implored the congregation to treat me and other queer Christians compassionately, hoping that they would respond with more than, "Be quiet." Many did—they found courage to not only hold my story, but also to advocate for others' belonging in the family of God.

I grew up evangelical (though I no longer describe myself as such), became a missionary with evangelical organizations and pastored in an evangelical church. I know that world well—one rife with tensions about purity and impurity, which bleed into all sorts of theological and ecclesiological debates

129 I requested that people who attended the second service refrain from giving a standing ovation, given that so many people's hearts were breaking in discovering that one of their pastors was gay. I wish now I had let people respond the way they wanted.

and practices.[130] The evangelical system was and is a pump primed for scapegoating.[131]

Much of this anxiety ultimately springs from the question of the authority of Scripture. *Sola Scriptura* proved highly inadequate over the last five centuries for many on the underside of power—gender and sexuality being only the latest "issues" poorly served—and that the living spirit of Jesus must be our primary beacon through stormy waters, in conjunction with other means of grace.[132] The Bible became an idol for the Church, to whom we regularly sacrifice vulnerable people for the sake of keeping our god on its throne—slaves, women, divorcees. Now queers. When will we stop slaughtering our own children in order to uphold an ideology?

We are not the first to identify the Bible as an idol—that's not *new* news—but we recognize the desperate need for a coherent theology of ritual sacrifice, given the mess made over the last 500 years appeasing a book rather than a living being. How can we heal when we don't understand how we incurred the wounds?

After my own outing, firing and subsequent planting of a new faith community, I felt like the apostle Thomas for a long time—touching Jesus's punctures and scars, trying to make sense of both the brutality and vindication enveloped in one body. If the God I love and serve is not the author of violence

---

130 For more information on the human biological inclination toward categorizing both things and people as "clean" or "unclean," see Richard Beck's *Unclean: Meditations on Purity, Hospitality, and Morality* and Jonathan Haidt's *The Righteous Mind: Why Good People are Divided by Politics and Religion.*

131 In *Violence and the Sacred,* Girard discusses the intricate connections between sex, violence and religion. His work shows that sexualizing people makes them prone to violent attack—and Western Christianity is especially good at sexualizing marginalized people—be it non-white men, women who don't follow prescribed sexual rules or LGBTQ+ people (34-36). Kelly Brown Douglas writes in *What's Faith Got to Do With It?: Black Bodies/Christian Souls,* " … the sexualization of a people serves a dual purpose in a Platonized Christian tradition. It allows for the religious legitimation of their vile treatment at the same time that it compels violence against them. A sexualized people is thus virtually fodder for violent sacrifice." Then she reminds us that "It bears repeating that sexual misconduct was often given as an excuse for the lynching of black men" (Douglas, 67-68).

132 See Chapter 3.

but, instead, is its redeemer, I needed to contend with the sacrificial system of the Torah. I wanted to better understand the scapegoat and its role in our larger collective story.

The scapegoat in the Torah

The first use of the term "scapegoat" appears in the book of Leviticus. Leviticus outlines the extensive sacrificial system requirements for Israel, complete with incense, blood sprinkling and the burning of animal flesh. Leviticus 16 records that each year, YHWH required the high priest (Aaron) to present two goats to the Lord—one sacrificed for the collective sins of the Hebrew people, and one sent into the wilderness as a scapegoat, "used for making atonement". Why were there *two* goats? And why does sacrificing and exiling animals "cleanse" people of sin or "make" atonement?

To approach these questions, we need to back up a bit.

Humans offered sacrifices—both animal and human—prior to God calling Abram, and long before the Law of Moses demanded ritual animal sacrifices of Israel. As Girard persuasively argues in *Violence and the Sacred* and *The Scapegoat*, sacrifice provides a way for people to maintain a false peace at the expense of the most vulnerable; we discovered the mechanism in ancient times and employed it generously. Even in the story of Cain and Abel, Cain offered a portion of his crops as a sacrifice to YHWH while his brother offered "fat portions from the firstborn of his flock" (Gn. 4:4).

In addition to crop and animal sacrifices, child sacrifice was also rampant in the ancient Near East (Goldingay, 236-237; Rohr, 47). In fact, human sacrifices likely preceded animal ones, with animals eventually replacing people as the practice evolved (J. Williams, xv).

But what if animal and human sacrifices are *our* invention, as Girard insists, and not God's? And what if the God of Israel is actually in the business of slowly eliminating it?

Leon Kass, a Jewish bioethicist, writes:

> *Sacrifice is of human origins. God neither commands nor requests it; we have no reason to believe that he even welcomes it. On the contrary, we have reason to suspect ... that the human impulse to sacrifice is, to say the least, problematic, and especially from God's point of view. To be sure, God will eventually command sacrifices, though then only under the strictest rules. As in so many other matters, the problematic is permitted but only if regulated. (Kass, 133)*

From Girard's perspective, the Bible tells a story of God eradicating all sacrifice—beginning with child sacrifice, which is probably the most ancient and certainly presents the greatest ethical obstacle of all ritual killings. When God had Abraham offer a ram on Mount Moriah, rather than his son Isaac, child sacrifice categorically ended in the Jewish tradition (Gn. 22).[133] This story marks a turning point in history, because the Abrahamic faiths graduated from offering humans as sacrifices to offering animals. James Warren writes, " ... the shift from human to animal sacrifice is one giant step forward for humanity nonetheless. The text as we have it represents a fundamental rejection of the validity of human sacrifice, and associates this move with the worship of Yahweh" (166).

Abraham's descendants eventually spent approximately 400 years in Egypt. After the Hebrew people fled from that land and found themselves wandering the desert of the Near East, it is as if God said, "OK, humans, you feel the need to offer sacrifices in order to prevent large-scale violence in your newfound society, free from Egypt? Once a year, under these supervised conditions, here is how it is done: the victim is to be an innocent goat—not one of your offspring, not your brother and surely not an entire minority group."

---

133 Also in Quran 37 (As-Saaffat)—Islamic tradition holds that Abraham went to sacrifice Ishmael on Moriah, rather than Isaac. Regardless, the story marks the end of child sacrifice in both Judaism and Islam—a break from a pagan past.

During those 40 years of wandering, God established the rituals, which included the one requiring the sacrifice of two goats—one for slaughtering on the altar once a year, and one for releasing into the wilderness. The first one chosen was "for the Lord," and the second "for the scapegoat."

> *Aaron is to offer the bull for his own sin offering to make atonement for himself and his household. Then he is to take the two goats and present them before the Lord at the entrance to the tent of meeting. He is to cast lots for the two goats—one lot **for the Lord** and the other **for the scapegoat**. Aaron shall bring the goat whose lot falls to the Lord and sacrifice it for a sin offering. But the goat chosen by lot as the scapegoat shall be presented alive before the Lord to be used for making atonement by sending it into the wilderness as a scapegoat.*[134]

Newer translations (such as Robert Alter's *The Five Books of Moses: A Translation with Commentary* or the New Revised Standard Version) translate the words "for the scapegoat" as "for Azazel." Azazel means "fierce or angry god," and is thought to be an ancient, demonic goat-like figure associated with the wilderness. Rabbis debated this passage through the years— one goat for YHWH, and the other for Azazel? Why are the ancient Israelites told to present a goat before the Lord that is then sent to a pagan god?

Perhaps the passage means to reveal that when we scapegoat, we sacrifice to a fierce, angry god. Scapegoating exists not for God but for us, to appease what humanity's dark, demonic side demands.

The way the ancient Hebrews practiced ceremonial animal sacrifice unmasks the psychological projection described by Girard. According to Leviticus, the priest placed his hands on the scapegoat and confessed all the sins his people had committed during the previous year, before releasing the goat

---

134 Lv. 16:6-10, emphasis mine.

into the desert. In this way, the process reveals that scapegoating is more about *our* sins—the sins of the people—and *not* the sins of the animal. The scapegoat is innocent. The fact that the sins of a group are projected onto a scapegoat is almost always hidden in human scapegoating dynamics. It is so very difficult to see when it happens. The ancient Hebrew animal rite in Leviticus clearly exposes it (Warren, 265-266).

Rather than presenting a blueprint for describing how God demands death for sin, the scapegoat custom in Leviticus begins a long process of reform, the goal of which is to end scapegoating altogether.[135]

First-century Judea: the unmasking continues

Let's now look more closely at the story of Jesus's life through a Girardian lens, to evaluate how it fits into the larger narrative.

Jesus was born into a large-scale system of envy, rivalry and anxiety. On the one hand, his people lived in the land they venerated, the land that was promised to them by God. King Herod I had reconstructed the Temple in Jerusalem one generation prior to Jesus, allowing for the regular celebration of rites and festivals and the offering of sacrifices. The Temple played an important role in how the Jewish people practiced their faith.

On the other hand, even though the Israelites lived in their ancestral land and could worship in the Temple on Mount Moriah, the Roman Empire ruled Palestine. The land was (and is) significant for commerce, lying on major trade routes between Europe, Asia and Africa. Its strategic significance (for military control) enticed Rome, and its leaders sought to maintain command of the land surrounding the Mediterranean Sea. The Romans taxed the people living there heavily, placing substantial burdens on them as an occupied people.

---

135 For a modern take on the ceremonial aspect of slaughtering the goat, Rabbi Maurice D. Harris has a great chapter in his book, *Leviticus: You Have No Idea* called "Animal Sacrifice is Gross? The Supermarket is Gross!"

Several Jewish revolts against the Romans took place before, during and after Jesus's life. Rome crucified people who protested too boldly (Josephus, 143-152, 310, 326).[136] Kelly Brown Douglas points out that Rome reserved this most brutal death sentence for "slaves and captured enemy soldiers," as well as for those "the state held in particular contempt ..." who were "considered outcasts or a threat to social stability" (85-86). Crucifixion represents Rome's scorn for lower-class people, and most especially those challenging and/or resisting the political power of the empire.

In addition to rivalry with the Roman Empire, feuding persisted *within* the Jewish community.[137] Sadducees, vested in controlling the Temple, often colluded with the Romans and did not always get along with the Pharisees. The Essenes rejected both groups, believing them to be corrupt, and started a utopian community in the desert near the Dead Sea. The Zealots, intent on overthrowing the Roman government by force, permeated the hills of the Galilee, creating chaos from the points of view of those intent on maintaining peace with Rome.[138]

Girard's theory informs us that war can be averted by identifying a series of scapegoats to temporarily relieve group pressure. This was the case during Jesus's lifetime and all the way up to the fall of Jerusalem, in 70 C.E., as various "false messiahs" and rebel groups hung on crosses throughout the land. The people of ancient Palestine found in Jesus an unusual rabbi from the Galilee whom Rome and others in power were able to use as one of their many scapegoats, someone on whom they could channel their violent energy, to temporarily avert widespread violence. Jesus was not the first nor the last, but rather was one of *many* scapegoats on whom

---

136 Josephus reports that Roman General Titus killed 500 people per day after a revolt in the Galilee around 4 C.E. General Varus crucified thousands.

137 Additionally, there were smaller-scale rivalries with neighboring people in the land, like the Samaritans.

138 Some believe Judas was, or had been in his past, a Zealot, in addition to his fellow apostle, Simon the Zealot.

Rome channeled its anxious energy. Once a group uses scape-goating to maintain peace, it will do so over and over again until—or unless—the violence overwhelms them.

Jesus, a classic scapegoat

As a Jewish man in Roman-occupied territory, Jesus perfectly suited the role of scapegoat. He hailed from the Galilee, a much-disparaged rural part of northern Israel. (Recall Nathanael's reply to Philip in the Gospel of John: "Nazareth! Can anything good come from there?") Jesus was also rumored to be illegitimate—a *mamzer*, a child of ques-tionable paternity. He was different, and his followers were different—they were the poor, the unclean, women, tax collec-tors and other so-called sinners.

Yet while he stood apart, Jesus was also deeply rooted in the traditions of his people—of the line of prophets (Thurman, 80).[139] Jesus stirred people up and both spoke and acted against unjust structures through stories, teachings and healings; many in power found his sizable crowd of disciples to be threatening.[140] People started murmuring that Jesus might be the messiah, the anointed one who would establish God's reign on earth. How would Jesus do that? Would he lead a violent rebellion, as many imagined the messiah might? Would he overthrow the Roman Empire? Would he become high priest in the Temple?

Jesus forged a different path. He encouraged people to lay down their power rather than seek it. He taught his followers to renounce violence and love their enemies. The Sermon on the Mount (Mt. 5-7) remains Jesus's most famous teaching.

---

139 "Jesus himself announced that his death would resemble that of the Servant of the Lord in Second Isaiah and other prophets who were collectively assassinated or mistreated under circumstances similar to those of the Passion" (Girard, *The One by Whom Scandal Comes*, 33).

140 "The way in which he [Jesus] preaches can only make him appear to be totally lacking in respect for the holiest of institutions, guilty of hubris and blasphemy, since he dares to rival God himself in the perfection of the Love that he never ceases to make manifest" (Girard, *Things Hidden Since the Foundation of the World*, 208).

Girard writes, "Look again at the Sermon on the Mount. We can see that the significance of the Kingdom of God is completely clear. It is always a matter of bringing together the warring brothers, of putting an end to the mimetic crisis by a universal renunciation of violence" (Girard, *Things Hidden*, 197). He urged the faithful to submit their desires to God and renounce rivalrous relationship patterns.

Jesus challenged the authorities of his day through his teachings on nonviolent resistance, and in openly accepting and championing people despised by their communities (Wink, 98-110).[141] As he did, those hoping to keep peace with Rome became increasingly afraid that Jesus's message might upend the tenuous entente.

"What are we accomplishing?" they asked. "Here is this man, performing many signs. If we let him go on like this, everyone will believe in him, and then the Romans will come and *take away both our temple and our nation*" (Jn. 11:47b-48, emphasis mine).

That's what some people believed was at stake: that both the Temple and the nation would be seized from the Hebrew people. And they were right, as the Roman destruction of both, in 70 C.E., proved. The pressure was real and it was intense. Sometimes entire structural systems are at stake when we follow Jesus. By the time people realize entire systems may crumble, the time is ripe for a scapegoat.

> "Then one of them, named Caiaphas, who was high priest that year, spoke up, 'You know nothing at all! You do not realize that it is better for you that one man die for the people than that the whole nation perish ... '
>
> ... So from that day on they plotted to take his life" (Jn. 11:49-50, 53).

---

141 Walter Wink talks about how Jesus's instructions in the Sermon on the Mount—to turn the other cheek, walk the extra mile and give your second cloak—are creative strategies of nonviolent resistance.

Caiaphas understood the power of channeling group energy onto one person. He knew that if Jesus could be accused of blasphemy and of plotting to overthrow the Romans, enough people would rally around the charges to relieve the pressure valve.

The very next chapter of John opens the week of Jesus's death with Mary of Bethany anointing her rabbi's feet with perfume, prophetically preparing him for burial. His death is imminent.

How a crowd becomes a mob

Right after Mary anoints Jesus, we read the story of him riding a donkey into Jerusalem. Crowds of Jesus's followers line the streets leading into the ancient city, waving palm branches and shouting, "Hosanna! Blessed is he who comes in the name of the Lord! Blessed is the king of Israel!" (Jn. 12:13b). The mob cries out in support of Jesus, giving him their clothes to sit on and laying their cloaks on the ground before him (Mt. 21:8)—but oh, how fickle crowds can be. They so quickly fall in line once a scapegoat is identified. On Sunday the mob shouted, "Hosanna!" and by Friday they shouted, "Crucify him!" What happened between those days? Girard's theory tells us that when fear and rivalry reach a fever pitch, false accusations against a potential scapegoat surface. That's exactly what happened to Jesus that Passover week.

People otherwise inclined to support potential scapegoats almost always coalesce around false accusations, even if they do not entirely believe them. They will sacrifice, almost every time, an innocent person or minority for the sake of what appears to be peace for the larger in-group (Thurman, 14-15).[142] Girard calls it *mimetic contagion*—the idea that once

---

142 "The opposition to those who work for social change does not come only from those who are guarantors of the *status quo*. Again and again it has been demonstrated that the lines are held by those whose hold on security is sure only as long as the *status quo* remains intact. The reasons for this are not far to seek. If a man is convinced that he is safe only as long as he uses his power to give others a sense of insecurity, then the measure of their security is in his hands. If security or insecurity is at the mercy of a

a core set of people begins forming a mob, other humans imitate their desire.

Under the right conditions, it only takes one person making a public accusation against another to ignite the process. After a few people reinforce the charge, it becomes difficult for others in the group to disagree (Kaplan, 89). Marketing professor Jonah Berger says, "Watch a focus group share opinions or a committee decide who to hire, and whoever goes first has a big impact on the outcome," because the other group members mimic the initiator's thoughts and desires (58). The impulse of the original accusers to project the group's anxiety onto an individual or small group of individuals spreads like wildfire, consuming people who did not know they were kindling.

Two charges against Jesus materialize that week: blasphemy and subversion. When Jesus appears before Pontius Pilate, the Roman prefect over Judea, the crowd " … began to accuse him, saying, 'We have found this man subverting our nation. He opposes payment of taxes to Caesar and claims to be Messiah, a king'" (Lk. 23:2). Surely not everyone in the crowd felt confident of these accusations, but on the whole they mobilized around projecting their own disloyalties onto Jesus.

Neither Pilate nor Herod could come up with anything with which to legally charge Jesus. Pilate, the Roman ruler, knew Jesus was innocent of accusations of plotting a revolt; he says so three times in the Gospel of John (Jn. 18:38, 19:4, 6). Even so, the crowd of people who so vehemently cheered Jesus's arrival into Jerusalem a few days prior now convinced themselves he needed to die. Jesus's innocence became buried in groupthink rationalizations as people called for an end to his life.

---

single individual or group, then control of behavior becomes routine. All imperialism functions in this way. Subject peoples are held under control by this device" (Thurman, 14-15).

An age-old story repeats

The Roman authorities then dressed Jesus (the scapegoat) like a buffoon, with a false crown and purple robe, and beat him until he looked nothing like *them*. They disfigured, mocked and paraded him around town for all to see, forcing him to carry his own cross until he could carry it no longer. The more different—the more *other*—he appeared, the easier it would be to dehumanize and kill him.

Humans killed Jesus, not God. Some members of both communities—Jew and Gentile alike, *representing all humankind*—executed Jesus. We took an innocent man and accused, condemned and sacrificed him because of our sin (Schneiders).[143] We sacrificed him to Azazel because of our need to appease our false gods. When Scripture tells us that Jesus bore the sin of the world, he was bearing our projected anxiety, sin and shame. He represented all of the innocent victims—past, present and future—who have ever been excluded, harmed and murdered.

The very words Jesus spoke as he hung on the cross, "Father, forgive them, for they do not know what they are doing," unmask the scapegoating system at work. An innocent man spoke for them. Not a *somewhat* innocent man. Not a man guilty of many things but not the thing of which he was accused. A *wholly* innocent man, carrying the envy, rivalry and violent energy of the world projected onto him.

He spoke out to God concerning *us*, all of humanity. *We do not know what we are doing.* A hallmark of the Girardian cycle is the complete and utter belief held by oppressors that they are innocent. They are convinced *they* are, in fact, the actual victims. Having lived through my experience of being scapegoated, this dynamic was perhaps the most surprising for me: the fact that *victimizers view themselves as victims.*

When people view themselves as victims, they justify discarding the people whom they believe cause them harm.

143 Schneiders makes a compelling case that scapegoating is, indeed, the "sin of the world."

An obvious example would be the extermination of the Jews leading up to, and during, World War II. On the whole, people throughout Nazi-occupied territory allowed themselves to be convinced that Jews were harming "their" culture and robbing "their" national coffers. Then, feeling victimized, Aryans felt free to do harm to Jewish people—or at least to ignore their mistreatment, as rumors swirled about concentration camps and forced exiles.

On a more intimate plane, a family who shuns its LGBTQ+ child is convinced that the child's "impurity" will harm the relational unit. Whether fearing that the child might "influence" younger siblings or cousins, or that their "sin" might evoke God's displeasure, the family projects its own insecurities about purity and the goodness of God onto the queer child, exiling the teen. The banishment might not be absolute; the child may still live in the house with the parent(s) and siblings. But the quiet judgment and exclusion from the full closeness of familial life resonates, communicating loud and clear to the LGBTQ+ child that their orientation is unacceptable. The victim is the queer child, but other family members conceptualize themselves as the sufferers. Their imagined victimhood justifies the ongoing ill treatment of the child.

Overturning the verdict of the mob

Girard tells us that the full exile or execution of a scapegoat brings peace to a troubled group. Once Ken and I left our former community and planted a new church, I knew that there would be a sense of tranquility in the church that had asked us to resign. The people who remained might be weary, but a sense of camaraderie would prevail as they pulled together, feeling they'd survived the ordeal shoulder-to-shoulder. Girard describes that sensation as feeling so good—so unifying—that people create myths about *what happened,* vindicating the violence against others' humanity.[144]

The communal sacrifice of Jesus brought hushed relief to the watching crowd, as darkness covered the land. The ritual killing marked the finale of a period of such intense turbulence that, after Jesus died, the bystanders simply "beat their breasts" and walked away.[145] Those who knew him, including the women from the Galilee, stood at a distance in silence, watching. Preparations for the burial of the body commenced and were carried on until evening, since it was the Sabbath and they did not want to leave the bodies on the crosses through the next day. There was silence, followed by the dutiful cleanup of the mess all had wrought.

Jesus's death remains unremarkable in that it bears resemblance to the stories of so many other scapegoats, including many crucified before and after him by the Romans. Yet his story also remains immensely remarkable in that he does not stay sacrificed.

Jesus died, but Jesus also rose.

In doing so, God overturned our human verdict of the scapegoat. With the resurrection of a completely innocent man, God revoked our human pronouncement of guilt and declared the entire scapegoating system—the entire cycle of human violence—foolish and void (Alison, 27). It is as though God said to humans: "I have been trying to wean you off of sacrifices since the beginning. First I had you channel this scapegoating energy onto animals instead of people, and then I had you do it under very specific conditions. Now I declare it done. *It is finished.* No more. Go and learn what this means: *I desire mercy, not sacrifice.*"[146]

> *It is finished.*
> *I desire mercy, not sacrifice.*

---

144 "The Bible is more concerned with victims than mythology is and with the possibility that individuals might be unjustly victimized. The ethical difference is obvious enough to be widely, although not universally, acknowledged" (Girard, *Oedipus Unbound*, 109).

145 Lk. 23:48

146 Mt. 9:13—Jesus quoting Ho. 6:6

The resurrection of Jesus ended the need for the sacrificial system, rendering it powerless. It thoroughly laid bare the purpose of continuous ritual killings—which is to maintain group stability—and displayed the futility of such acts. Long-term peace cannot be achieved through scapegoating. When we follow Jesus, we renounce our proclivity to do such violence to others.

This is, in fact, the essence of what it means to follow Jesus. The Greek word for "spirit," in the New Testament, is *paraclete*, which means "the advocate." Curious, isn't it, that *paraclete* means "advocate" when the Hebrew word *satan* means "accuser"? When we renounce our scapegoating ways—when we convert, so to speak—we move from operating in the spirit of the accusing mob to being infused with the spirit of the advocate, championing the vulnerable and oppressed.

Girard's theory shows us that the crucifixion was an act of barbarism, carried out by an empire fixated on keeping peace within its territorial conquests with the support of religious elites intent on maintaining stasis with Rome. The event itself displayed the effects of power used against the oppressed. As Jesus hung, dying, most of his followers hid in Jerusalem; his execution struck fear into most, if not all, of his disciples.

In reading the cross as a human endeavor, rather than a sacrifice required and sanctioned by God for his own appease-ment—or as a ransom payment given to the "evil kidnapper" of humanity (Satan)—we locate the spiritual power of the story in the *entirety* of Jesus's life. We find guidance for our own lives in understanding how Jesus *lived* his (what led him to be put to death); in the utter selflessness of his sacrificial love, demonstrated in his willingness to continue living a godly life in spite of the threat of his lynching on a Roman cross; and in his faith in God that resurrection would follow as the vindication of his righteous life.

The cross is the hinge of the story, but it isn't, in and of itself, the good news. The life of Jesus—teaching us how to exist in solidarity with the poor and oppressed—and the resurrection, substantiating that way of life, contain the real treasures.

Jesus is more than his trauma (and so are we)

A small group of people at my church have been reading through Gregory Boyd's latest two-part tome, *The Crucifixion of the Warrior God*. Though I balk at his choice to exclude LGBTQ+ people from fully participating in the church community where he pastors, I have appreciated his work on open theism, and figured I would join some thoughtful people in digging into his latest thesis.

In the book, he introduces and expounds on a concept he calls *cruciform hermeneutics*, in which he insists that the entire Bible be interpreted in light of the cross. He acknowledges that Jesus's life and resurrection also need attention, but the self-giving sacrificial love embodied in the death of the Christ should be, in his opinion, the central and primary lens through which we illuminate Scripture.

Two things struck me as noteworthy in reading it. First, his sources are almost entirely straight, white men. Nothing against straight, white men, but the perspective is monotone. All I could think was, "If he had read outside the straight, white, male author sphere, he might rethink his proposed theory." James Cone's *The Cross and the Lynching Tree* alone (which every Christian—and every American, Christian or not—should read) would highlight the intense response of most African-Americans to the idea that Jesus should be construed chiefly in light of the torment and fear of the lynching tree. That community understands full well the horror of the cross—our nation imposed that same terror on the black community for most of our shared history.

Second, I have been a scapegoat. It is difficult to convey the trauma caused by being publicly outed—just two weeks after I came out to my parents—and having to bear witness to my experience on a public stage amidst people with hostile intentions. I spent two years in trauma therapy treating my post-traumatic stress disorder. I had nightmares of that morning for months. If not for my now-wife, I might have taken my own life in the midst of that ordeal; I certainly understand the reasons why suicide rates are higher among LGBTQ+ youth than among the general population. *But my life is so much more than that day.* And my life is so much more than the night I walked out of that church building after the board of directors asked for my (and Ken's) resignation. My life is filled with four decades of events and relationships shaped by the God I love and follow, in addition to the continued abundance and joy generated from my marriage, my church, my family and friends and my community involvement. I am more than my trauma, and it would make me feel both sad and deeply misunderstood if people chose to interpret my entire life through the events of those days.

Jesus was a person, too. He had (and has) feelings, and I do wonder if he feels misread when we insist on reading the Bible primarily through the lens of his torture and killing.

The scapegoating theory of atonement affirms what the oppressed experience: the cross is a lynching tree, and only a lynching tree. I place far more importance on learning to live as Jesus lived—practicing love, justice, hospitality and peace—and on the resurrection, where the God-Who-Is-Love upended the world in clearing his son's name and calling us to stop crucifying the innocent for our own self-satisfaction.[147] The cross is simply what happens to us when we live our lives as Jesus beckons that we live them. He bids us "come and die," and each disciple will experience this in some way or another if they live as Jesus invites us to live. Not because God wills us violence and death, but because those are the natural consequences of living lives of abundant love.

The good news is that the dying does not define us; in fact, the dying portends new life and bountiful living. The

---

147 Ted Grimsrud's *Instead of Atonement: The Bible's Salvation Story and Our Hope for Wholeness* is a lovely book focusing on the way Jesus lived his life.

resurrection (if the early apostles are to be believed) changed the entire world. The day Jesus walked out of a garden grave marked a new beginning, whereby humans are shown how to live in non-rivalrous relationships with God, each other, themselves and all of creation. When we step into living courageous, vulnerable, principled lives—protecting and advocating for the equal humanity of all people (including ourselves)—we find freedom, and peace becomes a possibility.

9

The Path of Non-rivalry

Emily

THE MORNING I write this marks the three-year anniversary of the day my wife, Rachel, and I legally wed. Another eight months would pass before we held a public ceremony (which Ken officiated), followed by her moving to Michigan to be with me. That day three autumns ago, we woke up, drove to the Mall of America in Minneapolis, walked up to the third floor with two witnesses in tow, and entered the Chapel of Love. Two minutes later, we signed the marriage paperwork and rode a roller coaster to celebrate. The best three years of my life.

When I flew to Minnesota to see Rachel two days prior, I had not planned on getting married. We were engaged and had picked out rings, but spoke of tying the knot the following summer to let what was happening in my church play out. So I was surprised when she suggested that we go downtown and make it legal.

It made sense, though. I came out to my church just one month before and we were in the midst of the mess leading to the ouster of LGBTQ+ people and their allies. Our entire staff spent the previous year having one-on-one conversations with more than 60 leaders about treating LGBTQ+ inclusion as a disputable matter before three staff members withdrew their support for transitioning the church to being inclusive—triggering the drawn-out church split, a process that lasted four and a half months. I updated Rachel about the discussions happening around that ordeal—conversations that included congregants asking me if I would consider cancelling my wedding the following summer for the sake of the church. One member asked if I would consider simply *postponing* it so the church would have more time to hash through the "gay issue."

To which I replied: "I'm a 36-year-old woman. I waited a long time to find my mate, and it is not fair to ask me to put my personal life on hold any longer for the benefit of a church openly debating my relationship. I already spent time—years—not dating, in order to best serve this organization and help it work through the 'gay issue.' No time will be enough time for those anxious about the morality of it. Would you postpone your own wedding for the sake of church infight-ing—especially if the dispute were specifically about you and your fiancée? Would you walk away from your most cherished relationship?" The man sheepishly admitted that it sounded cruel when I put it that way, and that no, of course he would not postpone or ignore his own relationship needs. He would rather be asked to leave than do that. (Me, too!)

A leader sent out a congregational letter to all members saying that, in a conversation with the national director of our denomination, the director indicated that he would be fine with me remaining on staff so long as I did not marry. That conversation about my love life took place, of course, without my knowledge or permission, with the details of it then being sent out to be consumed by people trying to figure out what to think and how to respond. That letter led to more congregants urging me not to marry. Which led to someone else asking me if I could perhaps marry and never have sex … would that satisfy the national requirements?

Umm … that would satisfy no one.

Rachel's response to all of this was: "They do not get to dictate our relationship. Let's take the conversation off the table. Marry me now. This is our decision to make, not theirs."[148]

That resonated with me, because the inappropriate questions some people asked made me feel infantilized and patronized. Would you want your sex life discussed in public? Would you want your colleague going to the CEO of your company, talking about whether your employment should depend on your upcoming nuptials or whether or not you have sex? If I agreed to those terms—and broke up with Rachel to remain on staff—the entire church's belonging and standing within the denomination would then depend on whether or not I ever slept with someone. Such an old story, a woman's sexuality causing a war.[149] Which suitor would win out—my wife or the church? No contest from my perspective. Only the purity culture and its spawn could produce this kind of madness.

For so many years, I remained in rivalry with myself over my sexual orientation. When I confessed "what I really wanted" to Jesus (see my story at the beginning of Chapter 6), and entered a time of fasting and prayer for a wife, I attended a women's conference organized by my former denomination. During a time of worship—of the contemporary, charismatic sort—a woman from Oklahoma (whom I'd never met before) approached me. She asked if she could lift my right arm up in the air. I said, "Sure." She did, and then she said, "I felt like God gave me a picture for you. I was praying and I think God

---

148 I understand full well that I work in the "faith business," and so there are moral concerns about gay unions for those who are more conservative. Ken addressed those concerns adeptly in his book, *A Letter to My Congregation: An evangelical pastor's path to embracing people who are gay, lesbian, bisexual, and transgender in the company of Jesus, 2nd edition* published earlier that same year. Ken had opted out of the dichotomous thinking proffered by many churches and offered space for us all to hold differing views—leaving the judging to Jesus (where it belongs) and fully including the LGBTQ+ community. At the time I met Rachel, there was no official national policy on gay pastors and gay marriage in my denomination. The denomination's board of directors issued those positions less than one month after I came out in a letter that effectively outed me. They then enforced the newly minted guidelines without listening to or giving consideration to my story.

149 Helen of Troy would understand.

said you've been in a years-long boxing match over some personal issue and you're exhausted. But you recently won whatever battle you've been fighting."

That woman may or may not appreciate the application of what she said, but I found significance in its meaning and timing. It felt like God gave me a wink. I met Rachel two weeks later.

After I finally made peace in that area of my life, I found myself in rivalry with others in my faith community because of this newfound serenity. I intensely desired marriage, while others vied for me to "marry" the church instead. The rivalry literally took place over my body and what I could do with it. Rivalries also existed between parties with varying levels of power. Another pastor on staff publicly presented an alternative vision for our church, which placed him in open rivalry with Ken. I sensed a younger staff member felt rivalry with me. Various factions in the church—including a cabal of large tithers—contended for this pastor or that to "win out." The competitive stew boiled over, uncontrolled. With my Girardian lens it seemed anathema to God's ways and how he called us to behave in relationship with one another.

Jesus exposed the very nature and being of God as both nonviolent and non-rivalrous. We explored God's nonviolent nature in the last chapter, but I think it worthwhile to press further into the latter, as God's lack of rivalry with anything in the cosmos forms the foundation of his pacifist nature—the nature that he calls us to emulate. If humans act in harmony with, and for the good of, everyone and everything in all creation, it has the effect of renewing the entirety of what is known (and perhaps of what remains as yet unknown).

Non-rivalry within the Trinity

The inherent relationship of the Trinity requires reciprocity between the three persons (Father, Son, and Holy Spirit); there is no rivalry within the Godhead. While it is outside the scope of this book to dig too deeply into Trinitarian theology, Jürgen Moltmann's classic book *The Crucified God*, and his student Miroslav Volf's *After Our Likeness: The Church as the Image of the Trinity*, detail the mutuality between Father, Son, and Holy Spirit. God is not in rivalry with God-self, nor with any aspect of the Trinitarian essence.

I find myself drawn to David S. Cunningham's suggestion that we use the words *Source, Wellspring,* and *Living Water* to describe the Father, Son, and Holy Spirit, respectively. These words vanish cultural assumptions that may imply a pecking order within the Godhead; presumptions about gender; and conjectures about what it means to be a "person" within the Trinity. Cunningham chooses his metaphors carefully, explaining that "God is always in the process of 'giving place,' of moving out of the way so that a new divine manifestation can be recognized as 'fully God.' The Wellspring is always coming forth from the Source ('eternally begotten of the Father,' in the most common English translation of the creed), and the Living Water is always flowing out to nurture the believing community" (Cunningham, 197).

In describing God in such a way, Cunningham circumvents problematic language, whereby the word *persons* suggests an individualism more informed by modernity than the original intent. It also removes any hierarchy implied by the Father-Son relationship; the credal understanding of that bond is one in which the Son is "eternally begotten of the Father," and therefore the Father did not exist before the Son and the Son is not subordinate to the Father (more specifically, they are mutually subordinate to each other, as well as to the Spirit). This is how Jesus can say, "I and the Father are one" (Jn. 10:30). Additionally, the language removes any gendered expectation of a subservient Spirit—since *Spirit* is neuter or feminine throughout the Bible—by theologians with patriarchal bias.

Source, Wellspring, and *Living Water* paints a dynamic picture of a God bringing life to all in his/her purview.

Non-rivalry between God and humans

God is also not in rivalry with humanity. Humans might feel the need to contend with God, as seen in the opening chapters of Genesis (where the people eat of the tree of the knowledge of good and evil in order to become like their Creator), but God does not reciprocate or encourage humanity to be in rivalry with the Godhead (Warren, 42-51).

The Gospel of Luke records an account of Jesus telling a story about two brothers, better known as the tale of "The Prodigal Son," in which one of the sons feels intense rivalry with his brother. Many of us know the parable well: Two men stand to inherit their father's wealth, but instead of waiting until his father's passing to receive his inheritance, the youngest son asks for his share of the money while his dad still lives. The son then goes off to a distant land and squanders his fortune. Completely destitute, the man eventually comes home to his father's house, begging forgiveness and offering to be his father's servant. The father lavishly welcomes his wayward son and throws a party, celebrating the return of his child. The older son, meanwhile, becomes jealous, and asks his dad why he never threw *him* a festive reception. "'My son,' the father said, 'you are always with me, and everything I have is yours. But we had to celebrate and be glad, because this brother of yours was dead and is alive again; he was lost and is found'" (Lk. 15:31-32).

Regardless of whom you interpret the older son and younger son to represent—whether the people of Israel and Gentiles, factions within Judaism, self-righteous leaders and sinners or anyone who feels spiritually entitled and those who feel shame and unworthiness—an underlying point remains that the father is not in rivalry with either brother. One of the brothers (maybe both) feels rivalry with his sibling, but the father, representing God, embraces *both* of his children and makes all at his disposal available to them, without reservation. Neither does he pit them against each other, but rather encourages the older sibling to offer the same grace to his brother that he, the father, models. God doesn't ask us to earn, build or compete for our place in the family of the beloveds, but rather makes space for us to do so without turning either God-self or each other into rivals.

Non-rivalry between God and nature

In 2010, nearly 200 million gallons of oil leaked from an underwater drilling site and into the Gulf of Mexico. I grew up vacationing on the Florida Panhandle with my family, and reading about the thick, black sludge polluting the turquoise water and white-sand beaches broke my heart. Birds died, their feathers slicked down with petroleum; the toxicity of the spill poisoned countless fish and dolphins.

Trying to tame and control nature persists as one of the quintessentially human endeavors. As our species seeks dominance over the earth's resources, we find ourselves in an increasingly antagonistic wrestling match with Mother Nature. It's no longer simply about battling weeds and animals to grow food; now, we are fighting earthquakes and oil spills as we dig deeper into the earth's crust, in search of oil, gas and minerals. We will lose, in the end—and not without significant cost in the meantime. The book of Genesis describes this aspect of life—of trying to wrangle nature—as a curse.

The God we see in Scripture isn't in rivalry with nature, but rather is Lord over it. Genesis 1-2 is, first and foremost, a story about God creating the earth as a giant temple and installing humans as priests (Walton, 72-92; Watts; Enns, 70). Priests, we understand, are stewards of temples and sacred spaces. "And the LORD God took the human and set him down in the garden of Eden to till it and watch it" (Gn. 2:15).[150] The Hebrew words for "till and watch" are later translated as "serve and guard," and are used for describing the role of

---

150 Alter, *The Five Books of Moses: A Translation With Commentary*, 21.

priests in the tabernacle and temple.[151] It is the distinct role
of the human to work, steward and guard the earth-temple of
Yahweh.

In our role as caretakers of the earth, we humans are
pictured naming the animals in the Garden of Eden, walking
naked and unafraid through the foliage, and communing with
God uninhibited. The dream for humanity is harmony with
nature. This same vision of being at peace with nature is found
in the prophetic imagination of the first prophet Isaiah. After
God's justice is brought about by the "rod of his mouth" and
the "breath of his lips," then:

> The wolf will live with the lamb,
>   the leopard will lie down with the goat,
> the calf and the lion and the yearling together;
>   and a little child will lead them.
>
> The cow will feed with the bear,
>   their young will lie down together,
>   and the lion will eat straw like the ox.
>
> The infant will play near the cobra's den,
>   and the young child will put its hand into the viper's nest.
>
> They will neither harm nor destroy
>   on all my holy mountain,
> for the earth will be filled with the knowledge of the Lord
>   as the waters cover the sea. (Is. 11:6-9)[152]

---

151 "The two Hebrew words for "cultivate and keep" (respectively, 'ābad and shāmar)
can easily be, and usually are, translated "serve and guard." When these two words
occur together later in the Old Testament, without exception they have this meaning
and refer either to Israelites "serving and guarding/obeying" God's word (about 10
times) or, more often to priests who "serve" God in the temple and "guard" the temple
from unclean things entering it (Num 3:7-8; 8:25-26; 18:5-6; 1 Chr 23:32; Ezek 44:14).
Therefore, Adam was to be the first priest to serve in and guard God's temple." (Beale,
7-8)

152 Also, note in Verse 4 that God's justice isn't brought about with violence, but by
the words and breath from Jesus's mouth.

The apostle Paul tells us that all of creation has been groaning for this process—of creation being in balance—to unfold (Ro. 8:22-25). As followers of Jesus attempting to live as connectedly as possible with the world around us, we should try to care for what's entrusted to us, use as few resources as possible, and support community endeavors that protect and preserve the earth-temple of God. We live out, as best we can, this idea of living in equilibrium with the environment as priests of Yahweh.

Imitate Jesus in practicing non-rivalry

This, then, becomes the invitation to all humans: to live in non-rivalry in every area of life.[153] When humans imitate the non-rivalrous nature of the Trinity, the sinful and life-depleting mechanism that leads to death and destruction is exposed, defeated, and made impotent. If we join with Jesus in practicing non-rivalry with all of the created order, with the help of the *Paraclete*—the Advocate—the whole world will be made new.

We begin this process by acknowledging our participation in this system and turning our faces toward Jesus, whose desire we are called to mirror. The authors of the New Testament summon us to reject mimicking the crowd, and instead invite us to emulate Jesus.

When people around us get riled up, we reflect their anger, anxiety, and desire. It's biological. Girard calls this mimetic contagion; we call it herd mentality, or mob mentality. People do things in crowds that they thought they would never do.

Imagine a college campus erupting after their football team wins a championship game, and young people surging into the street, knocking down signs, burning couches, and ransacking parked cars. I presume that many of those young adults never imagined themselves as vandals or drunken arsonists. Yet, in

---

153 Note that competition, in and of itself, isn't necessarily bad. But when it turns to rivalry, we're in dangerous territory. Healthy competition doesn't wish ill on the other, but rivalry celebrates harm to the competitor.

a crowd—when people mimic the emotions and desires of those around them—people act in ways contrary to how they view themselves. Instead of crowd imitation, what God offers is mimetic contagion oriented toward Jesus as we allow our minds and our desires to be transformed by the Holy Spirit.

Understanding the importance of turning our desire toward Jesus and imitating his ways, the writers of the New Testament reiterate this concept over and over again. Consider the following examples, all of which direct us to mimic Jesus or his disciples:

> When [Jesus] had finished washing [the disciples'] feet, he put on his clothes and returned to his place. "Do you understand what I have done for you?" he asked them. "You call me 'Teacher' and 'Lord,' and rightly so, for that is what I am. Now that I, your Lord and Teacher, have washed your feet, you also should wash one another's feet" (Jn. 13:12-14).

> Jesus said, "A new command I give you: Love one another. As I have loved you, so you must love one another" (Jn. 13:34).

> Jesus said, "My command is this: Love each other as I have loved you. Greater love has no one than this: to lay down one's life for one's friends" (Jn. 15:12-13).

> Paul writes, "Follow my example, as I follow the example of Christ" (1 Co. 11:1).

> Paul writes, "Be kind and compassionate to one another, forgiving each other, just as in Christ, God forgave you" (Eph. 4:32).

> Paul writes, "Bear with each other and forgive one another if any of you has a grievance against someone. Forgive as the Lord forgave you" (Col. 3:13).

> Paul writes, "You became imitators of us and of the Lord, for you welcomed the message in the midst of severe suffering with the joy given by the Holy Spirit. And so you became a model to all the believers in Macedonia and Achaia" (1 Th. 1:6-7).
>
> The author of Hebrews writes, "We do not want you to become lazy, but to imitate those who through faith and patience inherit what has been promised" (Heb. 6:12).
>
> Peter writes, "To this you were called, because Christ suffered for you, leaving you an example, that you should follow in his steps" (1 Pe. 2:21).
>
> John writes, "This is how we know we are in [Christ]: Whoever claims to live in him must live as Jesus did" (1 Jn. 2:5b-6).

I once heard pastor and author Brian McLaren say, "This is what prayer, it seems to me, most deeply is: Prayer is the formation and direction of desire."[154] We open our hearts and minds to Jesus, allowing him to either reinforce or redirect our desires toward God's—and we mimic those aspirations, instead of the passions of the mob. Our hearts become shaped and formed in love, by love.

The shaping of desire

James Alison makes two points along this line of thinking.

First, we can imagine that the spirits—the powers and principalities—are both systemic and personal. Prayer supposes that we can be moved by such spirits. The traditional word we use for the spirits that move us in the direction of accusation, rivalry, and violence is *possess*, which Alison points out contains a "note of violence concerning the relationship between the spirit and the possessed person" (Alison, *Jesus the Forgiving Victim*, 405). The traditional word we use for the

---

154 Convergence Music Conference presentation, February 7, 2017

Holy Spirit moving us in the direction of advocacy is *indwelling*, which lacks the implication of violence against the person praying. Either way: humans can be shaped, but the effect of the shaping on us, as humans, is different depending on which spirit(s) we employ.

Second, Alison refers to Jesus's instruction to his disciples to pray in secret, give in secret, and "practice piety" in secret so that the temptation to receive praise from others is suppressed. "The danger of seeking approval from the social other is that you will get it, and thereafter you will be hooked on that approval. It will literally give you to be who you are and what you will become. You will act out of the pattern of desire which the social other gives you" (Alison, *Jesus the Forgiving Victim*, 408-409). Jesus notices and understands the urge to be fawned over by peers, but also warns us that our addiction to praise from anyone other than God causes us to do harm to ourselves.

We see this dynamic manifest in politics. I watched a news segment recently in which reporters interviewed a longtime politician. They showed clips of him saying contrary things about policy—sometimes within days of each other. I thought, "This man doesn't even know what he really thinks about anything anymore. He only knows how to play the game." We lose *ourselves* when we turn our faces toward public approval. Prayer is meant to shape the way we conduct ourselves, and if we seek approval from others for how frequently or fervently that we pray, we train ourselves to thrive on that admiration— rather than allow our hearts to be molded in such a way that helps us buck against the approval of the crowd when the Holy Spirit leads.

The Rev. Mihee Kim-Kort says, "Spirituality does not have to do simply with quiet or passive meditation in a dark room, though it often can begin here. Rather, it calls for brave and courageous engagement of life" (71). The shaping of our desire translates not into others' approval, but into loving, justice-centered hearts. Kim-Kort talks about how a

Spirit-infused heart often begins in private, but that we must also look for the Spirit in others and within our communities in order to better understand both ourselves and the work of the Advocate. This takes discernment. She writes that the new creation is born "with the pieces of our lives connecting in beautiful and surprising ways" (78).

We practice prayer to become more like God, imitating the desires of the *Source,* the *Wellspring,* and the *Living Water.* We allow the river of the Holy Spirit to slowly erode our ego, so that we become increasingly filled with love for more than just ourselves. Then that love compels us to work toward the liberation, justice and well-being of the world around us.

Resist rivalrous desires

The process of imitating the Trinitarian God means that we learn to resist imitating rivalrous desires. In fact, resisting rivalry is a hallmark of our "theology of resistance." Before his crucifixion, Jesus told his disciples that he would soon go to Jerusalem, suffer at the hands of those in power, be killed, and then "on the third day be raised to life." Peter pulled him aside and said, "Never, Lord! This shall never happen to you!" Jesus said to Peter, "Get behind me, Satan! You are a stumbling block to me; you do not have in mind the things of God, but merely human concerns" (Mt. 16:21-23).

We see Jesus resist being affected by Peter's desire—a very real temptation. Jesus was fully *human* (as well as fully divine), so his temptations and biological instincts to mirror the desires of those around him—as opposed to the desires of the Father—acted the same way they do for the rest of us. Jesus's strong response to his friend indicates how much he *wanted* to take on Peter's desire, even though he knew his imitation would be misdirected.

The temptations of Jesus in the desert offer another look at how the accuser tried to get Jesus to reroute his desires.

When I was in the midst of coming out publicly (and with all that ensued), a friend came by my office at the church and reminded me of a text from the Gospel of Luke, in which Jesus spends 40 days in the wilderness before starting his public ministry (Lk. 4:1-13).

After reminding me of the passage, he said this to me: "First, don't try to create your own strength. You'll be tempted, like Jesus in the wilderness, to try and make bread out of stones, but you can't. The only bread you need is the bread of life: Jesus. He is all the strength you'll need, because you won't be able to find enough of your own strength to do this without him. Talk to him about what you need and ask him to provide for you. He is your sustenance.

"Second, don't play political power games. Remember, Satan told Jesus that if he'd bow down then all the kingdoms of Earth could be his, without having to walk the road of suffering Jesus would *need* to walk to achieve that same end without selling his soul. Our power on this earth does not rely on power games; power in the kingdom of God is upside down— it works by laying down power. We lay down our power to control situations and people (who can't be controlled—many of us have surely tried!) and instead wholly trust in the person of Jesus. He has the ability to walk with us through the suffering that leads to life. He brings life out of death and he knows suffering. Don't play power games—follow Jesus.

"And third, don't look to dramatic acts that prove God's on your side. You don't need that. You don't need to throw yourself off a building to prove that angels will catch you. Rest in the knowledge that God is good, God is here, and God wants what's best for you. Be like a child resting in the arms of your dad, because that's the safest place and it's the place from which you will operate with the most spiritual authority. Rest in God and lean in to his person."

Trust God.

It's all you have.

It's your best way forward.

He's either real or he's not. This works or it doesn't.

And I thought: *All of my discipleship, all of my serving throughout my life, all my ministry leading, my pastoring, all of my Scripture study, all of my overseas ministry work—it all boiled down to whether or not I'd learned to trust God when I most needed her. Did I know and trust Jesus enough to model his desires, as opposed to the many fluctuating, dehumanizing, self-serving, and chaotic desires swirling in people around me? As Jesus was tested in the wilderness, so we will be tested by God to see how much he can trust us with authority and influence.*

How do we learn to trust Jesus? We practice. And, even when you've found that you can trust God in most circumstances, you still need to practice. *I* still need to practice. This is part of our lifelong work.

Resisting rivalry is a long-term strategy

The counterintuitive aspect of our Gospel message is that imitating Jesus will not lead to peace and unity in the short-term. Jesus said:

> *Do not suppose that I have come to bring peace to the earth. I did not come to bring peace, but a sword. For I have come to turn*
>
> *a man against his father,*
>   *a daughter against her mother,*
> *a daughter-in-law against her mother-in-law—*
>   *a man's enemies will be the members of his own household.*

Anyone who loves their father or mother more than me is not worthy of me; anyone who loves their son or daughter more than me is not worthy of me. Whoever does not take up their cross and follow me is not worthy of me. Whoever finds their life will lose it, and whoever loses their life for my sake will find it. (Mt. 10:34-39)

This passage used to baffle me. Jesus is the Prince of Peace and we are called to be ambassadors of peace, reconciling the world to God (2 Co. 5). But in the short-term, standing against the mob will not bring peace, and Jesus knows that.

Unmasking the scapegoat mechanism robs the crowd of its harmonious feeling. Remember: It is unifying to have a scapegoat. It is *not* unifying when the scapegoat is revealed for what it is: *a false peace at the expense of the vulnerable.*

In light of Girard, the apocalyptic books and passages in the Bible make sense. Girard says that the apocalyptic literature, like John's *Revelation*, remains crucial to the larger scriptural narrative. Apocalypse means "revealing," or "unveiling." When we reveal and unveil the violent mechanism of scapegoating, divisions previously hidden become exposed. If enough witnesses talk about what Jesus has done in declaring the scapegoating system unjust, God's justice will, eventually, reign. *But apocalyptic-scale conflict will come first, because we remove the false sense of peace.*

We live in an age when the stories of the oppressed are being told and sizable numbers of people speak out against scapegoating. Think of the backlash that Donald Trump's Muslim travel ban stirred up. Or of the reactions of many Americans to the news that our government separated immigrant children from their parents. More and more people stand with victims and potential scapegoats than ever before in history, and that creates social anxiety.

Amnesty International didn't exist until 60 years ago, and human rights are a relatively new concept in human history.

In just the last few decades, academia has become interested in the voices of the marginalized. We now have African-American history classes, women's histories, First Nations' histories and postcolonial histories. We build museums, helping us remember events such as the Holocaust; memorials, reminding us of the lynchings of African-Americans in the South, at the turn of the 20th century; and, most recently, an African-American history museum at the Smithsonian, allowing us to collectively remember how white Americans enslaved and abused fellow humans. We've started listening to and remembering the voices of the oppressed, humanizing history's scapegoats. These are signs of the kingdom of God, and the work does, eventually, lead to peace. However, the ensuing social strain is what we call *apocalypse*, and it will probably get worse before it gets better. When people speak up for and protect victims, dissension and disunity erupt.

Any resulting violence will not be of God, but will be of our own making—just as the cross was a violence of our own making. "It will be the result of an escalation to extremes, provoked by the mimetic mirroring of rivals no longer capable of resolving disputes at the expense of sacrificed scapegoats. In a world where nobody can be sacrificed for the sake of the general good, the general good will destroy itself unless it can find an alternate way to resolve rivalries" (Warren, 298).

Come, Lord Jesus.

Some division is inevitable in the short-term

Division within groups is not necessarily a sign of poor leadership, even within churches and other faith organizations. Some might object: "But, the unity of the Holy Spirit! Our call is to guard the unity! We must bear with one another!" Yes, the apostle Paul calls us to keep the unity of the Spirit in the letter to the Ephesians, but we so often misunderstand his meaning.

Make every effort to keep the unity of the Spirit through the bond of peace. There is one body and one Spirit, just as you were called to one hope when you were called; one Lord, one faith, one baptism; one God and Father of all, who is over all and through all and in all. (Eph. 4:3-6)

The unity of the Holy Spirit is a unity that holds diversity without making anyone a second-class citizen. Paul calls us to protect the table of fellowship, reminding us that we share the same Lord, faith and baptism. Baptism is the great equalizer. Prior to baptism being the physical symbol of membership to God's family, circumcision carried that distinction—though it was available only to men. Baptism, both water baptism and the baptism of the Holy Spirit, opened the doors to belonging on equal terms and to every living person. Paul iterates that we have one God who is over all, through all, and *in* all. Everyone bears the image of God, none more than anyone else.

Any table where one group receives less respect and dignity falls short of God's table. There is no unity without justice. People of color in the United States would not feel they were in unity with the majority culture if white people said, "You can sit at the table, but only white people can serve the food because you make some of us uncomfortable." There must be justice for true unity to exist. Otherwise, we pretend there is unity while, in reality, resentment abounds.

My experience is that most people understand Paul to say we should maintain peace for the majority at the expense of the minority. When the topic is full LGBTQ+ inclusion in the church, some leaders call for inclusion not to happen "too fast," on the basis that it disrupts church unity. Churches will fall apart! We need to honor the traditionalists!

Every person or group seeking justice faces the command to slow down. When writing from his jail cell in Birmingham (to white pastors giving him pushback for his nonviolent tactics), the Rev. Martin Luther King Jr. said, "We know through painful experience that freedom is never voluntarily given by the oppressor; it must be demanded by the oppressed. Frankly, I have yet to engage in a direct action campaign that was 'well timed' in the view of those who have not suffered unduly from the disease of segregation. For years now I have heard the word 'Wait!' It rings in the ear of every Negro with piercing familiarity. This 'Wait' has almost always meant 'Never.' We must come to see, with one of our distinguished jurists, that 'justice too long delayed is justice denied'" (King, *Letter from Birmingham Jail*).

I do not see my pastoral role as gathering a group of people and doing everything in my power to keep those same people together forever, because doing so most often takes place at the expense of the most vulnerable in the group. My job is to protect everyone's God-given gift to sit with everyone else in equal fellowship, and if some people at the table do not want certain groups to serve them, lead them, share the same silverware or cut the turkey, then (to be blunt) they have agency to leave the table. We are welcome at God's table so long as we welcome others.

Everyone is still welcome at any time they choose to return—relinquishing their entitlement to make the rules—but they cannot exclude or place special burdens on others based on their own judgments. Jesus is the only judge. "Who are you to judge someone else's servant? To their own master, servants stand or fall. And they will stand, for the Lord is able to make them stand" (Ro. 14:4). The call of Jesus beckons us, in the name of the Gospel, to practice the lavish love and grace of God that seems inordinately good and excessively easy.[155] All are welcome so long as we, in turn, welcome all.

---

155 In *Disunity In Christ: Uncovering the Hidden Forces that Keep Us Apart*, Christena Cleveland fleshes out the concept *of perspective divergence*: "When we adopt a group identity and surround ourselves with similar in-group members, we essentially create our own alternate universe in which we believe that the standards, ideals, and goals of our in-group should become the "new normal"—not only for our specific group but for the entire larger group, including the out-group. Since we think that our way of doing things is the most normal, we interact with others while thinking that our alternate universal laws and way of life are the gold standard for the larger group.

Protecting this understanding of unity produces conflict. King went on to say in *Letter from Birmingham Jail*, " … I must confess that I am not afraid of the word 'tension.' I have earnestly opposed violent tension, but there is a type of constructive, nonviolent tension which is necessary for growth." People will demand table rules and ask that women, people of color, divorcees, single mothers, LGBTQ+ people, immigrants or the scapegoat of the day be relegated to a side table. When we insist on *unity based on justice*—a unity created by sitting at the same table and with the same rules—it is as if a sword has been brought down, and sons fight against their fathers and daughters quarrel with their mothers. Many of us know that dynamic both literally and figuratively. When the sword appears, our instinct is to find a scapegoat to avoid the in-group fighting. Telling a less powerful person that they must have limits at the table "for the sake of the group" is less demanding than bearing the stress of fighting with family and friends in demanding equal treatment for all. *We regard those with less power as expendable in order to protect our comfort and our ability to continue making the rules.*

Loving our neighbors *as ourselves* is the narrow road. Let's hope more than a few find it.

Forgiveness vs. reconciliation: lessons from South Africa

It fascinates me that, after his resurrection, we have no account of Jesus appearing to people who could cause him further harm. He revealed himself to those who were contrite, who mourned their part in his death, and who learned from it. He *forgave* those who repented as well as those who did not, but he *reconciled* with the former while inviting the latter to take steps to be reconciled to God.

Essentially, we believe that we are the model citizens of the larger group and that other subgroups can only hope to be as relevant and valuable as we are. This particular attitude powerfully widens the divide between groups in the body of Christ because each group believes that they're better members of the body of Christ than individuals in other groups." (70-71)

There is a difference between forgiveness and reconciliation. Forgiveness of others is expected of all Jesus followers; reconciliation, however, can remain elusive even while we hope and pray for it. To better understand the distinction, let's look at both concepts.

As disciples of Jesus we forgive (*pardon, don't seek vengeance toward*) those who harm us for two reasons: First, because we are forgiven by God, and we imitate our rabbi, Jesus, in pardoning others (Eph. 4:32, Col. 3:13); and second, because it releases us from their power over us.

When we cannot forgive, we continue to be harmed by our perpetrators in very real physical and emotional ways. Desmond Tutu writes in a powerful book, cowritten with his daughter Mpho:

> *Without forgiveness, we remain tethered to the person who harmed us. We are bound with chains of bitterness, tied together, trapped. Until we can forgive the person who harmed us, that person will hold the keys to our happiness; that person will be our jailor. When we forgive, we take back control of our own fate and our feelings. We become our own liberators. We don't forgive to help the other person. We don't forgive for others. We forgive for ourselves. Forgiveness, in other words, is the best form of self-interest. This is true both spiritually and scientifically. (Tutu, 16)*

Unconditional forgiveness shifts power back to the victim. The abused controls forgiveness; it is not contingent on anything the perpetrator says or does.

Jesus prayed, "Father, forgive them, they know not what they do," even while he hung on a Roman cross, showing us the importance of forgiving others even if they embrace their own innocence. God gives us this wisdom for our benefit—to free us from power used against us, even if the process takes months or years. Forgiveness, especially for deep trauma, takes time.

If we have been harmed or scapegoated, it is our responsibility to forgive as Jesus forgave those who hurt him. Additionally, the scapegoat is to renounce any instinct to retaliate in order to surrender continuing the cycle of violence. God put a mark on Cain's head to limit its vicious cycle. Jesus calls us to love our enemies and do good to those who hate us, with the same intent (Lk. 6:27).

Loving our enemies, however, does not mean discarding healthy boundaries.

Forgiveness is not reconciliation, and reconciliation happens under specific conditions: It can only be accomplished when the ones who participate in the scapegoating mob (or the ones who sin against us) name and take responsibility for their sins. That is what Archbishop Desmond Tutu discovered when he ran the Truth and Reconciliation Commission in South Africa after apartheid.

Those who harmed others during the years of apartheid sat with the people they abused, named their crimes, asked for forgiveness, and made any reparations needed for forgiveness to take place. Perpetrators took personal responsibility for their role in others' suffering and owned their offenses. If Person A killed Person B's sister, then Person A needed to name their specific crime to Person B's family, be accountable for that action, and ask for forgiveness.

For example, if you were a victim and a perpetrator stole your car (and still had it), then you might ask them to return the car or buy you a new one. If a person killed your family member, you might ask them to set up a scholarship fund in your loved one's name—whatever it is that could help ease the pain of the wrongdoing. After forgiveness is granted, those harmed could *then* decide whether they could renew the relationship with the person who mistreated their family or release the relationship. Both options were valid.

Reconciliation requires making amends

It is not always beneficial for a victim to be reconciled to an oppressor if they have been abused. For example, a battered woman should not reconcile with her abuser. Forgive, yes; reconcile, no. Additionally, it might not be healthy for a battered woman to reconcile with the people who watched her abuse but did nothing to stop it. As Korean-American theologian Grace Ji-Sun Kim writes, "… the work of reconciliation begins with our wounds, which affect the deepest areas of our hearts" (150). Trauma must be addressed and tended with compassion and justice before reconciliation is possible.

In race relations in America, there will be no real reconciliation unless white people collectively say, "We have participated in—and benefited from—racist systems. We are sorry, and we will do our best to learn and repent. Please forgive us and allow us to return, in whatever ways we can, what we took from you."[156] African-Americans repeatedly share and discuss both the pain inflicted on them and their distrust that American institutions either can or will work for justice on their behalf. With every unarmed black person killed by police, the wounds fester. Black people say, time and again, that reforming the justice system and having reparations paid to the descendants of slaves will help heal the many injuries inflicted on them, as a people. Both of these requests are doable if we do the heart work necessary to recognize the need to move forward quickly and assertively. Why would we not support and pursue these options? It is the only way to move forward, toward healing our racial divide.

It should always be the job of the oppressors, and not the oppressed, to name their sin and repent. If the victim names the sin against them and the oppressor refuses to acknowledge it, the dismissiveness re-injures the victim by invalidating

---

156 We could make reparations the same way the U.S. government paid money to those confined in Japanese internment camps during World War II, or the way the German government paid reparations to Holocaust survivors.

them.[157] This is tricky, though, because the mob will, most often, not own the harm caused by group participants because their sin is not even recognized. They know not what they do.

A few months ago, I ran into someone who treated me terribly during my public outing and firing from my former denomination. I saw them at the entrance to a public space, and they said, "Hey, Emily! How are you? Good to see you." I walked on, ignoring them, but on my way out of the building, they tried again to communicate again: "Don't you remember me, Emily? From church? I'm trying to say hi." I walked out to my car, shaking. Then I walked back in and said to this man, "You advocated policies requiring my termination because I'm gay. You were horrible to me, your wife was horrible to me, and I don't consider us friends." He then looked baffled (a.k.a. refused to recognize and own his scapegoating).

Perhaps that conversation sounds harsh. I feel pressure, especially as a pastor, to smooth things over and help others move forward. But that does not help my Gospel witness as I understand it. Making things "seem OK" communicates that what happened to the scapegoat(s) was justified. It *needed to happen*, and it *probably didn't affect me much*. "We're cool," is what people desperately want to hear. If I convey that message, it becomes easier for scapegoating to take place again, because it seems there was no real harm done in the process. But harm was done; the incident did affect me, greatly. I'm human. It affected others, too. It is neither honest nor healthy for me to pretend to be friends with people who hurt me.

Desmond Tutu said:

> *Forgiving and being reconciled to our enemies or*
> *our loved ones is not about pretending that things*
> *are other than they are. It is not about patting one*

---

157 It strikes me that, in race relations in particular, this is not cut-and-dry, because some white people recognize their blindness and so are attentive to listening and learning, while others continue to invalidate (or unknowingly, we do both). So it seems that people of color have to weigh the cost and benefits of naming sins against them—another burden. The same could be said for sins against women, queer people or any other minority.

another on the back and turning a blind eye to the wrong. True reconciliation exposes the awfulness, the abuse, the pain, the hurt, the truth. It could even sometimes make things worse. It is a risky undertaking, but in the end it is worthwhile, because in the end only an honest confrontation with reality can bring real healing. Superficial reconciliation can bring only superficial healing. (qtd. in Keltner, 258)

We must honestly name the harm done—otherwise, myths get created that justify the violence, which lends credence to future rationalizations for violence. As author Zora Neale Hurston aptly said, "If you are silent about your pain, they'll kill you and say you enjoyed it."

If you want to understand why LGBTQ+ people fly rainbow flags, and why Black Lives Matter proponents insist their message not become diluted; why First Nations people camp for months, resisting continued colonial aggression against their traditional lands; or why intersectional support exists between many minority groups; it is because those who know oppression also understand that, to prevent further violence against them, they must speak. *They must let others know they hurt.* They must prevent the myth-making process. Otherwise, aggression against them continues; the people ignoring their message would rather believe minority groups are fine, because then nothing has to change. If you speak loudly enough, though, others have to at least hear your voice, crying out, and make a deliberate effort to dismiss it.

In *Between the World and Me*, Ta-Nehisi Coates urges his son to push back against narratives that would have him accept the status quo.

Never forget that we were enslaved in this country longer than we have been free. Never forget that for 250 years black people were born into chains— whole generations followed by more generations who knew nothing but chains. You must struggle to truly remember this past in all its nuance, error, and humanity. You must resist the common urge toward the comforting narrative of divine law, toward fairy tales that imply some irrepressible justice. The enslaved were not bricks in your road, and their lives were not chapters in your redemptive history. There were people turned to fuel for the American machine. **Enslavement was not destined to end, and it is wrong to claim our present circumstance—no matter how improved—as the redemption for the lives of people who never asked for the posthumous, untouchable glory of dying for their children.** *(Coates, 70, emphasis mine)*

Resisting the myths telling us that violence, submission, and oppression will eventually wrangle themselves free from our collective systems—without the diligent work of remembering, naming, owning, forgiving, and reconciling—is part of the work of Jesus's followers. This is no small task, but I believe that Christianity offers tools we can use to go about it.

Be reconciled to God: repent of scapegoating

My experiences as a public scapegoat opened my eyes to how Jesus and the New Testament writers talk about our relationship with God. I addressed reconciliation between humans and other humans above, but the Bible also speaks of reconciliation between humans and God. The Scriptures reveal that we are all part of the mob that turns on scapegoats. To be reconciled to the divine, we have to confess our sins; we must admit how we hurt both others and God.

Sometimes, those sins against others are specific and personal; sometimes they are systemic. I, Emily Swan, have perpetuated sexism, homophobia, racism and classism because oppression is intertwined with our culture. We swim in injustice. Being an American who buys food and clothing, I surely purchase goods from companies utilizing slave labor or underpaid immigrants. None of us gets to be completely innocent; we all are guilty, even if not equally guilty.

Our human tendency is to dodge feelings of guilt. We want them to go away, but we have to take responsibility for the oppressive systems that have been handed down to us. If we do so, and become aware of how they get passed along, we can be a part of bringing justice and peace to this world by opposing those structures. Guilt is not a bad feeling; shame is detrimental, but guilt leads us to change (B. Brown, 71-74).

It strikes me that Jesus *chose* to keep his scars and not pretend like the crucifixion and all that came before it did not happen. It's written on his body; the horror took place. His scars forced the disciples to come to terms with the story for what it was—not for what it was glossed over to look like. He became wholly human to embody the fullness of identifying with those who suffer. As a human, he experienced trauma of the worst sort. He forgave us for rejecting him, torturing him and crucifying him, but we cannot be reconciled until we confess our sin.

When we confess that we, too, are part of the mob that turned against Jesus (who represents all victims, everywhere), and we repent of scapegoating and of projecting our own sins onto others—of not loving God and our neighbors and our natural world like we could—we find that God is faithful and just and not only forgives us, but *wants* to renew our relationship and be reconciled with us. And then we are invited to go and summon others into this project of healing, to bring about the reign of God on earth.

And this, then, is grace. That we all participate in the violence and rivalry of this world, and yet our sin is declared null and void by a God whose table is open. At that table we practice extending to others the same grace and forgiveness shown to us.

Sometimes I operate in a highly prophetic mode, calling people to an ideal. And I can be—I think rightly, given my gifts—*blunt* with those doing harm to others, just as Jesus reserved his harshest words for those condemning the vulnerable. But my wife reminds me not to forget grace, because without grace, none of us experiences the life-giving community of fellowship. A place for every single person exists at the banquet feast of the slain Lamb, with room for more. Some will choose not to come—whether because they are not interested in the project, or because they want to insist on their own table rules being practiced, or they do not want to sit on equal terms with those they view as "unclean." Those more likely to edge up to the dining area are the social outcasts, as the parable of the great banquet suggests (Lk. 14:15-24). But that doesn't change the fact that the table is indeed open to all people, on equal terms. We are invited into a project where we celebrate love, peace and justice. Protecting that endeavor can be costly, but also worth selling everything to pursue.

Jesus emblematically cried out, "Father, forgive them, they know not what they do," mustering all the energy he could as he hung on that Roman cross, directing us to forgive others in the same way we receive forgiveness from God. Jesus unconditionally forgave the mob because he knew that they remained blind to their own actions and sin. I, also, am required, as a follower of Jesus, to forgive those who remain ignorant of their desire to sacrifice others in the same way I have been forgiven by Jesus for my ignorance. This, too, is grace.

A lens for peering more deeply into the Gospel

The work of René Girard remains a gift in my life as I continue learning from his writings and the work of scholars expanding on his breakthrough insights. I feel as though I have stumbled upon a profoundly deeper revelation of grace, love and inclusion in the body of Christ, while also encountering the high cost of discipleship described by Bonhoeffer. Belonging to and with Jesus is delightfully effortless and uncomplicated, but following his path of standing with the scapegoats and seeking the same justice for the vulnerable that God showed to his scapegoated son exposes us to suffering and sacrifice. Grace is unearned, but costly.

These days, I find myself weeping when I prepare to share the Gospel message. The standard evangelical Gospel I inherited claimed radical welcome, but in fact, there was no room at the inn for out-group members. There was no room for me. The signs of this Gospel read "Vacancy: Rooms Available," but the fine print requires me to dismantle my own emotions and humanity. What the Gospel of evangelicalism gave with one hand, it took away with the other. It was a Gospel riddled with rivalry toward others, and embracing it put me at rivalry with myself. The effect was not life-giving, but exhausting. At times, I wondered why I bothered at all. The only thing that kept me going was the unrelenting experience of Jesus, with whom I felt not a trace of rivalry—an experience that tasted more authentic than my experience within the evangelical faith-frame.

This Jesus saved me. He helped me accept myself, despite being immersed in a powerful religious culture that regarded my deepest desires as disordered. He freed me from the expectations of others. He comforted me in my anguish, walked with me when I became a scapegoat and vindicated me by his constant reassurance. As I have discovered others who share a similar experience, I am energized to participate in fleshing out this deeper understanding of the Gospel—one that can be self-evidently, and not by assertion alone—good news.

10

Scapegoaters Anonymous: Our Stony Silence

Ken

IT'S TIME TO tell more of my story as it intersects with Emily's. Emily met Rachel in 2014—an epic year in my personal life, as well. As I shared in Chapter 3, my wife had died suddenly and unexpectedly two years earlier. It had happened on the very Sunday I preached the key sermon in our process to reverse years of discrimination against LGBTQ+ people in the evangelical church I founded. Nancy's death launched a whirlwind of change for me.

In 2013, I presented a paper at the Society of Vineyard Scholars that advocated a path for the full inclusion of sexual minorities. It was met with stony silence—not a good sign. I quickly became a controversialist within my denomination and knew that things could get ugly. Partly in response to my increasing isolation, I called Julia Huttar Bailey, the clergy friend of a clergy friend, to see if we could meet for coffee. Julia was an Episcopal priest and a widow. I needed a friend outside my own religious circle, one that understood loss and the challenges of pastoring. We fell in love, and like many

older couples who have lost spouses, we both knew that life
was short—*time's a-wastin', you only have today*—so in the
summer of 2014, we got married. After the honeymoon, Emily
invited me into her office for a chat.

"Ken, I met a wonderful woman named Rachel and I'm in
love with her." As if I didn't know by looking at Emily's face. I
knew that feeling of new love dawning after a dark night of
the soul. Without a moment to reflect, I burst into tears—not
my typical response.

Emotion is often mixed and multi-layered. I knew this
development would heighten tensions in our church, bringing
the change process we had undertaken to a head. It's one
thing to walk up to a line—another to cross it. But I had been
walking up to this line for many years. And those tears spoke a
truth I couldn't deny, because they were tears of joy for Emily.
Joy, unbridled by fear. But they were also tears of relief. Of
course, I knew things could get complicated. But I also knew
that if it were not for the concerted work of the Holy Spirit
on—in spite of, but also in—me, I might have responded differently than I did in that moment. I might have let fear hold
sway. I had felt its oppressive power, keeping me in line with
the faulty judgment of the crowd—religion at its worst. I knew
its bullying grip on the heart. In that emotional release to
Emily's news, I understood that all the hard work I had done
in response to the Spirit was in preparation *for this moment*—
so when Emily said, "Ken, I met a wonderful woman named
Rachel and I'm in love with her," I could respond with tears
of joy. I hadn't blown it, as a younger version of myself most
certainly would have.

Let me take you to an experience of that younger version
of myself, some 10 years earlier. In retrospect, it was key to
my willingness to rethink the received tradition of the Church
regarding its LGBTQ+ members. I was praying early one
morning in my office at church.

"What's happening?" *The part of my brain that observes
wanted to know. Because what started as an experiment in*

praying the Jesus Prayer[158] *was morphing into something that had never happened before. I felt the center of my thinking-feeling self descend from my mind into my chest, as one might be lowered down an elevator shaft, slowly. I let it unfold and found myself in what looked like a cave, sitting near a fire, with Jesus on my left.*

His right arm was around my shoulders and I felt from him a sympathetic awareness of my humble estate as a sinner. As though he knew how miserable it can be, sometimes, to be a sinner. I felt no guilt or shame. I was only aware of what he seemed to be feeling, and it was pure sympathy without a trace of judgment. As if to say: "I know."

And so we sat there together, he and I, looking into the fire. My observing self became excited, not wanting this to end. So I began to simply mention, by name, my loved ones, knowing that he would stay there, listening: Nancy, Jesse, Maja, Amy, Judy, Grace … Marilyn and her husband, Nick, Nancy and her husband, David, and their sons (my nephews) Danny and Kevin. The sisters of my wife, Nancy, and their children. Loved ones who had died: my mother, my father, Nancy's parents. My mother's brother George. Then, to keep this going, my coworkers at church, including Don and his wife, Julie, and Julie's sister (whose name I couldn't remember at the time). That's when he spoke for the first time—quietly, as one might around a fire: "And another one's on the way."

My observing-self thought was, "That's a data point!" *Julie's sister had one child, but I didn't know about a second.* "I need to check that out when this is over." *When I saw Don later that day, I asked if Julie's sister, by any chance, was pregnant. He acted surprised:* "How would you know that? We just found out ourselves!" *I couldn't explain, but this connection to the real world meant it was hard to dismiss the experience in prayer as a mere figment of my imagination.*

---

158 A repetitive use of the prayer, "Lord Jesus Christ, son of the living God, have mercy on me, a sinner" practiced especially within Eastern Orthodoxy.

It has taken years to absorb the original impact of that morning's praying—years of reflection, engagement with Scripture, study and consultation with friends, colleagues, scholars, a spiritual director and a therapist.

What I didn't know at the time is that that morning's praying was as much about leaving one form of closeness behind as it was about enjoying the closeness with Jesus that I felt beside that campfire.

Peter, founding member of *Scapegoaters Anonymous*

The Gospel of John tells the story of Peter around two very different campfires. It is the story of Peter, as one of the founding members of *Scapegoaters Anonymous*. The first is in the courtyard of the high priest during the interrogation of Jesus; around this campfire, Peter aligns himself with the scapegoating mob. The other is on the shore of a lake, where the risen Jesus prepares a meal for his friends, including the one who denied him.[159]

At the time, Israel was in a state of intense rivalry and escalating violence. The nation was not just in rivalry with the Roman occupation force, but also wracked with fierce internal rivalries. (Communities under intense stress of any kind are vulnerable to turning on each other.)

These intensifying conflicts were triggering the scapegoat mechanism. Israel's ruling council was understandably anxious. They were managing a delicate political situation and were concerned, as good leaders ought to be, for the safety of their fragile community. They met to consider how to handle this latest destabilizing messianic movement. Caiaphas addressed the assembly, frustrated by their inability to face the hard reality of their situation: "You know nothing at all! Don't you realize it's better for one man to suffer, than for the whole nation to perish?" (Jn. 11:49-50). He was saying, in effect, "Messianic uprisings aren't good for anyone. The Romans will

---

159 I am indebted to Girard's discussion of Peter and scapegoating (Girard, *The Scapegoat*, 149-164).

crush this one and it won't be good for our people. We don't have the luxury of debating the finer points of this Messiah's claims when national interest—perhaps our very survival as a people—is at stake." Leaders face tough choices between bad options and sometimes have to choose what they judge to be the lesser of evils.

Leaders often *go along* with what amounts to scapegoating for what seems a noble reason: to preserve the institutions they lead. When I disclosed my changing views about LGBTQ+ to my evangelical pastor colleagues, some confessed sympathy—especially those who had gay children, siblings or parents. When it was clear that Vineyard would not tolerate my dissent, one prominent Vineyard pastor told me, "I'm afraid we're on the wrong side of history with this one." Likewise, a well-known theologian told me he agreed with my thesis—thought there ought to be room for it in the Church— then added, "Of course, this is not my issue." I knew not to expect public support from him. I can only imagine these leaders didn't want to subject themselves or their communities to the inevitable conflict that might ensue if they were to be more candid about their personal views. I understood the dilemma. The harmony of the many compared to the distress of the few is a compelling justification for the status quo. There is logic to the scapegoat mechanism that holds powerful sway as we make our moral choices. These choices are easier to make when the suffering of sexual minorities is at least partially hidden, their voices muted and their place at the power table denied.

Add this factor: Our personal security, our sense of safety in a hostile world, is bound to the acceptance of our communities. We are very careful not to threaten this.

In John 18, we find Peter and another disciple tagging along behind Jesus after he is arrested. In the clear light of history, Jesus is the innocent victim thought to be guilty, in the process of being scapegoated. In the moment, however—amid the swirl of competing and befuddling forces—this stark reality may have been obscured. We make choices that we later regret, if we pause long enough to reflect on them. As did Peter.

> *The soldiers, their officer and the Jewish police arrested Jesus and bound him. First, they took him to Annas, who was the father-in-law of Caiaphas, the high priest that year. Caiaphas was the one who had advised the Jewish leaders that it was better to have one person die for the people. Simon Peter and another disciple followed Jesus. Since the high priest knew that disciple, he went with Jesus into the courtyard of the high priest, but Peter was standing outside at the gate. So the other disciple, who was known to the high priest, went out, spoke to the woman who guarded the gate, and brought Peter in. The woman said to Peter, "You are not also one of this man's disciples, are you?" He said, "I am not." Now the slaves and the police had made a charcoal fire because it was cold, and they were standing around it and warming themselves. Peter also was standing with them and warming himself. (Jn. 18:12-18)*

Peter and the "other disciple" (probably John) are following Jesus, intending to support him. They love him. They don't think he is guilty of any crimes, though they may sharply disagree with his choices. Peter is frightened, cold and tired. He's doing a brave thing by getting this close to the authorities who arrested Jesus. Could we imagine that he feels betrayed by Jesus for putting him in this dangerous position—resentful that Jesus didn't listen to his objections to this course of action? Is it so inconceivable that, standing around the fire to warm himself, he denies even knowing Jesus?

In order for a community to transfer its internal conflicts to a scapegoated person or group, it needs a small faction accusing an individual or group as the source of the community's ills. But the community also needs many more people to go along with the accusers—either by remaining silent or by distancing themselves from the scapegoated individual or group. The mechanism for the acquiescence-of-the-many is the power of mimetic desire—often at work unconsciously, spreading like a contagion through the group.

In other words, Peter's denial is entirely predictable and understandable. We should not be surprised to find ourselves mirroring his actions when our own sense of security, within the communities that we depend on for safety, is at stake.

We get swept along, too

Why was it so hard for me to change my mind about LGBTQ+ people? Why did it take me 10 years of excruciating internal wrestling—listening, reading, thinking, questioning, talking, worrying, praying—to change my mind? Looking back, 10 minutes should have been enough. It took 10 years because I was embedded in a community that made stigma-tizing sexual minorities a loyalty litmus test. As one national leader told me when I disclosed my changing views, "If you land where I think you're landing, its outside the circle." For better and for worse, our communities corral us, even as we maintain an illusion of our independent-mindedness.

The fire surrounded by people warming themselves is a picture of community. It represents our basic need for the acceptance and approval of the crowd. When the community we depend on turns against an innocent victim, it becomes a majority-mob, doing what communities do to maintain internal cohesion. The power of the group's collective (and imitative) desire intoxicates us, hypnotizes us and pulls us along. The desire of the crowd becomes our desire—all the more difficult to resist, for being a largely unconscious mechanism.

I grew up in racially segregated Detroit during the 1950s and '60s. Compared to my white friends and neighbors, I was racially enlightened. My dad, raised in lily-white Dearborn, supported the civil rights movement. I once came home from first grade using the N-word and my mother sharply rebuked me. But I grew up surrounded by people who told jokes about the "Japs, WOPS, Krauts, Spics and Coloreds"—it was everywhere.

My first father-in-law told racist jokes, like so many people in that time. I did not have an auspicious beginning with my in-laws—married at 18 for the usual reason—and so I did not want to further rock the boat.

When my father-in-law told one of his jokes, what was I supposed to do? Say, "Dad, I do not want to hear those jokes"? Actually, yes, that's exactly what I was supposed to do. But I was afraid to spend my already-depleted equity in that way. So, I deflected at times. I pretended not to hear at times. There were probably times when I faked a chuckle, with my mother's voice ringing in my ears, "We do not use that word in this house!" Eventually my wife and I got up the gumption to object. And to his credit, my father-in-law realized the error of his ways and changed. But for too long we went along.

Why did I violate my own values and upbringing like that? Because I was like Peter—let into the courtyard, frightened, insecure and warming himself by the fire. We are wired to seek the approval and acceptance of a circle gathered around the fire, and sometimes we'll do anything to get it. If that means being silent, we'll be silent. If it means distancing ourselves from the scapegoats, we'll do it—especially if we are cold, tired and frightened enough.

Conversion requires leaving the mob

Have you ever found yourself laughing in a group and someone whispers in your ear, "I didn't hear that. What was so funny?" and you realize you didn't hear, either—and you're just laughing because everyone else is laughing? It's awkward. You don't want to admit that you are ignorantly following the group. We unconsciously and automatically imitate others (something we hate to admit), and things spread through groups by means of this powerful—but often unacknowledged—process.

Researchers have long been aware of the tendency of bystanders to respond passively in the face of group violence. The larger the group attacking a victim, the more violent the attack is likely to be—an effect seen especially in lynchings. When there are multiple bystanders to any emergency (a person passed out on the street, for example), the sense of responsibility to act is diffused and people are likely to be more passive. And when the victim looks different than the bystanders (for example, a black victim in the presence of white onlookers), bystanders are even less likely to intervene (Marsh, Keltner).

If Peter, who left his fishing business and family to follow Jesus, could be affected in this way—well, welcome to the human race, because we can, too. We are the kind of people who participate in scapegoating—if only by our silence, by our standing at the edge of the crowd and pretending that what's going on is not really going on.

The prayer Jesus uttered on the cross, "Father, forgive them because they don't know what they are doing," applies to people like us. We are never more ignorant about what we are actually doing than when we are swept into the hypnotic contagion of a crowd resolving its internal tensions by scapegoating someone.

Participating in a scapegoating mob is among the worst things we humans do to one another and, by extension, to God, whose image we bear. This complicity, conscious or unconscious, is what empowers genocide—whether against the Jews in Nazi Germany or the indigenous peoples of the Americas at the hands of European conquerors. It's what fuels the crimes of slavery, racism, sexism, xenophobia and homophobia. It's what happens in our schools, jobsites and homes when intensifying tensions are resolved and a temporary peace is restored by the many turning on the few.

It's how we—to use the graphic language of St. Paul, who knew our tendency—"devour one another" (Gal. 5:15). Do we obsess instead over lesser sins, in ourselves and in others, to avoid facing this greater one?

The evangelical church world (buttressed by Roman Catholicism, Eastern Orthodoxy, and much of the mainline Protestant Church) is composed of a rich network of families, congregations, parishes, communities and institutions offering love and safety to many of its members. In relation to its LGBTQ+ members, evangelicalism also *functions* as a scapegoating mob. The peace, comfort, stability and financial security of these communities is maintained, in part, by policies that stigmatize sexual minorities. This means we can all be wonderful, warm, kind, generous and compassionate toward some people, but also acquiesce as our faith communities protect the interests of the many at the expense of the few—blending in with a community that is, in fact, functioning as a mob.

It's no accident, then, that the two paradigmatic conversion stories in the New Testament feature recovering scapegoaters: Go-along Peter and Ringleader Paul. Despite asserting his righteousness under the Law (Phil. 3:16), Paul referred to himself as "the worst of sinners" (1 Tim. 1:15)—the latter a reference to his role as a scapegoating instigator.

Closeness with Jesus comes at a cost: We must be willing to leave our place (as ringleader or as accomplice) in the scapegoating mob—hence, the demand to leave father, mother, brother and sister for his sake. In many cases, unless we are willing to do so, such loyalty bonds will bind us to the scapegoating mob.

Three questions around another campfire

In John 21, Jesus has been raised, but what it all means for the disciples is unclear. He appears and disappears over the course of a few weeks, delivering various messages in preparation for his new mode of connection with his followers.

Peter and six other disciples are together, feeling aimless. Peter says, "I'm going fishing," and they join him. Out all night, the accomplished fishermen catch nothing. A man calls to them from the shore: "Friends, no fish? Try casting on the right side of your boat." They do—and they haul in a massive catch. John says to Peter of the man on the shore: "It's the Lord!" Peter jumps out of the boat and swims ashore. The others follow in the boat, finding Jesus preparing a meal for them over a charcoal fire.

Jesus and Peter have their first recorded conversation after Peter's three-fold denial.

> When they had finished breakfast, Jesus said to Simon Peter, "Simon son of John, do you love me more than these?" He said to him, "Yes, Lord; you know that I love you." Jesus said to him, "Feed my lambs." A second time he said to him, "Simon son of John, do you love me?" He said to him, "Yes, Lord; you know that I love you." Jesus said to him, "Tend my sheep." He said to him the third time, "Simon son of John, do you love me?" Peter felt hurt because he said to him the third time, "Do you love me?" And he said to him, "Lord, you know everything; you know that I love you." Jesus said to him, "Feed my sheep. Very truly, I tell you, when you were younger, you used to fasten your own belt and to go wherever you wished. But when you grow old, you will stretch out your hands, and someone else will fasten a belt around you and take you where you do not wish to go." (He said this to indicate the kind of death by which he would glorify God.) After this he said to him, "Follow me" (Jn. 21:15-19).

This harkens back to the three-fold denial around that other charcoal fire in the courtyard of the high priest. Jesus was a scapegoat, and the worst pain a scapegoated person feels is not the pain of the angry accusers accusing; it's the pain of the friends standing by, saying nothing. The Rev. Martin Luther King Jr. once said, "In the end, we will remember not the words of our enemies, but the silence of our friends," (King, "Loving Your Enemies").

To renounce scapegoating, we must see the humanity of its victims, always obscured by the contagious dynamics of the mob. As an evangelical pastor, I was shielded from the suffering, and thus the vulnerable humanity, of sexual minorities. For many years, the only gay people who confided in me about their sexuality believed it was wrong and sought a way to be rid of it.

What was going on? I was subject to "sampling error." Those who accepted their sexuality and weren't trying to change it would never approach an evangelical pastor for counsel; they would generally stay far away from evangelical churches. Within the conservative church world, many LGBTQ+ people—often the children raised in the church—know to remain in hiding, which is often a key skill for survival. They are especially careful not to reveal themselves to pastors, knowing that clergy have the greatest financial stake in the institutions they serve. Why would you confide your most sensitive information to someone who might lose their job if they didn't represent the party line? This serves to hide the suffering of sexual minorities from pastors like me, when I functioned within evangelicalism. As the humanity of sexual minorities remains hidden, the humanity of sexual minorities is dishonored—a vicious circle, literally.

While Emily and I had an intense experience around the suffering of LGBTQ+ people, white pastors are, in similar ways, shielded from the suffering of people of color; clergy in male-dominated systems are shielded from the suffering of women. Meanwhile, pastors are supposed to communicate God's heart represented in the suffering of the Son of Man (more properly, "Son of Humanity") on behalf of all humanity!

This may be why resurrection appearances in general are striking in their counterintuitive emphasis on the *humanity* of Jesus. Mary, at the empty tomb, mistook him for the gardener. The two disciples on the road to Emmaus saw the risen Lord as just another fellow traveler. Thomas was shown the wounds in his side. But it is Peter, in his after-breakfast walk with the risen Jesus, who may have witnessed Jesus at his most vulnerably human.

Jesus calls them a term that denotes his shared humanity—"Friends!"—and then eats breakfast with them. After breakfast, Jesus gives Peter a chance to reverse his three-fold denial with a three-fold assertion of love. But it's also possible that Jesus wants to show Peter a different wound than the physical wounds he showed Thomas. Jesus may be showing the emotional wound that he suffered when Peter, his friend, betrayed him. The still-human Jesus may have needed the three-fold reassurance as much as Peter needed to assert his love three times.

Peter's rivalry with John addressed

As the episode draws to a close, Jesus speaks to the rivalry between two of his leading disciples:

> *Peter turned and saw the disciple whom Jesus loved following them; he was the one who had reclined next to Jesus at the supper and had said, 'Lord, who is it that is going to betray you?' When Peter saw him, he said to Jesus, 'Lord, what about him?' Jesus said to him, 'If it is my will that he remain until I come, what is that to you? Follow me!' So the rumor spread in the community that this disciple would not die. Yet, Jesus did not say to him that he would not die, but, 'If it is my will that he remain until I come, what is that to you?' (Jn. 21:20-23)*

Scapegoating is a function of rivalry spawned by mimetic desire. Peter and John were rivals. At the time when John's Gospel began to circulate, the respective churches that identified with Peter (Rome) and John (Ephesus) may have been in rivalry over the pre-eminence of their founding apostles. In the Gospel, it is most likely John who refers to himself as "the disciple Jesus loved." Daniel William O'Connor notes that in the Gospels of Mark, Matthew and Luke, Peter seems to be given a sole place of preeminence—whereas in the Gospel of John, Peter's preeminence is shared with "the beloved disciple" ("Saint Peter the Apostle").

On Easter morn, Peter and John run together to the empty tomb, but John (to whom the Gospel is ascribed) says, "the other disciple" (his term for himself) "outran Peter." When Peter denies knowing Jesus, the person reporting this abysmal failure of nerve, is, in all likelihood, John. Their rivalry is leaking out through the texts.

It is fitting, then, that the Gospel of John ends with Jesus addressing this rivalry. Remember that in the boat, John was first to recognize Jesus; but Peter jumped in and got there first this time (as opposed to John's outrunning Peter to the empty tomb). Then Peter and Jesus go for a walk after breakfast for some one-on-one time. This time, John is catching up from behind. Now, immediately after Jesus says to Peter, "Follow me!" what does Peter do? He turns away from Jesus to focus on John, then asks, "What about him, how is he going to die?" Jesus responds, "If I want him to remain alive until I return, what's it to you? Follow me!"

Jesus understands by painful experience: Rivalry breeds scapegoating. The community formed by leaving the mob, to stand in solidarity with the victim of scapegoating, must renounce rivalry as well. This is the heart of the teaching of Jesus in the Sermon on the Mount: stop judging; no contempt; forgive; no vengeance; serve one another.

The first charcoal fire, in the courtyard of the high priest, represents the warmth of a community forming into a scapegoating mob to insure its survival. Why don't we object when our community is forming itself into such a mob? Because we don't want to upset our parents or alienate our friends. We don't want to rock the boat that is our safety in a world of stormy seas.

What's the alternative? We can prefer a different kind of closeness. We respond to the invitation of Jesus to jump out of the boat and swim to the shore, where he has a meal ready for us. We seek a sense of intimate community created by Jesus for us and with us. Such is the community Jesus builds among the scapegoated and the recovering scapegoaters. When we come together to eat the meal Jesus prepares for us, we leave all of our bragging rights behind. We bring our failures with us. And we offer gratitude for gifts needed and gifts received. Thus, we share connection with Jesus and each other.

Back to the campfire in the cave

This chapter's opening account of praying early one morning is missing one significant detail—which occurred toward the end of the time, when I was mentioning loved ones by name in the presence of Jesus.

I offered one final person in order to prolong the experience of sitting with Jesus in that interior cave, staring into the fire: Phyllis Tickle. As soon as I uttered her name, I shot out of the presence of Jesus and out of the cave. Startled and confused, I had to will myself back—and, eventually, the praying was over.

Why would the mention of Phyllis Tickle—then a new friend who was 25 years my senior—produce this effect? And yet, I was not entirely surprised. I had started a correspondence with Phyllis after discovering *The Divine Hours*™, which she compiled as a resource for prayer at set intervals through the day. Our friendship was largely a matter of sharing our respective prayer experiences over email. Eventually, I invited Phyllis to speak at our church. That's when Phyllis told me that she attended a gay church led by a partnered gay man. She wanted to give me the option of reconsidering the invitation.

It was 2004. The so-called "gay issue" was looming ever more ominously over evangelicalism. I was just beginning to doubt the traditional view. I was afraid—not of Phyllis, *per se*, but of what she represented: a person who had crossed a line that would get anyone else who crossed it with her ejected from evangelicalism. I wondered if the sudden ejection from the presence of Jesus was a warning: *Beware of Phyllis Tickle and what she represents!* But on reflection, that didn't make sense. Fear like that—enough to eject me from the most intimate connection with Jesus that I had ever known—had no place in the presence of what seemed, to me, like perfect love.

Instead, I had to admit a different intuition. The closeness with Jesus that had begun that morning came at a cost. It would not continue if I allowed fear to prevent me from embracing the queer people who I sensed were getting a raw deal from the Church. I became increasingly aware that Jesus stood in solidarity with them and, if I refused to join him, I would be choosing to distance myself from him.

Tentatively; fearfully; in fits and starts, I began to reassess my support of the traditional teaching about same-gender sexual relationships.

It took me a long time—much too long—to change my mind. The anxiety was palpable whenever I spoke about this with pastors in my denomination. I was warned about the implications of my changing views. Those who agreed with me often did so secretly; tentatively; anxiously.

It's a long story, and the conclusions reached were told elsewhere (Wilson, *A Letter to My Congregation, 2nd edition*). Eventually, despite the fact that I was a founding pastor—the church had begun in my living room, and grown to about 600 in average attendance on Sundays—my decision not to enforce the traditional practices of discrimination aimed at LGBTQ+ people led to a series of losses. Let me state that

less abstractly: my refusal to fire Emily when she fell in love
with Rachel, and my refusal to go along with further calls for
long-suffering people to suffer just a little bit longer, until the
rest of us feel more "comfortable"—led to a series of losses.

I lost a denomination and a local church I loved; I lost any
standing I had gained within evangelicalism; and I lost some
of my closest friendships. I still feel those losses deeply, but
I'm also free to follow my conscience. The joy of co-pastoring
with Emily and launching a church that offers real inclusion
makes it all worthwhile.

When all else fails: *solus Jesus*

From the very beginning, *sola Scriptura* proved insufficient
to settle many matters of dispute in the Church. Reformers
who filled the void left by Luther's absence from his beloved
Wittenburg (he was in hiding from the authorities seeking
to arrest him after his excommunication from the Catholic
Church as a heretic) interpreted the Bible differently than
Luther. They took the Reformation he sparked in Germany
in directions that Luther regarded as prompted by the
devil. Mutual anathemas flew back and forth between rival
reformers.

Later, the dispute over slavery was not settled by *sola
Scriptura*. Nor disputes over the morality of killing in war or
the ordination of women. In each case, polemicists appealed
to Scripture, citing chapter and verse. Biblical texts could be
summoned on either side. But at least some explicit textual
evidence could be garnered to challenge a previously sacro-
sanct tradition in these cases. A case from Scripture could be
made that God allowed slavery as a concession rather than
commanding it ("If you can gain release from your bondage
take it"). A case from Scripture could be made that women
could serve as leaders (Deborah, in the time of the Judges;
Priscilla and Phoebe, leading in the earliest Christian communities). A case could be made from Scripture that Christians

are forbidden from killing in war ("turn the other cheek"). But the best case that can be made about the question of gay marriage is that the handful of texts on which the traditional view is founded address orgiastic, pederastic or other idolatrous or exploitative male-with-male or female-with-female sex. The Bible doesn't *explicitly* address whether or not members of the same gender may have sex within marriage. While this has been the case for other important and disputed questions (What does the Bible explicitly teach about birth control?), the intensity of the dispute over homosexuality means that this controversy functions like the straw that broke the camel's back of *sola Scriptura*.

Sola Scriptura was an overreach. It is insufficient as an answer to the question, "Who gets to decide what God requires?"

We find that we are dependent—perhaps frighteningly dependent—on a living, risen Jesus, with a mind of his own and a capacity to communicate it even when the Bible is less than clear on a matter. We are dependent on One who is able to speak (or refrain from speaking) according to his often opaque purposes. This is no guarantee that, in the short-term, the Church will achieve a common mind on every contested matter or that we won't vigorously disagree over how the living, risen Jesus is guiding us on such matters. That level of unity may be reserved for the long-term—the very long-term—and we will struggle in the meantime, as seems to be our lot before all things are fulfilled.

So be it: *solus Jesus.*

11

Scapegoaters Anonymous: Our Blinding Privilege

Ken

I WAS THE popular guy in high school—a little brainy, but also an athlete and adept at the art of the classroom quip. I was the odds-on favorite to be senior class president, except for a stubborn obstacle in my rise to power: As an under-performing student who didn't bother much with homework, I could only manage a 2.9 grade-point average. A run for office required a 3.0, and so Gary Rosenberg—a close friend since junior high (though we had drifted apart by our senior year of high school)—was elected class president.

Memory gets a little fuzzy, especially for those episodes of which we are least proud. But rumors began to circulate— vague complaints about Gary's class-officer performance. On a lark, a couple of buddies and I thought it would be fun to start a recall petition. There was no protocol for recalling class officers, but we didn't take it seriously enough to care. We started making phone calls: *Would you sign a petition to recall Gary Rosenberg?* To our surprise, the recall gained traction. Before we knew it, the faculty advisor for our senior class called a class meeting, where complaints against Gary were solicited. The soap opera ended with Gary resigning, followed by the election of one of my co-conspirators.

Fast-forward to 2015. After Emily and I were forced out of church (Emily for being gay; me for refusing to fire her) and had planted Blue Ocean Faith Ann Arbor, I took a three-month sabbatical to recover. At Emily's recommendation, I decided to study the works of René Girard. It felt as though scales fell from my eyes. At a granular level, I could relate to what happens when an anxious community, rife with rivalries in the face of religious controversy, organizes itself to assuage the concerns of its most anxious members at the expense of a relative few. What had simply bewildered me then now began to make sense in light of Girard's subtle understanding of the scapegoat mechanism. While the basic concepts of scapegoat theory are simple, how they interact is not. It took me a full three months of intensive study coupled with attending a weeklong workshop led by Girardian scholars James Alison, Andrew McKenna and Curtis Gruenler—and endlessly talking over these discoveries with my wife, Julia, on our daily walks—for the picture to become clear.

Girard helped me understand how communities organize themselves into scapegoating mobs whose members are blithely unaware of what they are doing. As our old church devolved into chaos in 2014, I was baffled by the unfolding dynamics. Especially painful was how so many previously vocal "supporters" of full LGBTQ+ inclusion were swayed, by a smaller group of objectors, to remain passive—silently acquiescing to the denomination's demands to fire Emily, to promise never to perform a gay wedding and, most bizarrely, to vow never to publically criticize a national policy that had not yet even been established. Accusations about my leadership (an online annoyance, after the publication of my book) now circulated in my church family. While many privately told me that these accusations were ridiculous, no one objected openly until our board, on my final Sunday as senior pastor, publically declared my innocence. It was dizzying. Only Girard's profound understanding of mimetic desire—a mostly unconscious mechanism empowering the human instinct to protect group cohesion over minority rights—made sense of what happened.

Having experienced the butt end of this equation, I was even more attuned to how my younger self had supported a system that discriminated against LGBTQ+ people—all the while ascribing the best possible motives to myself. A Vineyard colleague told me he was deeply offended that I characterized the Vineyard policy forbidding gay marriage and ordination as a form of stigmatizing exclusion. I understood his offense. In his mind, "welcome" meant "you're perfectly welcome to be part of the community"—a compassionate concession from those with a sympathetic pastoral heart. Refusing to perform a gay wedding or ordain a non-celibate gay person was a noble stand for truth in a culture swayed by the ascendant tide of the "gay agenda." The perfect reconciliation of mercy and holiness! Thus do we reassure ourselves about ourselves when doling out a welcome with an asterisk. What this fails to reckon with is the experience of the gay person on the receiving end of the asterisk: "You're welcome* to a seat on our bus!" (*as long as it's in the back of the bus). The crucible that Emily and I went through together in 2014 was painfully enlightening: Institutions that preserve themselves at the expense of a vulnerable minority are adept at putting lipstick on the pig. Girard's theory was no longer abstract and conceptual, but vividly concrete and particular.

Only then did I remember my part in what happened to Gary Rosenberg in 1969.

In that case, I was a *ringleader* in a classic scapegoat mechanism, and like many ringleaders, was oddly unaware of the injustice of the whole thing. I didn't see myself as mean-spirited, or driven by envy. But I was a key player in a process that—for Gary, at least—was socially brutal. Can you imagine a class meeting in which complaints against you are raised, with no judicial proceeding to establish evidence and no due process to allow for a reasonable defense—just a group of adolescents allowed to reenact their own adaptation of *Lord of the Flies*? I shudder now and feel ashamed of my part in it. With Girard's theory to enlighten me, I could see how I might well have been motivated by rivalry—Gary had what I wanted, and I took it away from him. I was the perfect candidate to initiate what became a classic scapegoating event, even if I thought it was little more than a high school prank.

Newly convicted, I reached out to Gary through social media, and we got together for dinner. I owned up to what I had done so many years earlier and heard his side of the story. Then Gary did something that blew me away. He carefully and gracefully—I would even say brilliantly—let me know that he didn't hold what I had done against me. He didn't use the words, "Father forgive them, for they don't know what they are doing," but he conveyed to me the freedom those words are meant to convey. It turns out that after college, Gary had experienced an awakening of his Jewish identity, studying for years under a wise rabbi. The more we talked the more we realized how much we held in common.

The process I underwent over a period of years was a kind of conversion. It seems obvious to me now that the most detailed accounts of conversion in the New Testament involve the stories of two recovering scapegoaters: Peter, the acquiescent participant, and Paul, the ringleader. Their stories tell us something about the *nature* of Christian conversion.

The author of Luke-Acts connects the conversion stories of Peter and Paul by emphasizing, in each case, a searing and catalytic epiphany—a sudden unveiling of unwitting complicity in scapegoating the innocent. While all four Gospels record Peter's betrayal, Luke's Gospel alone records this intimate moment in Peter's story of betrayal: "The Lord turned to Peter and *looked straight at Peter* and Peter remembered the Lord's words, 'Before a rooster crows today, you will deny me three times.' And Peter went out and cried uncontrollably" (Luke

22: 61-62). In the very act of denying Jesus—thereby securing
and aligning himself with the scapegoating mob—Peter steals
a glance at his teacher, who looks straight at him, and Peter
weeps in deep remorse for what he's done.

Paul (also known as Saul)[160] will have a similarly intimate
encounter with Jesus that will forever change him. This
moment occurs in Acts 9, but Luke sets the stage with a
primer on scapegoating.

Paul, cofounder of *Scapegoaters Anonymous*

We first meet Paul at the stoning of Stephen—one of several
examples of scapegoating in the book of Acts, when escalating rivalries provide the Petri dish for scapegoating. In Acts,
crowds are frequently getting riled up. In these episodes, Luke
emphasizes a buildup of rivalry that threatens the cohesion of
the community, followed by accusations against a vulnerable
individual—often an outsider. Luke is teaching us to pay
careful attention to these details. Sometimes the mechanism
is aborted before a victim is expelled, but often there is an
expulsion or even a death. Such is the case with the stoning of
Stephen, which Luke includes as a dramatic introduction to
Paul (who approved of the stoning).[161]

The backstory is important to Luke, who is interested in
exposing the dynamics of scapegoating. Jesus is one in a
long line of innocent victims thought to be guilty "since the
foundation of the world" (Lk. 11:47-51). In Acts, Luke shows

---

160 Raised in Tarsus, Paul would have been known there as "Paul", the Hellenized
form of his name. He later adopted the Aramaic, "Saul," when he went to Jerusalem
to study under Gamaliel, and returned to the original "Paul" when living among the
Gentiles (Chilton, 29).

161 Given the shameful history of anti-Semitism within the Gentile-dominated
Church of a later era, it is important to emphasize that Luke is often describing a
conflict *within* the Jewish community. Like most communities, especially those under
the intense pressures of foreign occupation, Israel is rife with internal conflicts. All the
protagonists and antagonists in Luke's account are Jewish. When Gentile Christians
later used these accounts to inflame a pre-existing anti-Semitism (interpreting them
as "Jewish persecution of Christians"), they ignored this important history. Any use of
these texts to support anti-Semitism is a gross perversion of Scripture.

that scapegoating doesn't end with Jesus. We're to expect to see more of it and be alert to its unfolding. In this way, we can become conscientious objectors when we are tempted to be drawn into yet another scapegoating mob. The life, death and resurrection of Jesus is part of God's long-suffering effort to expose the scapegoat mechanism for what it is—a gross injustice—so we can join the ranks of those who see it, resist it, refuse to join in, call it out and stand with the victims.

Stephen's last words at the point of his death ("Lord Jesus, receive my spirit" and "Do not hold this sin against them") mirror the words of Jesus at the point of his death, as Luke records them (Lk. 23:34,46). These words are meant to end the cycle of violence. Stephen signals to his own supporters that faithfulness to Jesus requires renouncing vengeance. The account ends with the observation that Saul was present, perhaps in a semi-official capacity, approving the mob's verdict. Luke takes great pains to show that Paul, such a prominent figure in Acts, is a *recovering scapegoater*. As the story unfolds in subsequent chapters, we learn that Paul was not simply a passive witness of such actions, but an active agent—a *ringleader*.

Saul's moment of truth

Luke, a master storyteller, has set the scene for Saul's epiphany in Acts 9.

> *Meanwhile Saul, still breathing threats and murder against the disciples of the Lord, went to the high priest and asked him for letters to the synagogues at Damascus, so that if he found any who belonged to the Way, men or women, he might bring them bound to Jerusalem. Now as he was going along and approaching Damascus, suddenly a light from heaven flashed around him. He fell to the ground and heard a voice saying to him, 'Saul, Saul, why do you persecute me?' He asked, 'Who are you,*

> *Lord?' The reply came, 'I am Jesus, whom you are*
> *persecuting. But get up and enter the city, and you*
> *will be told what you are to do.' (Acts 9:1-6)*

This story is so important that Luke repeats it twice in speeches made by Paul (Acts 22 and 26). In both of these retellings, we learn that this episode happened around noon. It is possible that Saul had stopped to observe the noonday prayers when he had his mystical experience.[162] Jews—like Muslims today, and many Christians—observed prayer at fixed intervals through the day. Noon was one of those times (Tickle, *Divine Hours,* vii-ix).

The three accounts of Saul's conversion in Luke include some conflicting details. Bystanders hear what Saul heard, or they don't; they fall with him, or they remain upright. Such discrepancies are par for the course when Scripture bears witness to what defies description: disorienting mystical experience. None of these divergent particulars seem to matter to Luke. What matters is a voice, saying (in Aramaic), "Saul, Saul, why do you persecute me?" This is the moment that mirrors Luke's rendering of Peter's excruciating courtyard revelation: a world of hurt in the eyes of his master, looking at him, while Peter warmed his hands around the charcoal fire, denying that he ever knew Jesus.

Both moments are marked by the vulnerability of Jesus. Under interrogation by the temple guard, Jesus is vulnerable—pained at the denial of Peter a short distance away. But here, in Saul's conversion, the vulnerability of Jesus is all the more striking because the plaintive words, "Saul, Saul, why do you persecute me?" are spoken by the risen Jesus, no longer subject to the powers of death. Jesus is still speaking as a vulnerable victim, harmed by the injury done to his followers at the hands of Saul. To see someone's *vulnerability* is to see their *humanity*. As Emily has emphasized, it is precisely the *humanity* of the scapegoated that we fail to see.

---

162 For a credible rendering of Paul's experience, see Chilton, pp. 48-53.

When African-American men organized protests against Jim Crow laws in the 1950s, they carried signs that stated, "I am a man." Just that: "I am a man." Sign after sign read, "I am a man." These men understood by experience that the scapegoating mob is blind to the humanity of its victims.

Saul might have replied to the voice, "I haven't laid a hand on you!" He doesn't. As a Jewish rabbi, versed in the Law and the Prophets, he knew Israel's God was the God who hears the cry and takes the side of the victim—whether Abel, Joseph, Hagar, Tamar or Job. If the people he, Saul, was rounding up in an effort to purify Israel were *victims*, and not *perpetrators* (as he supposed), then he knew in a flash that he was on wrong side of the God revealed in history.

The heart of Paul's conversion, and by inference, the heart of all conversion, is to understand the murderous violence that so easily hides beneath the costume of our religious devotion, piety and zeal. For Saul of Tarsus, conversion is the necessary and shocking revelation of the grotesque underbelly of religion—especially manifest in our claims to religious certainty, which Paul later came to regard as "unenlightened zeal."

It's telling that the paradigmatic scapegoaters in the New Testament are Peter and Paul, not Caiaphas or Pilate. We are given so much more insight into how Peter and Paul were caught up in the scapegoating mob than were these formal antagonists in the Passion accounts. It's as if the writers of the New Testament are not interested in fueling our antipathy toward Caiaphas and Pilate. They want us to see that it is the protagonists in our own story—our *heroes*, not our villains—who were once perpetrators of the injustice inherent in the scapegoat mechanism. Why? Because pointing our fingers and clicking our tongues in self-righteous indignation at Caiaphas and Pilate doesn't *lead us to conversion*; it only reinforces the ignorance from which we need to be saved.

The contagious dynamics of anxious crowds, seeking to relieve the multiplying tensions that threaten their beloved

community, are driven by mimetic desire—our tendency
to mirror the desires of others that, suddenly, begin to feel
very much our own. The effect is to conceal *from us* what
is happening *to us,* when we find ourselves drawn into a
scapegoating mob. We are driven by a sense of our own
righteousness when we scapegoat others. We see ourselves as
protecting the community from threats. The words of Jesus,
the scapegoat, apply to us: "Father forgive them, for they don't
know what they are doing."

The blinding power of privilege

While it's true that Saul of Tarsus was a minority in relation
to the Gentile oppressors of the Roman Empire, in relation
to Stephen and the early disciples, he occupied a position of
civic and religious privilege. As a Roman citizen, he was less
vulnerable to Roman harassment (though he endured plenty),
and his religious credentials were surpassed by only a few of
his fellow Israelites. The most prolific author of the writings
that compose the New Testament was a privileged man who
used his misreading of Scripture to victimize people he never
regarded as victims until after his conversion. Saul saw himself
as purging Israel of perpetrators; not persecuting victims. He,
Saul, was on the side of the real victims, against *their* persecutors, and he had chapter and verse to support his views—or so
he believed.

I can relate. I'm a straight, white, male baby boomer, a
member of a demographic slice that is, if anything, *in charge*
of the most powerful nation on earth. I was born in 1952,
when 94 percent of the world's wealth, after the devastation
of World War II, was in American hands. This meant that
94 percent of the world's wealth was in the hands, mostly, of
straight, white, American males. (Women couldn't even open
a bank account without a male cosigner!)

As I write this, American society is extremely anxious
because many white men see themselves as victims in

comparison to other groups. White men do exert a slighty smaller share of influence, relative to women and minorities, than was once the case. Yet white men still occupy a secure position of privilege relative to other groups. As a member of this demographic group, I didn't have a one-in-four chance of being sexually assaulted while in college. I grew up in a house owned by my father, who had received a low-interest rate mortgage under the GI Bill. Of the first 67,000 mortgages made available through that program, 66,900 were for white GIs. I have never—ever—been questioned by the police for no reason. The only time my car was searched by custom agents at an international border crossing, I was with an African-American pastor friend; he told me that this happens to him frequently.

Members of my demographic group suffer because we share in the essential vulnerability of the human condition, and not for the added cause of our race or gender. The fact that many in my demographic category have fallen on difficult economic times lately has nothing to do with our race or gender and everything to do with big transitions in our economy, the effects of which are not aimed at us because of our race or gender. There is no cultural "war on men" just as there is no "war on Christmas."

When those who enjoy relative privilege in a society also see themselves as an aggrieved victim group, the potential for scapegoating increases. If left unchecked, it will be channeled into this ages-old mechanism for relieving social tension. When the scapegoat mechanism is triggered, otherwise decent people will be swept into bullying others, thinking that they are defending their own rights; "protecting our women and children"; or "Making America great again."

Saul's conversion was triggered when he realized that he was playing a different role in Israel's story than he thought he was playing. He thought he was rushing to Israel's defense, but he was persecuting fellow Jews who were just trying to be faithful to Israel's God. This perception-reversal took place when the risen Jesus presented himself to Saul as a vulnerable victim in solidarity with the people Saul was victimizing. Thereafter, Saul left the scapegoating mob. He stopped accusing and started defending the victims that he had previously regarded as perpetrators. That's a hard turn to make. Or, to use the iamge of Jesus: it's a narrow gate through which to pass.

From the realm of the accuser to the realm of the advocate

The shift from accuser to defender is tied to a major component of the Bible's unmasking of the scapegoat mechanism. Accusation and defense against accusation signify two realms, two modes of being, conceived of as the realm "of Satan" and the realm "of the Spirit."

The Hebrew term, *satan*, or more commonly, the *satan*, is both a character in the biblical drama and a force at work in the world. We don't have much perspective on what a philosopher would call the "ontology" of Satan—meaning, we don't have good answers to questions like, "What mode of existence does the figure called Satan occupy?" or "What kind of being or entity is Satan a reference to?"

Maybe it's helpful to simply face the ambiguity in order to hold more loosely to our opinions on this matter. To speak of Satan as a "personal being" is perhaps misleading—or, at least, more ambiguous than it seems. In classical Christian thought, Satan occupies the category of "non-being" (Girard, *I See Satan Fall Like Lightning*, 45). Keep in mind that the Hebrew doesn't require the capital "S" of a proper noun: It would be equally correct to translate the Hebrew as "satan" or "the satan". This rendering would convey the paradox of a being who is "non-being," and the ambiguity this entails.

The Hebrew *ha-satan* means "the adversary." Another term used to refer to Satan is the Greek *diabolos*, which means "accuser." These terms describe the hidden dynamics of a scapegoating mob, always triggered or fueled by accusations against innocent victims thought to be guilty. Remove the power of accusation, and you've undone Satan. René Girard identifies Satan with the power that animates scapegoating, citing the following description of Jesus regarding "the devil" (Gk. *diabolos*): "He was a murderer from the beginning and does not stand in the truth" (Jn. 8:44). The accusations that single out a scapegoat are lies that focus the energies of the group to an expulsion, which then brings about a false peace—all done in a paroxysm of crowd deception. If you've ever experienced it, you know that it is creepy and feels very much like a brush with evil.

Of the four Gospels, Luke and John seem to most antic-ipate the age of the Holy Spirit inaugurated on the day of Pentecost, weeks after the death and reported resurrection of Jesus. Toward the end of Jesus's ministry, John introduces the Greek term, *paraclete*, to refer to the Holy Spirit. This means "advocate," or "counselor for the defense." It can be understood as the opposite of the accusatory spirit designated by the *satan*, or *diabolos*.

Is John introducing this designation of the Spirit because the crisis in Jerusalem is beginning to organize around Jesus as a targeted victim? It seems so. Something that lies at the heart of what's wrong with the way human beings resolve their conflicts—resorting to violence to fight violence, ensuring a never-ending pattern of recurring violence—is playing out in the events surrounding Jesus. Good people, well-intentioned, are getting caught up in something that feels suprahuman; something that seems to happen only when we come together in groups and find ourselves afflicted with multiplying rivalries. The effect is trancelike, inevitable and seemingly unstoppable. Girard says the mimetic power of scapegoating mobs is such that even many innocent victims come to regard themselves as guilty.

What if, in the middle of such a trance, an innocent victim chose not to fight back against the violence aimed at him—without succumbing to the accusations of the crowd? Jesus

didn't resist the violence of the crowd, but he never embraced
the verdict of the crowd, either. By asking God to forgive
them, he affirmed their guilt; not his. But he did so on the
most generous grounds, because he knew they were acting
in ignorance. What, then, if his innocence were confirmed
by a divine act, prompting some to experience the now-dead
victim as a transfigured and fully alive person operating in
a realm beyond death and interacting with us in this realm?
Wouldn't it make sense that the Spirit, released into the world
to advance the demise of scapegoating, would be designated
paraclete—a defense advocate—for everyone who would ever
be subject to such treatment by scapegoating mobs?

Paul clearly knew the Holy Spirit as a *paraclete*, the opposite
of a condemning or accusing spirit. His most theological
understanding of the Spirit is found in Romans 8, which
begins and ends with God's work to defend us against condemnation and accusation. The chapter begins with, "So now
there isn't any condemnation for those who are in Christ Jesus"
(Ro. 8:1), and its concluding section returns to this theme:
"Who will bring a charge against God's elect? It is God who
acquits them" (8:13). Between these framing statements, the
Spirit is named 20 times, making this the most concentrated
exposition of the Holy Spirit in any of his writings (besides his
instruction about gifts of the Spirit, in 1 Corinthians).

The references to the Holy Spirit in this section end by
invoking the Spirit's role as defense advocate, who "pleads our
case" and "pleads for the saints." In his magisterial commentary on Romans, Robert Jewett says that Paul's understanding
of the Spirit as an intercessor (a function of the Spirit as
paraclete) is unusual. It isn't found in the Hebrew Bible or in
the literature between the Old and New Testaments. Jewett
quotes another scholar who regards this as a "Pauline novelty"
(Jewett, 523).

The echoes of this understanding resound throughout
Paul's writings. Ephesians, written either by Paul himself or
in his name, includes an admonition to put away falsehood,

anger, bitterness, slander and malice, so as not to make room for the devil. He is concerned about the community members turning on one another, as he had once turned on his Jewish brothers and sisters who believed in Jesus. Paul exhorts his readers to "put away your former way of life" (Eph. 4:22)—a possible allusion to his "former way of life" as a persecutor of the Church, elliptically referred to in the previous chapter (Eph. 3:8). Paul adds tellingly, "And do not grieve the Holy Spirit of God, with which you were marked as a seal for the day of redemption" (Eph. 4:30). The image of an aggrieved Holy Spirit corresponds to Paul's first encounter with the aggrieved Messiah, saying, "Saul, Saul, why do you persecute me?"

Paul's experience on the road to Damascus burned this like a branding seal on his heart: When we accuse, rather than defend, the vulnerable, we are *wounding* the vulnerable God revealed in Jesus. What a reversal! Saul of Tarsus had been known as a warrior for God, pursuing those he viewed as threats to Israel and accusing them of crimes while doling out punishment; this same man becomes the rabbi of the Holy Spirit, a Spirit whom he experienced as a *paraclete*—God's defender against accusation and condemnation. This turn, from accuser to defender, is the heart of the transfer from the realm of the Satan to the realm of the Spirit.

I picture myself many years ago: founding pastor of Vineyard Church of Ann Arbor, leader in an evangelical denomination and teaching a membership class. I remember stating clearly that people in same-gender sexual relationships were not allowed to become members of the church so long as they remained in such relationships. Of course, I stated this in terms that seemed to me, at the time, to be very "pastoral"— even "gentle"—but the message was nevertheless clear: LGBTQ+ people were being "warmly excluded" from membership. Yet there's nothing at all gentle about exclusion. When my position softened, allowing LGBTQ+ people as members but without the full privileges of membership, the effect was the same—stigmatization, a form of exclusion. Oh, the stories we tell ourselves to feel good about ourselves! More than a few Vineyard colleagues told me how deeply offended they were to hear me characterize the Vineyard national position as "exclusionary." In their minds, exclusionary meant "harmful" or "mean," and the national policy was "pastoral"—not harmful or mean. The parties harmed—not those enforcing, supporting or acquiescing to the policies, of course—best measure harm.

I didn't regard my exclusionary stance as harmful (and would have avoided characterizing it as "exclusionary"). I would have defended it as "helpful." I was "upholding Godly standards" and helping gay people understand how to please God. I didn't regard what I was stating—insistence on lifelong celibacy, without of hope of ever being intimate with someone they desired—as an unbearable burden. I saw it as an act of discipleship, albeit one I was unwilling to take on myself.

My conscience was clear—until it wasn't.

I know several other pastors from the evangelical orbit who publically supported full inclusion for LGBTQ+ people. I don't mean they merely changed their opinion; there are innumerable pastors in the Roman Catholic, mainline Protestant and evangelical world who disagree with the traditional teaching on sexual minorities. But they don't challenge the traditional practices of their denomination or local parish, and thus tacitly support them. Withdrawing support for policies that discriminate against LGBTQ+ people, and refusing to enforce those policies—that's what gets you into trouble. In every case, the pastors who changed their minds—and were willing to do so publically, not merely privately—regard their change as a kind of conversion: a transformation wrought by the Spirit against deep internal and external resistance.

We are presented with Saul's conversion as though it were instantaneous—a flash of light at midday, a voice. But Saul was merely stunned at first. His "conversion" might be more aptly described as an apprehension. He who chased others was apprehended instead. Remember: he suffered a temporary physical blindness that kept him from pursuing anyone. Luke records that Paul was baptized shortly thereafter and began to bear witness to Jesus in the synagogues. But how long did it take Paul to understand the implications of this experience, and integrate it into a coherent reading of Torah; an understanding of the mission of Israel; and a perspective on the inclusion of the Gentiles? We don't know. But judging from some fragmentary biographical details in Galatians, this process may have taken years (Gal. 1:13-2:10).

Conversion from two different angles

All of this makes me wonder: Have we missed an essential understanding of how conversion is experienced by some people? If conversion means, among other things, leaving the scapegoating mob behind (as it did for Peter and Paul), what does it mean for the targets of the scapegoating mob?

For some, conversion means coming to grips with their guilt.

For others, it means coming to grips with their *innocence*.

My wife is an Episcopal priest who recently performed a wedding for Tom and Eddie, together for nearly 40 years. They raised two grandchildren whose parents were not able to raise them. They cared for each other through thick and thin, over many years. Most recently, Tom has been caring for Eddie after cancer led to a leg amputation. Julia and I visited them in the hospital, and their devotion to each other was evident. They invited us over for dinner recently. I asked Tom about his return to faith. (Eddie, raised Catholic, had always identified as a Christian; Tom hasn't until recently, when he and Eddie started attending Julia's parish.)

Tom told me about growing up Baptist—the fundamentalist version of Baptist. He loved to read the Bible and attended a Bible college as a young man. He was growing in faith and considering going into Christian ministry when he heard his first sermon calling out homosexuality as a grievous sin.

Tom knew he was attracted to men, not women. He couldn't imagine living his life alone, without a partner he desired. So he left faith behind—assuming the preacher was right, which meant that he, Tom, was profoundly wrong and unfit for God. That is, until a few years earlier, when he and Eddie started to go back to church again—a church that had changed its mind about gay people and God.

As may be clear by now, I am curious about how people experience God. So I asked Tom, "When you came back to God a few years ago, what was that like? I mean, was there a moment or an experience that prompted you to make that turn? What was that moment like, if there was one?"

Tom thought for a moment, then looked up and said, "It happened when I said to myself, 'You're not such a bad person, Tom.' That's when I turned back to God."

I sat there, stunned. Of course. My evangelical framework emphasized conversion as a realization of one's status as a sinner, with little appreciation for the pervasive sin of scapegoating. But if the Spirit is, in fact, a defender of the innocent-thought-to-be-guilty, then Tom's experience would constitute a true moment of conversion. "It happened when I said to myself, 'You're not such a bad person, Tom.'" That was his confession of faith.

Religious people who don't know better (people like me, at one point) saw Tom as guilty of sexual sin. He had internalized their accusations, regarding himself as a bad person and unfit for God. He lived with that devilish lie for decades. He did so, that is, until he encountered the real Jesus at work (if you don't mind my saying so, with pride) at my wife's Episcopal parish. The Spirit called by Jesus, *Paraclete*, whispered in Tom's heart the word of his innocence—not his guilt. And as Tom internalized that word, he turned his heart toward the God whose heart had always been turned toward him. No one had to tell Tom this was good news.

When the Church lost most of its Jewish members and became, instead, a Gentile religion, embraced by the mightiest empire on earth as a privileged religious community, it lost something dear. It lost an understanding of the meaning of Jesus's dying and rising in solidarity with all victims of scape-goating. It lost a sense of the Spirit, poured out on all people in his name, as *Paraclete*—defender of those accused by an encircling mob. In losing its message, it lost its way.

Following Jesus is about choosing sides. I'm with Tom and Eddie because God is with Tom and Eddie. Their witness, and the witness of marginalized people like them, have helped me understand how the Gospel—the message of a God whose image-bearing child suffered, died and rose again, to change the world—really is good news for modern ears.

Part 3:
A New Way Forward

In this final section, we sketch the outlines of a new way forward, based on our framing of *solus Jesus* as a theology of resistance. First, we step back to restate the gospel for modern ears through the lens of René Girard. Then we tackle the problem of religion—our misuse of morality—combining Dietrich Bonhoeffer's intuition of a "religionless Christianity" with the clarifying work of Girard, both informed by the Holocaust. We then describe a robust spirituality of resistance informed by Pentecostal and monastic spiritualities, alongside practices drawn from the Sermon on the Mount. We end by describing a non-rivalrous engagement with other world religions as a more attractive and faithful expression of the Gospel.

12

The Gospel for Modern Ears

Ken

INFORMED BY THE writings of René Girard, alive in our own experience—Emily and I have taken you, our patient readers, on a lengthy stroll through scapegoat theory. We've told some of the more painful parts of our respective stories to put some "flesh on the bones" of scapegoat theory, and to reveal some of the experience that has informed the proposal we call *Solus Jesus: A Theology of Resistance*.

The basic elements of scapegoat theory are easy to grasp, but how they *interact* is much more subtle, and takes a while to sink in. Chief among these interactions is the way the scapegoat mechanism is fueled, from start to finish, by the mostly hidden dynamics of mimetic desire—a phenomenon we are loath to admit or recognize in ourselves, because it seems so, well, *imitative*, and thus beneath our dignity. It's easy to see how people (especially *other* people!) tend to scapegoat, but Girard's genius is unpacking how mimetic desire draws us unconsciously into the rivalries and spreading accusations that transform a loving community into a scapegoating mob. We hope that by now, the subtlety, persistence and pervasiveness of scapegoating is coming into focus for you: the light bulbs are flickering on as you use this lens for yourself, to interpret more of what you observe and experience.

We're now in position to take another look at how all of this illuminates the meaning of Jesus and his message—how it can justifiably be characterized as "Gospel," or the announcement of good news. The Church is in a communication crisis, struggling to communicate a Gospel formed in a pre-modern era to modern ears. We think scapegoat theory can make a considerable contribution to solving this problem. How does all that we've learned about scapegoat theory help us understand the heart of the Gospel message—and its significance in our world? What did Jesus *accomplish* by dying the way he did? How does his death *affect* us? What *meaning* can we make of it?

Our favorite atheist

Carl Safina is the most spiritually astute atheist we know. An acclaimed science writer, his *Beyond Words: What Animals Think and Feel* is one of our all-time favorites. Carl and I met at a retreat in 2006, composed of a dozen top scientific leaders paired with a dozen evangelical leaders. I was, as the British say, "above my station"—filling in for a more prominent leader who couldn't attend. Plus, there just weren't that many pastors in the sector of Christianity that I inhabited at the time who were willing to attend an event with "secular scientists" devoted to fighting climate change. In fact, before the retreat, we were admonished to keep it hush-hush—some of the evangelicals didn't want to be known to their constituencies as climate-change sympathizers. (Yes, such was my religious world not too long ago.)

Carl and I hit it off, and we developed some bridge-building events for evangelical leaders and environmental scientists at a handful of secular universities. In the process, we became friends-at-a-distance and naturally learned more about each other's respective paths in the realms of science and religion.

One day I received this email from Carl, recounting his loss of faith as a child growing up on Long Island:

> *My uncles had a boat and occasionally invited my dad. But an invite to him was not an automatic to include me ... When I was about 9, I did get one of the very rare invitations. I'd been fishing and on the boat before, so I knew it was the most exciting thing imaginable. When my father said I could go, I was leaping for joy. One problem: it was this Sunday. Sunday! I was in Catholic school and knew missing mass on Sunday was a mortal sin, period. You died before confession (any time in the next 5 days), and you were in the middle of a hundred burning Christmas trees forever.*
>
> *But by then I could think a bit. So I went to talk to the priest. Gotta be some wiggle room. Could I go on Saturday? No. Twice on Monday? No. Every day the whole next week? No. TWICE on Saturday ... No. He said, "I'm sorry, but you have to go to mass on Sunday." I could not believe the creator of the universe would demand I sit in church again, and only on that one day while missing time with my father and uncles, doing the most exciting thing possible—being out on His glorious ocean.....*
>
> *But the thing is I stayed home and went to mass. And the church lost me that day. Because, as I thought, "This just can't, it just cannot, be right. It can't be what God wants ... what he cares most about. These people ... are capable ... of getting it wrong." And as far as the Catholic Church and me; that was that. I went to church off and on for a few more years. But every time, I could see the wizard behind the curtain; the gloss was off. I don't remember going to confession any more, or*

worrying about missing a Sunday. And by the time I was about 12, I was pretty much gone ... God might be, but he could not possibly be that rigid or small.

It was gonna hafta be between him and me. And eventually, early 20s, my praying could no longer drown out all those suffering innocents. (I do thank the church, though, for telling me I should care about those suffering innocents. I think I would have gotten there from any of several directions, but the church was first to get me there.)

Carl's innocent question

Soon thereafter, I received this brief email from Carl: "When you get a moment, explain how Jesus died 'for our sins.' I've never gotten that. ... Keep it short or I won't understand."

Carl couldn't have known it, but his question is one that plagued me for 35 years. Not that I thought Jesus *didn't* die for my sins, but the usual explanations for *why* he did left me dissatisfied (Wilson, *Jesus Brand Spirituality: He Wants His Religion Back,* 155-160). I had always identified more with the notion of following Jesus—as the disciples in the Gospels felt compelled to do—than with "getting saved from my sins," as so many evangelicals emphasized. That left me a bit of a misfit within evangelicalism, but my options were limited. So much of "mainline Protestantism"—usually the oldest churches in town, near the center of the city—shared my lack of enthusiasm with the common explanations for why Jesus had to die, yet I couldn't find help for the open pursuit of a personal God-connection, through Jesus, in that sector of faith. And that was the only appeal I found in Christianity. (No doubt, I wasn't looking hard for this in the mainline sector, but that's another issue.)

If Carl had asked, "What do you love about Jesus—and how might a person come to experience that love?" I'd have been off to the races, pouring out my heart to him. Instead, good probing scientist that he is, Carl hit on the nub of what had been a longstanding faith dilemma for me. I composed the best answer I could summon, but as soon as I hit "send," I knew I hadn't answered Carl's question to my own satisfaction—let alone his. Years later, thanks to Emily introducing me to the work of René Girard and a little more life experience, I'm in a better position to respond.

Carl's question was provoked by a line from Paul, in one of the earliest written summaries of the Gospel that we have:

> For I handed on to you as of first importance what I in turn had received: that Christ died for our sins in accordance with the scriptures, and that he was buried, and that he was raised on the third day in accordance with scriptures and that he appeared to Cephas, then to the twelve. Then he appeared to more than five hundred brothers and sisters at one time, most of whom are still alive, though some have died. Then he appeared to James, then to all the apostles. Last of all, as to one untimely born, he appeared also to me. For I am the least of the apostles, unfit to be called an apostle, because I persecuted the Church of God. (1 Cor. 15:3-9)

There it is as an assertion without direct explanation: *Christ died for our sins (in accordance with the scriptures)*.

Christ died is a relatively uncontested historical fact. And *our sins* is a widely recognized, if highly unspecified, fact of our existence. The word translated as "sin" means "missing the mark" and most of us can recognize that we miss the mark of our own expectations, if nothing else. Certainly, we can acknowledge that human society is inclined to miss the mark. Then, sandwiched between these two phrases is the connecting word: "for." Therein lies the nub of Carl's question: "What does it mean to say Christ died *'for* our sins'"?

First, here's an explanation in paragraph form (for Carl, per his request to keep it short):

"Christ died for our sins" in order to unmask the scapegoat mechanism, in accordance with a distinctive feature of the "scriptures" Paul knew—the Hebrew Bible. Christ died, as so many scapegoats have, at the hands of humans unconsciously projecting their own guilt on him, to resolve their own community's destabilizing internal conflicts. His death is the most famous example of this in history, and his innocence (the key characteristic of scapegoats being "an innocent victim thought to be guilty") was proclaimed far and wide, by persistent rumors of his resurrection and by the witness of those who experience his Spirit. As more humans realize how we can all unwittingly participate in scapegoating others, and as more of us renounce the root of scapegoating—our amped up rivalries—the circle of compassion will expand to include more people and creatures— and that's good news.

What follows is the expanded version, applying what we've learned of the scapegoat mechanism to Paul's Gospel summary.

The word translated as "for," in "Christ died for our sins," is *huper* (pronounced 'who-pear') in the original Greek. It's a preposition, and its definition is fluid, depending on context. It can mean "in behalf of" or "for the sake of"; it can mean "beyond" or "more than" (as in the English derivative, "hyper"). Like most prepositions, "for" only makes sense in a larger backstory, just as "I'm here for you" means different things if the speaker is your best friend at the door or an immigration and customs enforcement officer.

The Gospel's backstory: atonement theories

Paul alludes to our preposition's backstory with "in accordance with the Scriptures." We can derive many backstories out of the Hebrew Scriptures; the question is, which of these backstories makes sense of "Christ died for our sins"? In the more technical jargon of theology, the backstory to this question is called "atonement theory." Think of "atonement" as "at-one-ment." Atonement is how we are made one again, or reconciled with God, ourselves, others and the wide world.

Emily introduced us to atonement theory at the beginning of Chapter 7, just as she was introducing us to the work of René Girard. We don't have to think of atonement theories as correct or incorrect. The Scriptures are a living word, adaptable to many different cultural contexts in many different ways. Instead, we can evaluate atonement theories by their helpfulness to us in our given historical and cultural context. Which atonement theories help make sense of a statement like "Christ died for our sins"?

Some of this will be a (brief) repetition of what Emily wrote in Chapter 7, but I think it is worth understanding how different explanations for why Jesus died for our sins (atonement theories) have held sway at different times. This will help us decide which atonement theory makes sense to us now, and which ones are simply a record of what made sense to people in other periods of history. After all, we get to decide what makes sense to us.

Died to ransom us from the devil?

In the second century, the backstory to "Christ died for our sins" went like this: When we sinned, we became the property of the devil, who held us captive. Christ died in order to pay the devil a sufficient ransom to set us free. For those of you who enjoyed *The Lion, the Witch, and the Wardrobe* from the *Chronicles of Narnia*, by C.S. Lewis, this is background to the death of Aslan. The atonement theory known as *Christus Victor*, described by Emily in Chapter 7, is a later variant of this older theory (promoted today by the scholar N.T. Wright).

We can imagine how this atonement theory may have helped make sense of "Christ died for our sins" in a world in which other people owned a large percentage of humanity and moral objections to slavery were rare. But today, this backstory raises more questions than it answers: Who—or *what*—is the "devil"? How does the "payment of a ransom" apply to our sins? How would my view of reality have to change for this to make *any sense to me at all*?

First, I'd have to be convinced that my sins (or collectively, *our sins*) somehow gave a figure known as the devil, or Satan, legitimate ownership rights over me (or us). Maybe, if I focused and possibly amplified all the things I've ever done that I feel bad about, I could get there. But when I try to picture, say, one of my kids—getting older and, somewhere along the line, doing enough horrible things that they had effectively sold their soul to the devil (who had rightful ownership of them now)—I'm sorry, I just can't get there and I'm not sure why I would even try. Speaking in all candor, if I started believing something like this, what would prevent me believing that the moon landing was a fake or that humans are not contributing to a warming climate, as some intelligent people I know also believe?

Died to satisfy God's wrath?

This was replaced a thousand years later with what is arguably the most influential atonement theory within evangelical forms of Christianity: Christ's death satisfied the just demands of God the Father who was so filled with appropriate wrath because of our sins that he required the bloody sacrifice of his son, Jesus. Since he has done that (and if we accept it) we are no longer subject to that wrath.

I can imagine how this may have made sense in a world in which the only reliable peace was kept by a strongman-authoritarian dictator (warlord, patriarch, king, emperor) who could quell disorder by displays of overpowering violence. Even today, the prospect of spreading violence through anarchy can make this an appealing option. If I lived in Iraq and could keep myself out of trouble with Saddam Hussein, I might long for his return, given the violent chaos that replaced him. But as we come to regard God as a loving parent to whom we can draw close, this backstory presents obvious problems. Let me just say it plainly: A God who kills his son to pacify his own wrath seems creepy to me, and I can't get over it. I've heard the thoughtful explanations that attempt to make sense of this, but they don't work for me. These explanations stress God's holiness, so deeply offended by sin, and our reciprocal inability to appreciate the gravity of our sin, given our immersion in it (much as we might imagine fish not understanding what "wet" is). But even the most thoughtful of these explanations are not only unsatisfying to me, but viscerally repugnant. I'm plagued by the pesky thought that I can forgive people who sin against me without requiring a bloody sacrifice. Is it too much to ask God to be more loving than I am? I certainly hope not, for all our sakes.

By now you get the gist: Atonement theories can be better or worse at helping us understand why Christ died for our sins. These theories can "explain" one thing (if accepted), only to raise new questions that are even more difficult. And most of us are well past the point of accepting something just because those in authority assert it is compelling.

Safina anticipates Girard's alternative explanation

What backstory makes better sense of "Christ died for our sins" than these? A backstory that, as Paul said, is "in accordance with the Scriptures." The answer was hidden in plain sight in Carl's email and I missed it until I became familiar with the work of René Girard. You may recall that in Carl's email about losing his faith as a child, he wrote: "And eventually, early 20s, my praying could no longer drown out *all those suffering innocents*. (I do thank the Church, though, for telling me I should care. I think I would have gotten there from any of several directions, but the Church was first to get me there.)"

Carl was referring to a problem that many of us wrestle with: How can there be a good God who allows the suffering of so many innocent people and creatures? As one who has read all of Carl's books, I can say that concern for "all those suffering innocents" is his animating passion. In particular, Carl knows animals in a way that causes him to love them (starting with birds) in spite of the fact that many people around him are oblivious to their existence and, therefore, oblivious to their suffering (often at our hands, directly or indirectly). We're unnaturally detached from nature, so we do things to needlessly increase the suffering of other creatures. All of his books are about reconnecting us to the natural world *so that we care* about all those suffering innocents.

Concern for suffering innocents provides an explanatory backstory to the meaning of "Christ died for our sins." As René Girard suggests, the crime of humanity that is distinctively exposed in the Scriptures of Israel is scapegoating—the crime in which innocents, thought to be guilty, are mistreated in order to give anxious communities a false sense of peace. This is a crime that a smaller number of us participate in as ringleaders (vocal accusers, perpetrators) and which a much larger number of us participate in as silent, non-objecting, going-along-with-the-crowd-to-save-our-place-in-it, acquiesors (a word I've been forced to coin for lack of another).

Girard's writings are informed by his interest in great literature, in archaic myth and in medieval persecution narratives, all of which he studied before studying the sacred writings of Israel. He believes the ancient world was awash with stories of guilty people whose death or expulsion restored their communities to peace, harmony and health. This is the story of Oedipus and the story of Rome's founding by Romulus and Remus. It is the theme of later stories of a plague only stopped when the community expelled its Gypsies, Jews or "witches." In all these myths and stories, Girard claims, the storytellers assume the guilt of the expelled. But in so many stories found in the sacred texts of Israel, and the apostolic writings of what began as a Jewish sect—stories that often have their parallels in ancient mythic tales—these figures are relatively innocent, not guilty. Abel is innocent. Joseph, left for dead in a well by his brothers, is innocent. Hagar, sent into wilderness by jealous Sarah, is innocent. Job is innocent, though his friends assumed his guilt. The maligned prophets of Israel are innocent. And Jesus is innocent, along with Stephen, and others who followed in his footsteps. The texts that tell their stories present them as unjustly accused: present them as what we now call "scapegoats."

Later in life, as Girard studied the sacred texts of other religions, he came to see traces of scapegoating in them, as well. But his life's work was animated by the discovery that the writings of Israel seem uniquely—or at least distinctively— concerned with unveiling the crime of scapegoating to a world largely blind to it. Unveiling the injustice of murder, adultery, stealing and dishonoring the elderly—these are not the distinctive contributions of Israel's sacred writings to the catalog of human sins. The sins that enable scapegoating are. Now you know why we've spent so much time on this.

In a sense, our worst—our distinctly human—crime is this: fueled by mimetic desire, we resolve our internal group conflicts (in families, on the job, in society) by targeting a vulnerable member or minority group. We accuse them of faults we are blind to in ourselves, projecting onto them what we are loath to face in ourselves. As we write this, the "scape-goats *du jour*" include Muslims, immigrants, global financiers (code for the Jews), advocates of Black Lives Matter, members of the "dishonest" press—always, there is some "other" causing our problems. We stigmatize, isolate, silence and oppress "those people" … and it brings a temporary sense of unity to the crowd organizing itself around these accusations. We resort to this mechanism again and again, forever blind to the innocence of those we target—the guilty ones who are, in fact, the objects of our own projected guilt.

Scapegoating is "that thing we do." And the way to *undo* it is to unmask it. This is surely one—perhaps the primary—purpose in the history of God's dealings with Israel, in accordance with the Scriptures.

Are we simply reading this into our text? I don't think so. After *Christ died for our sins in accordance with the Scriptures,* Paul adds that the risen Christ appeared first to Cephas (the Aramaic form of "Peter") and finally appeared to him: "Last of all, as to one untimely born, he appeared also to me. For I am the least of the apostles, unfit to be called an apostle, because I persecuted the Church of God."

He features, in other words, the founding members of the Church as a manifestation of *Scapegoaters Anonymous*—those who face, renounce and seek to recover from their scapegoating ways.

If this is the backstory, then "Jesus died *for* our sins" means that he died "on account" of our scapegoating ways. His death (and rising) was a ripening, or a culmination, of God's long effort to unmask the scapegoat mechanism. In this reading, the resurrection isn't just about Jesus beating death; it is God's declaration of the *innocence* of all who are scapegoated. Thus, the risen Jesus gives voice to all of the scapegoats who have been silenced by their oppressors.

By emphasizing the appearance he received of the risen Jesus—the culmination of his summary of the Gospel—Paul invokes what would have been a well-known part of his biography within the churches that recognized his apostleship. Paul's readers would have known that his relationship to the scapegoating mob was transformed from instigator to conscientious objector on the road to Damascus. He hardly let them forget it.

The Gospel for modern ears is an answer to the question, "Where is God in this world?" The good news is that God is standing with the scapegoated—defending them, comforting them and declaring their innocence. The more we see this, the more we understand God's heart toward humanity (and Carl

Safina's influence bids me add, "his heart toward *all creatures*"). God stands with and for all the suffering innocents, and we keep God's company when we stand with God, standing with them.

To follow Jesus is to undergo a spiritual awakening—to see scapegoating for what it is and to stand with whomever it is this mechanism is targeting.

To be immersed in the spirit of Jesus is to be immersed in the Holy Spirit he named *Paraclete*, defender of the accused.

If you have ever been scapegoated, you know that the verdict of the group you belong to—which is now turning against you—is difficult to resist. Cognitive scientists tell us that the brain processes a lie by first considering it plausible; only later does it override that assessment. This is one of the reasons aspiring strongmen incessantly repeat their lies—the repetition wears us down. As Mark Twain said, "A lie travels half way 'round the world while the truth is putting on its shoes." When we are repeatedly subjected to false accusations, they fatigue our brains and a part of us will wonder if the accusations aren't true.

Furthermore, we are so attuned to the opinion of the groups we belong to that, by a process of unconscious imitation, we often internalize such accusations. The verdict of the group becomes a voice within our own heads, subjecting us to a damning accusation from within. The Spirit that raised Jesus from the dead as a sign of his innocence enters us, and from within us, bears witness that we are children of God— that we do not stand condemned.

From this perspective, the God who becomes so enraged by our sin that his wrath can only be assuaged by the bloody sacrifice of his own son, may be an echoing voice of the scape- goating mob, rather than its contravening voice. The former is a God we might understandably fear, in the sense in which Saint John says, "Perfect love casts out all fear." The latter is a God with whom we can let down our guard, abandoning ourselves to divine love.

This is a God we can get close to, to comfort, calm, guide, challenge and transform us.

Did I mention that Carl's first book is titled *Song for the Blue Ocean*? It was the first of his books that I read after meeting him, and I wrote him to say that I thought he was a flipping mystic, based on some of his descriptions of being out on the ocean. When Emily and I planted our church as an aspiring, fully inclusive community, we called it Blue Ocean Faith Ann Arbor.

To us, the blue ocean is a symbol of the wide world God loves and inhabits. Situated on our respective landmasses, we are all connected by the ocean, which is something none of us dare claim as our own—no billionaire, no corporation, no authoritarian strongman, no religion or religious authority and no nation-state.

This understanding of the Gospel is our song for the blue ocean.

13

The Problem of Religion

Ken

THE PROBLEM OF religion, simply put, is the ubiquitous use of morality to oppress others—so much so that any preoccupation with morality, as a category, seems to spell trouble.[163]

Try a little free-association exercise: Consider the word "morality." Let it roll around in your brain for a moment.

What feelings does the word elicit? Does it make you cringe? Does it evoke a sense of smugness … or perhaps a feeling of conditioned shame? Are you associating the latter, in particular, with something having to do with sex?

So many ugly battles are fought over morality in the name of religion. Judging by the overriding concerns among Christians over morality, one might assume that the religion Jesus founded is all about getting things right—in particular, knowing the difference between what is good and what is evil (especially in others) in order to embrace the former and shun the latter. We might have a "liberal" version of this in mind, or a "conservative" one. Either way, it triggers an ugly

---

163 This is not to deny the positive contribution of religion through advocacy of ethic codes that promote well being. It is simply to acknowledge that the track record of religion in the moral realm is mixed, and that the institutions of religion can hinder, rather than support moral reforms.

swirl—notwithstanding on which side of any purported moral God-line we may find ourselves.

But wait. How could *this* be the point of *walking with God*?

Bonhoeffer, the problem of religion and religionless Christianity

We turn again to Dietrich Bonhoeffer, who was pressed by experience to wrestle with the problem of religion at depth (and especially religion's framing of the category "morality").

Perhaps this is a good time for a word of caution. Dietrich Bonhoeffer is everyone's darling, claimed by liberation theologians, progressive Christians and conservative Christians alike. President George W. Bush quoted Bonhoeffer to justify the invasion of Iraq and the war on terror.[164] And here we are—Emily and I adding our voices to that cacophony. I suppose Jesus would sympathize with the tug-of-war endured by Bonhoeffer. So we advise you, dear reader: Whenever Bonhoeffer is invoked, do your homework, check the footnotes and keep the salt shaker handy.

Never is that more the case than when treading into the territory that Bonhoeffer labeled "religionless Christianity."

Bonhoeffer wrote several letters to friends and colleagues during his two years in a Gestapo prison, before his execution, as the war in Europe was ending. Many were written to his beloved friend Eberhard Bethge (pronounced Bet-geh.) In a few of the letters, Bonhoeffer offered preliminary thoughts on what he called a "religionless Christianity." He raised the issue again in a sermon he wrote for the baptism of Bethge's infant son. His thoughts are provisional and provocative—classic Bonhoeffer and, like so much in his writings, open to widely varying interpretations and applications.

Two words of caution, then, are in order before we proceed. First, the meaning of religionless Christianity is hotly contested by scholars today. Bonhoeffer offered *musings* on a religionless Christianity—as much intuitions as thoughts. But

---

164 For a discussion of Bonhoeffer's disparate fans, see Pugh, 2-7.

even a half-formed thought from this man, in prison for resistance to Hitler and providing pastoral care to fellow prisoners and guards alike, is worth exploring. Second, in the post-war period, there were several attempts to implement a religionless Christianity, especially among privileged white Christians. These attempts were abject failures. In addition to throwing off institutional structures and a hyper-rigid orthodoxy, experiments in religionless Christianity also abandoned aspects of faith that were precious to Bonhoeffer: Christian community, interior devotion and a steely-eyed commitment to follow Jesus, come what may.[165]

You can imagine the difficulty. How does one separate the chaff of "religion" from the wheat of "Christianity"? Are they, in fact, distinguishable—let alone separable? Are all ecclesial structures religion? How about distinctive Christian beliefs? When all that is religion—whatever it may be—is stripped away, is there even a nub left that is worth pursuing, or might we all just be better off getting a degree in one of the helping professions and doing our best to improve the world in other ways?

So, yes—religionless Christianity is a fraught concept. And yet, it resonates. The post-war period in the West witnessed three positive and powerful manifestations of Christianity that substantially transcended institutional forms and structures associated with the term "religion": the civil rights movement; Alcoholics Anonymous; and, a bit later, the spiritual renewal among (mostly white) baby boomers, called the Jesus movement (or Jesus freaks) and various versions of charismatic renewal in the Catholic and mainline Protestant tradition.

All of these movements got their start in church basements across the United States. All three had roots in the Church, yet they moved well beyond the confines of its institutional structures. And though they transcended the organizational

---

165 For a robust analysis of various failed attempts to implement "religionless Christianity" inspired by Bonhoeffer, see Ryrie, 302-304.

and doctrinal boundaries of the Church (often bypassing the clergy), each movement tapped into deep streams of spirituality languishing within those institutional structures. We see traces of this influence in ecclesial arrangements that have been described as "post-denominational" (Miller).

So what did Bonhoeffer mean by the term "religionless Christianity"?

Bonhoeffer was struggling with a constellation of concerns when he coined the term. What does Christianity become when we don't think "religiously" anymore? What happens when the secular realm continues to expand, and the sacred begins to shrink into increasing irrelevance? And, especially: What happens when religion as we know it proves to be powerless in the face of an atrocity, such as the Holocaust?

The following statement, in a letter to Bethge, on April 30, 1944, is an example:

> *How do we speak of God—without religion, i.e. without the temporally conditioned presuppositions of metaphysics, inwardness and so on? How do we speak (or perhaps we cannot now even 'speak' as we used to) in a 'secular' way about 'God'? In what way are we 'religionless-secular' Christians ... those who are called forth, nor regarding ourselves from a religious point of view as specially favored, but rather as belonging wholly to the world? In that case, Christ is no longer an object of religion, but something quite different, really the Lord of the world. But what does that mean? (Bonhoeffer, Letters and Papers from Prison, 280-281)*

The Christianity we have received, and attempt to pass on, emerged within a thought-world that many no longer inhabit. It recognized a sharp divide between the sacred and the profane. It explained naturally occurring phenomena that could not be explained by observable cause-and-effect with claims of supernatural intervention: a God-of-the-gaps theology. But the gaps shrunk over time, leaving less need for God as an explanation. In this older view, an overarching divine authority accounted for human authority structures (of men over women, masters over slaves, rulers over subjects). Human beings were regarded as the pinnacle, aim or ultimate purpose of divine creation—the central object of God's concern. With time, these presuppositions eroded. As a result, religious explanations are less compelling than they once were.

For example, my Roman Catholic friend explained the meaning of "transubstantiation"—how bread and wine become, in reality, the body and blood of Christ in a Roman Catholic Eucharist. When I made the usual objection—"Then why, on closer inspection, doesn't it appear as human flesh and blood?"—my friend offered the distinction between the "substance," or "essence" of a thing (its essential being or nature), and its "appearance" (how the thing-in-itself is perceived by our senses). This distinction was rooted in the physics of Aristotle. But I don't regard material things in these terms—as having a substance, which is their essential being, and a separate appearance, which may be something different. I asked my friend: "Are you saying I have to accept Aristotelian physics to accept transubstantiation?" What if Aristotle's understanding of physical reality doesn't make any sense to me? How can I accept the doctrine of transubstantiation—defined as Catholic dogma—other than to say, "If the Church says so, I'll say so, too"?

Scandal-ridden religion

The appeal of "religionless Christianity" is powerful, whether or not we have the philosophical vocabulary of a Dietrich Bonhoeffer. We live in an age of intense religiosity and profound disillusionment with religion. Consider the modern scandals that wrack the Abrahamic faiths alone. Judaism struggles with the moral dilemmas posed by the State of Israel, and its relationship with the Palestinian people; Jimmy Carter, a close friend of Israel during his presidency, later described the policies of Israel toward the Palestinians as a form of "apartheid." Our Muslim friends are deeply distressed by the rise of groups like Al-Qaeda and ISIS, performing acts of terror in the name of Islam. Closer to home, Donald Trump rose to power on a wave of nationalistic populism and barely-disguised appeals to the dark forces of white supremacy; support from a substantial majority of Roman Catholics, evangelicals, Mormons and even a razor-thin majority of "mainline Protestants" (regarded as a liberal stream of Christianity) was a form of collusion with frank attempts to scapegoat Muslims, Mexican immigrants, the press, scientists and people of color (Smith and Martinez).

When Bonhoeffer wrote to Bethge about a religionless Christianity, he also prepared a sermon to be read at the baptism of his friend's son. He wrote the sermon as though speaking to a grown-up version of the infant. Near the conclusion, he tells of his disillusionment with the Church:

> Our church, which has been fighting these years only for its self-preservation, as though that were an end in itself, is incapable of taking the word of reconciliation and redemption to mankind and the world. Our earlier words are therefore bound to lose their force and cease, and our being Christians today will be limited to two things: prayer and righteous action among men. All Christian thinking, speaking and organizing must be born anew out of this prayer and action. By the time you have grown up, the church's form will have changed greatly. We are not yet out of the melting pot, and any attempt to help the church prematurely to a new expansion of its organization will merely delay its conversion and purification. (Letters and Papers from Prison, 300)

I was born eight years after the infant to whom that sermon was addressed. I came to faith as a young adult in the Jesus movement—a revival among then-young baby boomers who fancied themselves part of a "counterculture." Left-leaning, anti-war and pro-ecology, the "Jesus freaks" I knew in Detroit in 1971 were reading C.S. Lewis, Søren Kierkegaard, Watchman Nee and Dietrich Bonhoeffer. We regarded the institutional Church as hopelessly irrelevant and were happy to operate beyond its boundaries. We prayed for revival, even as the institutions of conservative Christianity absorbed the Jesus movement. Before long, what had begun as a counter-cultural movement was simply another force powering the religious right, along with racism, sexism, homophobia and a corporately funded resistance to environmental science.

Eventually, I stopped praying for revival—at least for what Bonhoeffer called "a new expansion of the Church's organization." And I did so for the reason Bonhoeffer cited: A revival of Christianity, in its current form, would fuel much that is antithetical to the kingdom of God and would, in Bonhoeffer's words, "merely delay its (the Church's) conversion."

Bonhoeffer was not raised in a devout family. His Christian commitment was intentional, and not merely cultural. He earned his doctorate in theology by age 21 and became a rising voice in the Church. His disillusionment with religion is all the more noteworthy for his deep personal commitment to the Christian faith, lived in the context of Christian community.

Bonhoeffer had reason to be disillusioned with religion. Hitler rose to power with the overwhelming support of the people and institutions of the Christian religion.[166] German pastors were prey to Hitler's anti-Semitism—endemic in the Church and deeply rooted, with Luther himself having been a brazen anti-Semite. Hitler wooed German Christians with appeals to morality, including "moral purity" and the epic

---

166 Alec Ryrie describes Jehovah's Witnesses as "the one major Protestant group that openly defied the Nazi state" even though many Protestants would regard Jehovah's Witnesses as "heterodox" (285).

battle between good and evil. Noting this appeal, religious scholar Jeffery Pugh describes the German Church at this time as filled with "great protests against secularism and godlessness, against Catholicism, disbelief and immorality" (76).

Let's pause to digest this. Many Christians celebrate Bonhoeffer's courageous resistance, but this admiration often cloaks a form of historical denial—as though Bonhoeffer represented a vigorous underground Christian resistance to Hitler, called the Confessing Church. The fact is, Bonhoeffer was an outlier even within the Confessing Church. By 1938, when Hitler was firmly in power, 85 percent of Confessing Church pastors had signed a loyalty oath to Hitler (40). While Bonhoeffer is regarded as a Christian martyr, his co-conspirators were members of the German military intelligence community—not fellow Christians in the Confessing Church. As Pugh observes, "He would find people who would take up the challenge of his time, but they would not do so out of commitment to Christ" (40).

To sharpen that point just a bit: If we regard Islam as a violent religion (compared to our beloved Christianity) we had better be prepared to account for Christianity's own violent tendency. By now, I hope we're all feeling just a hint of the mental anguish Bonhoeffer must have felt, reflecting on Christianity and the problem of religion in his prison cell.

A hidden cause of Bonhoeffer's religious problem?

There may also have been a hidden factor contributing to Bonhoeffer's disillusionment with religion. In Chapter 6, Emily referred to a recent biography by the respected Bonhoeffer scholar Charles Marsh. Using newly available sources, Marsh describes Bonhoeffer's relationship with Eberhard Bethge as marked by unrequited sexual desire on Bonhoeffer's part. I found the evidence compelling: Dietrich Bonhoeffer was gay.

Think of it: being gay in Germany at this period, when homosexuality was viciously stigmatized. A gay Bonhoeffer would have grown up deeply conflicted about his sexuality and terrified to be found out. During this period, homophobia was as widespread, institutionally protected and unchallenged in the Church as anti-Semitism. The pink triangle became an icon within the gay rights movement because it marked gay prisoners in the concentration camps (Steakley). As Christian ethicist David Gushee points out, Christian homophobia—like Christian anti-Semitism—was grounded in a pernicious and, until recently, fixed traditional interpretation of a handful of biblical texts. The unavoidable horror and shame of the Holocaust precipitated the relatively rapid abandonment of the traditional reading of these texts (Gushee, *Changing Our Mind*, 126-146). As it becomes more evident and unavoidable—the harm done to sexual minorities by a traditional reading of a handful of texts —we can hope for a similar repentance, but it is just beginning in our day and wasn't even imagined in Bonhoeffer's time.

Bonhoeffer was well situated to experience the problem of religion within a national, as well as an intimate, frame of reference. As a modern-day prophet, he confronted it by going deeper than simply criticizing a particular form of religion: Bonhoeffer thought there was a problem with religion itself and that we are moving out of a time when religion works. He developed these ideas in his two latest works, published posthumously as *Ethics* (dealing with morality) and *Letters and Papers from Prison*.

Cold water on our moral enterprise

Dietrich Bonhoeffer startles us with the opening lines of what he hoped would become his life's work, *Ethics*: "The knowledge of good and evil seems to be the aim of all ethical reflection. The first task of Christian ethics is to invalidate this knowledge" (21). Bonhoeffer grounds his approach to ethics in Israel's origin story in Genesis, where the "tree of the knowledge of good and evil" appears in the Garden of Eden story.[167]

Origin stories are powerful tales that shape our imagination for a long, long time. Consider the rise of the Tea Party—a political reaction to the election of Barack Obama, claiming title to the Boston Harbor protest against King George in 1773. A community's origin stories are used to frame a communal narrative over many years. In a sense, a nation's arguments are over the meaning of its origin stories. The Eden story can be framed as a classic morality tale, or as a critique of the instinctive way that we do morality. The latter goes to the heart of "the problem of religion," in light of Girard and Bonhoeffer.

To retell it briefly: *Two characters, Adam and Eve, walk with God in a lush garden. At the center of this garden stood two trees: the tree of life and the tree of the knowledge of good and evil. One day, God called out to the humans with a word of freedom: "You are free!" God said, "…to eat the fruit of any tree in the garden!" adding, "Just keep away from the fruit of the tree of the knowledge of good and evil. The day you eat of it you will surely die."*

Soon, another voice arose in the garden—a seductive voice, claiming to be wise: "Are you sure you don't want that fruit from the tree of the knowledge of good and evil? The day you eat of it, you will become wise, like God! Don't you want what God has?" They listened to that voice, and things did not go well for them.

The Eden story introduces two paths: not good and evil, per se, but the path of childlike trust in God (which leads to life)

---

167 In *Creation and Fall: A Theological Interpretation of Genesis 1-3*, Bonhoeffer had already begun his exploration of religion as tied to the knowledge of good and evil.

and the path of rivalry with God (seeking the knowledge of good and evil, so we can "be like God," which leads to death). That sentence might be worth rereading, as it runs counter to our assumed binary. The notion of two paths emerges again and again in Scripture, under various guises: the way of wisdom vs. the way of foolishness; the house built on solid rock vs. the house built on sand; the way of the Spirit vs. the way of "the flesh." But all these versions of "two paths" are an echo of an original binary facing Israel—and, by extension, all of humanity: the way of *life*, represented by the tree of life, and the way of *death*, represented by the tree of the knowledge of good and evil. By invoking *these* two trees in his treatment of ethics, Bonhoeffer invites us to think differently about morality.

A mystery hidden in plain sight

Bonhoeffer describes the Eden story as a children's fable: "The language is extremely childlike and shocking for those who want to 'understand' to know anything" (Bonhoeffer, *Creation and Fall: A Theological Interpretation of Genesis 1-3*, 50). That Jesus said entry into the kingdom of God requires us to become "like little children" should alert us to the possibility that our assumed "mature perspective" on morality may be misleading. Israel's Eden story is told as a children's story (replete with talking snakes and naming animals, a classic trope for small children) because there is something childlike in the human connection to the divine that we long for and are not yet ready to "grow out of."

However, this story invites us to do some very adultlike, critical self-reflection on the way we go about our moral enterprises—that is, in our supposed moral wisdom, which may simply be a kind of foolishness in religious guise. Bonhoeffer invites us to approach our understanding of ethics with deep sorrow and suspicion. After all, our ethical concerns are, themselves, mired in our sinnerliness. According to our origin story, this is not at all intuitive. We did *not* become sinners by choosing evil over good; instead, our sinnerliness is a profound personal disconnection from an immediate experience of God as our loving and guiding parent. This disconnection is portrayed by our choosing what had been forbidden to us: to eat from the tree of the knowledge of good and evil, even though the good fruit of all the other trees in the garden was freely available to us.

We moved, that is, beyond a position of childlikeness, in which all that we knew was known in relation to God and mediated through God—as a child experiences and navigates his or her way through the world through the mediation and guidance of parents. We stepped out of this sphere to inhabit a middle ground between God and the world, from which we hoped to assess the world (and God) for ourselves. So suggests Dietrich Bonhoeffer in his unfinished work, *Ethics* (21-24).

Think how counterintuitive this is. How easily we revert to a different binary than the one presented us. Our version of "two trees" might be the tree of good and the tree of evil, making the religious project choosing good over evil (and thus needing, above all, to be able to tell them apart). But the mystery standing in plain sight is quite different than that. The reason we are "ethically challenged" is not that we *lost* our knowledge of good and evil, but that we *gained* it. In grasping for the knowledge of good and evil, we've lost our childlike connection with God. In the aftermath of this loss, our knowing—including, maybe even especially, our *religious* knowing, in its moral aspect—is our own knowing, and not God's.

Girard confirms Bonhoeffer's intuitions about religion and morality

As Jeffrey Pugh observes in *Religionless Christianity: Dietrich Bonhoeffer in Troubled Times,* Bonhoeffer "never really develops a theory of religion, nor is there a fixed place in him that one can point to and think they possess the interpretive key to Bonhoeffer's concept of religion" (73). Where would Bonhoeffer have taken his intuitions about ethics and a religionless Christianity if he had been familiar with the writings of René Girard—who *did* develop a theory of religion?

Remember, Girard sees the violence of the scapegoat mechanism as the *origin* of what we call religion. Or, to use his language, it is the origin of "the sacred"—the transcendent-seeming awe that archaic societies felt when the chaos of spreading conflict was suddenly "resolved" by identifying and expelling (originally, murdering) a scapegoat. Girard sees the sacred (a term for what we are calling "religion") as intrinsically violent. This is the theme of *Violence and the Sacred*, one of Girard's earlier works. Girard scholar Robert G. Hamerton-Kelly understands that the so-called Axial Age, during which the major world religions emerged, represents a significant development beyond the violence of the "archaic sacred" though much of the "violent sacred" remains (Kaplan, 107).

Would Bonhoeffer agree with Girard that the "problem of religion" can be traced to the violence at the heart of the origin of religion? We can't know. Both were inescapably confronted with scapegoating at a massive scale. Born in pre-war France, Girard was only 17 years younger than Bonhoeffer, and would have understood even better than Bonhoeffer could the sheer scope and brutality of the Holocaust. This must have sensitized Girard to the ubiquity of the scapegoat mechanism in human culture and religion.[168]

Whether or not Bonhoeffer would agree with Girard's assessment about the origin of religion in "sacred violence,"

---

168 Furthermore, according to Girard's biographer, Cynthia Haven, Girard would have witnessed the public abuse of 20,000 women by French mobs after the Germans were defeated. Haven describes the collective guilt felt by many of the French for putting up relatively little resistance to the Nazi invasion. When the German armies were finally driven out, the women were accused of collaboration—sleeping with German soldiers, and so on. They were rounded up and their heads shorn as a mark of public shame (Haven, *Evolution of Desire*, 37).

he understood violence as the problem of our age and religion's complicity with violence as the problem of religion. At
the very least, we can say that Girard's hypothesis regarding
the origin of the sacred, and his later call for a Christianity
purged of violence, is tantalizingly resonant with Bonhoeffer's
yearning for a religionless Christianity.

Let's explore Girard's view of religion a bit further. Girard
saw religion as the foundation of human culture; not a mere
expression of it. In Girard's view, archaic society couldn't
exist without the relief valve of scapegoating. Human culture
began with a founding murder (Girard, *I See Satan Fall Like
Lightning*, 82-94). What we call "the gods" emerge in the
aftermath of a scapegoating event. After experiencing what
seems to be a miraculous peace in the wake of the scapegoat's
expulsion, the community begins to regard the victim as a
divine being, responsible for the community's newfound order.
The practice of sacrifice to the god (first of human victims, and
later of animals and other human replacements) originated
as a way to extend the ordering effects of scapegoats before
internal disputes threatened the community's survival (Girard,
Violence and the Sacred, 1-19).

Girard also sees the emergence of law (in the form of
taboos, moral codes and so on) as connected to the scapegoat
mechanism. After communities are threatened by rivalries run
wild, they resolve these tensions in a scapegoating event and
institute taboos to contain the rivalries that nearly destroyed
the community. These taboos include strictures against
excessive vengeance and social arrangements, like sex between
family members, that heighten rivalry (218-22). The scapegoating event, then, is the origin of central aspects of religion:
the gods, sacrifice and law. While religious cultures revere all
three, Girard sees them as rooted in the violence of a founding
murder. They play a key role in maintaining order and their
removal comes with significant dangers to the social order, but
their origin in violence is real and must be confronted. This

provides a framework within which Bonhoeffer's concerns about religion and morality cohere.

A love-beyond-rivalry ethic

Girard's understanding of law (with its connections to sacred violence in the scapegoat mechanism) is attached to morality. This is a deep dive into the ambiguous origins of our moral reasoning, and it mirrors Bonhoeffer's thought. Bonhoeffer did not question the legitimacy of ethics (or morality) *per se*, but challenged the way humans regard attaining "the knowledge of good and evil" as the aim, or the center, of the moral enterprise. Like Girard, he is concerned with helping us become suspicious of our largely unexamined moral impulses.

Girard and Bonhoeffer call for a fundamental re-centering of "ethics." Girard calls for the renunciation of envy-fueled rivalry—and its inevitable devolution into violence—as the center of ethical concern. Bonhoeffer calls us to renounce "the will to power" that seems to characterize so much religion, in favor of the embrace of a God who identifies with us in our vulnerability and powerlessness.[169] These two perspectives are closely related and we might imagine that they represent intuitions toward the same reality.

What might such a re-centering look like?

Girard, echoing Bonhoeffer, emphasizes the importance of the Sermon on the Mount (Mt. 5-7) in a Christian ethic. In the sermon, Jesus exposes religion's potential to distract us from, rather than lead us to, God. It is a growing dispute between Jesus and the "scribes [teachers of the law] and Pharisees [a particular party of teachers]".

---

169 "Here is the decisive difference between Christianity and all religions. The Bible directs man to God's powerlessness and suffering; only the suffering God can help. To that extent we may say the development towards the world coming of age outlines above, which has done away with a false conception of God, opens up a way of seeing the God of the Bible who wins power and space in the world by his weakness" (Bonhoeffer, *Letters and Papers from Prison,* 361). One might have hoped that Bonhoeffer had recognized Judaism (at least) as sharing in this development, which he ascribes to Christianity alone.

In light of a demonization of the Pharisees, fueled by an underlying anti-Semitism affecting so much Gentile Christianity, we need to remind ourselves of a few things before proceeding. The "Judaism" of this period could better be described as a collection of often-competing "Judaisms" (Neusner, 6-9)—just as any contemporary religion is an extended family engaged in intra-family disputes, some of them quite sharp. The Pharisees, in particular, promoted a more democratized form of Judaism that would have appealed to the disciples of Jesus. Jesus is critical of some teachings of the Pharisees that would distract his disciples from following his instruction. So, in the Sermon on the Mount, we have a series of "You have heard it said, but I say to you" sayings (Mt. 5: 17-48).

In the face of this sharp polemic, we can forget that Jesus also honored Israel's teachers (Mt. 13:52)—and many Pharisees, in particular, did, in fact, come to follow the instruction of Jesus. In the book of Acts, Pharisees are portrayed as speaking on behalf of tolerance toward the vulnerable Jesus sect (5:34-39), protecting Paul from perse-cution (23:9) and belonging to the Jesus movement (15:5). In commenting on the "woe to you Pharisees" passage in the Gospels, Girard urges us to see the Pharisees as the best of religious people in his time, so that we see ourselves in them and understand that his condemnations apply to aspects of all religions—including Christianity (Girard, *Things Hidden Since the Foundation of the World*, 160-164).

Echoes of Eden in the Sermon on the Mount

The Sermon on the Mount bears strong echoes of Israel's origin story (the Eden story), and can be viewed as a form of *midrash* on the binary involving the tree of life vs. the tree of the knowledge of good and evil. The sermon commends the childlike faith of the first humans in the garden. The Lord's Prayer is of a child speaking to God as a benevolent parent, providing daily bread, forgiveness and deliverance from tests beyond the child's ability to endure. In Matthew 6:30, the sense of childlike dependency is affirmed in the counsel not to worry about being provided for: "But if God so clothes the grass of the field … will he not much more clothe you—you of little faith?"

The prohibition against judging others (Mt. 7:1-5) can be seen as an interpretation and extension of the prohibition against eating the fruit of the tree of the knowledge of good and evil. The Pharisees are portrayed in the Gospels as presenting Jesus with moral test cases for his ruling (often in an effort to trap him in polemical binds). They approach him with confident knowledge about the tricky moral concerns of their day, and not with a childlike faith. They are preoccupied with discerning the difference between good and evil, regarding such knowledge as the aim of their religious project.[170] We do the same today. Jesus is concerned, instead, with what gives "life," rather than what gives "knowledge." In a different context, Paul perceives the focus on knowledge as a distraction from the pursuit of love.[171] The subtleties of the Eden story are being worked out here.

Focus on renouncing rivalry

René Girard highlights how Genesis 2 introduces the Jewish concern with envy and rivalry as the fuel sustaining the engine of violence among humans (and affecting all creatures). This is a concern we see throughout the book of Genesis, with its several sibling rivalries: Cain-Abel; Isaac-Ishmael; Jacob-Esau; Leah-Rachel; and Joseph-brothers. Here we have sacrifice, prohibition, envy-rivalry and violence—all of a

---

170 See *Ethics,* 30-41 for Bonhoeffer's treatment of the prohibition against judging and the knowledge of good and evil.

171 This is a major theme in 1 Corinthians, dealing with a party claiming special knowledge. See, for example: "… we know that 'all of us possess knowledge.' Knowledge puffs up, but love builds up. Anyone who claims to know something does not yet have the necessary knowledge; but anyone who loves God is known by him" (1 Cor. 8:1).

piece in the beginning. And it was all foreshadowed when the original humans were seduced into thinking that prohibition against the knowledge of good and evil comes from a god in rivalry with them: not wanting them to have what would surely be good for them, because it would make them equal to God.

The prohibition of envy, enshrined in the Tenth Commandment ("Thou shalt not covet") is seen throughout the Sermon on the Mount. The Beatitudes can be seen as instruction not to envy those things desired by so many religious people: riches, power, good reputation and freedom from suffering. The rivalry powered by envy is prohibited in the instruction about murder, anger toward the brother and contempt. Similarly, leaving one's wife to have another's is prohibited. Swearing oaths to gain advantage is prohibited, and simple truth-telling enjoined. Vengeance and retaliation for wrongs done is prohibited and forgiveness enjoined. The commandment to love the neighbor is expanded to include even one's enemy. Practicing one's piety before others, to provoke their envy, is prohibited; sincerity before God is enjoined.

As Girard reminds us, Jesus is squarely in the tradition of Israel, to expose the scapegoat mechanism. When this mechanism is exposed, it loses its power to contain and constrain escalating human violence—leaving us, in a sense, more vulnerable to our own violent ways. This calls for all people to confront their own mimetic desire whenever it leads to rivalry and the violence that rivalry breeds.

Let's pause for a moment and compare this emphasis with so much of our moral rhetoric today. The dangers of envy, rivalry, contempt and judging others—especially as precursors of violence—can hardly be regarded as the center of our moral concerns. The religious world within the United States, at least, is preoccupied with anything having to do with sex—while the moral "conversation" seems to be *characterized* by envy, rivalry, contempt and judging others.

Two paths known by their fruit

In the "summing up" section of the sermon (Mt. 7: 12-28), Jesus invokes the metaphor of two paths: one leading to life, the other to death. It is yet another echo of the two trees at the center of Eden, coming after the prohibition against judging, which Bonhoeffer ties to the pursuit of the knowledge of good and evil as a characteristic of the religious project. The allusion to Eden's two trees continues with Jesus's metaphor of a tree and its fruit:

> Beware of false prophets, who come to you in sheep's clothing but inwardly are ravenous wolves. You will know them by their fruits. Are grapes gathered from thorns, or figs from thistles? In the same way, every good tree bears good fruit, but the bad tree bears bad fruit. A good tree cannot bear bad fruit, nor can a bad tree bear good fruit. Every tree that does not bear good fruit is cut down and thrown into the fire. Thus you will know them by their fruits. (Mt. 7:16-17)

The Gospels describe differing approaches to discernment. The Pharisees are depicted[172] as modeling a kind of moralism, which Bonhoeffer regards as the illicit pursuit of the knowledge of good and evil. Jesus advocates a different approach to discernment: notice the effects, and thereby discern their source (as a tree is known by its fruit).

Jesus discerned how and where to proceed in ministry by paying attention to the Spirit at work around him, summed up in the saying, "Very truly I tell you the Son can do nothing on his own but only what he sees the Father doing" (Jn. 5:19). This observational approach would seem woefully inadequate

---

172 It's important to note that the Gospel material on the Pharisees was shaped by the concerns of the early Church in its various localities, including disputes between various factions of the Jesus movement and disputes within the broader Jewish and/or Gentile communities. The depiction of the Pharisees in the Gospel is not simply driven by a desire to provide the most accurate historical record of this sect within Judaism at the time of Jesus.

if we didn't regard God as a powerful agency at work in the world, whose presence can be detected through open-hearted attention.

Absent this, we crave a different method. But what if that's the point: absent this, there *isn't* a satisfactory method?

Paul, who had a robust experience and understanding of the Spirit at work in the world, advocates a similar approach, in his letter to the Galatians.

Sinners in the hands of an angry Paul

We discover Paul at his angriest in his letter to the Gentile churches scattered throughout the region of Galatia (modern-day Turkey). The churches of this region were different than the churches addressed in Paul's other letters. In many other places, the Church was a mix of Jewish and Gentile followers of Jesus, and in some places, the Jewish believers were dominant. The churches of Galatia were composed almost entirely of Gentile converts.

In Galatians, Paul is in an intense dispute with a group of itinerant teachers who claim the endorsement of the church in Jerusalem—the center of messianic Judaism. These teachers have been characterized in the past as "Judaizers", but this is misleading; following the lead of J. Louis Martyn, we will refer to them as simply "the Teachers" (Martyn, 117-126). The older term suggests that Paul was engaged in a dispute between Christianity and Judaism. In fact, what we now call "Christianity" was, at this time, a movement *within* Judaism (albeit in tension with other expressions of Judaism) that was now strained by the inclusion of so many Gentiles—and in the case of the churches of Galatia, churches that were almost entirely Gentile. Paul was a Jewish teacher himself, from the party of the Pharisees, who was educated under Gamaliel, the founder of a prominent rabbinic school of the period (Acts 22:3). Paul is writing as a founder himself—as he calls himself, in the letter, their "father in Christ." He regards the Teachers as interlopers, bringing a different version of the Gospel than the one he introduced. This is a Gospel so flawed (at least, for proclamation to the Gentile converts of Galatia) as to be false. Paul's tone is immoderate, like a spurned lover.

Within a few centuries, what we call "the Church" had become almost entirely dominated by Gentiles. The voice of the Jewish believers had, by then, been suppressed—either by the accidents of history (centered, as many were, in regions ravaged by war, so their writings have been lost to us) or by the comparative volume of Gentile voices. Until recently, this Gentile Church has been afflicted by an unchallenged and toxic combination of incipient anti-Semitism and simple ignorance regarding the diverse Judaisms of the period when the New Testament was written. All to say, we have to do a lot more learning from Jewish scholars (and the Christians informed by them) before confidently weighing in on what Jews who were not Jesus followers believed and practiced regarding the law, salvation, sacrifice and the rest.[173]

Stepping back for a moment from the details of the controversy addressed in Galatians, we can say that the Teachers were raising a moral alarm: "Unless you Gentile converts are circumcised and follow the obligations of Torah, you will find yourselves cut off from the life of God." In response to this moral alarm, Paul raises a Gospel alarm: "This message from the Teachers is not the Gospel I preached to you."

Paul begins by reminding his readers of his spiritual biography. It is the story of an overconfident young man enforcing his (mis)understanding of Torah on the early Jewish followers of Jesus. Paul's moral reasoning blinded him, and this blindness justified violence toward others. He then underwent a stunning redirection from the Jewish messiah, who sent Paul as envoy to the Gentile world—perhaps

---

173 A good place to start is *Judaism When Christianity Began,* by Jacob Neusner, and *Siblings: Rabbinic Judaism and Early Christianity at Their Beginnings,* by Hayim Goren Perelmuter. See also, *The Jewish Annotated New Testament,* edited by Amy-Jill Levine and Mark Zvi Brettler, and *The Misunderstood Jew: The Church and the Scandal of the Jewish Jesus,* by Amy-Jill Levine.

knowing what a profound reassessment such a mission would require of him.

Paul's approach to faithful living for Gentiles

We turn now to Galatians 5, in which Paul confronts the question of ethics. Paul turns to themes emphasized in the Sermon on the Mount. He begins by referring to the crisis in the church, provoked by the influence of his opponents—the interloper Teachers, claiming Jerusalem credentials, who are pursuing a competing "Gentile mission" in the wake of Paul's pioneering work.

> *You were running a good race. Who cut in on you to keep you from obeying the truth? That kind of persuasion does not come from the one who calls you. 'A little yeast works through the whole batch of dough.' I am confident in the Lord that you will take no other view. The one who is throwing you into confusion, whoever that may be, will have to pay the penalty. Brothers and sisters, if I am still preaching circumcision, why am I still being persecuted? In that case the offense of the cross has been abolished. As for those agitators, I wish they would go the whole way and emasculate themselves!* (Gal. 5:7-12)

The Teachers have been imposing the burden of circumcision on the Gentile converts, signifying the obligation to come under the yoke of the Mosaic Law. Paul, who likely continued his own Torah observance (Kinzer, 71-88), bristled at the idea that his Gentile converts would have to become Torah-observant. This was not a burden imposed on Gentile converts by his Gospel. The Teachers might have been scandalized by Paul's view that Gentile Jesus followers could be faithful to God without also becoming Torah-observant. The Teachers regarded Torah as God's gift, to ensure faithfulness among those who receive it; how could Gentile converts please God without the benefit of Torah observance?

Echoes of Eden: opposing regimes

As the apostle of a new creation, Paul's appeal is replete with allusions to Eden:

> *You, my brothers and sisters, were called to be free. But do not use your freedom to indulge the flesh; rather, serve one another humbly in love. For the entire law is fulfilled in keeping this one command: 'Love your neighbor as yourself.' If you bite and devour each other, watch out or you will be destroyed by each other. For the flesh desires what is contrary to the Spirit, and the Spirit what is contrary to the flesh. They are in conflict with each other, so that you are not to do whatever you want. But if you are led by the Spirit, you are not under the law. (Gal. 5:13-18)*

Listen for the echoes of Israel's origin story: walking with God in a new creation (an earlier theme in the letter); being led by the Spirit/Breath/Wind; bearing the fruit of love; and renouncing the path of envy. Paul also sets up a binary that echoes the subtlety of the choice between two trees in the middle of the garden.

As in the Eden story, Paul presents two paths, but his are designated the way of the Spirit and the way of "the flesh." The former leads to life, following the Breath/Wind/Spirit of God. The Teachers represent the latter path, characterizing it as wise, which invites us to remember an earlier appeal to wisdom made by Eden's talking snake: *Why not eat from the tree of the knowledge of good and evil and be like God?* This overtly religious path actually leads to death.

Paul's term for this other path, marked by "works of the flesh" (fueled by the desires of the flesh) is notoriously difficult to pin down. It's not a reference to the body, per se, nor is it a reference to material reality, as opposed to spiritual reality—both common misconceptions. The term probably contains an allusion to the rite of circumcision imposed on the Gentiles. The fact that "the flesh"—in this context—is a religious term is a clue that it may correspond to another path with religious appeal: the tree of the knowledge of good and evil, representing or conveying the power of death; as opposed to the tree of life, representing or conveying the power of life. Without drawing this comparison, J. Louis Martyn makes a credible case that the "Spirit" and the "flesh" represent two "warring powers," brought into conflict as the kingdom of God invades this present evil age (Martyn, *Galatians: A New Translation with Introduction and Commentary*, 97-100).

Martyn's use of the term "warring powers" to describe Paul's Spirit-flesh binary suggests something more vigorous than two paths. Perhaps a term closer to Paul's thinking is the term "regime." The inhabitants of my home state, Michigan, have been under three major regimes. The Algonquian peoples came first ("Michigan" is an Algonquian word), then the rival British and French colonial powers, battling for ascendancy as a second regime. Some European settlers then broke free of their British overlords and completed the near-destruction of the indigenous people, to set up the current regime. Each regime has affected virtually every aspect of life in this territory—the forests, flora, fauna, lakes and rivers, air quality, economic structure, language, currency, values, norms, *etc.*

Paul is writing as a Jewish man whose nation—Israel—is under occupation, so the militaristic imagery has a different resonance than it does in our time, when so much Christianity is linked with empires established through massive military power. A less warlike metaphor might be the concept of high-pressure and low-pressure weather systems. These systems cover large portions of territory, affecting all living things under their influence. As one system bumps into another, there is often a period of turbulence in the form of storms.

As Martyn points out, the realm of the Holy Spirit is moving into the space occupied by the realm of the flesh, so there is bound to be conflict at their point of intersection—in this case, the controversy that occasioned Paul's letter.

Whether seen as a regime or a system, this is the fundamental binary for Paul—one that overshadows all previous binaries, including Jew-Gentile, slave-free and male-female. The significance of these other binaries is reduced by comparison because the age in which they matter is nearing its end (Martyn, 570). The regime of the Spirit vs. the regime of the flesh—this is the binary that should command our attention and discernment.

Paul's mission as a messenger of Jesus (or as an ambassador of the regime of the Holy Spirit) is not to bring the Gentile converts to Jesus "under the Law" of Moses—that is, to impose the obligations of Torah observance on them. Paul is after a more fundamental regime change—from the regime of "the flesh" to the rescuing regime of "the Spirit."

Regard the fruit to discern the tree

What does this mean for how the Gentile converts should now conduct themselves—especially in the new community forming around Jesus and empowered by the Holy Spirit? For this, Paul relies on the approach advocated by Jesus in the Sermon on the Mount: "by their fruits you shall know them."

He writes:

> *The works of the flesh are obvious: sexual immorality, impurity and debauchery; idolatry and witchcraft; hatred, discord, jealousy, fits of rage, selfish ambition, dissensions, factions and envy; drunkenness, orgies and the like. I warn you, as I did before, that those who live like this will not inherit the kingdom of God. But the fruit of the Spirit is love, joy, peace,*

forbearance, kindness, goodness, faithfulness, gentleness and self-control. Against such things there is no law. Those who belong to Christ Jesus have crucified the flesh with its passions and desires. Since we live by the Spirit, let us keep in step with the Spirit. Let us not become conceited, provoking and envying each other. (Gal. 5:19-26)

We can discern the flesh (the misleading path) by observing its effects. As Paul says, "the works of the flesh" are obvious, observable and easily recognized. He then offers a list of things that characterize a community rent by multiplying conflicts that are fueled by rivalries and envy. You just have to see these "works" (a word that emphasizes effects) to know where they come from. Likewise, the regime of the Holy Spirit is known by its fruit, followed by a list of things that characterize a community that anyone in their right mind would want to be part of.

The phrase "against such thing there can be no law" is a tip-off: the Eden garden is in view. Eden represents a more direct communion with God, before the Law was given.

In Eden, there is only one prohibition, preceded by a word of freedom: "You are free to eat from any tree in the garden (against such things there can be no prohibition), but of the tree of the knowledge of good and evil you shall not eat, for in the day you eat of it, you shall die (this tree alone is prohibited because its fruit leads to death)" (Gen. 2:16-17).

We can hear the echoes of Eden in Paul's earlier lines regarding freedom and a single command: "You, my brothers and sisters, were called to be free. But do not use your freedom to indulge the flesh; rather, serve one another humbly in love. For the entire law is fulfilled in keeping this one command: 'Love your neighbor as yourself.'" (Gal. 5:13-14).

As noted by many commentators, while Paul lists several good effects of the Holy Spirit, the "fruit" of the Spirit is singular in Greek. The significance of this—like so much else about this letter—is in dispute, but it is possible that Paul regards the fruit (singular) as love, expressed in the particular virtues of "joy, peace, patience, kindness, generosity, gentleness and self-control." This would correspond to Gal. 5:14, rendered by Martyn as, "For the whole law has been brought to completion by one sentence: 'You shall love your neighbor as yourself!'" In other words, the fruit is love, in the same way that the Torah is fulfilled or completed in keeping the one command: Love your neighbor as yourself. In support of this reading, it is worth noting that these two ideas are also connected in Jesus's summary statements in the Sermon on the Mount (Mt. 7: 12-18).

Martyn and others suggest that Paul's view of Torah is not comprehensive in Galatians and that Romans elaborates on this question in a more dispassionate way, since Paul was not the founder of the churches in Rome (and these house churches included a much stronger contingent of Jewish believers in Jesus). We would add that a more comprehensive view of the role of Torah in the life of believers in Jesus, not to mention in the life of the Jewish people, is well beyond our scope. We would further suggest that it is beyond the ken of the Church in general at this time, without much closer dialogue with the inheritors of Torah, the Jewish people. May God bless all such dialogue wherever it occurs. In the meantime, a humble caution—especially on the part of Gentile Christians—is advised.

Humbled as moral agents

What we can say is this: Jesus seems to challenge the notion that faithfulness to God is about gaining knowledge—especially knowledge regarding good and evil. He challenges the notion that faithfulness to God is about becoming an expert in morality. There's something deeply distorted about the way we human beings go about the moral enterprise.

Facing the question of whether Gentile converts should be placed under the obligation of Torah observance, Paul is informed by his searing experience as a recovering scape-goater. He is painfully aware that, in his zeal for morality, he actually used something given by God—Torah—to oppose the work of God. This realization—something that came to him by divine revelation, not moral knowledge or moral reasoning—humbled him as a moral agent.

The radical significance of Paul's teaching in Galatians has been obscured in the Christian tradition by the tendency to paint the Law of Moses as inherently odious. Preachers glibly refer to Torah's 612 commands as an example of legalistic sophistry bordering on the ridiculous—as something that necessarily evokes an insecure scrupulosity among those who seek to observe it. But the witness of Torah-observant Jews is quite different than the tortured perspective of Martin Luther, reacting to the legalism of medieval monastic (and Gen-tile-dominated) Catholicism. Rejecting Torah doesn't free us from the distortion that lies at the heart of our instinctive way of engaging morality.

The adequacy of Paul's instructions was predicated on his understanding that he and his converts *experienced* "the Spirit" (a power invading the realm of "the flesh," if Martyn is correct) as an active and pursuing agency whose efficacy can be trusted to prevail, is sufficient, and will get the job done. As Paul reminds us in the beginning of his letter, he is convinced that something has been unleashed in the world—something that pursued and overtook him; something that is bearing witness to and effecting not simply a better way through this world, but a transformation so radical as to be called a new creation.

You are not alone

All to say, dear reader, that if you have a problem with religion despite an appreciation for Jesus, you are not alone. If you think that there is something fundamentally off about religion (as a way to do what religion purports to want), you are not crazy. Others before you and many around you have had the same intuition. The problem of religion is nettlesome—that's why it cuts, and that's why it seems to be the cause of so much suffering in the world. Self-evidently, it is.

This is why it can be so reassuring to see within the Jesus tradition, which is the tradition of Israel as well, an acknowledgment of this crazy-making dilemma—that something about religion *itself*, and especially the kind of moral meaning-making that religion produces, seems to be keeping us from God. And this acknowledgment is present from the beginning, in one of Israel's origin stories. The prophets and sages of Israel who question the validity of things that seem so central to religion—like sacrifice, and whether all religious wisdom is ultimately wise—take up the problem. And Jesus, learning from them, takes it up as well.

Yes, he does. And he subjects himself to the problem of religion—the violence it produces—in order to expose it for all to see.

All that remains is for the rest of us to add our experiences (and the insights they generate) to the likes of René Girard and Dietrich Bonheoffer, until we all enter what St. Paul called "the glorious liberty of the children of God" (Ro. 8:21).

14

A Spirituality of Resistance: Pray and Act

Ken

SO MUCH OF the writing, speaking and marketing about spirituality has been shaped by the advantaged perspective of those with the best media access in a consumer culture. Maybe that's why so much of the contemporary Christian approach to spirituality seems to mirror the self-help, how-to-improve-my-life literature, un-tethered from a Gospel concern for justice. What does spirituality look like if it supports faith as a form of resistance to the powers oppressing people, other creatures and creation itself?

Let's take a closer look at those words of Dietrich Bonhoeffer, disillusioned by the impotence of a spirituality of the advantaged to resist the nationalist demagoguery of Adolf Hitler:

> Our church, which has been fighting these years only for its self-preservation, as though that were an end in itself, is incapable of taking the word of reconciliation and redemption to mankind and the world. Our earlier words are therefore bound to

lose their force and cease, and our being Christians today will be limited to two things: prayer and righteous action among men. All Christian thinking, speaking and organizing must be born anew out of this prayer and action. By the time you have grown up, the church's form will have changed greatly. We are not yet out of the melting pot, and any attempt to help the church prematurely to a new expansion of its organization will merely delay its conversion and purification. (Bonhoeffer, Letters and Papers from Prison, 300)

The phrase "prayer and righteous action among men" echoes the Jewish term *mitzvah*—righteous deeds of compassion that constitute the heart of a Jewish *spirituality*. Such deeds are the heart of all major religious traditions of our time. It's not an accident that Bonhoeffer chose this Jewish idiom when his church was enabling a massive scapegoating operation against her sibling, the Jewish people.

The critical failure of the Christian Church had exposed the utter inadequacy of "all Christian thinking, speaking and organizing"—which, Bonhoeffer said, "must be born anew out of this prayer and action." Prayer and action would become the source of whatever repentance and renewal might rise from the ashes of the Church's failure.

This turns on its head the classic Reformation thinking that correct belief, grounded in the correct interpretation of Scripture, leading to the correct construal of the Church—e.g., as the place "where the Gospel is rightly preached and the sacraments are rightly administered"—would inevitably lead to correct actions. All of that had been proven grossly inadequate in Bonhoeffer's experience. In its place, Bonhoeffer commends a painfully stripped-down spirituality, one that might otherwise be considered hopelessly naïve: pray and act. "All Christian thinking, speaking and organizing must be born anew out of this prayer and action."

Circumstance pressed Bonhoeffer to adopt this approach when he was invited to join a plot to assassinate Hitler. Consider his dilemma: Bonhoeffer's theological work had focused on the pacifist teaching of the Sermon on the Mount, and now he is trying to decide whether to lend a hand to an assassination plot. His theology—let alone the Christianity surrounding him—was wholly inadequate to guide him at such an important juncture. He joined the conspiracy, having been reduced to a kind of childlike position in which he could only, in the end, pray and act.

Pray and act: this is the spirituality of the vulnerable, the poor, the oppressed, the disinherited—and any who wish to align with the God who aligns with them.

Bonhoeffer meets pray-and-act spirituality in Harlem

Bonhoeffer saw this spirituality at work during his time in New York City. His host, Union Theological Seminary, was the intellectual center of liberal Christianity, nestled among the historic (and powerfully privileged) Protestant denominations. It was a heady time of deconstruction, based on form and textual criticism combined with the emergence of what would be known as "the social Gospel." But Bonhoeffer was unimpressed with the spiritual vitality at Union. For sustenance, he turned instead to an African-American church in nearby Harlem, throwing himself into the life of the Abyssinian Baptist Church. The congregation was less than 70 years removed from slavery and well acquainted with slavery's then-contemporary offspring: the Jim Crow laws of the South and the overt-systemic racism of the North. The pastor of this large (10,000-member) church was Adam Clayton Powell, Sr.—a spiritual leader, community activist, founder of the Urban League and active member of the NAACP. The church was a leader in the African-American faith-based resistance movement.

The spirituality of Abyssinan Baptist was robust. It was a center of the Harlem Renaissance, marked by the work of artists like James Weldon Johnson, who wrote the lyrics of "Lift Every Voice and Sing" (also known as the African-American national anthem.) Consider the first two verses:

Lift every voice and sing,
Till earth and Heaven ring,
Ring with the harmonies of liberty;
Let our rejoicing rise,
High as the listening skies,
Let it resound loud as the rolling sea.
Sing a song full of faith that the dark past has taught us,
Sing a song full of the hope that the present has brought us;
Facing the rising sun
Of our new day begun,
Let us march on till victory is won.

Stony the road we trod
Bitter the chastening rod,
Felt in the days when hope unborn had died;
Yet with a steady beat,
Have not our weary feet
Come to the place for which our fathers sighed?
We have come over a way that with tears has been watered,
We have come, treading our path through the blood of the slaughtered,
Out from the gloomy past,
Till now we stand at last
Where the white gleam of our bright star is cast

Johnson also wrote *God's Trombones: Seven Negro Sermons in Verse,* which artistically conveys the heart of inspired black preaching. Read the lyrics to Johnson's "The Judgment Day":

And I feel Old Earth a-shuddering—
And I see the graves a-bursting—
And I hear a sound,
A blood chilling sound.
What sound is that I hear?

It's the clicking together of the dry bones,
Bone to bone—the dry bones.
And I see coming out of the bursting graves,
And marching up from the valley of death,
The army of the dead.
And the living and the dead in the twinkling of an eye
Are caught up in the middle of the air,
Before God's judgment bar.
(Johnson, 58).

Not a timid, tentative, beset-by-doubt-from-the-latest-form-criticism example of spirituality here! If spirituality means hoisting our sails to catch the wind of the Holy Spirit, then there are two sides to every sail: one side facing the wind, and the other side facing the direction the wind is blowing—toward the cry of the victim.

Bonhoeffer met unapologetically *experiential* Christianity at Abyssinian Baptist Church. Worship was intellectually, emotionally and physically expressive. Scripture was employed as salve for weary souls and inspiration for courageous action—but read with the critical eye of those who suffered under white supremacist interpretations of Scripture. Bonhoeffer found the combination of robust spirituality, critical thinking and risk-taking, community-building, resistance activism compelling. He returned to Germany with a new vision, prepared to engage in his own form of faith-based resistance.

Bonhoeffer shifted from academic theological work to increasing activism against the Nazi regime. He felt summoned to follow the Jesus revealed in the Gospels; the teacher of the Sermon on the Mount. His prayer life deepened as he discovered prayer practices of the monastic movement, including *lectio devina* (a contemplative form of Scripture reading that emphasizes the Gospels). In 1935, Bonhoeffer assumed leadership of an underground seminary at Finkenwalde committed to serving the resistance movement; several of these spiritual practices were incorporated into the common life of the seminarians. Within two years, the Gestapo had closed the seminary and arrested many of its students. By the time he wrote these words in 1944—"our being Christians today will be limited to two things: prayer and righteous action among men. All Christian thinking, speaking and organizing must be born anew out of this prayer and action"—they had already been seared into his soul.

These words resonate still as we witness a church scrambling to preserve its power and privilege, while resisting the work of the Spirit; a church co-opted by authoritarian voices preaching nationalism and fueled by a thinly veiled white supremacy—all framed as noble resistance to a much-despised "political correctness." The genie has been released from its bottle again. It will no doubt morph into different shapes as befits the particulars of the fear growing among us.

The work of René Girard reminds us that our cultural moment is simply another iteration of the scapegoat mechanism—the tendency to project our collective guilt and the pent-up tensions of our conflicts onto a vulnerable few, in order to preserve a fragile order serving "the many" at their expense. Seeing this and then renouncing our participation in it requires a *spiritual* renewal; "born anew" is Bonhoeffer's phrase.

What kind of praying and what sort of spiritual practices can empower the work of resistance in our hearts, our communities and our world?

The Pentecostal practices

The Pentecostal movement is a global work of the Spirit originating among the disinherited, notwithstanding its more recent promulgation through the sophisticated marketing organs of American evangelicalism (of which the charismatic movement is now but a wing.) Ignore the televised forms of Pentecostalism, the hip marketing and the fog-machine reverence of celebrity worship leaders. Consider instead the treasures buried beneath this array of religiously dressed-up consumerism. Let's start with some of the least-expected-in-a-book-like-this practices from this spirituality of the margins.

Speaking in tongues

Pentecostalism is best known for the permission it grants to pray in ways that can be described as trans-rational—beyond the boundaries of logical-reasoned thought and speech. "We don't know how to pray as we ought," wrote Paul, "but the Spirit helps us in our weakness giving voice to sighs and groans too deep for words" (Romans 8:28). Wonder is trans-rational. Praise can be, too—sorrow, loneliness and grief, as well. Heavy metal music. A Jackson Pollock painting. Much human expression is trans-rational, because rationality is only one of our many "heart capacities."

As a young man, I had a mentor in faith named Joseph—a grad student from India at the University of Michigan, who belonged to the Ceylon Pentecostal Mission. The charismatic renewal was in full swing, so I had plenty of peers who were eager to get me speaking in tongues. I was curious and wanted to please them. Perhaps I wanted to reassure my religiously insecure self that I was not bereft of the Spirit. They coached me: "Start praying out loud in English, then stop praying in English and just let the sounds keep coming." I did it, and I liked it a lot.

My wife, Julia, is an Episcopal priest who wasn't caught up in this charismatic fervor. When I recently demonstrated what I call "speaking in tongues," she said, "Oh, that sounds like making up a language—what Oceana [now my stepdaughter] and I used to do when she was a kid." Julia did her own demonstration, stringing random syllables together in what sounded like a language made up on the fly. Was my speech "the real gift of tongues" and hers, something else? The answer to that question seems irrelevant to me.

Many religious traditions have a form of "glossolalia" (the sociological term for speaking in tongues), and I suspect that on a continuum between "ordinary" and "wildly supernatural," the gift of tongues is often closer to the former. Which doesn't make it any less a gift of the Spirit. Besides, I like doing whatever it is I do and find there are times when I'm able to express things that words can't convey—and that expression is a kind of praying. (I do not usually do this within earshot of others, but often when I'm driving in my car.) Sometimes I'm perplexed or frightened or frustrated, and have to give voice to something that I don't yet have words to convey. Other times I'm delighted for no particular reason but need to express it. Sometimes I sing while I'm doing it—setting the words in a made-up melody, usually just riffing in a key. When the world is too heavy, it helps. When I need to interrupt ruminating thought-loops or the unwanted fragment of a song stuck in my head ("You're so vain, you probably think this song is about you … "), it helps.

When I think about what it means to pray in tongues, I wonder if it doesn't do us some good to speak things that don't lend themselves to words now and again. I wonder if God doesn't enjoy hearing us prattle on like this, momentarily untethered to our known tongue. I wonder if it doesn't help us to venture beyond our known languages from time to time—bound as they often are to social arrangements like patriarchy and rigid gender binaries that may not have much at all to do with God. If language contains and promotes ways of thinking and being that fall short of God, maybe it's a small act of resistance to speak in tongues. I'm grateful for my sojourn through the charismatic movement where I learned to appreciate speaking in tongues—this culturally marginal, but helpful-to-me, way of praying.

Prophecy

"For those who speak in a tongue do not speak to other people but to God; for nobody understands them, since they are speaking mysteries in the Spirit. On the other hand, those who prophesy speak to other people for their up building and encouragement and consolation" (1 Co. 14:2-3).

Prophecy is a form of speaking to others that is inspired by the Holy Spirit. Its forms are as "manifold" (to borrow an old English word) as any inspired speech—no "thus saith the Lord" or wild-eyed looks required. The function of the gift of prophecy in the New Testament is congruent with the Gospel of John revelation of the Holy Spirit as "Paraclete"—Greek for "defender, comforter, one called alongside to encourage." In Girardian terms, prophecy is a work of the Spirit to counter the effects of accusation—characteristic of scapegoating mobs. The gift is meant to build up those whose inherent dignity, as children of God, is under assault.

I had a dramatic experience as the beneficiary of a prophetic encouragement when I presented a paper urging full inclusion of LGBTQ+ people at the Society of Vineyard Scholars meeting in 2013. The paper proposed a biblical justification for full inclusion of sexual minorities in the Church. I once thought it had a chance of working in our renewalist denomination, since we had no national policies forbidding full inclusion. A conversation with our new national director in 2012 assured me that he was inclined to allow dissenting views on the topic in local congregations. But things were heating up, and I knew that if Vineyard allowed any of its churches to practice full inclusion, it would be cutting across the grain of American evangelicalism.

Before my scheduled session, J.P. Moreland, a distinguished professor of philosophy at Talbot School of Theology, presented a paper to warn Vineyard against "gravediggers" in the camp (Moreland). He used the term to refer to insiders promoting views that would be harmful to the denomination.

Moreland offered three examples of current threats he saw at work in Vineyard: gravediggers who advocate "theistic evolution"; those who use neuroscience to understand prayer experiences; and those who advocate revision of long-accepted matters of Christian doctrine or ethics. I was the primary voice in Vineyard for allowing theistic evolution; Moreland footnoted my book, *Mystically Wired: Exploring New Realms in Prayer,* as an example of the second danger; and the third, we all knew, was the subject of my paper scheduled for later in the conference (summaries of the papers were available in advance).

I sat there stunned and befuddled. To anyone with ears to hear, Moreland was using his considerable academic prestige to warn conference participants that I was a "gravedigger." Or was I just being paranoid? It was more than a little unnerving. I was not a distinguished professor of philosophy. I held a Bachelor of Science (in nursing). My thesis—full inclusion of sexual minorities on the ground that this was a "disputable matter" à la Romans 14-15—was an application of that text not advanced by any scholars at the time. N.T. Wright, who was the most progressive-leaning scholar with credibility in Vineyard, had explicitly rejected my thesis. And I was still six months into mourning the sudden death of my wife of 42 years—making the "gravedigger" characterization an added, if unintended, dig.

I presented my paper at a later session to a packed room, in which key national leaders were present. The tension was palpable. After a brief Q & A in which the main leaders did not participate, my paper was met with an icy and eerie silence. Weeks, and then months, would pass without anyone in authority engaging me about the issues raised in the paper—despite my invitations to do so. The silence said: "What you are saying cannot be discussed in this setting. It's the sort of thing people who don't belong here say." The ensuing months proved the point.

It's uncanny how you can intuit an outcome from the feel of a crowd in a room, as I did the afternoon I became a controversialist in Vineyard. But later I learned that just before my session started, Emily (who was present) got a premonition—that there would be a significant earthquake somewhere in the world before the talk was over; that this would be an indication that the Holy Spirit was at work to "change the landscape" on the question of LGBTQ+ inclusion. Emily sent herself an email describing her hunch so it would be time-stamped. It turns out that there was an earthquake, in the short time-window specified—a large one, 7.0 on the Richter scale—and it occurred in a region where Emily had served as a missionary. I had seen Emily operate in a prophetic mode before, but this one was a doozy.

Do I believe God *sent* an earthquake to encourage us? No. Correlation is different than causation. The plates that shifted to cause the earthquake were bound to shift when the pressure built up enough. The earthquake, combined with Emily's intuition, was a serendipity—a concurrence of events given a particular meaning though the message Emily received; a message I regard as a prophecy. Was my talk of such big significance that it warranted an earthquake? No. The metaphorical earthquake corresponding to the premonition took place in my relatively small world; a world that would, in fact, be shaken (for me and others) more than I could imagine. But the strange concurrence encouraged, bolstered and consoled us. Surrounded by a broader faith community whose collective disapproval was turning its disapproving eye on us, the assurance was needed. We were not, despite claims to the contrary, doing something unfaithful or disloyal.

The point of an example like this is simply that *this stuff happens.* But the gift of prophecy doesn't need a dramatic, unusual or predictive element to do its job. Simple words, inspired by the Spirit to offer a timely encouragement to someone who needs one, will do. The inspiration of prophecy is measured by its effect on the recipient.

Loud vocalizations

"In the days of his flesh, Jesus offered up prayers and suppli-
cations, with loud cries and tears, to the one who was able to
save him from death, and he was heard because of his reverent
submission" (He. 5:7). We detect echoes of the scapegoat
mechanism in this text. The "suffering servant" of Isaiah,
representing Israel—the called-by-God community that represents all scapegoated people of all time—was silenced by the
scapegoating mob. But through Isaiah's writings, the suffering
is recorded—a sign that it is, indeed, heard by the God who
remains after the mob has dispersed. The "loud cries and tears"
of Jesus were made in solidarity with Israel and all who thus
suffer.

The letter to the Hebrews speaks of the end of the sacrificial order (rooted in the scapegoat mechanism). Hebrews
assures us that God hears the cry of the victim: "By faith
Abel offered to God a more acceptable sacrifice than Cain's.
Through this he received approval as righteous, God himself
giving approval to his gifts; he died, but through his faith he
still speaks" (He. 11:4). After what Girard calls "the founding
murder," God says to Cain, "Listen! Your brother's blood is
crying out to me from the ground"(Gn. 4:10). God hears the
victims' cries—from Abel to Jesus, and all who cry out in
anguish. Later in Hebrews, the cry of Jesus, calling for mercy,
is favorably contrasted to the voice of Abel, calling for vengeance.[174] But God hears both of their voices.

The global Pentecostal movement has given voice to
countless disinherited people. In the United States, it gave
voice to black preacher William Seymour, who sparked the
Asuza Street Revival that would become the epicenter for
the Pentecostal movement in the United States and beyond.
Seymour preached the importance of racial equality to
an integrated crowd in a time when that was unheard of.

---

174 "But you have come to Mount Zion and to the city of the living God … and to
Jesus, the mediator of a new covenant, and to the sprinkled blood that speaks a better
word than the blood of Abel" (He. 12: 22,24).

Similarly, Pentecostalism—especially in its early days—gave voice to many women previously silenced by the Church, including Aimee Semple McPherson, founder of Angelus Temple in Los Angeles and of the Foursquare Gospel Church, an early Pentecostal denomination.

Much Pentecostal prayer is marked by loud vocalizations—whether in praise, loud intercessory cries, weeping or the freedom to voice complaints in the tradition of the psalms.[175] (I wonder if we would yell less at each other if we had the freedom to yell more at God).

We are embodied beings. Worship is a bodily function.[176] My friend Sharonda, who grew up in the Pentecostal Church, introduced me to "Lift Every Voice and Sing," suspecting that I was unfamiliar with it. (She was right.) Sharonda told me to speak and sing and shout those lyrics out, until they made an impact on my soul—which I did, for several days in a row, until it worked. Pentecostal worship forms, including loud vocalizations, teach us that we are not to be silenced—that God hears our cries of highest praise and deepest distress.

The monastic practices

The monastic movement began as a form of resistance. Within the Judaism of the Second Temple period, the Essenes gathered in proto-monastic communities in the Judean desert and in cities. These communities were a protest against what they saw as the corruption of Israel's temple worship through accommodation with the ruling Roman Empire. The Essenes had their own practices, including daily ritual immersions in water.

After the Roman Empire absorbed Christianity in the fourth century, Anthony and others retreated to the Egyptian

---

175 Psalm 55 is the complaint of a man surrounded by enemies, a classic scapegoat situation. At one point he cries out: "Evening and morning and at noon I utter my complaint and moan, and he [God] will hear my voice" (18).

176 "I appeal to you therefore, brothers and sisters, by the mercies of God, to present your bodies as a living sacrifice, holy and acceptable to God, which is your spiritual worship" (Ro. 12:1).

desert. These "Desert Fathers and Mothers" developed prayer practices featuring stillness, silence and the communal chanting of psalms—practices that were further developed in the later and more structured monastic communities of Eastern Orthodoxy and Roman Catholicism.

The Jesus Prayer

The Jesus Prayer involves repeating "Lord Jesus Christ, Son of the living God, have mercy on me, a sinner."[177] The prayer can be joined to the rhythm of one's breathing, repeating for several minutes until the prayer recedes into the background of one's awareness.

Here's how it works: When distracting thoughts intrude, as they always do, return your focus to the prayer. Over time, you learn to pay less attention to your inner dialogue, including thoughts that may be generated by the words of the prayer itself. As thoughts, feelings and impressions vie for your attention, look over their shoulder, so to speak—or simply notice them with disinterest, and with an "oh, well," return your focus to the rhythmic use of the Jesus Prayer, tied to your breathing. (If coordinating the prayer to your breathing is itself distracting, don't bother with that part).

Now here's the interesting bit: the Eastern Orthodox learned that prayer can stimulate an experience described as "descending with the mind into the heart." This phrase refers to a shift in awareness—from the everyday thinking we do with our minds to a slower, calmer, less anxious or frenetic kind of awareness. It's not an attempt to "turn off the mind"; rather, as the phrase suggests, it is a descent with the mind, into the heart.[178]

As anything else, it takes a bit of practice. What you may discover is that it can be incredibly calming. The

---

177 This is the longest version, but shortened or adapted versions are also used. For example: "Lord Jesus, child of God, have mercy on me" or "Lord Jesus, have mercy."
178 A classic on the Jesus Prayer is *The Way of a Pilgrim and The Pilgrim Continues His Way,* translated by Olga Savin. For a summary of the Eastern Fathers' teaching see 193-238.

hyper-vigilant alarm system running in the background of so much of our everyday thinking calms down, allowing for a more peaceful, less fearful and less fretting interior landscape. Pictures, images and thoughts can emerge from our "held-in-the-loving-arms-of-God" self, perhaps unlocking powerful insights and perceptions.

In an earlier chapter, I mentioned a time when praying the Jesus Prayer for several minutes initiated a vivid interior experience of being with Jesus in a cave, sitting beside him as we looked into a fire. Jesus had his arm around my shoulder. I was aware of my mortality, my limitations; my tendency to miss the mark. But I felt not the slightest reactivity or disapproval from Jesus—just a sympathetic understanding of the burden that my condition placed on me.

I've mulled over this experience for several years now. What was it about Jesus that I found so compelling and astonishing? The work of James Alison, a gay Catholic priest and theologian (who is also a leading Girard scholar) has helped me a great deal. He describes the God revealed by Jesus as a being who is in no way in rivalry with us. This is how Allison puts it:

> *If the "social other" tends to teach us a pattern of desire such that what is normal is reciprocity, which of course includes retaliation, then Jesus presents God as what I call, "the Other, other," one who is entirely outside any being moved, pushed, offended or any retaliation of any sort at all. On the contrary, God is able to be **towards** each one of us without ever being **against** any one of us. God is in no sort of rivalry at all with any one of us: he is not part of the same order of being as us, which is how God can create and move us without displacing us. (Alison, Broken Hearts and New Creations: Imitations of a Great Reversal, 166)*

Yes, that's it. The figure sitting next to me was a fellow human, and yet also a being of absolute non-rivalry with and toward me. Any two humans can so easily, given the right circumstances, enter into an overt or covert, mild or intense form of rivalry with each other, against their best intentions.

Have you noticed that the primary source of intra-human conflict in the book of Genesis is manifest in a series of relationships marked by envy/rivalry and the misery it generates? Cain and Abel, Noah and his sons, Abraham and Lot, Sarah and Hagar, Isaac and Ishmael, Jacob and Esau, and Joseph and his brothers, just to name a few? So much rivalry leading to so much violence. What if we could learn to step away from the magnetic pull of rivalry and learn to be with each other differently? Imagine being in a place where envy, rivalry, competition, jealousy or even comparison doesn't even exist as a potential state of being.

Prayer practices that calm us, lower anxiety and quiet our fears can decouple us from the automatic reactivity that otherwise drives us. When my old church was in crisis over the LGBTQ+ inclusion issue, things got pretty ugly. Dear colleagues intervened in ways that effectively outed Emily, stirred accusations against me and eventually led to our expulsion. This all took place just after I had moved out of my house of 26 years to get married and become a new stepdad to a teenage daughter—all in the wake of publishing a book advocating full inclusion for sexual minorities that triggered hostile pushback. My alarm system went into overdrive, as you can imagine—but I got through those awful days by taking two, and often three, 12-minute meditative prayer periods every day. Research shows that 12 minutes of meditation triggers the relaxation response that lowers anxiety throughout the day (Benson, Proctor). I'm sure that practice helped me to be less reactive to the anxious religious forces swirling around me, and several times I received words from God to guide me. Looking back, these messages were always in support of a non-rivalrous response.

The calming prayer practices help decouple us from the dynamics that lead to violence. We will be less likely to mirror hostility from others with our own reciprocal hostility. We will become more able to regard others with sympathetic understanding and compassion—even those with whom we may find ourselves in conflict.

The key mental skill developed by habitual use of the Jesus Prayer and similar contemplative prayer practices is learning to gently shift our attention away from a particular line of thought, feeling or image and return to the designated focal point. Over and over, thoughts, impressions and feelings vie for our attention, and over and over again, we learn to gently "look over their shoulder" and shift our attention back to our chosen focal point. In effect, we're learning not to be in rivalry with ourselves. This is precisely the skill that we need in order to step away from rumination (repetitive thoughts that preoccupy us, generated by anxiety). It helps us to stop mentally rehearsing an argument with a coworker and trying out more effective rhetorical "checkmate" moves; it interrupts our tendency to mull over injuries we have endured from others, and to plot out various forms of retaliation or vengeance.

It's no accident that the monastic setting became such a repository for these practices. A monastery is a learning laboratory designed to require participants to get a grip on their rivalrous ways. The clear authority structure of monastic life—commanding obedience in everyday matters—is another mechanism designed to put a lid on rivalry. And yet, if you've ever been in a highly hierarchical social setting (the military, the police force, a symphony orchestra, high-level athletic teams, any workplace with clear supervisory lines of authority), you know that rivalries inevitably still form, fester and eventually break out, despite these external structures—as they would in a monastery. But if members of the monastery are committed to "work it out with each other, come what may" through vows of stability, then other internal mechanisms to help dial down the reactivity that fuels rivalry would have to be developed. Like the Jesus Prayer.

Cognitive scientists have conducted brain-imaging studies on Catholic nuns engaged in these sorts of prayer practices. The studies show that as we repeatedly concentrate on returning to a chosen focal point, and the part of the brain that differentiates the self from the surrounding non-self (the parietal lobe association area) becomes "de-afferented," or less stimulated. When this happens, we feel more connected to our surroundings, to others and to whatever it is that we would otherwise view as "non-self." This is called a "unitive experience" (Newberg and d'Aquili, *Why God Won't Go Away: Brain Science and the Biology of Belief,* 115-116). It's incredibly calming, and it primes our brains to experience empathy, sympathy and compassion toward others and ourselves (Newberg and Waldman, *How God Changes Your Brain: Breakthrough Findings from a Leading Neuroscientist,* 123-127). No wonder many of the mystics made Church authorities nervous by their "all-is-one-and-let's-love-everybody" inclinations. They were having unitive experiences on a regular basis that made their brains more comfortable with inclusion.

René Girard's biographer, Cynthia Haven, reports that Girard underwent several months of mystical experience ("altered states") in 1958-59 during two-hour train rides from Baltimore to Philadelphia. Haven quotes Girard reporting that, "Everything [his 'mimetic theory'] came to me at once in 1959. I felt that there was a sort of mass that I've penetrated little by little. Everything was there at the beginning, all together." Quoting Girard again, Haven describes his "altered states": "I remember quasi-mystical experiences on the train as I read, contemplated the scenery and so on ... my mental state transfigured everything [the industrial landscape] and, on the way back, the slightest ray from the setting sun produced veritable ecstasies in me." This is significant, because many regard Girard's work as a rational deconstruction of religion— whereas his "system" came to him in the context of a recurring series of mystical experiences over several months (Haven 109-110, 118-119).

The uncensored Psalter: giving voice to the oppressed

The regular use of the psalms is another feature of monastic life adopted by Bonhoeffer and many others—the book of Psalms being the most widely used book of Scripture in all Christian traditions. But I'd like to suggest that we often censor the psalms, focusing on beautiful psalms like Psalm 23 ("The Lord is my shepherd … ") while avoiding the psalms of complaint (especially complaints against God), of crying out in distress, and psalms that include the venting of words of angry retribution. This censorship often is a kind of unintended complicity with the silencing function of a scapegoating mob, which as Girard points out, is always invested in silencing the complaints of its victims.

Take Psalm 137 for example. In the lectionary and many prayer books, this psalm is presented in censored form:

By the rivers of Babylon—
   there we sat down and there we wept
   when we remembered Zion.
On the willows there
   we hung up our harps.
For there our captors
   asked us for songs,
and our tormentors asked for mirth, saying,
   "Sing us one of the songs of Zion!"
How could we sing the LORD's song
   in a foreign land?
If I forget you, O Jerusalem,
   let my right hand wither!
Let my tongue cling to the roof of my mouth,
   if I do not remember you,
if I do not set Jerusalem
   above my highest joy.

A poignant, aching and devout lament—as it stands. As it stands, the Psalm is a lovely version of *saudade* (so-da-duh): "an intense emotional state of melancholic longing for an absent person or thing."

But that's without the final verses:

Remember, O LORD, against the Edomites
    the day of Jerusalem's fall,
how they said, "Tear it down! Tear it down!
    Down to its foundations!"
O daughter Babylon, you devastator!
    Happy shall they be who pay you back
    what you have done to us!
Happy shall they be who take your little ones
    and dash them against the rock!

Without these final anguished, injured, angry verses, the suffering of the people who generated this psalm is obscured. What was that suffering? A large segment of the Jewish population was forcibly removed from their homeland by the Babylonian occupation force. The Babylonians were cheered on by the Edomites, a local ethnic group. King Herod, no friend to the Jewish people, was half-Edomite. When you are facing oppression or exclusion, you are as galled by those you know who stand by silently as by those who egg on your abusers.

When those who are subjected to fierce hostility begin to give voice to their anger, they often shift into a higher gear … just as the psalmist does in the final lines of the psalm:

O daughter Babylon, you devastator!
    Happy shall they be who pay you back
    what you have done to us!
Happy shall they be who take your little ones
    and dash them against the rock!

There, we've read it twice now. For those of us worried about whether this is included in sacred text as encouragement to vengeance, we have the sage words of translator Robert Alter:

> *No moral justification can be offered for this noto-rious concluding line. All one can do is to recall the background of outraged feeling that triggers the conclusion: The Babylonians had laid waste to Jeru-salem, exiled much of its population, looted and massacred; the powerless captives, ordered—per-haps mockingly—to sing their Zion songs, respond instead with a lament that is not really a song and ends with this bloodcurdling curse pronounced on the captors, who, fortunately, do not understand the Hebrew in which it is pronounced. (Alter, The Book of Psalms: A Translation with Commentary, 475)*

Reading the psalm in its uncensored form forces us to face the injury that these people—and so many others—suffer. The God of the victims hears their outrage, but do we? This outrage is prayer—and not merely private prayer, but public prayer, now, because this God does not participate (nor should we) in silencing the outrage of those who suffer.

Let people have their anger! Minorities are often punished for their anger because majority people are shocked by it or consider it disproportionate. Our tendency to "shush" the anger of the oppressed has roots in the scapegoat mechanism by which the majority mob drowns out the cries of those it is circling 'round. If you haven't seen it yet, check out "Luther, Obama's Anger Translator," a video in which the president and comedian Keegan-Michael Key teamed up at the White House Correspondents Dinner to make comedic commentary on how African-Americans are placed under pressure from the majority culture to restrain their justified anger.

Injustice breeds outrage as surely as a hammer strike to your thumb releases an expletive. The fact that these troubling final lines of the psalm haven't been edited out of Scripture tells us something about the God these exiles were getting to know: This is a God who will not participate in attempts to silence the oppressed who give voice to their pain.

De-escalation practices from the Sermon on the Mount

We often get tangled up in the teaching of the Sermon on the Mount by approaching it as a kind of rulebook. We naturally examine a statement like "give to anyone who asks of you" and quickly think of situations in which it would not be the ethical thing to do. What if, instead, we approached the Sermon on the Mount as a repository of spiritual practices that de-escalate our tendency to engage in reciprocal aggression leading to violence? A spiritual practice is a patterned behavior that allows us to habituate responses that are difficult to generate "from scratch," without the momentum of a preexisting habit.

The sermon contains several spiritual practices that seem especially adept at helping us more easily bypass rivalry in our interactions with others. Luke's Gospel provides a condensed version called "The Sermon on the Plain."

The spiritual practices can be summarized in two groups, as follows:

- Cultivate love rather than reciprocal aggression toward enemies and those with whom you find yourself in conflict (Lk. 6:27-36).
- Refrain from judging others and fault-finding; instead practice forgiveness and self-reflection (Lk. 6:37-42).

These are expanded in Matthew's Sermon on the Mount, but the framework is the same: Foster practices that reduce rivalry and reciprocal violence. Both versions of the sermon end with a section that emphasizes the need to translate his teaching into habitual action—by practice.

I will show you what someone is like who comes to me, hears my words, and acts on them. That one is like a man building a house, who dug deeply and laid the foundation on rock; when a flood arose, the river burst against that house but could not shake it, because it had been well built. But the one who hears and does not act is like a man who built a house on the ground without a foundation. When the river burst against it, immediately it fell, and great was the ruin of that house. (Lk. 6:47-49)

Bold leadership and inspired preaching

In the book of Acts, one of the chief effects of the Holy Spirit was boldness to speak the truth in the face of risk. As Emily and I learned, the evangelical Church world is unwilling to practice full LGBTQ+ inclusion, and only a little less inclined to effectively support the equality of women in ministry. Leaders in this world will need to operate outside the camp of evangelicalism—a move that comes with a high cost.

The historic Protestant (mainline) Churches have more freedom to move forward in theory, but there is less forward movement than progressive national policies suggest. A clergy friend from the Episcopal Church told me that in the 1960s, mainline clergy were challenged in their seminary training to become change agents within their future parishes. This corresponded roughly, with the beginning of severe membership losses in those denominations, which in turn led the seminaries to urge new caution on clergy. The preferred clergy role shifted from change agent to a leader who helps an existing parish discern its call and helps them to accomplish it. Clergy became more timid about advocating changes that might lead to membership losses. We now have entire denominations—the Episcopal Church, Presbyterian Church (USA), Evangelical Lutheran Church in America and United Church of Christ, for example—that have national policies supporting full LGBTQ+ inclusion, while many of the parishes within those denominations are unwilling or unable to implement the national policies. Finances play a key role: Often, these churches are disproportionately dependent on conservative givers (who are more generous givers on the whole). If the parish is not attracting new members, there's a great reluctance to alienate existing ones.

These institutions will have to find a way to foster more bold, risk-taking leadership that is savvy at change-agency. Rather than transitioning reluctant congregations, the mainline churches will have to attract and equip leaders of a more entrepreneurial bent—a specialty of the evangelical post-denominational church networks, more so than the mainline Church institutions. This will inevitably require bold, risk-taking, entrepreneurial leadership, rather than a cautious leadership model that is about maintaining existing institutions, largely unchanged (and shrinking).

As Emily wrote in Chapter 7, clergy in the historic Protestant Churches often simply avoid preaching and teaching about the meaning of Jesus's death in terms that make sense to the modern ear. They don't preach "penal substitutionary atonement," but neither do they present a compelling alternative—leaving a gaping hole in the Gospel.[179] Why commit to a Christian spirituality that doesn't present a compelling case for its central message?

We think Girard's scapegoat theory, and the biblical and theological reflection it has stimulated provides a promising lens for reading, teaching and proclaiming the Gospel anew. The Christian calendar provides two important seasons in which this lens is especially helpful. The first is Advent, the four weeks leading up to the 12 days of Christmas. A theology of resistance is tuned into the significance of the Gospel as a

---

179 In fact, in my former evangelical denomination, I recall a speaker at a national conference urging us all not to abandon preaching penal substitutionary atonement. He must have been concerned that we were slipping in the same direction as the mainline churches.

challenge to prevailing empires, grounded in violence and the logic of scapegoating. Christmas Day is followed by the feast of St. Stephen, the first Christian martyr—a veritable primer in scapegoat theory, as Stephen's story is told in the book of Acts. The second is the season of Lent, the 40 days leading to the remembrance of the death and rising of Jesus, followed by the gift of the Spirit on Pentecost. These seasons are ripe for preaching, informed by the lens of scapegoat theory.

The privilege-releasing practices

Paul wrote his letter to the Philippians while in prison, having lost his freedom of independent movement. If the letter is any indication, Paul was learning to let go of his previous status while he was in prison. The themes of the letter are humility, joy and relation to our own advantaged position (privilege).

The prayer of love and remembrance

Paul opens the letter by echoing a theme found in other letters: "I thank my God every time I remember you, constantly praying with joy in every one of my prayers for all of you" (Phil. 1:3). It would be easy to skip past this as an opening greeting and nothing more. But I think Paul is actually referring to a spiritual practice that he developed—a practice that helps him to be less reactive toward others (something he obviously struggled with, as his correspondence clearly indicates): a prayer of love and remembrance.

Too often, our private praying for others can be a form of fault-finding: "God, help my spouse (child, roommate, coworker, *etc.*) to be more (fill in the fault-finding blank)." I imagine Paul nurturing a different prayer practice: holding loved ones in memory, as a form of prayer, and surrounding the remembered loved one with gratitude.

To do this, one has to take quite literally this injunction: Don't judge—that is, renounce any sense of superiority, advantage or moral privilege you may consider yourself to have in relation to the other person. As fault-finding thoughts intrude, gently let them go and return your focus to the loved one with gratitude. Later in the letter, Paul says, "Whatever is true, whatever is honorable, whatever is just, whatever is pure, whatever is pleasing, whatever is commendable, if there is any excellence and if there is anything worthy of praise, let your mind dwell on these things" (Phil. 4:8). That could be a guide for regarding others when practicing the prayer of love and remembrance.

This is a simple matter of applying the Golden Rule to the way we pray for others. "In everything do to others as you would have them do to you" (Mt.7:12). Wouldn't this be the way you would want others praying for you? Focused on whatever is true, honorable, pleasing, commendable about you and surrounding that focus with gratitude for you?

Using (or losing) your privilege for others

You wonder if Paul wasn't meditating on what it means to have unearned advantages, having lost his freedom in pursuit of his mission to the Gentiles. He opens with what most scholars regard as a hymn:

> *Let the same mind be in you that was in Christ Jesus,*
> *who, though he was in the form of God,*
> *did not regard equality with God*
> *as something to be exploited,*
> *but emptied himself,*
> *taking the form of a slave,*
> *being born in human likeness.*
> *And being found in human form,*
> *he humbled himself*
> *and became obedient to the point of death—*
> *even death on a cross*
> *Therefore God also highly exalted him*
> *and gave him the name*

that is above every name,
so that at the name of Jesus
every knee should bend,
in heaven and on earth and under the earth,
and every tongue should confess
that Jesus Christ is Lord,
to the glory of God the Father.
(Phil. 2:2-11)

The Divine Son had the ultimate privileged status and he willingly relinquished it—and this is precisely the kind of attitude or mind we are to foster in ourselves. There's no following Jesus that leaves our privilege intact. Later, Paul personalizes this, when he records his list of lost privilege.

> *If anyone else has reason to be confident in the flesh, I have more: circumcised on the eighth day, a member of the people of Israel, of the tribe of Benjamin [the tribe of Israel's first king], a Hebrew born of Hebrews; as to the law, a Pharisee; as to zeal, a persecutor of the church; as to righteousness under the law, blameless. Yet whatever gains [advantage/ privilege] I had, these I have come to regard as loss because of Christ. (Phil. 3:4-7)*

Like most people, Paul jealously guarded his privilege. Like most of us with privilege, we can imagine he regarded it as something earned, rather than an advantage granted by circumstance of birth, geography, *etc.* He was, like most of us with privilege, used to asserting his privilege and loath to lose its advantages. His encounter with Jesus changed all that. Following Jesus resulted in the loss of his privilege—in many cases, for the sake of others, just as Jesus freely relinquished his divine privilege for the sake of others.

Protective reactivity to the loss of privilege is a sign we've missed Paul's message. If we have privilege, then sharing power that we haven't earned should be easy—as we regard our privilege as unearned and already lost, as Paul did. And there's the rub. We'd much rather assume our privilege is something else—something we've earned and thus have a right to. Paul's ongoing spiritual awakening seems to have been a process of waking up to this fundamental reality. In Philippians, we meet him at the end, not the beginning, of this awakening.

So here we have a spiritual practice: recognize your privilege for what it is and regard it (consider it, account it) as loss. That is, act as if you have already lost it, so that when opportunity arises to use it or give it away, you don't react defensively. Share power with those who have less ... and question your internal resistance to do so.

Systems of privilege manifest in many ways, including the ubiquitous assumption that the less privileged are less qualified. Ruthlessly question that assumption. I functioned as the "senior pastor" for many years in a system that privileged men. I normalized to that system, which means it felt "natural" to me. It operated at a conscious and unconscious level—as any cultural systems do. When Emily and I planted Blue Ocean Faith Ann Arbor, we wanted to break out of that male-privileged model, so we did so as co-pastors, sharing power equally. We expanded the size of our church board and included a bylaw that requires gender equity in the board's composition. We have lots more to learn about the effects of privilege, especially in matters of race, but it was an important start.

Use whatever power you have to benefit those who have less.

In a democracy, that means using whatever political power we enjoy as citizens on behalf of those who are on the short end of the power stick. As a straight, white male, that means weighing in with my political power when policies are harmful to women, people of color, or sexual minorities—even though the harmful policies don't threaten me. Remaining passive as though it is a virtuous form of "rising above politics" is a cop-out. That passivity is a function of privilege—when we're not likely to be harmed by policies in the realm of politics, we instinctively diminish the value of political activism. If we're theologically inclined, we might regard it as less than "Jesus-centered." But most churches led by women or people of color don't see political action as opposed to spiritual action. They intermingle the two as easily as does the humanity and divinity of Jesus.

While addressing questions of privilege and minority rights seems like a politically liberal concern, there are steps we can take which are more at home in a conservative philosophy. Conservatives typically emphasize values like personal responsibility and the power of individual actions, like charitable giving, to alleviate suffering. Conservatives give a significantly higher percentage of their income to charitable causes (including to non-religious charities) than liberals do. (As I sometimes tell our liberal congregants, "Put your money where your bleeding heart is!") We know that slavery and ongoing discrimination against African-Americans has led to a massive racial wealth-gap. Wealth doesn't die with its owners; it is passed on to the owner's offspring through inheritance. After the Emancipation Proclamation, the U.S. government planned to provide "40 acres and a mule" to emancipated slaves. This plan was aborted with the presidency of Andrew Jackson, one of our more overtly racist presidents. Today, political prospects for making financial amends for slavery and racial discrimination seem remote. But what prevents individuals from including a person of color in their will? If you currently have four heirs, why not add one and divide your estate among five heirs instead? Pray—ask the Spirit to identify a person of color in your life who has no prospect of receiving an inheritance. Then, act—change your will to include them as an heir.

Pray-and-act: a spirituality of resistance for our cultural moment

Bonhoeffer conceived of a pray-and-act spirituality in response to his cultural moment: the existential crisis of religion brought on by the nightmare of the Holocaust, in which the powers of the Christian religion were complicit. Empowered by the Holy Spirit, Bonhoeffer raised a lonely voice of resistance that resonates today. While the cultural memory of that moment has dimmed, the crisis it precipitated lingers. It's a crisis with a long shelf life. Today, much religion functions as an aid to the resurgent forces of nationalism, white supremacy and Fascism.

Pray-and-act also describes an approach to spirituality that fits how Jesus announced his ministry in his hometown synagogue. He was given a scroll from the prophet Isaiah to read, and read it he did in that place of prayer.

He unrolled the scroll and found the place where it was written:

> "The Spirit of the Lord is upon me,
> because he has anointed me
> to bring good news to the poor.
> He has sent me to proclaim release to the captives
> and recovery of sight to the blind,
> to let the oppressed go free,
> to proclaim the year of the Lord's favor."
>
> And he rolled up the scroll,
> gave it back to the attendant, and sat down.
> The eyes of all in the synagogue were fixed on him.
> Then he began to say to them,
> "Today this scripture has been fulfilled in your hearing"
> (Lk. 4:17-21).

The Spirit moving through Jesus is rearranging things, advocating for a new way of sharing power that benefits those who have labored on the short end of the power arrangements

of this world. Prayer and action, indeed. As Bonhoeffer prophesied, "all Christian thinking, speaking and organizing must
be born anew out of this prayer and action."

Solus Jesus. Let's get going.

15

Jesus Among the World Religions

Emily

I WORSHIPPED WITH an underground Chinese church for a few months during the three years I lived in Qinghai. They meet secretly, evading registration with the government.[180] A local friend invited me to come with her to services; we often met on Sunday afternoons, rotating the location in various apartments via word of mouth. The group of 30-40 people gathered to sing, pray and listen to a teaching. They regularly sang hymns familiar to me—only in Mandarin. On the one hand, singing shared songs with brothers and sisters in Asia moved me; on the other, I knew that the presence of these hymns, at the foot of the Tibetan Plateau, indicated that Western missionaries had infused portions of their own culture into the Gospel narrative and ritual practices.

Over the last 400 years, missionary work was closely intertwined with colonialism and empire-building. Wealthy Western nations collected foreign territories to rule and exploit, while their well-meaning (nearly always white) apostles traveled abroad to the new protectorates to convert the (nearly always non-white) "natives." When these

180 For more information on the Chinese underground churches, see: Xi, Lian. *Redeemed By Fire: The Rise of Popular Christianity in Modern China*, Yale University Press, 2010, 204-232.

pioneering missionaries proselytized, they transferred their own Euro-American-shaped church customs and theologies to those non-Westerners, who became Christian. These missionaries participated—sometimes tacitly, sometimes overtly—in the subjugation of peoples all over the world (Twiss, 62-64; Kidwell, 8; Tamez, 13-26; Dube, 297-318; M. Smith, 236).[181]

Singing "Amazing Grace" and "Blessed Assurance" in an underground church is part of the colonial legacy.[182] I wasn't surprised that the songs were sung, so much as conflicted. How much of what I was doing was also naïvely enmeshed in racism and/or a sense of national, cultural or religious superiority? Is sharing my faith with people of different backgrounds inherently disrespectful or oppressive? How has the legacy of colonialism affected interfaith relations—including both our willingness to engage in conversations and the distrust surrounding such interactions?

In this final chapter, I explore questions of power and some possible implications of Girard's scapegoating theory on interfaith relations, and I advocate a humble approach to our neighbors of different spiritual traditions. Skilled interfaith scholars like Paul Knitter, Raimon Panikkar and others have thought broadly and deeply about such things, and I am indebted to their scholarship. I've also learned from and tried to engage theologians born in subjugated territories. I hope my perspective as a queer, white Western woman, who has

---

181 "... European missionaries and imperial colonialists claimed that God made black people naturally inferior and innately servile to whites. Thus, some missionaries indoctrinated Africans by imposing upon them the belief that they were obliged to serve Jesus Christ *and* their masters. Many missionaries, in collusion with European colonizers, separated the physical unjust, inhumane treatment and oppression of Africans and slaves from the saving of their souls. It was more important for colonized Africans and enslaved blacks to submit to missionary teachings, to learn to recite Scriptures and creeds, and be added to the membership to expand the Church's geographical presence as evidence of the successful propagation of the Gospel among them and in foreign lands." (M. Smith, 236)

182 The network of such churches contains as much diversity as Chinese cuisine, so my particular experience can not be taken to be emblematic of the whole. Not all underground churches sing Western hymns; but enough do to testify to the colonial legacy.

lived abroad with some knowledge of the colonial legacies, provides interesting angles to explore in this chapter. I also hope that people coming from colonized areas continue challenging both the Church and me to press in deeper, so that our blind eyes may see.

More people and more religion than ever

The question of how to interact with other faith traditions increasingly affects large numbers of Jesus followers, who encounter people of other faiths in the course of day-to-day life. We live in a world crowded with humans, many with enough resources to travel, work or study around the globe. People residing in cities commonly live near people of other ethnicities and faith traditions. As our global village continues trending toward mega-cities—with agrarian populations shrinking rapidly— more people will associate with humans who hold myriad perspectives on the *how's* and *why's* of life.[183]

Even those in rural or monocultural regions of the world can easily access the vast data contained on the internet— many of them from developing nations and some 89 million from the least developed nations (Sanou). More than 70 percent of youth are online. The accessibility of information about other religions and ways of life continues to grow. More people, more interaction, better technology: these trends will not go away anytime soon, barring a massive global disaster.

Religion, also, will not go away. According to Rodney Stark, a social sciences professor at Baylor University, "The deeper one digs into the data, the clearer it becomes: The popular notion of an increasingly secularizing world is not merely wrong but actually the *opposite* of what has been taking place" (Stark, 11-12, italics in original). Faith and spirituality

---

183 United Nations, Department of Economic and Social Affairs, Population Division (2014): "In 2014, 54 percent of the world's population is urban. The urban population is expected to continue to grow, so that by 2050, the world will be one-third rural (34 percent) and two-thirds urban (66 percent), roughly the reverse of the global rural-urban population distribution of the mid-twentieth century."

continue to influence us, and the world is becoming *more* religious—not less.

A faithful posture toward other faiths

As contact with those from other faith traditions increases, we need wisdom about how to follow Jesus with and among people of other spiritual backgrounds. We need an approach that is both faithful to God as we understand God, and loving toward all. Weaving together themes we have explored thus far, we think a coherent Christian posture emerges. The following Gospel motifs point the way forward.

Non-rivalrous, non-sacrificial

In Chapter 9, I wrote about how applying René Girard's scapegoat theory to the story of Jesus reveals that we follow a completely non-rivalrous God. The Trinitarian godhead—*Source, Wellspring* and *Living Water*—remains non-rivalrous within itself; additionally, God does not compete with either humans or nature. God invites all of humanity into this same way of being, as God's good realm unfolds. The path we tread, imitating Jesus, leads us to behave as if we, also, are non-rivalrous. Vying for power, respectability and standing loses its appeal in the reflection of the Son of God on a cross. It follows, then, that Christianity must be non-competitive in its relationships with other belief systems.

When I lived in China, I came home to spend a couple of months with my family. I missed being in Asia, so I found a Tibetan Buddhist temple to visit. I pulled up to a small house on the east side of Indianapolis that had been converted into a worship space.

I went inside and chatted with a few people, waiting for the meditation hour to begin. I also spoke with the monk leading it, letting him know that I am Christian, but that I studied Amdo Tibetan in Qinghai and wanted to join them in prayer. He welcomed me with a large smile and tea. Turns out he was born in a town not far from where I lived in China, and we knew some of the same places.

We sat on pillows in rows along the floor, and the monk led us in prayer. As he guided us, he specifically made space for me, as a Christian. He would say things like, "We're going to meditate on compassion, but you can meditate on whatever you'd like. If Jesus is meaningful to you, you can meditate on Jesus." His eyes crinkled as he looked at me. So I meditated on Jesus—which is what I would have done anyway for my own nourishment.

This monk treated me the way I wanted to be treated: with respect, hospitality and genuine welcome to be fully myself. He had no secret agenda to make me into a Buddhist. I aspire to treat people of other traditions in a similar way—I want to love others with the same generous spirit with which I was accepted in that space. We are, after all, instructed to love our neighbors as ourselves—to do unto others as we would have them do unto us.

Maintaining a non-rivalrous posture doesn't mean that we turn into wishy-washy people who lack conviction. We bear witness to that which we believe, but we also recognize that it is not our job to either judge or change others. I can have full confidence in Jesus as the path to life without the kind of certainty that leads me to try to *dominate* or *conquer* another; I have no need to do either of those things. Jesus did not seek to dominate or conquer us. Instead, he *witnessed* to a thoroughly good God through his embodied sacrificial love and showed us how to do likewise. In doing so, he did vanquish *something*: namely, the powers and principalities—rivalry-ridden power structures that use accusation and sacrifice to maintain false peace (Col. 2:15). Jesus subjugated and overpowered the realm of the Accuser.

Non-rivalrous and non-sacrificial postures toward "the other" go hand-in-hand, since the first leads to the second. Just as we do not wish to be falsely accused and scapegoated ourselves, so we should not falsely accuse and scapegoat those of other faiths, misconstruing their beliefs and acting as experts in traditions of which we have only superficial knowledge.

A prophetic posture

That said, Jesus prophetically denounced rivalrous, sacrificial religion—most especially that embodied in the Roman Empire and its practices, but also within his own tradition (Horsley, 79-104). He addressed and warned those susceptible to doing violence or colluding with the empire's violence, teaching them spiritual tactics of de-escalation; the Sermon on the Mount reads like a manual in restraining rivalries. In his preaching and teaching, Jesus stands in the long line of Hebrew prophets who warned their people about what happens when an imperial mindset blinds us to the suffering of others.

Ken and I are Americans. We live in the wealthiest, most heavily armed consumer culture the world has yet known. Its resources allow some good to be done in the world, but the arm of our empire also damages lives—and even entire nations. If Christianity lacks the tools and equipment to counter the harm and oppression done in the name of mammon, American exceptionalism, white supremacy, patriarchy and heteronormativity, then our spirituality remains impotent. It is a sounding gong, a clanging cymbal.

In order to follow Jesus in his prophetic mode, we need conviction to unequivocally condemn white supremacist rallies. We need spiritual empowerment to champion policies benefiting the poor and vulnerable. We need courage to stand with victims of sexual harassment and assault. And we need the guiding presence of Jesus to bring healing to those traumatized by our national sins. We bring about God's good realm by imagining a better future and reimagining social structures that take advantage of those with less power. We do so by prophetically speaking into the empire and its adherents, calling out its willingness to sacrifice the sick, the poor and the vulnerable for the sake of the healthy, the rich and the powerful.

Productive interfaith dialog with people from the developing world is enhanced when Christians from the developed world understand how themes of liberation from oppression intertwine with the Gospel narrative, and how the power of Jesus's life, death and resurrection requires magnanimous love of neighbor. We must allow Jesus's direction to disconnect us from earthly possessions, to sink in deep. When we talk about what these teachings mean for those of us benefiting from the current global system—at the expense of the poorest among us—I suspect that it will sound like tangible good news to those on the underside of global economics.

A voice in my head protests: "But isn't calling out rivalrous, sacrificial religion/empire creating rivalry?" No—because rivals desire the same object. We can hold systems to account without making false accusations or hoping to gain any power lost by that system. Our hope lies in Jesus and the foolishness of the cross; we do not aspire to worldly power. As the apostle Paul wrote, "For when I am weak, I am strong" (2 Co. 12:10b).

When we speak prophetically, we speak not "as a Christian" to "non-Christians"; we speak as people refusing to take part in toxic, power-seeking and power-maintaining religion, following the way of Jesus. This means that we make prophetic declarations to those within our own tradition as much as—if not more than—we do to others. And we embrace and bless those of other faiths following a path of love and justice.

A posture of non-judgment

A third Jesus-shaped posture toward people of other faiths is one of non-judgment. A young man attending a church membership class I taught some years ago asked me, "Do you think my Hindu grandmother in India is going to hell? Because I don't know if I can come to this church if you believe that. She's the most loving, generous, kind and wise woman I know. I would be lucky to be as spiritually mature as she is."

The person who said this to me identifies as a secular Hindu who likes Jesus. His wife is Christian, and they sought a faith community where they could both agree to worship and in which they could raise their children with a spiritual framework. It's a scenario playing out in churches around the world, as people wed spouses from different spiritual backgrounds. Interfaith relationships are as old as we humans; even the prophet Moses was in an intercultural, interfaith marriage with Zipporah, whose father was a priest of Midian.

I shared a passage with the young man that reads, "Dear friends, let us love one another, for love comes from God. Everyone who loves has been born of God and knows God. Whoever does not love does not know God, because God is love" (1 Jn. 4:7-8).

> *Everyone who loves* has been born of God and knows God.
> *Whoever does not love* does not know God.

"'*Everyone who loves*' seems inclusive of your grandmother." I continued, "However, I'm not the judge of anyone's soul. I've never met your grandma, and God alone knows her heart."

In *Buddhists Talk About Jesus, Christians Talk About the Buddha*, Rita M. Gross expresses a similar sentiment to the young man above. Writing about Jesus as a practicing Buddhist, the author says she fears talking with Christians because our claims of Jesus being a higher, indispensable truth feel as though Christians prejudge her religious path as inferior (34). This fear presents a hurdle for interfaith dialog and violates the Golden Rule. I don't want to talk to someone who automatically assumes I'm wrong, unintelligent or less spiritually evolved. Does anyone?

Removing the barrier of judgment requires genuine humility, an ancient Christian value. When we start with humility, we move from speaking out of a place of *certainty* to speaking out of a place of *confidence*. We addressed the distinction between certainty and confidence more fully in the introduction to this book. Suffice it to say, Christians can be fully Christian—embracing the Jesus path completely and confidently—while acknowledging that we humans can never be *certain* about anything. We follow Jesus and can be declarative about this path, but only under the auspices of, "But I could be wrong."

That, "But I could be wrong," must permeate our very being. Because we *could* be wrong, and likely are about at least a portion of what we hold to be true. And the person we're talking to *could* be right—without our recognizing it. Paul Knitter describes this dynamic beautifully, as tending a "relationship of mutuality" (Knitter, *Introducing Theologies of Religions*, 110).

People fear judgment because we need belonging, and we can only have meaningful relationships with those who are different than we are if we relinquish judging and instead offer embrace (B. Brown, 98-101). In theory, this should be an easy barrier to overcome within a Christian framework, because the heart of our faith is just that: eat from the tree of life (Jesus), and not the tree of the knowledge of good and evil (judgment).

Jesus understood this relationship-killing aspect of judging. He said:

> *Do not judge, or you too will be judged. For in the same way you judge others, you will be judged, and with the measure you use, it will be measured to you.*
>
> *Why do you look at the speck of sawdust in your brother's eye and pay no attention to the plank in your own eye? How can you say to your brother, 'Let me take the speck out of your eye,' when all the time there is a plank in your own eye? You hypocrite, first take the plank out of your own eye, and*

then you will see clearly to remove the speck from your brother's eye.

Do not give dogs what is sacred; do not throw your pearls to pigs. If you do, they may trample them under their feet, and turn and tear you to pieces. (Mt. 7:1-6)

I find it intriguing that Jesus followed the plank-in-the-eye line with not throwing pearls to swine. Perhaps he means those who judge others become like ravenous animals—unsafe and worth avoiding.

A non-heroic posture

Finally, it's not helpful to approach those of other faiths as if we are the heroes. It is not our job to save others or prove ourselves with heroic feats. That task belongs to Jesus alone. "No one can come to me unless the Father who sent me draws them, and I will raise them up at the last day" (Jn. 6:44). When Jesus himself was tempted by the Accuser to produce a heroic miracle (jump from here and have the angels catch you!), he refused. That's not his way of attracting others.

In *To Love As God Loves: Conversations with the Early Church*, Roberta Bondi describes how we must relinquish this heroic image of ourselves (Bondi, 41-56). When we become aware of our dependence on God and others, we grow to understand that we are not the masters of our own fates nor knights in shining armor—for either non-Christians or the oppressed.[184] Rather, we embrace our common humanity and make ourselves available for God to work through us for the sake of others. The apostle Paul expressed this when he wrote:

184 The "white savior" mentality many white Christians maintain of themselves has been toxic to interfaith dialog, racial relations and missions work for centuries. That said, I hope it goes without saying that a good number of missionaries—especially those who provide medical care, education and support for orphanages—do so not because of any motivation to be heroes, but because they genuinely feel their faith compels them to supply valuable skills and goods where needed. I would hope anyone, of any ethnicity, would do the same for their neighbors—local or global—when aid is needed. Providing care does not always translate into a hero complex.

> *For I am the least of the apostles and do not even deserve to be called an apostle, because I persecuted the church of God. But by the grace of God I am what I am, and his grace to me was not without effect. No, I worked harder than all of them—yet not I, but the grace of God that was with me. Whether, then, it is I or they, this is what we preach, and this is what you believed. (1 Co. 15:9-11)*

We all stand before God and participate in enacting God's good realm by grace—the most beautiful and enduring revelation of the 16th-century Reformation. We can only bear witness to the truth claims of our own faith as reliably as possible, recognizing our limits: we can not save anyone, we can not possibly know everything, and we can not adequately judge the state of another's soul. But we *can* offer the treasures we've found as gifts, trusting that if God draws people to God-self, as we believe, then the attractiveness of this God is enough.

A living Buddha showed me how it's done

When I lived in China, a friend and I had an opportunity to visit a Tibetan Buddhist monastery at the invitation of a Buddhist nun. We rode public buses to the small town nearest the nunnery, located a few hours south of where we lived on the edge of the Tibetan Plateau, and then hiked 45 minutes down a valley and up a mountain to reach the building where approximately 40 nuns live. A monk resides in separate quarters just above the monastery—a living Buddha charged with overseeing the women and their spiritual education.[185]

When we first arrived, a Chinese official followed us to the monastery to register our stay and inquire as to why we were in that part of the country. The chief governmental concern, as

---

185 There are between 350-400 living Buddhas in Tibet. Living Buddhas are believed to be reincarnated Buddhist teachers who are custodians of specific schools of spiritual thinking.

I understand it, is with foreign journalists doing undercover work on the Chinese occupation of Tibetan areas. We were not journalists, but also realized our presence may have been controversial. In that light, we wanted to be transparent with our hosts so as not to either mislead them or put them in an awkward position with their local government offices.

My friend and I talked about how we might approach the monk to discuss our visit. Both of us were legitimate language students at a local university, and so we could honestly present as students. But I was really visiting the monastery because I was interested in holding spiritual conversations with the nuns. I wanted to talk about Jesus, but also to watch, listen and learn from the women and their understanding of the world. How do they think about their faith? What motivates them to devote their lives to monastic living? What is life like on a day-to-day basis for them, and how do their spiritual practices make their lives better? The historian in me was also curious about how Tibetan Buddhism developed in this part of the world and how it shapes culture and rituals.

On the edge of a mountaintop (where, for whatever reason, the world feels holier), the two of us prayed to ask Jesus what to do. We sensed the Holy Spirit saying, "Speak friend, and enter." It's a line from *The Lord of the Rings*, when the fellowship of nine travelers tries to find the entrance to the mountain dwellings of Moria and they discover an ancient door that says, "Speak friend, and enter." They eventually realized they needed to speak aloud the elven word for "friend" to open the door.

For us, "Speak friend, and enter" meant treating the monk and the many nuns with mutual respect and love—we felt we had instructions from Jesus to regard them as true friends. In that vein, we wanted to be completely truthful about who we were and why we were there, inviting shared discussion about spirituality and the world around us.

That evening, the monk invited us to have tea in his private quarters. He welcomed us lavishly, and we spoke openly about faith matters. In general, I've found Buddhists to be open-hearted with different religious traditions, and hope that I reciprocated that generosity of spirit. As we talked, he shared a personal vision of opening a building at the monastery where the nuns could explore other faith traditions. He expressed sincere gratitude at our being there and delighted in the idea of mutual dialog. He then made a blanket invitation to us to return later that summer for as long as we wanted. He said he would give us a room to stay in and we could be his guests. We took him up on that for a few weeks later that year.

While there are very real differences between Christianity and Buddhism—significantly distinct approaches to life and spirituality—there are also commonalities on which to base our dialog. Both traditions offer deep insights into the nature of suffering, though we vary on how to handle it. Both traditions care deeply about compassion and peacemaking. Both traditions value chanting, silence and meditation. I remember a nun telling us about waking up early to chant each morning, and asking if we chanted in our tradition. I pulled up a recording of *Taizé* singing on my iPhone, and my friend hooked it up to travel speakers she had in her backpack. The three of us sat on a hilltop overlooking the mountains, with the music creating a bond of shared serenity between us. It was a sacred moment, and remains one of my best memories.

I think I was able to prophetically speak peace to a Buddhist woman who confessed her deep fear of dying by sharing about the spirit of love, which holds all things together. And the nuns prophetically called me to treat animals—including insects!—with greater care and reverence, since they are living beings like myself. I became a vegetarian for five years after returning from China because of their influence on my life.[186]

In Chapter 6, I mentioned that these nuns gave me a Tibetan name that means *white woman in whom there are buried treasures.* I think they experienced what I brought as

---

186 I broke down and ate bacon last spring.

valuable, and I received their gifts as valuable in return—like the baby Jesus receiving gold, frankincense and myrrh from the astrologers of the East. If Jesus accepted foreign gifts, who are we to turn away the offerings of other cultures and faiths?

Mutual relationships hold and handle diversity. We practice this in our own lives all the time—acknowledging our differences with others while remaining in mutually respectful and loving relationships. When we approach people of other faiths charitably and humbly—relinquishing our instinct to become rivals, to sacrifice each other for the sake of our own gain, and our natural tendency to judge—we benefit and experience God's good realm in our midst.

Spirit-oriented theology of mission and interfaith relations

These four Jesus-shaped postures toward others free us up to be curious, open-hearted, charitable and able to learn. God is not contained in a Christian-shaped box. On the contrary, in our tradition, *every* human bears the image of God, so every human carries some element of the divine. Our view of God at work in the world goes far beyond God at work in Christians, or in the Christian Church. God's Holy Spirit has been unleashed onto the earth, blowing and roaming where she will. It is our good pleasure to watch for signs of the Spirit in mysterious places.

Clark Pinnock, a Canadian theologian of the Holy Spirit, long championed what he called a Spirit-oriented theology of missions and interfaith relations. He wrote:

> Openness to others does not imply that they have heard God's voice accurately and know only truth with no admixture of error. All of us make mistakes in our theologies, because God's ways are not coercive and because the truth can be suppressed by unrighteousness. But we should not prejudge such things. Spirit is present everywhere, and God's truth may have penetrated any given religion and

culture at some point. We should be eager to find out. (Flame of Love, 202)

First Nations theologians testify to a similar belief among some tribes. In *A Native American Theology*, Clara Sue Kidwell, Homer Noley and George E. "Tink" Tinker explore the idea that Jesus existed as *Logos* among ancient peoples long before becoming incarnate. They argue that if the *Logos* was there "in the beginning," then this Word-Spirit of God roamed the earth at will, giving revelation to people from all times and places (Twiss, 21-22). "Why would this *Logos*, which was so instrumental in the creation act, have lain dormant for so much of human history?" (Kidwell, 78). That would mean the *Logos* unveiled characteristics of the divine that various people groups still guard and pass along through stories, art, music, rituals and other means. We can access those stories and learn, should we have discerning eyes to see and ears to hear.

Our Scriptures allude to humans of different backgrounds operating out of the same spirit of love. Jesus tells us, "I have other sheep that are not of this sheep pen. I must bring them also. They too will listen to my voice, and there shall be one flock and one shepherd" (Jn. 10:16).

And elsewhere: "'Teacher,' said John, 'we saw someone driving out demons in your name and we told him to stop, because he was not one of us.' 'Do not stop him,' Jesus said. 'For no one who does a miracle in my name can in the next moment say anything bad about me, for *whoever is not against us is for us.* Truly I tell you, anyone who gives you a cup of water in my name because you belong to the Messiah will certainly not lose their reward'" (Mk. 9:38-41, italics mine).

The story of Cornelius, a Roman centurion in the Italian regiment, shows us in Acts 10 that people can be "devout and God-fearing" as evidenced by giving "generously to those in need" and praying to God "regularly" (Acts 10:2). Cornelius, a man of war who was part of the oppressing empire, was judged by God to be so faithful that he became the conduit for

the apostle Peter's acceptance of Gentiles into the wider family
of God. That's not who I would have laid my money on God
using, but God sees people differently than we humans do.
Perhaps God needed the oppressed to understand God's grace
extends to even those we might be tempted to exclude.

The story of Abram/Abraham tells us that God speaks
to humans outside the context of *any* religion or spiritual
framework, which is consistent with my experience of people
from all walks of life—many of whom have had some kind of
spiritual experience that they may or may not call God.

Could we go so far as to say that anyone who refuses to
scapegoat and sacrifice others for the sake of group peace—
anyone who stands up for the outcast—is a follower of the
God-Who-Is-Love, regardless of what they call the spirit by
which they live? Yes. I've recognized the Holy Spirit in people
who do not call it by the same name I call it. I look for love as
the marker of who walks a similar path to mine.

Why go, then?

In light of all this, how do we make sense of the Gospel
command to go and make disciples of (or among) all nations?
If God works beyond the confines of Christianity, why go and
tell anyone anything? I suggest three reasons.

Go, to discover buried treasures

First, if the Holy Spirit is at work among all people, it only
serves Christians to learn the perspectives of others. Buried
treasures abound. I personally continue finding more depth to
my faith in knowing practitioners of other traditions.

I think of Paul Knitter's book, *Without Buddha I Could not
be a Christian*. A lifelong Catholic, Knitter talks about how he
still has questions about his faith that he has not been able to
adequately answer, given his particular doctrinal framework.
He looked to Buddhism (his wife is Buddhist) to discover
other angles from which to approach his conundrums.

What he found is that Buddhism unlocked different ways of thinking about his issues—ways different than he had found from his Christian perspective. As the title of his book implies, some Buddhist approaches to faith and mysticism helped him better embrace his own Jesus path.

Our post-Enlightenment, Western ways of thinking can confine our spiritual access roads, so why be afraid of engaging a different perspective to get at our issues—especially if that search leads us to a better understanding of God?

Go, to sharpen and be sharpened

Second, we grow when we can accept critique, and we influence others when we are able to effectively give it. "As iron sharpens iron, so one person sharpens another" (Pr. 27:17).

All of us make mistakes in our theology. We should question one another when it seems our beliefs cause harm. We should also challenge the parts of other spiritual traditions that do not seem to bear good fruit—with the full understanding that Christianity has as much to renounce as any other tradition. We cannot, however, effectively challenge another faith's rivalrous and sacrificial practices if we are not in relationship with any practitioners or if we do not respect the goodness and richness of their path.

When Gandhi said, "I like your Christ; I do not like your Christians. Your Christians are so unlike your Christ," he communicated from a place of having studied our texts, talked with Christians and engaged in Jesus's nonviolent resistance tactics. We should deferentially accept his feedback, then—especially as it was a way of communicating to the West that we were hurting his people. The "Christian West" colonized his country, depleted it economically, enlisted its men for war, and painted Indians as weak, backward, effeminate people (*effeminate* being used, of course, pejoratively—what's new?)

who needed Christian guidance.[187] Gandhi knew the Jesus I
know better than the people professing faith in the triune God
sitting in judgment over the Indian subcontinent.

I can *hear* Gandhi because of his love and respect for my
faith tradition. It works no differently the other way around.
So many Christians want to armchair-critique other religions
(especially Islam) when they have never studied these traditions in depth, been in a friendship with an adherent, or
allowed themselves permission to respect any other way of
finding God.[188]

Every faith has terrorists, and I think that naming violence
done by those groups is called for because the harm done is
obvious. But sweeping generalizations will not be received
well, and will discourage productive relationships. Interfaith
friendships can not be built on assumptions or with the
motive of converting the other—real relationships acknowledge that the Spirit works in people and in ways that are, at
times, quite mysterious.

Go, because our news is good to share

Third, we "go and tell" because we have good news and
treasures of our own to share. A comprehensive narrative
of good news is what Girard provides for my spiritual life.
His writings on scapegoating bring together pieces of the
spiritual puzzle for me in a way no one else's work has done. It
equips the Church to tell a story in which God is thoroughly
good, God is nonviolent, God stands in solidarity with the
vulnerable, and God's embrace is wider than we could hope or
imagine. Other thinkers arrive at similar positions, but Girard
gives me the intellectual footholds that help me live with
integrity within the perimeter of my Christian identity. I find

187 "Thus the whole question of imperialism, as it was debated in the late nineteenth
century by pro-imperialists and anti-imperialists alike, carried forward the binary
typology of advanced and backward (or subject) races, cultures and societies" (Said,
206).
188 When the apostle Paul preached, he did so from the place of being an insider to
both Judaism and Greco-Roman culture.

it liberating, and want others in need of the same message to hear it.

Our good news also tells us that God lives and continues speaking and guiding us, and that the Spirit of this God of love is available to everyone. *I am not alone in this world. We are not alone.* In fact, love moves us toward a grand vision of equality and kinship. The Jewish prophet Isaiah spoke to this when he wrote:

> *On this mountain the Lord Almighty will prepare*
>   *a feast of rich food for all peoples,*
> *a banquet of aged wine—*
>   *the best of meats and the finest of wines.*
> *On this mountain he will destroy*
>   *the shroud that enfolds all peoples,*
> *the sheet that covers all nations;*
>   *he will swallow up death forever.*
> *The Sovereign Lord will wipe away the tears*
>   *from all faces;*
> *he will remove his people's disgrace*
>   *from all the earth.*
> *The Lord has spoken.*
> *In that day they will say,*
> *"Surely this is our God;*
>   *we trusted in him, and he saved us.*
> *This is the Lord, we trusted in him;*
>   *let us rejoice and be glad in his salvation." (Is. 25:6-9)*

All of the nations are invited to this feast. Everyone can come—the whole global family. No one is coming as a servant; no one is coming as a second-class citizen; no one has restrictions on their participation in the meal. All are invited as honored guests.

At this banquet, we're told, sadness will melt away, shame will be wiped from our experience, and the goodness, joy, abundance and companionship present will cause all those who attend the feast to say, "Surely this is our God. This is the Lord." It is visionary; it is romantic; it is an exquisite picture of connection between God and the people of the earth.

A non-rivalrous Gospel is a more attractive one

I'm attracted to a faith whose big idea is a giant family banquet table where everyone is welcome. Any meal where one group—be it women, or people of color, or LGBTQ+, or the poor, or any other *category* of human—receives less respect and dignity falls short of God's table. The only table rule is, "You are welcome so long as you welcome others."

My friend Jeff Chu once said: "The table I long for—the Church I hope for—has each of you sitting around it, struggling to hold the knowledge that you, vulnerable you and courageous you, are beloved by God, not just welcome but desperately, fiercely wanted."[189]

Creating a banquet table where all are welcome and wanted is not easy—it is hard-fought and hard-won. It requires self-giving love, learning to do the (sometimes drudgery) work of forgiveness and reconciliation, placing others' needs above our own, and living generously with each other's differences.

As followers of Jesus, we equip ourselves with the time-honored tools our tradition contributes to realizing such a world. We, in turn, offer these as means of grace to those who desire them—as medicine for the soul—while we listen for what tools others bring from their traditions. Because there are sheep not of this fold.

We bear witness to love and offer to help others along the path we walk. Scripture does not say "go and dominate," or "go and conquer," but rather, "go and make disciples." We prepare people wanting to be trained in a Jesus-shaped spirituality that leans into justice and belonging for all, renouncing scapegoating and violence and laying down our lives for the sake of love. Jesus tells us we should spread this message throughout

189 In his talk at the Gay Christian Network conference in Portland, 2015.

the earth like kneading yeast into unleavened bread—slowly, deliberately.

On this quest, we seek to find the image of God in every human, because every human bears the marks of love, regardless of how unredeemable they may seem. And we humble ourselves, knowing we cannot save anyone; that we do not know everything; and that it is not our job to judge. We embrace the path God presents us, and live with gratitude, joy and in peace with all people.

This feels like good news for the world.

Afterword:
Dancing in the Ruins

Emily & Ken

WE RETURN TO where we began in our Introduction to *Solus Jesus: A Theology of Resistance*. There is so much worrying about getting things right in matters of faith. So we search for the foolproof truth-safeguard system that we mortals can manage to insure certainty. But what if the pressure to discover, create, or adhere to such a system is wondrously off? And what if the wonder that removes it is simply a living Jesus, exercising his considerable agency to make God known through the means at his disposal? This doesn't remove the messiness that inevitably attends any communication involving humans. But perhaps the mess is just a given to accept, rather than a sign that something is horribly wrong. *Solus Jesus: A Theology of Resistance* has been our attempt to say that it is so and that it is enough.

As we conclude our proposal, we turn to two final questions having to do with time and place. First, is it time for *solus Jesus*? Second, where might we expect *solus Jesus* to take root?

Is it time for *solus Jesus*?

We think so, but only in the long arc of history. In other words, we think the time for *solus Jesus* is in the process of coming.

Our dear friend Phyllis Tickle had an eagle-eye take on Christianity. In her public life, Phyllis was known as an astute observer of the turbulent religious landscape. Privately, she was a Christian mystic and, like all mystics, had an appetite for connections and a feel for the shifting winds of the Holy Spirit. Phyllis was fond of seeing Christian history unfolding in 500-year shifts. Every 500 years or so, as Phyllis saw it, we enter a major hinge period: a bursting of old wineskins and a search for new ones. This is an image Jesus used to describe the tension between his message (new wine) and the existing religious structures (old wineskins) threatened by his message. Any given wineskin has its season of usefulness, but the divine and yearning Spirit, moving within the confines of time, seeks new wineskins lest the old and brittle ones burst. Tension builds as fundamental structures and ways of thinking lose their suppleness, and an especially messy period of epic transition ensues. This seems to happen every half of a millennium or so. All around us, old wineskins are bursting in slow-motion.

Phyllis called it an "epic rummage sale," during which the Church gathers up practices, perspectives, structures, consensus opinions, doctrines and even dogmas that seem to have outlasted their purpose—languishing in the attic, so to speak. What of all this should be kept, revised, tossed, fixed or replaced?

Historians are understandably skeptical of cycles-of-history schemes. Indeed, it may just be an imaginary structure imposed by our pattern-seeking brains to reassure us that the chaos of history has some underlying order—as if some purpose may be working itself out in history. But Phyllis, perhaps goaded by her mystic mode, dared to go where souls more concerned about peer-review than hers feared to tread.

Consider, then, the following Ticklean romp through history:

The dawn of the Jesus era, and its eventual separation from its sibling, Rabbinic Judaism, takes place roughly five centuries after the Axial Age (so named by the new ways of thinking forged by the Hebrew prophets, Confucius and Gautama Buddha). Roughly 500 years into the Common Era comes the fall of Rome and the rise of monasticism (and, in the Middle East, the emergence of Islam). The fall of Rome meant the end of the empire whose authority undergirded much of Christian faith and practice. What now? The answer emerged through the rise of tightly knit communities scattered throughout the chaotic ruins of the empire, seeking to order themselves around the Gospel mandates as they were understood at that time.

Another 500 years brings us Christendom's Great Schism, in 1054, as the Roman Catholic pontiff and the Eastern Orthodox patriarch pronounce mutual anathemas against each other. Which authority system (represented by pope and patriarch, respectively) would secure the unity of the one, holy, Catholic and apostolic Church? Neither. The Church split and the two major branches of Christianity would coexist in the fraught bonds of intense rivalry for at least another millennium.

The Great Schism of 1054 was followed, in 1517, by Luther's 95 Theses, which may or may not have been nailed to the door of All Saints Church in Wittenberg. The hallmark of the Protestant Reformation was (and still is) *sola Scriptura*—a different answer to the authority question in the Western (or, until that time, Roman Catholic) branch of the Church. This epic shift meant the Western Church had its own multiplying rivalries, between Rome and the new centers of Reformation.

If you've been tracking the math, *sola Scriptura* has had a 500-year run, and we are due for another rummage sale. This context has occasioned our proposal, *solus Jesus*.

We have to admit: We, too, can see the outline of what Phyllis discerned in history. Big-picture narratives help us make sense of things, especially when great historical shifts are impinging on our very short timescale lives. We last heard Phyllis's "500 year rummage sale" talk at a conference we co-hosted with Episcopalian friends in Ann Arbor. On the opening night, Emily met her soon-to-be future wife, Rachel, in the lobby. The religious turmoil that soon surrounded them—two people falling in love—was intense, and very much part of the story that became *Solus Jesus: A Theology of Resistance*.

When a hinge of history is turning in our vicinity, it's easy to get our fingers pinched—and consoling to see it as part of a bigger drama than our own.

So, yes, in the grand scheme of things, it's time for proposals like *solus Jesus* to emerge. In the previous rummage sale, *sola Scriptura* answered the question at issue in every 500-year rummage sale: Where lies the authority? *Sola Scriptura* is now a stately tree and one that has outgrown its root system, bearing diminishing fruit season by season, so that new proposals are needed.

We hurry to offer two caveats. First, we don't presume to say that *solus Jesus* (or *solus Jesus* as we have framed it) must be the Next Big Thing. We do know that *sola Scriptura* has failed us, but the same cannot be said for Jesus. And we know that our task is to propose it, and to continue to subject it to the test that only time can provide.

Second, we understand that transformations of this magnitude happen in fits and starts over many long decades. It's like taking out your gas-powered lawn mower in the late spring, after a long Midwestern winter. Maybe you didn't drain last season's gas like you were supposed to. Maybe the spark plug is getting old. After several pulls on the starting cord and a little muttered cussing, you replace the old gas and spark plug, followed by lunch, then more pulls on the starter cord until, at last, you get the dang thing going.

We see *solus Jesus* as a proposal for such a glorious springtime.

Where might *solus Jesus* take root?

This is the real conundrum: where, indeed? The epic transitions occasioned by Tickle's 500-year rummage sales don't sweep across the entire landscape: They add to the theological and institutional diversity of the Church, rather than forming a new monolithic consensus. We can only speculate about which pockets on that vast landscape might provide an early welcome to *solus Jesus*.

Roman Catholicism and Eastern Orthodoxy provide their own answers to the "Where lies the authority?" question, and they both work for those for whom they work and will continue to hold sway on their sectors of the landscape.

Similarly, it's difficult to picture *solus Jesus* taking root in churches tied to *sola Scriptura* as their institutional birth narratives (the Calvinist-Reformed and Lutheran sectors, in particular). Here, it will continue to serve as a rallying cry, with further refinements offered.

We (Emily and Ken) came from the intersection of two broad sectors of conservative Christianity: evangelicalism and Pentecostalism, marked by renewed appreciation for the role of experience.[190] Many of the institutions associated with these movements are bound by well-entrenched doctrinal boundaries that forbid *solus Jesus*. But, some are not. We came from a newer denomination (Vineyard) born in the free-wheeling Jesus movement. Vineyard blended evangelical and Pentecostal influences with a minimalist approach to doctrinal orthodoxy. It is an example of what some call "post-denominationalism," marked by more nimble and loosely affiliated Church structures. In the end, *solus Jesus* could not survive there. The post-denominational or nondenominational church networks, along with evangelical campus ministries like Intervarsity Christian Fellowship, have shut down debate over

---

190 In *When God Talks Back: Understanding the American Evangelical Relationship with God*, Tanya Luhrmann surveys this renewal and demonstrates how it has spread beyond Pentecostalism to affect non-Pentecostal evangelicalism, as well. Her research focused on two Vineyard churches in the United States.

full inclusion, under the "biblical faithfulness" rubric. But in time—decades, not years from now—this could change. As Emily argued in Chapter 5, "The Age of the Spirit," Pentecostalism may (where its earliest impulses prevail, at least) prove a testing ground for *solus Jesus*—but only at the periphery of any organized expressions and far from the reach of American evangelicalism in its current state.

In the United States, Roman Catholicism and evangelicalism-Pentecostalism represent the lion's share of the Christian landscape—and one openly unwelcoming to the signature issue that occasioned *solus Jesus*. This leaves us with the third largest (and still shrinking) sector: the so-called historic mainline traditions; to use the American titles, they are the Protestant Episcopal Church; the United Methodist Church; the United Church of Christ; the Presbyterian Church (USA); the Evangelical Lutheran Church in America; and so on. We suspect that the institutions not committed to *sola Scriptura*, and with a high tolerance for theological diversity, may be open to *solus Jesus*—at least at their institutional periphery.

Of the mainline denominations, two fit this profile (in the United States, at least). The Episcopal Church (part of the broader Anglican Communion) never adopted *sola Scriptura*, and is a theologically large-hearted tradition bound by the *Book of Common Prayer* (if not the Thirty-nine Articles, at the back of that book) and love of liturgical worship. *Solus Jesus* may find some resonance there. The high view of experience that marks *solus Jesus* will be a challenge, given the culture of caution regarding experience in the Episcopal Church (reinforced by reaction to the conservative tilt of the charismatic movement in that communion). The United Church of Christ is the first fully inclusive mainline denomination (at the level of national policy, if not local practice) and has a strong tradition of local autonomy that allows for experimentation.

Furthermore, its slogan—"God still speaks today"—resonates with a *solus Jesus* approach.[191] Time will tell.

While *solus Jesus* may find a welcome at the periphery of some mainline denominations, it is not theologically centered in any existing tradition.

It is something new.

Certain key features—an emphasis on social justice as integral to the mission of Jesus, non-violence (with its corollary, full inclusion) and a robust spirituality emphasizing the cost of discipleship and direct spiritual experience—have a home already in existing traditions. The 20th-century movement led by the Reverend Doctor Martin Luther King Jr. and based in the African-American Church world is an example of the power of this particular combination of influences—but King's movement was a bright light that transcended existing structures, just as the spirituality of *Alcoholics Anonymous* has done. *Solus Jesus* is an attempt to integrate these features into a new and coherent synthesis—with the integrating help of understanding Jesus as a manifestation of the divine intention to unmask the scapegoat mechanism so we can repent of the rivalry that drives it.

As a new thing, perhaps its proper place is in the wilderness.

Dancing in the ruins

For hopeful and theologically ambitious people like us, that assessment is pretty sobering. If one were a venture capitalist, *solus Jesus* would be a long bet. But the wilderness is a vast territory—one that occupies a venerable part of the faith landscape. A growing number of people find themselves outside the camp of existing ecclesial structures—in the wilderness. In particular, we think of our LGBTQ+ friends and their allies, who cannot make a home in churches that

---

191 We are especially encouraged by the fascinating intersection of full inclusion and Pentecostal theology in the work of Yvette Flunder, presiding bishop of The Fellowship of Affirming Ministries, and in and the recent book, *Filled with the Spirit: Sexuality, Gender, and Radical Inclusivity in a Black Pentecostal Church Coalition*, by Ellen Lewin.

do not extend a welcome without caveats (increasingly, these days, buried in the fine print). This is the wilderness in which we find ourselves.

But there is life in the wilderness. In March 2018, I (Emily) attended my brother-in-law's wedding in Antigua, Guatemala. He and his now-husband married on the front steps of the ruins of Ermita de la Santa Cruz, a Roman Catholic church destroyed by a series of 18th-century earthquakes. The church was surrounded by 1,200 candles and approximately 65 friends and family who had traveled to Central America to witness the vows of these two men.

The reception took place inside—between timeworn stone walls, and under stars shining through the missing ceiling. Throughout dinner, the grooms made their way down two rows of magnificently decorated dinner tables, to talk and laugh with their guests. Food was served and good wine flowed, followed by dancing. A rainbow of colors lit up the dance floor—set up on what would have been the altar—and people let loose under the stars.

It struck me that my brother-in-law and his husband started dating more than a decade ago, when gay marriage was illegal in their state and not yet federally protected. Meanwhile, they'd built a community of friends—mostly marginalized people of color and/or queer-identified—who cobbled together enough money and vacation time to travel to Guatemala to witness their wedding. And here we were, celebrating love, honor and commitment in the ruins of a church that would no more offer the sacrament of marriage to these men than it would ordain a woman.

Yet, this is where the party was. I'd never experienced a more joyous, magical and … well … *perfect* wedding. It seemed like the kind of place Jesus would gravitate toward. In fact, I think it's exactly the kind of place Jesus would be—in and among the oppressed and their friends, drinking and dancing and celebrating unconditional love. The spirit of Jesus wanders and woos outside the institutional Church and in spaces long neglected. There is life among those exiled into the wilderness. May we have eyes to see how and where God moves.

If *solus Jesus* resonates with you

If you've gotten this far with us, *solus Jesus* probably resonates—alongside questions, cautions and a good case of nerves, all of which are perfectly normal at a time like this.

And if *solus Jesus* resonates, you probably find yourself in a spiritual wilderness. If so, then we humbly offer these parting words of advice, especially for those who would pursue the formation of new faith communities informed by *solus Jesus*:

First of all, good for you, pursuing community in this time of so much communal dislocation. The Jesus vision of God is irreducibly communitarian. Jesus summons us to follow him with others, so keep your eye out for them and join with them. The shape, form and structures that such communities take is negotiable; that God is calling us with others is not.

Make the move, if you haven't already, to full LGBTQ+ inclusion. So long as our LGBTQ+ siblings are only afforded a seat at the back of your existing church bus, we would advise you to transfer to one that openly eschews these increasingly hidden and still harmful policies. We think one can make a credible case for full inclusion even within the constraints of *sola Scriptura*, but the rancor this generates is soul-wearying. And the presuppositions of *sola Scriptura*, which we don't see in Scripture itself, place a nearly impossible burden of proof on changes wrought by the Holy Spirit.

If you are part of forming new faith communities informed by *solus Jesus*, we urge you to implement gender balance in leadership structures. This is the first 500-year rummage sale in which such a thing is possible. It's too important a possibility not to realize. Men have had more than their fair share of the power pie in matters of faith for far too long, and faith—rooted as it must be, in the image of God—has been distorted as a result. Make the gender-equity move now. Our church bylaws require gender equity on the board—the best move we made in the heat of our traumatic beginnings.

Long for, pray for, look for and work for greater diversity—to more closely approximate the image of God in humanity. Read outside your cultural boundaries. Do the hard work of building relationships beyond them, too. Mourn the state of affairs that makes this work seem so difficult. Rejoice at small beginnings but don't be satisfied with them.

Relax into God. Martin Luther King Jr. led one of the most powerful spiritual movements of our time, and it was based on his commitment to nonviolence. *Solus Jesus*, aided by the insights of René Girard, is grounded in the vision of a God who is, in every respect and in all aspects of being, nonviolent love. Without a vision of God who is, in very nature, nonviolent, human beings will always have a guard up in relation to God.

We join with James Alison, a Catholic priest, Girardian scholar and gay man, in believing that it is our spiritual task to relax into God.

Alcoholics Anonymous, one of the first fruits of this present rummage sale, bears witness to the power that can only be found when we "let go and let God." The first move toward God is not bearing down or revving up, but letting go. This move honors a God who stands apart from all rivalry with and toward us. It honors our essential relatedness to God, that "in God we live and move and have our being."

The pressure we put on ourselves and internalize from others is off. The God of surrounding love is at work in us. The news that arises from voices in the wilderness is good, truly good and nothing but good.

Solus Jesus—if it resonates, come along. Let's see where God will take us.

Bibliography

Abraham, William J. *Canon and Criterion in Christian Theology: From the Fathers to Feminism*. Oxford University Press, 1998.

———. "Canonical Theism: Thirty Theses." *Canonical Theism: A Proposal for Theology and the Church*, edited by William J. Abraham, Jason E. Vickers and Natalie B. Van Kirk. Wm. B. Eerdmans Publishing Co., 2008.

Alison, James. *Broken Hearts and New Creations: Intimations of a Great Reversal*. Bloomsbury Academic, 2010.

———. *Jesus the Forgiving Victim: Listening for the Unheard Voice*. Doers Publishing, 2013.

———. *Raising Abel: The Recovery of the Eschatological Imagination*. The Crossroad Publishing Company, 1996.

Alter, Robert. *The Book of Psalms: A Translation with Commentary*. W.W. Norton & Company, Inc., 2007.

———. *The Five Books of Moses: A Translation with Commentary*. W.W. Norton & Company, 2004.

Anderson, Allan Heaton. *To the Ends of the Earth: Pentecostalism and the Transformation of World Christianity*. Oxford University Press, 2013.

Barth, Karl. *Church Dogmatics: The Doctrine of the Word of God, Vol. 1, Part 1*. T&T Clark, 2010.

Basile, Kathleen C., et al. "Stop SV: A Technical Package to Prevent Sexual Violence." Division for Violence Prevention, Centers for Disease Control and Prevention, 2016, https://www.cdc.gov/violenceprevention/pdf/SV-Prevention-Technical-Package.pdf

Beale, G.K. "Eden, the Temple, and the Church's Mission in the New Creation." *Journal of the Evangelical Theological Society, Vol. 48, Issue 1*, March 2005, pp. 5-31.

Beaman, Jay. *Pentecostal Pacifism: The Origin, Development, and Rejection of Pacific Belief Among the Pentecostals.* Wipf and Stock Publishers, 1989.

Beck, Richard. *Unclean: Meditations on Purity, Hospitality, and Morality.* Cascade Books, 2011.

Benson, Herbert and Proctor, William. *Relaxation Revolution: The Science and Genetics of Mind Body Healing.* Scribner, 2010.

Berger, Jonah. *Invisible Influence: The Hidden Forces that Shape Behavior.* Simon & Schuster, 2016.

Bondi, Roberta C. *To Love as God Loves: Conversations with the Early Church.* Fortress Press, 1987.

Bonhoeffer, Dietrich. *The Cost of Discipleship.* Simon & Schuster, 1937.

———. *Creation and Fall Temptation: Two Biblical Studies.* Simon & Schuster, 1997.

———. *Ethics.* Simon & Schuster, 1995.

———. *Letters and Papers From Prison.* Edited by Eberhard Bethge. Touchstone, 1953.

———. *Life Together: The Classic Exploration of Christian in Community.* Harper & Row Publishers, Inc., 1954.

Boyarin, Daniel. *The Jewish Gospels: The Story of the Jewish Christ.* The New Press, 2012.

Boyd, Gregory A. *The Crucifixion of the Warrior God: Volumes 1 & 2.* Fortress Press, 2017.

———. *God of the Possible: A Biblical Introduction to the Open View of God.* Baker Books, 2000.

Brown, Austin Channing. *I'm Still Here: Black Dignity in a World Made for Whiteness.* Convergent Books, 2018.

Brown, Brené. *Daring Greatly: How the Courage to be Vulnerable Transforms the Way We Live, Love, Parent, and Lead.* Avery, an imprint of Penguin Random House, 2012.

Brown, Robert McAfee. *Unexpected News: Reading the Bible with Third World Eyes.* Westminster John Knox Press, 1984.

Brueggemann, Walter. *Reality, Grief, Hope: Three Urgent Prophetic Tasks.* Wm. B. Eerdmans Publishing Co., 2014.

Bruce, F.F. *Paul Apostle of the Heart Set Free.* Wm. B. Eerdmans Publishing Co., 1977.

Bubbio, Paolo Diego. *Intellectual Sacrifice and Other Mimetic Paradoxes.* Michigan State University Press, 2018.

Chi, Kelly Rae. "Felipe De Brigard: The Purpose of Memory and Imagination." *Duke Today*, October 27, 2014. https://today.duke.edu/2014/10/debrigard

Chilton, Bruce. *Rabbi Paul: An Intellectual Biography.* Doubleday, 2004.

Christerson, Brad and Flory, Richard. *The Rise of Network Christianity: How Independent Leaders are Changing the Religious Landscape.* Oxford University Press, 2017.

Chu, Jeff. *Does Jesus Really Love Me?: A Gay Christian's Pilgrimage in Search of God in America.* HarperCollins Publishers, 2013.

———. "Together at the Table." Opening Keynote, Gay Christian Network Conference, Portland, OR., January 8, 2015. http://byjeffchu.com/together-at-the-table/

Ciszek, Walter S.J. *The Way of a Pilgrim and The Pilgrim Continues His Way.* Translated by Helen Bacovcin. Doubleday, 2005.

Cleveland, Christena. *Disunity In Christ*. InterVarsity Press, 2013.

Coates, Ta-Nehisi. *Between the World and Me*. Spiegel & Grau, 2015.

Coleman, Monica A. *Making a Way Out of No Way: A Womanist Theology*. Fortress Press, 2008.

Cone, James H. *The Cross and the Lynching Tree*. Orbis Books, 2011.

Cox, Harvey. *Fire From Heaven: The Rise of Pentecostal Spirituality and the Reshaping of Religion in the 21st Century*. Da Capo Press, 1995.

———. *The Future of Faith*. HarperCollins, 2010.

Cunningham, David S. "The Trinity." *The Cambridge Companion to Postmodern Theology*. Edited by Kevin J. Vanhoozer. Cambridge University Press, 2003, pp. 186-202.

Davies, Andrew. "What Does It Mean to Read the Bible as a Pentecostal?" *Journal of Pentecostal Theology, Volume 18, Issue 2*, 2009, pp. 216-229.

De La Torre, Miguel A. *Doing Christian Ethics from the Margins*. Orbis Books, 2014.

———. *Reading the Bible from the Margins*. Orbis Books, 2002.

Department of Economic and Social Affairs/Population Division, "2014 Revision of the World Urbanization Prospects." United Nations. https://esa.un.org/unpd/wup/publications/files/wup2014-report.pdf Accessed 2017.

Douglas, Kelly Brown. *What's Faith God to Do with It?: Black Bodies/Christian Souls*. Orbis Books, 2005.

Dube, Musa W. "Reading for Decolonization (John 4: 1-42)." *Voices from the margin: interpreting the Bible in the Third*

World. Edited by R.S. Sugirtharajah. Orbis Books, 2006, pp. 297-318.

Edwards, James R. "The Authority of Jesus in the Gospel of Mark." *Journal of the Evangelical Theological Society*, 37/2, June 1994, pp. 217-233.

Eire, Carlos M.N. *Reformations: The Early Modern World, 1450-1650.* Yale University Press, 2016.

Enns, Peter. *The Evolution of Adam: What the Bible Does and Doesn't Say About Human Origins.* Brazos Press, 2012.

Ewing, Walter, et. al. "The Criminalization of Immigration in the United States." American Immigration Council, July 13, 2015. https://www.americanimmigrationcouncil.org/research/criminalization-immigration-united-states

FBI Counterterrorism Division, "Terrorism 2002-2005," FBI, 2006. https://www.fbi.gov/stats-services/publications/terrorism-2002-2005 Accessed 2017.

FitzGerald, Frances. *The Evangelicals: The Struggle to Shape America.* Simon & Schuster, 2017.

Flinchbaugh, Hope C. "The Man Who Asked God for More." *Charisma Magazine.* March 31, 2000. http://www.charismamag.com/~charisma/site-arch/site-archives/120-features/unorganized/7-the-man-who-asked-god-for-more

Freire, Paulo. *Pedagogy of the Oppressed.* Bloomsbury, 2000.

Fuller, Dan. *The Unity of the Bible.* Zondervan, 2000.

Gagnon, Robert. *The Bible and Homosexual Practice: Texts and Hermeneutics.* Abingdon Press, 2001.

Garrison, David. *Church Planting Movements: How God is Redeeming a Lost World.* Monument, CO: WIGTake Resources, 2004.

Girard, René. *I See Satan Fall Like Lightning*. Orbis Books, 2001.

———. *Oedipus Unbound: Select Writings on Rivalry and Desire*. Edited by Mark R. Anspach. Stanford University Press, 2004.

———. *The Girard Reader*. Edited by James G. Williams. Crossroad Herder, 1996.

———. *The One by Whom Scandal Comes*. Michigan State University Press, 2014.

———. *The Scapegoat*. The Johns Hopkins University Press, 1986.

———. *Things Hidden Since the Foundation of the World*. Stanford University Press, 1978.

———. *Violence and the Sacred*. The Johns Hopkins University Press, 1977.

Gleick, James. *Chaos: Making a New Science*. Penguin Group, 1987.

Goldingay, John. *Old Testament Theology: Israel's Gospel, Vol. 1*. InterVarsity Press, 2003.

González, Justo L. *The Story of Christianity, Vol. 1: The Early Church to the Dawn of the Reformation*. HarperCollins, 2010.

Goodhart, Sandor. *The Prophetic Law: Essays in Judaism, Girardianism, Literary Studies, and the Ethical*. Michigan State University Press, 2014.

Gottman Institute. "Marriage and Couples." https://www.gottman.com/about/research/couples/

Green, David. "The Trump Hypothesis: Testing Immigrant Populations as a Determinant of Violent and Drug-Related

Crime in the United States." *Social Science Quarterly*, Volume 97, Issue 3, September 2016, pp. 506-524.

Gregory, Brad S. *The Unintended Reformation: How a Religious Revolution Secularized Society*. Belknap Press, an imprint of Harvard University Press, 2012.

Grimsrud, Ted. *Instead of Atonement: The Bible's Salvation Story and Our Hope for Wholeness*. Cascade Books, 2013.

Gross, Rita M. "Meditating On Jesus." *Buddhists Talk About Jesus, Christians Talk About the Buddha*. Edited by Rita M. Gross and Terry C. Muck. The Continuum International Publishing Group Ltd., 1999, pp. 32-51.

Grudem, Wayne A., et al. *Are Miraculous Gifts for Today? Four Views*. Zondervan, 1996.

Gushee, David. *Changing Our Mind*. Third Edition. Read the Spirit Books, 2015.

———. *Righteous Gentiles of the Holocaust: Genocide and Moral Obligation*. Paragon House, 2003.

Hackett, Conrad and McClendon, David. "Christians Remain World's Largest Religious Group, but Belief is Dying Out in Europe." Pew Research Center, April 5, 2017. http://pewrsr. ch/2o5CXFL

Haidt, Jonathan. *The Righteous Mind: Why Good People Are Divided by Politics and Religion*. Vintage Books, 2012.

Harris, Maurice D. *Leviticus: You Have No Idea*. Cascade Books, 2013.

Haven, Cynthia L. *Evolution of Desire: A Life of René Girard*. Michigan State University Press, 2018.

Hays, Richard. *The Moral Vision of the New Testament: Community, Cross, New Creation*. HarperOne, 1996.

Henry, Patrick. *We Only Know Men: The Rescue of Jews in France During the Holocaust*. The Catholic University of America Press, 2013.

Heim, S. Mark. *Saved From Sacrifice: A Theology of the Cross*. Wm. B. Eerdmans Publishing Co., 2006.

Horsley, Richard A. *Jesus and Empire: The Kingdom of God and the New World Disorder*. Fortress Press, 2003.

Huntington, Samuel P. Foreword. "Cultures Count." *Culture Matters: How Values Shape Human Progress*. Edited by Lawrence E. Harrison and Samuel P. Huntington, Basic Books, 2000, pp. xiii-xvi.

Isasi-Díaz, Ada María. *Decolonizing Epistemologies: Latina/o Theology and Philosophy*. Fordham University Press, 2011.

———. *Mujerista Theology*. Orbis Books, 1996.

Jenkins, Philip. *The New Faces of Christianity: Believing the Bible in the Global South*. Oxford University Press, 2006.

———. *The Next Christendom: The Coming of Global Christianity*. Oxford University Press, 2011.

Jeung, Russell. *At Home in Exile: Finding Jesus Among My Ancestors and Refugee Neighbors*. Zondervan, 2016.

Jewett, Robert, et. al. *Romans: A Commentary*. Fortress Press, 2006.

Johnson, James Weldon. *God's Trombones: Seven Negro Sermons in Verse*. Penguin Books, 1927.

Johnson, Luke Timothy. *The Gospel of Luke*. Edited by Daniel J. Harrington, S.J., Sacra Pagina series, Vol. 3, The Liturgical Press, 1991.

Johnson, Steven. *Emergence: The Connected Life of Ants, Brains, Cities, and Software*. Scriber, 2001.

Jones, Tony. *A Better Atonement: Beyond the Depraved Doctrine of Original Sin.* The JoPa Group, 2012.

Josephus, Flavius. *Josephus: The Jewish War (Books V-VII).* Penguin Books, 1959.

Kalilombe, Patrick A. "A Malawian Example: The Bible and Non-literate Communities." *Voices From the Margin: Interpreting the Bible in the Third World.* Edited by R.S. Sugirtharajah. Orbis Books, 2006, pp. 442-453.

Kaplan, Grant. *René Girard, Unlikely Apologist: Mimetic Theory and Fundamental Theology.* University of Notre Dame Press, 2016.

Kärkkäinen, Veli-Matti. *An Introduction to the Theology of Religions: Biblical, Historical & Contemporary Perspectives.* InterVarsity Press, 2003.

Kass, Leon R. *The Beginning of Wisdom: Reading Genesis.* The University of Chicago Press, 2003.

Keltner, Dacher, Marsh, Jason, and Smith, Jeremy Adam, editors. *The Compassionate Instinct: The Science of Human Goodness.* The Greater Good Science Center (W.W. Norton), 2010.

Kidwell, Clara Sue, et al. *A Native American Theology.* Orbis Books, 2001.

Kim, Grace Ji-Sun. *Embracing the Other: The Transformative Spirit of Love.* Wm B. Eerdmans Publishing Co., 2015.

Kim-Kort, Mihee. *Making Paper Cranes: Toward an Asian American Feminist Theology.* Chalice Press, 2012.

King Jr. Martin Luther. *Letter From Birmingham Jail.* April 16, 1963. African Studies Center, University of Pennsylvania, Accessed 2017. https://www.africa.upenn.edu/Articles_Gen/Letter_Birmingham.html

———. "Loving Your Enemies." Sermon delivered at Dexter Avenue Baptist Church, Montgomery, AL. November 17, 1957. https://owl.english.purdue.edu/owl/resource/747/09/

Kinzer, Mark S. *Post-Missionary Messianic Judaism: Redefining Christian Engagement with the Jewish People.* Brazos Press, 2005.

Knitter, Paul F. *Introducing Theologies of Religions.* Orbis Books, 2002.

———. *Without Buddha I Could not be a Christian.* Oneworld Publications, 2009.

Kruger, C. Baxter. *Jesus and the Undoing of Adam.* Perichoresis, Inc., 2003.

Kugel, James L. *How to Read the Bible: A Guide to Scripture, Then and Now.* Free Press, 2007.

———. *The Bible as It Was.* Belknap Press, 1997.

———. *The God of Old: Inside the Lost World of the Bible.* Free Press, 2003.

Kushner, Aviya. *The Grammar of God: A Journey Into the Words and Worlds of the Bible.* Spiegel & Grau, 2015.

Kyle, Richard. *Evangelicalism: An Americanized Christianity.* Transaction Publishers, 2006.

Lee, Deborah Jian. *Rescuing Jesus: How People of Color, Women & Queer Christians are Reclaiming Evangelicalism.* Beacon Press, 2015.

Lee, Michelle Ye Hee. "Donald Trump's false comments connecting Mexican immigrants and crime." *The Washington Post*, July 8, 2015. http://wapo.st/1J3uuEA?tid=ss_tw-bottom&utm_term=.311e2d782c8b

Levine, Amy-Jill and Brettler, Marc Zvi, editors. *The Jewish Annotated New Testament*, Second Edition. Oxford University Press, 2017.

Levine, Amy-Jill. *The Misunderstood Jew: The Church and the Scandal of the Jewish Jesus*. HarperOne, 2006.

Lewin, Ellen. *Filled with the Spirit: Sexuality, Gender, and Radical Inclusivity in a Black Pentecostal Church Coalition*. The University of Chicago Press, 2018.

Lightsey, Pamela R., *Our Lives Matter: A Womanist Queer Theology*. Pickwick Publications, 2015.

Lingenfelter, Sherwood G. *Transforming Culture: A Challenge for Christian Mission*. Baker Books, 1998.

Luhrmann, T.M. *When God Talks Back: Understanding the American Evangelical Relationship with God*. Vintage Books, 2012.

Manarin, Louis Timothy. *And the word became kigambo: Language, literacy, and Bible translation in Buganda 1875-1931*. Dissertation, Indiana University. ProQuest LLC, 2009.

Marsh, Charles. *Strange Glory: A Life of Dietrich Bonhoeffer*. Knopf, 2014.

Marsh, Jason and Keltner, Dacher. "We Are All Bystanders." *Greater Good Magazine*, September 1, 2006 https://greater-good.berkeley.edu/article/item/we_are_all_bystanders

Martyn, J. Louis. *Galatians: A New Translation with Introduction and Commentary*. Doubleday, 1997.

Mesters, Carlos. "A Brazilian Example: 'Listening to What the Spirit Is Saying to the Churches'—Popular Interpretation of the Bible in Brazil." *Voices From the Margin: Interpreting the Bible in the Third World*. Edited by R.S. Sugirtharajah. Orbis Books, 2006, pp. 431-441.

McLaren, Brian. "Convergence Music, Worship, and Liturgy." Keynote speaker, The Center for Progressive Renewal, February 7, 2017.

Miller, Donald E. *Reinventing American Protestantism: Christianity in the New Millennium.* University of California Press, 1999.

Moltmann, Jürgen. *The Crucified God.* 40th Anniversary Edition. Fortress Press, 2015.

Moreland, J.P. "Keeping Vineyard Distinctives in the Plausibility Structure: A Reflection on Kingdom Epistemology." Presentation, Society of Vineyard Scholars conference. Anaheim, CA., April 18, 2013.

Neusner, Jacob. *Judaism When Christianity Began: A Survey of Belief and Practice.* Westminster John Knox Press, 2002.

Newberg, Andrew and Waldman, Mark. *How God Changes Your Brain.* Ballantine Books, 2009.

Newberg, Andrew and D'Aquili, Eugene, et al. *Why God Won't Go Away.* Ballantine Books, 2001.

Newbigin, Lesslie. *Proper Confidence: Faith, Doubt, and Certainty in Christian Discipleship.* Wm. B. Eerdmans Publishing Co., 1995.

Noah, Trevor. *Born a Crime: Stories From a South African Childhood.* Spiegel & Grau. 2016.

O'Connor, Daniel William. "Saint Peter the Apostle." *Encyclopædia Britannica.* Encyclopædia Britannica, Inc. October 24, 2017. https://www.britannica.com/biography/Saint-Peter-the-Apostle Accessed November 2017.

Olson, Roger E. *The Mosaic of Christian Belief: Twenty Centuries of Unity and Diversity.* InterVarsity Press,, 2002.

Outler, Albert C. *The Wesleyan Theological Heritage*. Edited by Thomas C. Oden and Leicester R. Longden. Zondervan, 1991.

Perelmuter, Hayim Goren. *Siblings: Rabbinic Judaism and Early Christianity at Their Beginnings*. Paulist Press, 1989.

Petrella, Ivan. *Beyond Liberation Theology: A Polemic*. SCM Press, 2008.

Pinnock, Clark H. *Flame of Love: A Theology of the Holy Spirit*. InterVarsity Press, 1996.

Pinnock, Clark H., et al. *The Openness of God: A Biblical Challenge to the Traditional Understanding of God*. InterVarsity Press, 1994.

Piper, John. *The Future of Justification: A Response to N.T. Wright*. Crossway Books, 2007.

Plato. *The Collected Dialogues of Plato*. Edited by Edith Hamilton, et. al. Princeton University Press, 1961.

Polkinghorne, John R. *Quarks, Chaos, and Christianity: Questions to Science and Religion*. The Crossroad Publishing Company, 2005.

Pugh, Jeffrey C. *Religionless Christianity: Dietrich Bonhoeffer in Troubled Times*. T&T Clark International, 2008.

Reeves, Michael. *The Unquenchable Flame: Discovering the Heart of the Reformation*. B&H Publishing, 2010.

Robeck, Jr., Cecil M. *The Azusa Street Mission and Revival: The Birth of the Global Pentecostal Movement*. Thomas Nelson, Inc., 2017.

Robinson, Nathan J. "Wait, do people actually know just how evil this man is?." *Current Affairs Magazine*. August 26, 2017. https://www.currentaffairs.org/2017/08/wait-do-people-actually-know-just-how-evil-this-man-is

Rohr, Richard. *Things Hidden: Scripture as Spirituality*. Franciscan Media, 2008.

Roser, Max. *Our World in Data*. University of Oxford, 2011. https://ourworldindata.org/literacy/ Accessed 2017.

Ryrie, Alec. *Protestants: The Faith That Made the Modern World*. Viking Press, 2017.

Said, Edward W. *Orientalism*. Vintage Books Edition, 1979.

Sanou, Brahima. "ICT Facts and Figures 2017." International Telecommunication Union (ITU). https://www.itu.int/en/ITU-D/Statistics/Documents/facts/ICTFactsFigures2017.pdf Accessed 2017.

Schneiders, Sandra M. "Whose Sins You Shall Forgive. … The Holy Spirit and the Forgiveness of Sin(s) in the Fourth Gospel.", Special guest speaker. The Spirit in the New Millennium, The Duquesne University 5th Annual Holy Spirit Lecture and Colloquium, Pittsburgh, PA, June 12-13, 2009.

Smith, Christian. *The Bible Made Impossible: Why Biblicism Is Not a Truly Evangelical Reading of Scripture*. Brazos Press, 2011.

Smith, Gregory A. and Martínez, Jessica. "How the faithful voted: A preliminary 2016 analysis." Pew Research Center, November 9, 2016. http://pewrsr.ch/2fSNWBY

Smith, Mitzi J. "Knowing More than is Good for One." *I Found God in Me: A Womanist Biblical Hermeneutics Reader*. Edited by Mitzi J. Smith, Cascade Books, 2015, pp. 236-265.

Snyder, Timothy. *On Tyranny: Twenty Lessons From the Twentieth Century*. Tim Duggan Books, 2017.

Snyder, Timothy. "Why Did the Holocaust Happen? A History Lesson for the Future." Featured speaker. Inaugural Girard Lecture at Stanford University, Stanford, CA, March 13, 2013.

Stanley, Tiffany. "The Life of Dietrich Bonhoeffer: An Interview with Charles Marsh," *Religion & Politics*, July 30, 2014. http://religionandpolitics.org/2014/07/30/the-life-of-dietrich-bonhoeffer-an-interview-with-charles-marsh/

Stark, Rodney. *The Triumph of Faith: Why the World Is More Religious Than Ever*. ISI Books, 2015.

Steakley, James. "Homosexuals & the Holocaust: Homosexuals & the Third Reich." *The Body Politic*, Issue 11, January/February 1974, Jewish Virtual Library http://www.jewishvirtuallibrary.org/homosexuals-and-the-third-reich

Sugirtharajah, R.S. "Introduction: Still at the Margins." *Voices From the Margin: Interpreting the Bible in the Third World*. Edited by R.S. Sugirtharajah. Orbis Books, 2006, pp. 1-10.

Sutter, K. *Keys to Church Planting Movements*. Asteroidea Books, 2006.

Sweeney, Jon M. *Phyllis Tickle: A Life*. Church Publishing, 2018.

Tanfani, Joseph. "Donald Trump warns that Syrian refugees represent 'a great Trojan horse' to the U.S." *Los Angeles Times*, October 19, 2016. http://www.latimes.com/politics/la-na-pol-syrian-refugees-debate-20161019-snap-story.html

Tamez, Elsa. "The Bible and the Five Hundred Years of Conquest." *Voices From the Margin: Interpreting the Bible in the Third World*. Edited by R.S. Sugirtharajah. Orbis Books, 2006.

Thurman, Howard. *Jesus and the Disinherited*. Beacon Press, 1976.

Tickle, Phyllis and Sweeney, Jon M. *The Age of the Spirit: How the Ghost of an Ancient Controversy is Shaping the Church*. Baker Books, 2014.

Tickle, Phyllis. *The Divine Hours™ Prayers for Summertime*. Doubleday, 2000.

———. *Emergence Christianity: What It Is, Where It Is Going, and Why It Matters*. Baker Books, 2012.

———. *The Great Emergence: How Christianity is Changing and Why*. Baker Books, 2008.

Tutu, Desmond and Tutu, Mpho. *The Book of Forgiving: The Fourfold Path for Healing Ourselves and Our World*. HarperOne, 2014.

Twiss, Richard. *Rescuing the Gospel from the Cowboys*. InterVarsity Press, 2015.

Vanhoozer, Kevin J. "Scripture and tradition." *The Cambridge Companion to Postmodern Theology*. Edited by Kevin J. Vanhoozer. Cambridge University Press, 2003.

Vicker, Jason. "Medicine of the Holy Spirit: The Canonical Heritage of the Church." *Canonical Theism: A Proposal for Theology and the Church*. Edited by William J. Abraham, Jason E. Vickers, and Natalie B. Van Kirk. Wm. B. Eerdmans Publishing Co., 2008.

Volf, Miroslav. *After Our Likeness: The Church as the Image of the Trinity*. Wm. B. Eerdmans Publishing Co., 1998.

Volker, Ullrich. *Hitler: Ascent 1889-1939*. Knopf, 2016.

Wallace, Mark I. *The Second Naiveté: Barth, Ricoeur, and the New Yale Theology*. Mercer University Press, 1995.

Walton, John H. *The Lost World of Genesis One: Ancient Cosmology and the Origins Debate*. InterVarsity Press, 2009.

Warren, James. *Compassion or Apocalypse? A Comprehensible Guide to the Thought of René Girard*. Christian Alternative Books, 2013.

Watts, Rikki E. "Making Sense of Genesis 1." The American Scientific Affiliation, A Network of Christians in the Sciences, 2002. http://www.asa3.org/ASA/topics/Bible-Science/6-02Watts.html Accessed January 2014.

West, Traci C. *Disruptive Christian Ethics: When Racism and Women's Lives Matter*. Westminster John Knox Press, 2006.

Williams, James G. Forward. *I See Satan Fall Like Lightning*. By René Girard. Orbis Books, 1999, pp. ix-xxiii.

Williams, Reggie L. *Bonhoeffer's Black Jesus: Harlem Renaissance Theology and an Ethic of Resistance*. Baylor University Press, 2014.

Wilson, Ken. *Jesus Brand Spirituality: He Wants His Religion Back*. Thomas Nelson, 2008.

———. *A Letter to My Congregation*. Second Edition. Read the Spirit Books, 2016.

Wilson, Maja Joiwind. "Writing Assessment's 'Debilitating Inheritance': Behaviorism's Dismissal of Experience." Dissertation, University of New Hampshire. ProQuest LLC, 2013.

Wink, Walter. *Jesus and Nonviolence: A Third Way*. Fortress Press, 2003.

———. *The Powers That Be: Theology for a New Millennium*. Doubleday, 1999.

Wright, N.T. "Communion and Koinonia: Pauline Reflections on Tolerance and Boundaries." Paper given at the Future of Anglicanism conference, Oxford, 2002.

———. *Justification: God's Plan & Paul's Vision*. InterVarsity Press, 2009.

———. *The Resurrection of the Son of God*. (Christian Origins and the Question of God, Vol. 3). Fortress Press, 2003.

Xi, Lian. *Redeemed By Fire: The Rise of Popular Christianity in Modern China*. Yale University Press, 2010.

Yong, Amos. *The Spirit Poured Out on All Flesh: Pentecostalism and the Possibility of Global Theology*. Baker Academic, 2005.

About the Authors

Emily Swan is co-pastor of Blue Ocean Faith Ann Arbor. She received her B.A. in history from Butler University, and has worked toward her Master's degree at Fuller Theological Seminary. Additionally, she spent three years studying Mandarin and Amdo Tibetan languages at Qinghai Minzu Daxue Nationalities University in Xining, China.

Emily worked for two Fortune 500 companies and lived abroad for four years prior to serving as a pastor in the Vineyard movement, a movement which ultimately rejected ordaining queer pastors. She co-planted Blue Ocean Faith Ann Arbor with Ken Wilson in 2014. Emily is the author/creator of small group material, "The Earth is God's Temple," and occasionally speaks, or hosts workshops, at conferences.

She is married to author and therapist Rachel Murr. She lives in Ypsilanti, MI, and enjoys feasting with friends, playing tennis and making music. Emily blogs at: SolusJesus.com.

Ken Wilson was born and raised in Detroit, Michigan, is the father of six, grandfather of another six, and is married to Rev. Julia Huttar Bailey. Ken received a B.S.N. from the University of Michigan; before entering the pastorate, he worked in community mental health. Ken is the author of several books, including *Mystically Wired: Exploring New Realms in Prayer* (Thomas Nelson 2010); and most recently  *A Letter To My Congregation: An Evangelical Pastor's Path to Embracing Those Who are Gay, Lesbian, Bisexual, and Transgender Into the Company of Jesus, 2nd edition* (ReadTheSpirit, 2016).

Ken was the founding pastor of Vineyard Church of Ann Arbor, served for seven years on the national board of Vineyard USA, and now co-pastors (with Emily Swan) Blue Ocean Faith, Ann Arbor, a fully inclusive church. Ken enjoys walking, reading and writing—but arithmetic, not so much. Ken blogs at: SolusJesus.com.

Emily and Ken blog at SolusJesus.com.
Follow along and join the conversation!

CPSIA information can be obtained
at www.ICGtesting.com
Printed in the USA
LVHW09s0005240918
591148LV00001B/4/P